The Camden House History of German Literature

Volume 1

Early Germanic Literature and Culture

The Camden House History of German Literature

Volume 1

The Camden House History of German Literature

Edited by James Hardin

Vol. 1: Early Germanic Literature and Culture
Edited by Brian Murdoch and Malcolm Read,
University of Stirling, UK

Vol. 2: German Literature of the Early Middle Ages
Edited by Brian Murdoch, University of Stirling, UK

Vol. 3: German Literature of the High Middle Ages
Edited by Will Hasty, University of Florida

Vol. 4: Early Modern German Literature
Edited by Max Reinhart, University of Georgia

*Vol. 5: Literature of the German Enlightenment
and Sentimentality*
Edited by Barbara Becker-Cantarino, Ohio State University

Vol. 6: Literature of the Sturm und Drang
Edited by David Hill, University of Birmingham, UK

Vol. 7: The Literature of Weimar Classicism
Edited by Simon Richter, University of Pennsylvania

Vol. 8: The Literature of German Romanticism
Edited by Dennis Mahoney, University of Vermont

Vol. 9: German Literature of the Nineteenth Century, 1830–1899
Edited by Clayton Koelb and Eric Downing,
University of North Carolina

*Vol. 10: German Literature of the Twentieth Century:
From Aestheticism to Postmodernism*
Ingo R. Stoehr, Kilgore College, Texas

Early Germanic Literature and Culture

Edited by
Brian Murdoch
and
Malcolm Read

CAMDEN HOUSE

First published 2004
by Camden House

Camden House is an imprint of Boydell & Brewer Inc.
668 Mt. Hope Ave., Rochester, NY 14620, USA
www.camden-house.com
and of Boydell & Brewer Limited
PO Box 9, Woodbridge, Suffolk IP12 3DF, UK
www.boydellandbrewer.com

ISBN: 1–57113–199–X

Library of Congress Cataloging-in-Publication Data

Early Germanic literature and culture / edited by Brian Murdoch and
    Malcolm Read.
        p. cm. — (Camden House history of German literature; v. 1)
    (Studies in German Literature, Linguistics, and Culture)
    Includes bibliographical references and index.
    ISBN 1–57113–199–X (hardcover: alk. paper)
        1. Germanic literature — History and crticism. 2. Literature, Medieval
    — History and criticism. 3. Civilization, Germanic. 4. Germanic peoples.
    I. Murdoch, Brian, 1944– II. Read, Malcolm, 1945– III. Title. IV. Se-
    ries: Studies in German literature, linguistics, and culture (Unnumbered)

PN831.E28 2004
830.9'001—dc22

                                                            2004000336

A catalogue record for this title is available from the British Library.

This publication is printed on acid-free paper.
Printed in the United States of America.

Contents

Illustrations

Preface

This volume was planned initially by Professor William Whobrey, who drew up the original outline and commissioned individual chapters from a wide range of scholars, and we wish first of all to acknowledge his work. He was, however, unable to continue with the editorship, and at a relatively late stage we agreed to take this over. Although some three-quarters of the chapters had by then been sent in, several of them some long time previously, there were still gaps for which new contributors had to be found. Our debt of gratitude to the contributors, therefore, is two-fold. To those who submitted chapters within the original time-scale goes our gratitude for their patience; and to the second wave of contributors go our thanks for their willingness to produce the material to give the book, we hope, as useful a range as possible. Apart from the editing of the contributions and the re-commissioning of missing chapters, there were a number of technical problems regarding unusual characters, such as those comprising the runic alphabet, as might be expected in a work concerned with the very earliest stages of Germanic literature. We hope that the outcome has been a satisfactory one, and the editors are grateful to James Hardin and Jim Walker for all their assistance in the completion of the project.

Brian Murdoch and Malcolm Read
Stirling, 2003

Abbreviations

GIVEN THE RANGE of material included here, journal titles which may be familiar in one branch of the study but not others have as far as possible been given in full.

ABäG   *Amsterdamer Beiträge zur älteren Germanistik*

ASE   *Anglo-Saxon England*

ASPR   *Anglo-Saxon Poetic Records*

CUP   Cambridge University Press

DVjs   *Deutsche Vierteljahresschrift*

EEMF   Early English Manuscripts in Facsimile

EETS   Early English Text Society (O[riginal], E[xtra], S[upplementary] S[eries])

GRM   *Germanisch-romanische Monatsschrift*

MGH   Monumenta Germaniae Historica

MHG   Middle High German

OE   Old English

OHG   Old High German

ON   Old Norse

OS   Old Saxon

OUP   Oxford University Press

PBB   [Pauls und Braunes] *Beiträge zur Geschichte der deutschen Sprache und Literatur* (H[alle], T[übingen])

RGA   *Reallexikon der Germanischen Altertumskunde*, 2nd ed. by Heinrich Beck et al. (Berlin and New York: de Gruyter, 1976–)

UP   University Press

WBG   Wissenschaftliche Buchgesellschaft

Introduction

Brian Murdoch and Malcolm Read

WHY SHOULD A HISTORY of early medieval German literature contain a collection of apparently disparate essays, only a few of which — and those toward the end of the volume — have anything directly to do with literature at all? Indeed, even in the later chapters, some of the literature described either is not literary (at least in the sense that the modern world might understand it), or not German (but rather from England or from Scandinavia). The aim of this volume is to provide some insights into aspects of the culture of the Germanic world from which German literature in the modern sense originated. However, several preliminary caveats are necessary in the pursuit of what constitutes Germanic culture, and these derive partly from lessons that have been taught by the history of the last couple of centuries in particular.

It is, of course, simple enough to define German in terms of the modern language. However, what we now recognize as the German language is part of a far wider Germanic language family, sharing a common ancestry with other modern languages, such as Dutch, English, or Swedish, and also with earlier ones, either ancestors of those still spoken, such as Anglo-Saxon or Old Norse, or now extinct, such as Gothic. German is closer to all of these, however, than it is to other more distantly related languages throughout Europe. And thus, if we go back in philological history, we can, at least in theory, find some kind of common Germanic origin, get closer perhaps to the origins of that branch of the Indo-European language family whose speakers are known by the useful Roman name of *Germani*.[1] The Germanic branch separated from the Indo-European parent language between the fifth and second century B.C. (it is datable with reference to borrowings from other languages) and demonstrates various features not shared by, say, the Romance, Slavic, or Celtic language groups. These features include — and this is, of course, a great simplification — the effects of what is known as the First or Germanic Sound Shift. This is a series of sound-changes affecting one group of speakers, but not others, and the First Sound Shift affected the Indo-European stops, principally the "explosive" sounds /p/, /t/, and /k/ and their voiced equivalents /b/, /d/, and /g/. As representatives of the unvoiced changes only (to give an idea of what is meant by the sound shift) we may note the shift of Indo-European /p/ to Germanic /f/, still visible when we compare modern French *père* still showing the unshifted /p/ with a Germanic cognate, English *father;* for Indo-European /t/, which shifted to /þ/ (thorn, pronounced th), we can compare French *tu* against earlier English *thou;* and for the change from Indo-European /k/ to the Germanic guttural /kh/ usually represented in writing as h- we can compare in Indo-European languages not affected by the shift the Latin word *canis,* its Greek parallel *kyon,* or the Welsh word *ci* (all pronounced with a hard initial sound), and their modern German and English cognates *Hund* or *hound.* The voiced stops /b/, /d/, and /g/ became unvoiced as /p/, /t/, and /k/, so that we can compare Latin *decem* and Greek *deka* with English *ten.*[2] Another feature is the fixing in the Germanic languages of a stress on the root syllable of words, in contrast to French, for example. We might compare the French word *mouton,* "sheep" and the related English borrowing *mutton;* the French original stresses the end syllable, and the English has shifted the stress to the root. A third feature is the formation of a past tense in weak verbs with a dental (*-d, -t*) suffix: English *loved,* German *liebte:* compare French *aimais,* Russian *lyubil* and so on.

The search for Germanic origins is, of course, not without its dangers. Laudable as such a search might be, in certain political circumstances an insistence on a unified ethnicity might all too easily lead to a supposed exclusivity in the possession of certain characteristics, or indeed to the notion of superiority. The whole *Rassenkunde* of the Nazi period is a properly discredited area, but even in the sphere of literary criticism, the insistence in the nineteenth century on a *Nationalliteratur,* at the time simply an expression of the general striving toward political unity, had inherent in it the danger of an exaggerated stress on the *Volk.* Here is part of August Vilmar's preface to the fourth edition of his much reprinted *Nationallitteratur:* it is dated *1850, am Jarestage der Schlacht von Belle Alliance,* on the anniversary, then, of the defeat of Napoleon by Wellington and Blücher at what we now call Waterloo:

> Dem Leben aber hat diese Geschichte der deutschen Literatur dienen wollen, dem ganzen und vollen Leben meines Volkes, in der Kraft seiner Taten, wie in der Macht seiner Lieder, in dem Stolze seiner angebornen Weltherschaft, wie in der selbstverschuldeten Demütigung unter Fremde, in dem lachenden Glanze seiner Fröhlichkeit wie in dem tiefen Ernst seiner christlichen Frömmigkeit.[3]

> [This history of German literature is intended to serve life, the whole and complete life of my people, in the power of its deeds as in the might of its songs, in the power of its natural leadership and its self-

denigratory humility amongst foreigners, in the laughing splendor of its joy and the deep seriousness of its Christian piety.]

The late addition of Christian piety in that statement echoes at a distance of a thousand years the plea of Otfrid of Weissenburg that the Franks of the ninth century should not desist from producing Christian literature, since they are just as bold as the Romans and in no way inferior to the Greeks: *Sie sint so sáma chuani, sélb so thie Románi; ni thárf man thaz ouh rédinon, thaz Kríachi in thes giwídaron*[4] (They are just as bold as the Romans, nor may anyone say they are inferior to the Greeks in this respect). But both Otfrid and Vilmar had cause to boost what they felt to be their own people, even if Vilmar used the term *deutsch* and Otfrid thought of himself as a Frank. So too in original literary production, the *Heimatroman, Heimatkunst* and *Heimatdichtung,* the regional novel, regional art and poetry, though once extremely popular and part of a broad German cultural context in the concentration on the countryside and on farming or peasant life, was nevertheless given a negative twist in the link with the extreme nationalism of *Blut- und Bodenliteratur,* the literature of blood and soil in the Third Reich.

How, then, does one investigate the concept of what is Germanic? The word is rooted in language and ethnology, of course, rather than in geography, and the original homeland, the *Urheimat* of the *Germani* is not Germany in any modern sense, but (as far as it can be determined at all) probably what is now Scandinavia and the North Sea and Baltic coastal areas. There are all kinds of ways in which the groups who constituted the Germanic ethnos can be (and indeed have been) investigated, and in most recent times philologists and historians have begun working with geneticists to examine and establish similar DNA patterns.[5] The longer established use of field archeology is also useful to establish common practices and indeed beliefs among the *Germani,* and one group, the Goths, for example, may be traced by such methods from the Vistula to the Black Sea by examination of the archeologically established cultures. Even more graphically we can learn a great deal about, and even look into the faces of actual Iron Age *Germani,* preserved by the waters of the peat-bogs in Denmark and Schleswig-Holstein. The preservation of Tollund man, however, brings home to us forcibly precisely his inability to *speak,* and although forensic archeology permits us to know such details as diet, domestic habits, clothing and hairstyles, burial custom, and even matters associated with ritual murder, question marks, some of them large ones indeed, will always remain.[6]

A more specifically linguistic archeology, with reference to place names, may tell us a great deal, though it, too, can be inconclusive, especially in the early stages. Whether the Goths were really ever at Västergötland in Sweden is unclear, but in later historical times they certainly left their mark on place names such as Godega (in Italy), Godos (in Spain) and Gueuex (in France) just as firmly as the Vikings would later leave their inscriptions on physical monuments located as far apart as the Piraeus in Greece and the north of Greenland. Place names may also convey other information, on religion and cult practices amongst the early *Germani,* for example; theophoric place names — those that include or are based on the name of a god — provide clear examples, as with Wednesbury in England and Godesberg in Germany, both containing the name of the Germanic god Wodan (variously Odin, Woden and so on). In the general vocabulary of the Germanic languages, too, evidence of early contact with other cultures may still be preserved. Thus from the Celts, their predecessors in much of Europe, the Germanic Goths (who are often used as examples because theirs is the most completely preserved of the early Germanic languages) took the word *reiks,* ultimately giving us the word *Reich,* from Celtic (we find it in names like Vercingetorix, and in the Old Irish word for a king, *ríg*), and later we may point to the plethora of borrowings in the Germanic languages, especially those in the Western sub-group, after contact with the Romans. Germanic words were also taken over into Latin.[7] In terms of linguistic archeology in a general sense, it is worth noting that D. H. Green's *Language and History in the Early Germanic World* examines early Germanic vocabulary for information of practices in the precise areas of law, kinship, warfare, and the higher echelons of the social structure.

Most of the earliest direct information we have about the *Germani* in these respects in particular comes also from outside sources, from classical writers, the principal example being the *Germania* of Tacitus, which might of course have exaggerated some perceived qualities of the supposedly noble savages as a stick with which the author could beat his degenerate fellow Romans.[8] The literary topos of the *origo gentis* can also be helpful, of course — the concept itself and the written tale of the origins of the Goths as an early example are discussed in a chapter of the present volume. However, the history of Germanic interaction with the Roman Empire and indeed the filling of the vacuum left at the fall of that empire from the fourth century onward largely by Germanic tribes is a complex one, and eventually more than one Germanic group would claim to have assumed the mantle of that empire, some elements of which did indeed survive. Relations between the Germanic and the classical worlds, however, range from the great defeats of the imperial armies under Varus by Hermann at what we now know was Kalkriese, near Osnabrück, or by the Goths at Adrianople (now Turkish Edirne) in the fourth century, to the mixture of defense and trade along the *limes*-line, the fortified frontier between imperial Rome and Germania, to the ultimate hegemony of what was essentially a Roman Church over all the Germanic tribes.

The *Germani* may be split into groups in a variety of ways. Tacitus speaks of Ingaevones, Herminones and Istaevones, which philologists have tried to associate with tribal and linguistic subdivisions. Other distinctions, based on the supposed geographical origins of various tribal groups, divided them into *Nordgermanen* (who would develop into the various Scandinavian peoples) and *Oder-Weichsel-Germanen* (those originating around the Oder and the Vistula, and including Goths and a number of tribes with un- or only scantily recorded languages, such as the Burgundians, Herulians, Rugians, Vandals and Gepids). The languages of these two broad groups are usually referred to as North and East Germanic, and are linked more closely with each other than with the third, West Germanic group, made up of *Elbgermanen* (Lombards, Bavarians and Alemanni or Alemans — again the spelling varies), *Nordseegermanen* (Angles, Frisians, Saxons) and *Weser-Rhein-Germanen* (Saxons and Franks).

Although there is a rich literature in Old Norse as representative of North Germanic, and some surviving material, albeit a Bible translation, in the East Germanic language of Gothic, our principal focus of interest is on West Germanic, the common ancestor of modern German and English. Distinctive features of West, as opposed to North and East Germanic, include gemination, a doubling of consonants under certain circumstances, and also the loss of the strong masculine noun ending found in Norse as *-r* and Gothic as *-s* (compare *ulfr* in old Norse and *wulfs* in Gothic with *wolf* in both German and English). Within the West Germanic languages, another series of radical changes to the stops in particular, occurring around A.D. 500, beginning in the area of the Alps and moving north as far as, roughly speaking, Aachen, made for a division between what we now refer to as the High and Low German dialects. Those that were affected by this High German Sound Shift to any degree (the shifting of the stops or plosives becomes less noticeable as the shift progresses northwest) constitute the High German group, of which the modern standard German language is the descendant. The dialects of the Lombards, Bavarians, Alemanni, Thuringians, and many of the Franks fall into this group, even though some (the Lombards) gave up German in favor of a local language at an early stage and hence are barely recorded, while others (Thuringian) are not recorded in writing for some long time. By Low German then, those dialects not affected by the shift, is meant Low Franconian, the ancestor of Modern Dutch, and Saxon (linked with modern Plattdeutsch), plus the various dialects of Frisian and their close relative Anglo-Saxon, the ancestor of English. As a very simple example, and again using only the unvoiced plosives /p/, /t/, and /k/, the High German Sound Shift is the reason behind the contrast between modern

German *Pfad, zehn, machen* and their unshifted English equivalents *path, ten*, and *make*.[9]

The emergence of a standard and unified High German language was a long process, a unificatory progression involving political, social, and finally technological elements (in the arrival of printing). There is no unified language in any of the early stages, and when we speak of Old High German, the first written stage of German from about 750 to 1050, we are deliberately simplifying what should really be called Old Bavarian, Old Alemannic, and so forth. Written materials in the early dialects vary considerably, owing to dialectal peculiarities and the absence of an orthographic standard, and there are differences in vocabulary and syntax as well as just in spelling. Still more sound changes after the middle of the eleventh century within the High German dialects gave rise to a new stage, known as Middle High German, a kind of aristocratic literary language did emerge, and movement toward standardization, always linked with politics, would continue through the Reformation (with Luther playing a vital role). In any case, for many centuries, again down to the Reformation and beyond, the German language itself was seen in some social spheres at least as a secondary language, excluded from many spheres of intellectual life in favor of Latin, whose dominance throughout the Middle Ages cannot be overestimated. However clear it may be from later written material and from outside sources as far back as Tacitus, to say nothing of iconographical representations such as those of the story of Weland or Wayland, the mythological gold- and swordsmith depicted on the Franks Casket, that an oral literature existed in all the branches of Germanic, this can now only be reconstructed for individual cases with a great deal of conjecture.[10] The transmission of literature in any other way requires writing, and leaving the question of runic and the cul-de-sac of Gothic aside for the moment, the role of the Latin Church is formative in the simplest of ways. However inadequate the Latin alphabet may be for representing some of the sounds of early (and indeed to some extent also the modern) Germanic languages, it established itself through the offices of the Catholic Church for the purpose of transcribing German and English in particular. The runic alphabet, designed for carving and with mystical overtones as well, is sometimes linked with major works of literature,[11] and some letters made their way later into Germanic versions of the Latin alphabets. When he translated the Bible into Gothic, Ulfila had to design an alphabet, which he based largely upon Greek, though with some Latin and runic letters, but this did not last beyond the demise of the Gothic language. Runic, too, fell out of use. Although other alphabets have been used for Germanic languages (Yiddish uses a modified Hebrew system, for example), the alphabet of the Romans was victorious. The emergence of German (paralleled by other Germanic languages) as a

Schriftsprache, with a gradual and in some respects ad hoc standardization, led to a unification of language prior to, but linked with the search for a national identity. It should be added, of course, that even in the earliest stages of Germanic writing the culture depended upon the individually copied manuscript. Printing is a determinative and vital technology in the question of language standardization, but for the early period it is centuries away, so that we are faced with "the dynamic of the medieval manuscript matrix" — the citation is from an introduction to a series of essays on what has been called the "new philology" as applied to medieval studies.[12] The importance of the written language as the vehicle for memory, and hence for decisions, laws and government, needs no underlining, of course, so that the very fact of land ownership documents in, say, Gothic or Old High German have an importance that is more than simply linguistic.[13]

Germani from all three ancient language branches are in fact associated more with movement than with any clearly defined geographical locality, through what is known as the folk migrations (*Völkerwanderungen*). Although there is archeologically identifiable movement of some of the Germanic groups — the Goths are an example — in the first centuries A.D., the most significant periods of folk migrations came with the influx of Germanic tribes into the vacuum of the collapsing Western Roman empire in the old provinces of Gallia, Hispania, and Italia itself, to say nothing of the more remote outlying provinces, such as Britannia.[14] Dates such as that of the sack of Rome by the Goths in 410 and the eventual deposing of the last emperor in 476 are well known. If earlier Roman writers had identified a number of separate tribes beyond their borders in what they termed Germania, tribal movements are clearer from the fourth century on and especially in the fifth, as Germanic tribes moved from outside the old Roman Empire into virtually the entire area that the Romans had occupied.

We shall begin with the tribes that form the East Germanic language group, especially the Vandals, Burgundians and Goths: by the first decades of the fifth century the Vandals had moved from Eastern Europe into what is now Northern France, then into the Roman province of Hispania (Spain), and by 429 had crossed into North Africa, Roman Mauretania, the land of the Moors, where they set up a kingdom centered on Carthage, under Gaiseric, from which they could raid Southern Europe. They were eventually conquered in 534 by Belisarius, a general of the Byzantine Emperor Justinian, and their kingdom was virtually destroyed. It was only about a century and a half later taken over by the Arabs from the east, who took on the name of the Moors.

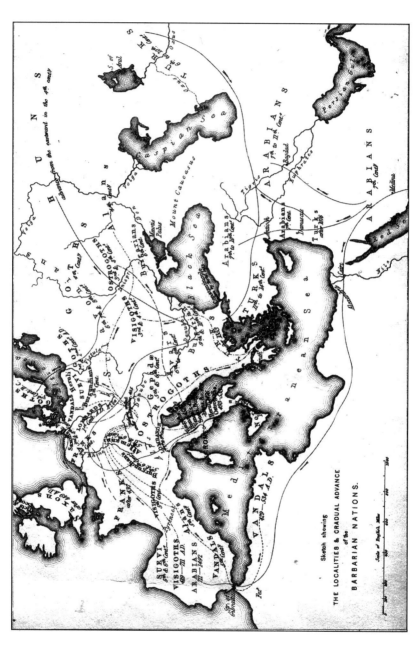

Map of the folk-migrations

The Vandals are the furthest traveled of the early Germanic tribes, even if they have given their name in modern English principally to a force of destruction. Their civilization was not well-structured and indeed they were not much more than a pirate kingdom in Africa. The Burgundians also moved southwest across Europe, settling first around the Rhine. But they were conquered by what was left of the Roman Empire, which meant effectively the soldiers in Gallia, modern France, in the fourth century, and then only because of a particularly effective general Flavius Aëtius, the Roman military leader in the Western Empire, one of whose most effective strategies was using barbarian auxiliary troops against each other. To defeat the Burgundians under their king Gundahari in 435–36 he brought in Huns, who in the next years destroyed the Burgundians completely. After 437 what was left of the Burgundians went southwest again to the territory that preserves their name, what is now known as Burgundy in France. The kingdom of Burgundy on the Rhine was in turn eventually ruled by the Franks.

A non-Germanic tribe, the Huns, had made a spectacular entry into Europe from Asia in the late fourth and early fifth century. Without a written culture, so that our information about them comes largely from hostile historians, they swept across Germany and France with enormous success, especially under their greatest leader, Attila, who ruled the Huns from 434 until his death in 453. Although he was not in fact involved at the fall of the Burgundians when they were attacked by the Roman general Aëtius and by Hunnish auxiliaries in 435–37 (an idea that becomes established in various branches of early Germanic literature), he continued the Hunnish tradition of incursive raids into Roman Gaul, and led the Huns against the combined forced of Aëtius's imperial army and the Visigoths at the Catalonian plains in 451. He was defeated, but in the following year ravaged northern Italy, dying in 453 on his wedding night to a Germanic princess, of a hemorrhage supposedly brought on by excessive drinking (Attila has a literary reputation for drunkenness), but also leading to the suggestion (again reflected in literature) that he had been murdered.

The Goths, another East Germanic group like the Vandals and the Burgundians, had originated (by tradition) in Scandinavia, and are attested at an early stage at the mouth of the Vistula in modern Poland. They moved in the first Christian centuries toward the Black Sea in a number of groups, developing eventually (but only after some time) into two groups, the Visigoths and the Ostrogoths. It was the Visigoth leader Alaric who first sacked Rome, but the Visigoths moved on to set up a kingdom within the Western Roman Empire in Aquitaine, based on Toulouse, and then later in Spain, where they were more successful than the Vandals, and their kingdom, with its capital at Toledo, lasted for two centuries, producing some notable rulers. They had been Arian Christians, adherents to a variant creed, that is, and which was later condemned as heresy, but they had served too as very early Christian missionaries to Germany and had indeed converted several other Germanic peoples to Arianism. In Spain they themselves eventually adopted Catholic Christianity, and survived as a political unit until they were subjugated at the beginning the eighth century, when the Moors under Tarik (whose name is preserved in the last element of the place-name Gibraltar) conquered and replaced them as rulers of Spain. The Ostrogoths, meanwhile, had themselves moved west to Italy, and at the end of the fifth century had set up a kingdom there under Theoderic the Great, but in their turn they too were defeated by the Byzantine generals Belisarius and Narses. Although there was still a handful of Ostrogoths in the Crimea in the seventeenth century, they disappeared, in effect, from history.

After the death of Justinian, the Byzantine emperor, in 565, a West Germanic tribe, the Lombards, invaded northern Italy, and their name, Lombardy, remains, together with other Germanic elements in the names associated with northern Italy in particular. The name of the great patriot Garibaldi, for example, is purely Germanic, containing the elements *gar* and *bald* [ready, strong], with only an Italian ending. Even though the Lombards gave up their Germanic language in favor of the local language (later Italian), as had the Visigoths in Spain and later the Franks in France, we do have some early relics of the Lombardic language. Their kingdom continued in northern Italy until they were subsumed into the Frankish empire under Charlemagne after 800.

Of other West Germanic groups, the Alemanni, who were not a tribe but a kind of confederation of smaller groups (their name means "all men"), settled in the southern part of Germany in the sixth century and in what is now central France. Although they were a coherent group, they were continually harassed by the most powerful of them all, the Franks, who had replaced the Burgundians on the Rhine and in central Germany, and who would push the Visigoths down into Spain. Eventually in the eighth century the Alemanni, too, were taken over into the Frankish kingdom. Their name, however, provided the Romance languages with designations for Germany such as Allemagne. Another confederation of Germanic tribes, the Bavarians, formed in the early part of the sixth century largely from tribes that had been subject to the Ostrogoths, were also defeated by various Frankish kings.

The Franks, the most significant of the West Germanic tribes, were originally a confederation of Germanic groups in what is now central and northwestern Germany, began to expand into Roman Gaul — France and the Low Countries. Chlodwig or Clovis, from a ruling dynasty known as the Merovingians, set up a kingdom at Tournai (now in Belgium), and gradually defeated and drove out or subsumed into his own lands the other Germanic tribes. Clovis adopted Catholic Christianity in 503, and this is extremely important for the history of the west of Europe, since it marked the end of the hitherto powerful Gothic Arianism, which the Church had pronounced heretical. Frankish territory gradually came to embrace what is now, roughly speaking, France and Belgium on the one hand, and north and central Germany on the other.

The ruling Merovingian dynasty itself degenerated gradually to a situation in which the lands of the Franks were ruled in effect by stewards, the most famous of whom was Charles Martel, the hammer, who came to rule the whole of the Frankish kingdom from 719–41, and whose defeat of a Saracen army in 732 at Poitiers was also of enormous importance to the later development of Europe, just as the defeat of Varus at Kalkriese had been centuries before. The battle at Kalkriese prevented further Roman expansion; the victory of Charles Martel at Poitiers stopped the further expansion of Islam into Europe.

Charles Martel was succeeded by his son, Pépin the Short, who ten years later, in 751, deposed the last Merovingian king and established the new royal dynasty of the Carolingians. Pépin's son, Charles, who came to the throne in 768 was to rule later as Charlemagne, and although earlier Germanic leaders had come close to assuming the mantle of the Roman emperors, he was on Christmas Day, 800, formally crowned emperor of a newly constituted Holy Roman Empire, marking the ultimate triumph of this West Germanic group and in fact laying down the foundations for modern Europe to a great extent, as Charlemagne's empire divided in the next generations into what we would now understand as France and Germany. Charlemagne's view of a divinely appointed kingship may not actually have made him into a Holy Roman emperor, but he ruled, for a while, a largely unified western Europe, working together with the Roman church, but accepting, although he legislated on church matters, that the Pope in Rome would be charged with the exposition of the faith. Walter Ullmann has noted that Charlemagne's rule in the west was in fact very like that of the Byzantine Empire, but that the Byzantine rulers did not acknowledge the primacy of the Roman church. "This important difference was to prove itself of crucial concern to later royal (and imperial) generations. In Charlemagne's reign this thin end of the wedge could not possibly be perceived in its complexity."[15] This dualism of state and church would be a more or less permanent problem for centuries.

If Charlemagne's empire was a parallel to that of Byzantium (with whose rulers he eventually reached an accommodation through a treaty with Nicephorus I, in 810, a year in which he made three separate peace treaties), his lands in the West were defined to a great extent by the enemies that he had to face: the Asian invaders on the eastern side — the Avars, known as the White Huns, and on that eastern side, the Slavs. To the south, the attacks came from a relatively new force in the world, the Arabs, unified with a new religion, Islam. In the north, too, a new and this time Germanic force was also gaining strength, the Vikings, but their own period of major expansion was yet to come. Charlemagne conquered the Avars and held back the Slavs, and in the north eventually reached an agreement of non-aggression with the Vikings, first with Godefrid and then with his son, Hemming, king of the Danes, also in 810. Finally, in that same year, and after years of fighting, Charlemagne made a peace treaty with Hakim, grandson of the great Caliph of Cordoba, Abd al Rahman. Indeed, he maintained a fairly cordial relationship, of course at a distance, with the ruler of Baghdad, his equally great contemporary Harun al Rashid (786–809), who famously sent Charlemagne the gift of an elephant, although Harun did play Charlemagne and western Christendom off against the Byzantines, his immediate neighbors.[16] We have moved on somewhat in time from the age of the migrations, but the age of Charlemagne, his sons and grandsons marks two important points for history and for literature. First, the establishment, after the division of his empire in 843, not thirty years after his death, of identifiable territories roughly corresponding to modern France and Germany, so that at last we reach a geographic approximation of what might be called Germany. And second, it is in the age of Charlemagne that we find the earliest writings in High (and Low) German. It is true that the Goths had a written language some centuries earlier, but what survives in Gothic comprises only a partial Bible translation (mostly the New Testament); early runic inscriptions, too, tend to be slight and are often difficult to interpret in any case; whether we may count an enigmatic single-line inscription on a horn from Gallehus as literature or even poetry is questionable.[17]

To round off the earlier stages of folk migration, a final West Germanic group, the Saxons, moved from North Germany, together with Angles and Jutes from Denmark to the most remote of the Roman provinces, Britannia, and took over much of the country. The legions had left, Britain was too far away from Rome to justify defending it, and the local Romano-British (that is, Celtic) forces could only hold them off for a while until they either retreated to the fringes, to Wales, to Cornwall, or indeed into mythology, led by the last Romano-British hero, whose mythological role is far better known than his historical one, namely Arthur. Later on, Charlemagne himself corresponded with some of the Anglo-Saxon leaders, including the king of Northumbria, and the king of Mercia, Offa, to whom in 796 he sent "a Hunnish sword-belt and sword, and two lengths of silk" — valuable gifts to demonstrate friendship. Charlemagne also took England's greatest scholar, Alcuin, away from York to his palace school.

Almost the last of the Germanic movements, not really part of the great folk migrations as such, but later and indeed by far the most far reaching, is the expansion of the Vikings, seafarers who, from the eighth century, began a series of major explorations and conquests. From Scandinavia they settled in the Faeroes and Shetland Islands (Faroese is a descendant of Old Norse, and the Shetlanders spoke Norse until the eighteenth century), and at the start of the eighth century they moved south from Orkney, off the north of Scotland (the Orkney Islands belonged to Denmark until 1469), through the Western Isles of Scotland (where Norse place names still share the map nearly equally with Gaelic ones), and established a kingdom in Dublin in 852 which was undefeated until 1014 at the Battle of Clontarf, and even then not decisively. Toward the end of the eighth century and all through the ninth, Vikings from Denmark and Norway attacked the Anglo-Saxons in England, and took over the land north of a line drawn roughly from London to Liverpool (known from 886 on as the Danelaw), and although they were held back in Southern England after the Saxon leader, Alfred the Great, defeated them at the battle of Ethandune (Edington) in 878, renewed their attacks particularly during the reign of Æthelred II, the Unready (978–1016). The Vikings were paid an enormous amount of what is effectively protection money, known as Danegeld, and by 1016 the Danish king, Cnut, son of Sweyn Forkbeard, was acclaimed king of England. In continental Europe the Vikings had turned their attention to what is now France and the Low Countries, then part of the kingdom of the West Franks, and after an initial defeat were, in the tenth century, given land centered on the city of Rouen, where they set up an independent state which they called the state of the Northmen or Norsemen, Normandy, from which England itself was again conquered in 1066.

Moving east, Swedish Vikings had colonized Finland, and moved into what is now Russia, at the same time as the kingdom was being set up in Ireland. By the later part of the ninth century a capital had been set up at Novgorod and the Duchy of Kiev, the political origins of the Russian state, founded. From here, the Vikings moved into southeastern Europe, with Vikings warriors serving in the palace guard of the Byzantine emperors, the Varangian guard. Evidence of their movements is provided by carved inscriptions such as those on the stone lion in the harbor at the Piraeus (taken to Venice in 1687) and that in northern Greenland at Kingitorsoak. From Greenland — a name given in the hope of attracting settlers — they moved at the end of the tenth century to what they called Markland or Vinland, which is a land where vines grow, presumably northern New England, and the expeditions by Leif Eriksson are well known. They also reached an area which they called Svalbarðr, which may actually be Arctic Spitzbergen.[18]

Echoes of the *Völkerwanderung* can be found in place names, but the spread of names lacks consistency. It is a philological pleasantry of some antiquity that Germany ought really to be called France, after the Franks, France Romania, since it used the language of the Romans (although Romania itself, where a Latin-derived language is still spoken, *is* appropriately named) and Switzerland Allemagne, after the Alemanni. But the Franks did give their name not only to France, where the local Gallo-Roman language predominated, but to Franken, Franconia in modern Germany. Roman imperial names predominate still in Europe, with the notable exception of France. Britain, Spain and Germany are all Roman names, although other languages preserve earlier tribal names, that of the Alemanni in Romance names for Germany, that of the Saxons in Celtic names (as modern Welsh *Saeson,* English, and the Scots word *Sassenach*), and England itself, deriving from the name of the Angles. As with Franken, tribal names are preserved in regions (Bayern, Sachsen, Thüringen); the Island of Rügen has the name at least of the Rugians, an East Germanic tribe; the extent of the migrations is still well illustrated by Bourgogne, Burgundy, the name of the East Germanic Burgundians who settled the area, and where Germanic tribes actually adopted the language spoken by the locals, names still remain, such as Lombardy.

Given the early tribal distinctions and the absence of a national unity, it is interesting to consider the rise of the national name *Deutsch,* which is still much debated. A Latin word *teudisca* or *theotisca* comes from a Germanic word represented in the earliest recorded Germanic language, Gothic, as *þiudisko* (in the Gothic Bible it renders "gentile," "heathen"), and comes in Latin during the early Middle Ages to mean something like Germanic, as opposed to Romance or Latin. Thus documents relating to Charlemagne — whose language was High German — and slightly earlier to the Anglo-Saxon king, Offa, use the word. Under Charlemagne it could mean any of the dialects — Otfrid called his first chapter *Cur scriptor hunc librum thodisce dictaverit* (why the author wrote this book in German), but in his own vernacular he refers always to *frenkisc,* Frankish. It is used in Latin, which was, after all, the dominant written language for many centuries, to define the language in opposition to a non-Germanic *lingua romana,* a Romance language deriving from Latin, and it is not until later that it comes to be used, still with the generalized linguistic sense, in German (as *diutisk, diutsch*); it is noticeable that no distinction is made between High or Low German, as the present use of the English word Dutch indicates; indeed, the phrase High Dutch continued in English as a periphrastic version of German. To speak of Old High German is in any case an unhistorical simplification, albeit a necessary and useful one. Otfrid was concerned about writing in what he thought of as Frankish, and Notker the German in the early eleventh century was also aware of the novelty of using the vernacular language. Martin Luther was perhaps the first modern writer to give a programmatic statement (in the context of translation) on what is good German, and to speculate upon how the Archangel Gabriel would have addressed the Virgin at the Annunciation *wan er hette wollen sie deutsch grussen* (had he wanted to greet her in German).[19]

From the Middle Ages, however, the word *deutsch* became part of political history, as it is identified with a concept of nationhood, even if we may trace the origins of a specifically German Reich to the Treaty of Verdun and the breakup of Charlemagne's empire in 843.[20] That was technically an East Frankish[21] empire, and only under the Saxon emperor Otto the Great (936–973) does the concept of a German empire, using the word *diutisk*, appear. The notion of a holy and then a secular *deutsches Reich* and the designation of a geographical rather than socio-political concept *Deutschland* remains a shifting notion throughout the centuries.[22] It is still forgotten too easily that Hoffman's line *Deutschland, Deutschland über Alles* is a plea not for superiority (it does not seek to place Germany above all others, of course), but for nationhood before anything else, although his *Deutschlandlied* does offer a precise set of geographical borders from the Meuse to the Memel and from the Adige to the Skaggerak. And of course, within the past century, Europe has experienced (under the Third Reich) a *Großdeutschland* which included Austria (renamed *Ostmark,* eastern marches), plus other areas that were not entirely German speaking, but which excluded Switzerland and the Netherlands, and which caused a generation of émigré writers to ask what *Deutschtum* now meant. Thomas Mann could in May 1945, addressing Germany by radio through the British Broadcasting Corporation, speak of the German as having been deprived by Hitler, the person least worthy of so doing (*der Allerunberufenste*) of his German-ness (*sein Deutschtum*), and would later in the same year ask whether Germany was even a geographic entity any more. Ernst von Salomon answered in 1951 in his extended response to the allied military questionnaire, the *Fragebogen,* the question of *Staatsangehörigkeit* (nationality) that in the absence of a proper German state, he was a Prussian.[23] The country — even so rather different from that drawn on maps issued under the Third Reich — divided into politically divergent eastern and western parts, and having sat uncomfortably (and with some linguistic division too) on a line between two conflicting ideologies, joined together again in 1989–90.

In a sense, the Roman definition of Germania was a negative one, the lands outside the empire. What constitutes Germany at any point after the turn of the millennium has depended, of course, upon the historical and political situation, from *Kleinstaaterei* (regional particularism) to the Third Reich, and whether there is now an identifiable ethnos remains debatable in the present multicultural society.

The language designation "German" now refers to West Germanic High German as spoken (and, perhaps more important, used as the spoken and written official language) within a specific geographical area, that covered by modern Germany, Austria and Switzerland, with some few remaining linguistic remnants elsewhere (and not very many in the past few centuries). Even within that area, dialect variations are always present, mainly spoken but also written, and Plattdeutsch, for example, as opposed to the official High German language, is still spoken in north Germany.[24] In the south, German in Austria and especially in Switzerland exhibits considerable variation, and in the latter case it is an historical accident, perhaps, that Schwyzertüütsch is not now regarded as a separate, if related, language, on the pattern of English and Dutch. The point was underlined by a film made by Rolf Lyssy in 1978 called *Die Schweizermacher,* hinging on the difficulties precisely for German speakers of learning Swiss German for citizenship reasons. Equally, German is still spoken in some areas outside this geographical area, and this feature has been the cause of conflict, of course, in relatively recent history: one need mention only the German-speaking groups in the Sudetenland, in Alsace, in the Italian Tyrol, in what is now Slovenia and elsewhere, and going back even further, in Danish Schleswig-Holstein.

Germanic languages have spread to cover most of the world, with the dominance of English as the primary example. Other Germanic languages have played a very small part in this modern migration, though we may point to Afrikaans in South Africa and the remnants of modern High German in Namibia, formerly German South West Africa, and even in North America to Pennsylvania German and one or two tiny Low German survivals (Plautdietsch).[25] There is no real colonial literature in German itself, and the rather different literature of exile during the Nazi period was a limited and temporary phenomenon. Language changes constantly, of course, perhaps more rapidly than usual in a period of great technological advance, and the globalization implied by the age of mass media has led in German not only to a media language of its own[26] but to a dominance of English influence, forced upon it by advances in technology.

Sociological change, patterns of thought or intellectual movements can and do also affect the language, and in the case of Germany one might consider supranational questions, such as the so-called feminization of the language (the word *entpatrifizieren,* ["de-paternalisation"] for example, is a neologism based upon the analogy with *entnazifizieren* ["denazification"] and thus has emotional as well as gender connotations). Gender correctness does lead to special problems in a language where the nouns have grammatical gender in any case.[27] There has been interest too in *Jugendsprache,* youth language, all this giving different kinds of linguistic divisions from those based on tribal, regional or latterly political differences. The multiculturalism implied by immigrant movements in Europe has led to language changes in Germany as elsewhere, and the problem of the German language after the re-unification of Germany of 1990, too, is demonstrated by that very word, given that *Wiedervereinigung* and *Vereinigung* were both used, the latter being preferred since the Germany that emerged had never previously existed either geographically or politically. None of these features matches even closely the dominant influence of American English on the current German language.

Of course there are some identifiable natural boundaries for what we may call modern Germania, albeit not quite those implied in the words of the *Deutschlandlied*, where the boundaries are the Meuse and the Memel, the Adige and the sea around Denmark. The Alps and the North Sea do form natural boundaries, as does the Rhine to the west; but the eastern boundary is far harder to pin down, and various rivers have been called upon to serve as a limit, but the borders with the Slav world are difficult to determine, and have fluctuated over the past centuries. The ranges of mountains in the south — the Alps and the Carpathians — certainly form frontiers, and the contrast with the plains in the north is striking, although we must, with Edward Sapir, be cautious about the ascription of environmental influences to cultural developments, especially of and within language.[28] The effect of landscape (or indeed the sea) upon literature is well known, especially in nineteenth- and twentieth-century German writers such as Theodor Storm, for example, or Siegfried Lenz.

Socio-economic factors and cultural factors have always affected the concept of Germany. One predominant factor which is at once potentially unifying and dividing is religion. We may speak of a pre-Christian Germanic religion (for which we may even name a still moderately familiar pantheon of gods), but must remain aware that much of the material is known to us from relatively late or outside sources, and that even archeologically we cannot gauge to any real extent the beliefs of the Germanic group, if indeed there was a coherence to that set of customs at all. The promotion of Christianity, first by the Romans after it had been adopted in the Empire, then via the Goths already implies a divide, given that the latter group were Arian Christians, with different views on the Trinity, and influencing very strongly other East and West Germanic tribes for a long period. The somewhat roundabout adoption of Catholic Christianity in all the territories has been well documented, with special reference in continental Germania to Irish and then to Anglo-Saxon missions. Important enough as a social factor, it also provided the basis for the writing of German. This effect had been seen already with the necessary invention of the largely Greek-based alphabet by Ulfila to translate the Bible into Gothic in the fourth century, but with the spread of partly new, partly revitalized Christianity in the seventh and eighth centuries in Germany the Roman alphabet was known and available. Equally important for the development of the German language some centuries later still was, of course, the effect of the Reformation of the sixteenth century, and the making accessible of the Bible to a broad spectrum of people, translated by Luther and assisted by the latest technology of printing. The cultural significance of the Reformation (on both sides of the Protestant-Catholic divide) cannot be underestimated, although of course this new religious division had an effect on literature. So, too, have other religious questions: the position of the Jews in German-speaking territories and more specifically their movement from them, has linguistic and literary implications in the development of another Germanic language, this time the Yiddish language, which achieved a real florescence, in spite of some earlier isolated high points, only in the nineteenth century. But it can arguably be traced back to the Middle Ages and to works written down in the late fourteenth century such as *Dukus Horant* (if we do not wish to describe that distant relative of *Kudrun* simply as Middle High German in Hebrew orthography), or to the later so-called *Tsena-Urena,* the storybook Bible designed for women. Nowadays in a society that can be and has been called both post-Christian and multicultural, religious conflict has thrown up further problems. In terms of linguistic history, of course, the layers are always present at the same time, so that a ceremony performed by the (Protestant) sovereign in Britain nowadays with a distribution of money on Maundy Thursday, combines in its name an earlier Latin Christianity (*mandatum* being the first word of the antiphon for that day), and the pre-Christian name of Donar/Þor in the name of the day of the week.

A volume intended to be introductory to a literary history will necessarily be disparate, since much of it is to do with the pre-literary period and the rest with — if such a formulation is permissible — the non-literary beginnings of literature.[29] It is for this reason that the volume is entitled "early Germanic culture," and as such it tries to consider some of the most important sources for the later development of what we understand by German literature, and also some of the early parallel developments, although clearly some aspects of this development process will be treated less fully than others. The first part of any literary history is a history of culture in general and of language in particular; consequently we attempt here first to move from the general consideration of what is meant by the study of Germanic antiquity in theory and in practice, to the classical literature of German origins. It would be possible to pick thereafter from a large number of cultural aspects of early Germanic society, or art, or what can be gleaned of social practices through archeology and in written history in other languages. However, two areas are of signal importance: the initial contact between the *Germani* and the greatest force of the ancient world, that of Rome; and the confrontation with what be-came the dominant religion of the west, Christianity. It is significant that it was only at the end of the twentieth century that an actual location was at last established for the *Hermannsschlacht,* a battle that had played a part for centuries in the German consciousness in particular, celebrated in one way by the victors, but with history being written in this case largely by the vanquished, so that Varus's famous loss of the Imperial Eagles in the Teutoburg Forest to Arminius (Hermann) and the Cherusci in A.D. 9 became a potent symbol of heroic resistance on one hand and of barbar-ianism in a modern sense on the other. Archeology — both field and lin-guistic — and to some extent literary sources may help provide a picture of pre-Christian Germanic religion, even if the name of the chief of the gods may vary (as will be clear in later chapters) from Odin to Wodan or Woden in different subdivisions of the culture. The methodologies and practices of these attendant disciplines, and a consideration of how they contribute to an understanding of Germanic culture and literature are extremely significant.

The earliest literature in most cultures is oral, and this requires at least a theoretical consideration as a transition from cultural considerations in general to more readily acceptable areas of literary study. "At least," be-cause empirical evidence (other than modern extrapolations, as in the work of Milman Parry or Albert Lord on twentieth-century oral bards)[30] is necessarily lacking. It has been pointed out that there is a strong distinc-tion between the language of record and the spoken language — the for-mer depending upon the status and context of what is being written and by whom, and this is of importance in the period when Latin dominates for written material in Germania.[31] But for the commitment of thought in more permanent form in general — with the use, that is, of writing — we must consider first the writing-system known as runic, which is not only pragmatic, but also has a mystic dimension (albeit one as exaggerated by modern romantics as it was abused by the Nazis), and then the language of the Goths and the first writings in manuscript form, before we reach the period in which the Latin alphabet provides more familiar written Germanic languages.

The final chapters of this collection, having arrived at that point, are more clearly literary, but now the problem must be confronted that was raised in the opening paragraph: of the chapters that look ostensibly at written records, only one is even (partly) to do with High German, the closest ancestor of modern German, and there, too, much of the material is not very literary. Even in the Old High German period, a self-conscious concept of *Hochdeutsch* is still some way off, and even the equivalent of our notion of *Deutsch* in the early stages meant simply Germanic rather than Roman. Runic monuments are extremely limited, however, in their literary content, even if a claim may be made for the first line of Germanic poetry ever recorded on the Gallehus horn. Gothic is the oldest Germanic language written down in manuscript, and is the one surviving fully documented East Germanic language, with a fourth-century Bible translation which makes a polyvalent cultural statement of itself, even if the language itself vanished. It was used in Spain in the seventh and eighth centuries, and far later in the east, in the Crimea, but much reduced. There is no other literature, although there are still echoes of Gothic history even in Old High German. North Germanic literature in the form of Old Norse-Icelandic comes a few centuries later, but by now we are in the territory of recognizable literary history. Old Norse offers a rich, important and ongoing literature, and one that preserves much to do with the earliest Germanic peoples — including in works like the *Hamðismál* the Goths once more, and the links between Norse poetry and the Nibelungen saga are a bridge to later High German writings.

Moving at last to the broad group of West Germanic languages, Low German is represented first by Old English with its rich literature, and, again, with links to German writings. Here the case of *Waltharius* might stand as a symbol of the linkage: there are a couple of fragments of a Walter saga in the Old English *Waldere,* a heroic saga based on historical antecedents, perhaps, from the Burgundian and Gothic worlds. In High German there are later references to the story, but the full version is in Latin, though it was written by a German. These early roots are greatly entangled.

On the continent, High German itself — that is, a group of dialects that share certain features known collectively as Old High German — begins to be written down in the eighth century, almost exclusively in the service of the Roman Church (the Goths had been Arian rather than Roman Catholic Christians), and with little material surviving that we might recognize as literature. But there is a conscious effort and a self-awareness for the first time, even if the writer who may stand as a symbol of this time, Otfrid of Weissenburg, in the middle of the ninth century, thought of himself as writing in Frankish rather than German, and worked in a monastery that is now called Wissembourg in Alsace. Otfrid, the first named writer, the first self-conscious German literary figure, may stand as a starting point, but he too did not spring fully armed from nowhere. Anglo-Saxon has a religious epic, and on the continent Otfrid had an important forerunner in the anonymous *Heliand*. It is fitting that a chapter be devoted to another Low German text, the Old Saxon *Heliand* here, since it is a work that can all too easily — but quite wrongly — be omitted or sidelined in a history of German literature. In continental Low German, the *Heliand* stands alone, however, and some other early High or Low dialects either died out, while others were committed to parchment only later (such as, in spite of the name, Old Frisian).

Where, then, is one to start the first volume of the history of German literature? A precise beginning is, of course, impossible to determine: claims can be made for the songs mentioned by Tacitus (though of course we do not have them), for the inscription on the Gallehus horn, or for Ulfila's Gothic Bible, just as much as for Caedmon (who lived, according to Bede, in the late seventh century), the *Heliand* or Otfrid's Gospel Book. Furthermore, many of these existed side-by-side with literature that is clearly Germanic, but which was written in another language. The history of the Goths written by the Senator Cassiodorus (ca. 485–ca. 580), and adapted by the Goth Jordanes (who lived and wrote in the middle and later part of the sixth century), the *Getica*, is in Latin, and so is Bede's (ca. 673–735) history of the English Church and people. Otfrid apologized to his ecclesiastical superior for *not* writing in Latin, the language used in the written works of his much respected teacher, the German prelate Hrabanus Maurus (776 or 784–856), and indeed of his teacher, the Anglo-Saxon pedagogue and scholar Alcuin (ca. 735–804). This volume is, as indicated, in some respects a fragmented one, and that is inevitable, since there are many contributory sources to a German literature, and at the beginnings these were indeed diverse. It provides introductions to some of the paths toward the determination of what is meant by Germanic culture — through classical writings, social and religious history, archeology, then through oral transmission on to the earliest written Germanic, and finally to the beginnings of literature proper.

Notes

[1] D. H. Green, *Language and History in the Early Germanic World* (Cambridge: CUP, 1998), uses the word *Germani* to render *Germanen*, and this will be followed here. Green's work will not be referred to specifically for every point, but it is a work of considerable importance in most of the areas indicated in this introduction. The concept *Germania* is equally useful.

[2] This is a highly simplified presentation, and it has to be noted that German itself has undergone further sound changes not always shared by English, which is why English words rather than German ones have been chosen to demonstrate this shift. There are many introductions to this area of study both in German and English, but a good (if outdated) brief introduction is provided by Arthur Kirk, *An Introduction to the Historical Study of New High German* (Manchester: Manchester UP, 1923, repr. 1961).

[3] A. F. C. Vilmar, *Geschichte der deutschen Nationallitteratur* (4th ed., Marburg and Leipzig: Elwert, 1850, still present in the 20th edition, 1881).

[4] *Otfrids Evangelienbuch,* ed. Oskar Erdmann, 7th ed. by Ludwig Wolff (Tübingen: Niemeyer, 1973) This is Book I, i, 59–60.

[5] See for example the work of Luigi Luca Cavalli-Sforza, *Genes, People and Languages,* trans. Mark Seielstad (New York: North Point Press, 2000). Some earlier anthropological-ethnological methods became tainted when used for purposes of racial discrimination rather than objective enquiry. This is a permanent danger.

[6] P. V. Glob, *The Bog People,* trans. Rupert Bruce-Mitford (London: Paladin, 1971).

[7] Green, *Language and History,* 182–235.

[8] The standard work remains E. A. Thompson, *The Early Germans* (Oxford: Clarendon, 1965), and see also Ferdinand Lot, *Les invasions Germaniques: La pénétration mutuelle du monde barbare et du monde romain* (Paris: Payot [1935], 1945), with good brief comments on the various tribal groups. A useful edition of Tacitus's *Germania* and *Agricola* is that by Henry Furneaux, revised by J. G. Anderson (Oxford: Clarendon, 1938), with a translation by H. Mattingley, *Tacitus on Britain and Germany* (Harmondsworth: Penguin, 1948). Several chapters in the present volume consider Germanic/Roman interaction. For a brief but useful survey of Germanic tribal usage, see William Stubbs, *Select Charters* ([1870], 9th ed. by H. W. C. Davis (Oxford: Clarendon, repr. 1966), 7–9.

[9] See Theodor Frings, *Grundlegung einer Geschichte der deutschen Sprache* (3rd ed., Halle/Saale: Niemeyer, 1957) for what are still extremely valuable basic essays on linguistic and cultural geography, the divisions of the German(ic) linguistic area, and the definitions of West Germanic. Modern histories of the language are plentiful, but see as another very useful small handbook: Werner König, *dtv-Atlas zur deutschen Sprache* (Munich: dtv, 1978).

[10] See D. H. Green, "Orality and Reading. The State of Research in Medieval Studies," *Speculum* 65 (1990): 267–80 and his *Medieval Listening and Reading* (Cambridge: CUP, 1994). There is another useful and brief, but thought-provoking study by Haijo J. Westra, "Literacy, Orality and Medieval Patronage," *Journal of Medieval Latin* 1 (1991): 52–59. The Franks casket (named after the collector Sir Augustus Franks rather the Germanic people) is housed in the British Museum, dates from around 700, and shows illustrations both of pre-Christian sagas and of the Gospels. See on this and other examples David Wilson, *The Anglo-Saxons* (Harmondsworth: Penguin, rev. ed. 1971).

[11] See the Ruthwell Cross inscriptions and the Anglo-Saxon *Dream of the Rood,* ed. Bruce Dickins and Alan S. C. Ross (London: Methuen, 1934).

[12] The quotation is from Stephen G. Nichols's introduction to an issue of *Speculum* devoted to the New Philology and containing a series of interesting papers: *Speculum* 65 (1990): 1–10. Most studies of the New Philology take as their starting point Bernard Cerquiglini, *Eloge de la variante: Histoire critique de la philologie* (Paris: Seuil, 1989). As with many critical movements, defining what precisely is meant by the key term is difficult.

[13] See Patrick J. Geary, "Land, Language and Memory in Europe 700–1100," *Transactions of the Royal Historical Society,* 6th Series, 9 (1999): 169–84. The paper is one of a series in the same volume on literacy, and several of the papers refer to such standard works as Rosamond McKitterick, *The Carolingians and the Written Word* (Cambridge: CUP, 1989) and her edited volume *The Uses of Literacy in Early Medieval Europe* (Cambridge: CUP, 1990).

[14] See for a clear introductory survey Peter Brown, *The World of Late Antiquity* (London: Thames and Hudson, 1971) and as a useful guide *The Oxford Illustrated History of Medieval Europe,* ed. George Holmes (Oxford and New York: OUP, 1988).

[15] Walter Ullmann, *Medieval Political Thought* (Harmondsworth: Penguin, 1975), 69–70. See Brown, *Late Antiquity* on the Byzantine world.

[16] See H. St. L. B. Moss, *The Birth of the Middle Ages 395–814* (London: OUP, 1935), 238 and such works as Henri Pirenne, *Mohammed and Charlemagne,* trans. Bernard Miall (London: Allen and Unwin, 1939). On the Slavs, see *Eastern and Western Europe in the Middle Ages,* ed. Geoffrey Barraclough (London: Thames and Hudson, 1970).

[17] The two horns from Gallehus, one with an inscription round the rim, are described and illustrated in great detail in Willy Hartner, *Die Goldhörner von Gallehus* (Wiesbaden: Steiner, 1969). See also David Wilson, *The Vikings and their Origins* (London: Thames and Hudson, 1970), 53–54 and ill. 31. The inscribed horn was stolen and presumably melted down in 1802, but an impression of it was made. Its inscription is discussed in various chapters in the present volume.

[18] Wilson, *Vikings* and such works as Johannes Brøndsted, *The Vikings,* trans. Kalle Skov (Harmondsworth: Penguin, 1965).

[19] In the 1530 *Sendbrief vom Dolmetschen,* ed. Karl Bischoff, 2nd ed. (Tübingen: Niemeyer, 1965), 18/19 (two versions). The words *verdeutschet, gut deutsch, der deutsch man, Deutscher, das beste deutsch* all occur within a very brief passage.

[20] The equation of nation and language is not always a simple one, certainly in the earlier stages, although it becomes clear later. See R. R. Davis, "The People of Britain and Ireland, 1100–1400," *Transactions of the Royal Historical Society,* 6th Series 7 (1997): 1–24, esp. 2. See also Leonard E. Scales, "At the Margin of Community: Germans in Pre-Hussite Bohemia," *Transactions of the Royal Historical Society,* 6th Series, 9 (1999): 327–52 for some interesting comments on the later medieval position.

[21] Even though both translate the German term "ostfränkisch," it is appropriate to use East Frankish as the historical-geographical term, and East Franconian as the name for the dialect.

[22] See Timothy Reuter, *Germany in the Early Middle Ages* (London and New York: Longman, 1991), 51–54 for a detailed discussion of *deutsch* and of *Germania.*

[23] Thomas Mann, *Deutsche Hörer! Radiosendungen nach Deutschland aus den Jahren 1940 bis 1945* (Frankfurt am Main: Fischer, 1987), 149, 154. Ernst von Salomon, *Der Fragebogen* (Reinbek: Rowohlt, 1961), 45–53.

[24] See R. E. Keller, *German Dialects* (Manchester: Manchester UP, 1961) and the older German work by Walther Mitzka, *Deutsche Mundarten* (Heidelberg: Winter, 1943). As a fortuitous example of modern written dialect, which could be multiplied, a series with the general title of *Fränkische Mundart in Vers und Prosa* (echoing Otfrid's insistence well over a millennium earlier on Frankish), opened with a collection of poems by Fritz Gronbach in the dialect of Hohenlohe: *Mir Hohaloher* (Gerabronn and Crailsheim: Hohenloher Verlagshaus, 1965).

[25] There is a good introduction to many of these languages, with examples, in W. B. Lockwood, *An Informal History of the German Language* (London: Deutsch, 1976). There are several publications on Plautdietsch (Plattdeutsch), including a rhyme dictionary, which certainly seems to indicate literary activity. As an extreme example, see Rogier Nieuweboer's 1998 Groningen dissertation, *The Altai Dialect of Plautdiitsch: West-Siberian Mennonite Low German* (Munich: Lincom, 1999).

[26] Harald Burger, *Sprache der Massenmedien* (Berlin: de Gruyter, 1984).

[27] See Luise F. Pusch, *Das Deutsche als Männersprache* (Frankfurt am Main: Suhrkamp, 1984).

[28] Edward Sapir, "Language and Environment," *The American Anthropologist* 14 (1912): 226–42.

[29] An indication of the range of non-literary materials is provided by R. C. van Caenegem's *Introduction aux sources de l'histoire médiévale* (with F. L. Ganshof), new ed. by L. Jocqué, trans. B. van den Abele (Turnhout: Brepols, 1997 = Corpus Christianorum, Cont. med.).

[30] Albert B. Lord, *The Singer of Tales* (Cambridge, MA: Harvard UP, 1960).

[31] See Michael Clanchy, *From Memory to Written Record, 1066–1130* (London: Arnold, 1979), 160.

The Concept of Germanic Antiquity

Heinrich Beck

THE STUDY OF GERMANIC ANTIQUITY (*Germanische Altertumskunde*), both as a concept and as a problem, is a peculiarly German affair. This is demonstrated by the fact that there is no entirely appropriate English translation of the term. It is worth considering why, and to what extent, the founders and subsequent representatives of this discipline saddled themselves with a conceptual term that exercises critical attention, today more than ever. Such critical considerations are concerned with both aspects of the term: "Germanic" on the one hand, and "antiquity" on the other. The *Reallexikon der Germanischen Altertumskunde*, which began to appear in its second edition in 1973 under the auspices of the Academy of Sciences in Göttingen and which is scheduled to be completed in 2005, may serve as an immediate point of reference.

The Concept "Germanic"

The term "Germanic" in classical historiography represents an initial problem. Historians in the ancient world, from Poseidonios, to Caesar and Tacitus[1] follow the tradition of a Germanic ethnonym. Alongside the scholarly discussion that continues to this day, there has been, since the humanist reception of Tacitus's *Germania,* a national adoption of the terms *Germani* and Germanic, which increasingly became more exclusively German. There were two main reasons for this: Tacitus's *Germania* covered a geographical area that allowed the German humanists to identify themselves within these boundaries. The then contemporary views of the geographical location of Scandinavia and the eastern areas in 1500 further promoted this identification of Germania with Germany. Scandinavia, by contrast, was linked with the sixth-century historian Jordanes and his ethno-geographical perspective, within which the Goths played a leading role.

Renaissance humanism led to a conscious nationalism in which the *Germani* rose to become a unique source of popular Germanic thought and culminated in the formula: Germanic equals German. The continued existence of this equation in subsequent centuries, down to the present, represents an important and much debated topic of recent German intellectual history. The ethnic and nationalistic view of antiquity was significantly consolidated by a new academic discipline that was beginning to establish itself at the start of the nineteenth century and, based on the name of the Germanen, termed itself *Germanistik*.

Jacob Grimm (1785–1863), one of the founding fathers of *Germanistik*, not only helped to give this discipline its name, but also ascribed to it a patriotic mission. Against the background of his time one can perhaps understand Grimm's attitude; for future generations this attitude was to culminate in a national-ideological development. In a dedication to the literary historian Georg Gottfried Gervinus (1805–71) in the first volume of Grimm's history of the German language in 1848, Grimm spoke of the fervently longed-for political unity, and of the unnaturally divided Fatherland.[2] Further, there is reference to a vision of linguistic imperialism linking a dreamed-of political order within Europe to linguistic boundaries. A "political Germanism" took its lead from this.

Scientific enquiry also gave Grimm an instrument with which to make differentiations within the area of Germanic-German, and with which to establish greater and lesser degrees of "German-ness." For Grimm, German was a comparative or relative term. For him, the first sound shift, the process of historical linguistic change that distinguishes Germanic from other Indo-European languages, as described in the introduction to this volume, constituted what was German (that is, Germanic). The repetition of this development[3] in the second sound shift amounted, in Grimm's view, to a renewal of the original "German-ness." In other words, for him, the "Germans" were the most German of the Germans — in today's terminology: the Germans represented the most genuine of the *Germani*. For Grimm this conclusion was linked to linguistic phenomena which he felt could be explained less physically than spiritually. The first sound shift, to his mind, was rooted in the disruption of the migration of peoples (the earliest *Völkerwanderung*). How could it not be, he argued, that such an intense disruption of the people would not also effect their language, shaking it from its traditional pattern and elevating it. When calm was restored after the end of the migration, he further argued, sounds also came to rest, and it may be taken as a demonstration of the superior control and mildness of the Gothic, Saxon, and Nordic tribes that with them the language halted at the level of the first sound shift, while the "wilder force" of High German pressed on to the second sound shift.[4]

It is almost an irony of history that Grimm provided with this concept of Germanic the arguments with which subsequent generations reduced "Germanic" to "German," since he at the same time wished to understand "Germanic" as the neutral and therefore more generally acceptable term. Posterity, however, determined the further development in such a way that German and Germanic came to be a relationship exclusive of others, and *Deutschtum* was identified with *Germanentum.*

The discussion of the role of Scandinavia did, however, contribute to a certain modification of this concept. Grimm had endeavored to win over the Germanic-speaking north to his terminology, and had tried to get Scandinavian scholars to accept the term Germanic. In his *Deutsche Mythologie* (1835–1844) he points out insistently the contribution of Nordic tradition — the German monuments, he says, are older but also poorer, while the Nordic are more recent but more pure.[5] The idea of the "purity" of the Scandinavian branch of the tradition determined the nature of further discussion from a German perspective. He believed that with Tacitus's *Germania* and other ancient sources the Germans have the older body of evidence, but the Scandinavians (with the Eddic songs, the sagas, and the Skaldic poems) provide the genuine and more pure sources — an opinion that is still widespread today.

The identification of Germanic with German was given further support in the late nineteenth and early twentieth centuries with the discussion of the *Urheimat,* the original homeland, the debate about the original home of the Indo-Europeans and the *Germani.* While in the nineteenth century the view prevailed that the home of the original Indo-European people was in Asia (or the southern parts of eastern Europe), now the hypothesis of the north German home of the Indo-Europeans became increasingly prominent. The year 1905 marked a high point in this radically revised view, in works by prominent scholars. For example, Victor Hehn in the foreword to the second edition of his *Kulturpflanzen und Haustiere*[6] had already complained that anthropologists and ethnologists now no longer sought the *officina gentium* (the womb of nations) in the headwaters of the Oxus, in the Asiatic Taurus, or in the Indian Caucasus, but in the boggy trackless forests of Germania. And in keeping with this view, the oldest form of language, Hehn observes, would have been that of the Celts and *Germani.* In 1907, Otto Schrader[7] complained that with these new views the notion of Indo-European becomes fused with that of Germanic. From the storm-swept strands of the North Sea or out of the primeval forests on the Baltic coast, according to this patriotic and therefore willingly accepted belief, the *Germani* and pre-*Germani* spread in time immemorial across the world by water and on land to the Oxus and the Ganges. Based on alleged pre-historical evidence, there was increasing acceptance of the idea that the former cultural greatness of this original Indo-European culture had existed not just in a material and social but also in an ethical sense. Some important aspects of a contemporary view of Germanic antiquity are: the merging or fusing of Indo-Europeans and *Germani* (and as a logical extension Germans); the belief

in the cultural greatness of the Indo-Europeans and of the *Germani;* and
the patriotic turn in the development of the study of Germanic antiquity.
With his reference to pre-history Schrader fixes on a new academic discipline which was to become a powerful proponent of the national idea:
prehistoric archeology. Gustaf Kossinna (1858–1931), who had moved
from German studies to that of prehistory, made a significant contribution to this development through his work.[8]

From an historical-linguistic point of view, Johannes Hoops is of particular interest since, as the editor of the later *Reallexikon der Germanischen
Altertumskunde* (1911–1919), he was a significant shaper of opinion. In
1905 Hoops put forward the view that the original home of the Indo-
Europeans had been in Germany, particularly in northern Germany, perhaps including Denmark. There were various theories supporting this
view, First, the beech argument: the Indo-Europeans were familiar with
the beech tree, as Latin *fagus,* Old High German *buohha,* Greek *fagós*
(oak), Kurdish *búz* (elm) demonstrate. However, the beech only occurs
west of a line between Odessa and Königsberg (Kaliningrad). It did not
appear in northern Europe until the Bronze or Iron Age. Second, the
barley argument: barley, which matures very quickly and was the Indo-
Europeans' main cereal crop, points to an area with short summers — also
to the west of the Odessa-Königsberg line — which would lead one to
think of Germany as the area of cultivation. Third, an argument *ex nega-
tivo:* in the later Stone Age, a number of cultivated plants were known in
the circumalpine area of Mediterranean culture (including the area of the
pile-dwellers on the alpine lakes) — plants such as the pea, lentil, poppy,
flax, apple. These were unknown to the Indo-Europeans. The original
homeland must therefore have been located further north.

The sum of these arguments pointed, in the view of Hoops, to northern Germany.[9] If one considers the obvious assumption of a continuity of
the population in this geographical area, then the conclusion was self-
evident: there is a geographical and ethnic continuity between the *Germani* and the original Indo-Europeans, and the Germans, in turn, are the
direct Germanic descendants.

The *Reallexikon der Germanischen Altertumskunde* puts forward similar
views. Rudolf Much wrote in the article "*Germani*" that Germanic folklore
certainly first developed in the area of the western Baltic basin, that is, at
the center of the oldest historical area of Germanic dissemination, and was
not brought there in some pre-existing form.[10] Most closely linked with this
issue is, for him, the question of the original home of the Indo-Europeans.
His view differs from that of Hoops. Much agrees with Schrader that the
southern Russian steppes and the adjacent wooded heath was part of the
settlement area of the original people, but he also agrees with Hoops that
they were located on the North Sea and the Baltic.

Questions about the extent to which the Nordic countries might be included in the original Indo-European or Germanic areas caused Hoops and Much some difficulty. Regarding woodland trees and cultivated plants, Hoops expressly excluded Scandinavia from the original Indo-European homeland. In the foreword to the *Reallexikon* he formulated his views on the *Germani* along the following lines: according to the now generally prevailing view, only northern Germany or the Scandinavian countries, or both, might be considered to have been the home of the *Germani* in ancient times.[11] Since he held to his belief in the original homeland in northern Germany, Scandinavia had, for him, to be an early area of diffusion. His concept of the study of Germanic antiquity therefore covered the geographical area of "central and northern Europe." On the question of how far north the Indo-Europeans and the Germani might have extended, Much had used racial features: complexion (light skin, hair, and eye color) and the elongated skull shape of the inhabitants. Both features belonged to the Indo-Europeans. Since dolichocephalism (elongated skull shape) has been observed in the Nordic countries from neolithic times, Much concludes that it is in the region of northern and central Europe, where elongated skulls dating from the Stone Age have been discovered, excluding the Alps at the time of the earliest period of pile dwellings, that the Indo-Europeans as a homogeneous group are to be found.[12] He took the area of the western Baltic basin to be the earliest location for the Germani. In his estimation of the Nordic development, Much was influenced by the eminent Swedish archeologist Oscar Montelius.[13]

The Study of Antiquity as a Concept

The seventeenth century appears to have been of particular significance in establishing a specific terminology for the academic and scientific study of antiquity. Here, for the first time, one can observe in German scholarly language, the use of the word *Altertum,* applied to classical, Graeco-Roman, ancient, and to domestic pre-history. Linked with this is also an extension of its meaning from "olden times" (*antiquitas, vetustas*) to "object from the olden times," mostly in the plural *Altertümer* (objects from olden times), based on the Latin word *antiquitates.* The seventeenth century also established the juxtaposition of the three German terms: *Kunde* (study), *Kunst* (art), and *Wissenschaft* (science). Whereas *Kunst* had already displaced the earlier word *list* in the sense of *ars, scientia* by 1270,[14] a new and subtle differentiation was possible with *Kunde* and *Wissenschaft. Kunde* obviously arose in the sphere of the German *Sprachgesellschaften* (language societies) of the seventeenth century and had from the first a markedly pedagogical tone. *Volkskunde* (study of folklore),

Heimatkunde (local history), *Kulturkunde* (study of culture) and so on were intended as programmatic efforts to place special emphasis on the educational idea — and this initially with regard to the sciences, which in the seventeenth and eighteenth centuries were endeavoring to establish a systematic structure and coherence, but also in more recent times in striving to serve the national purpose. In this context the distinction between *Altertumskunde* and *Altertumswissenschaft* also arose. Friedrich August Wolf spoke in 1807 of *Alterthums-Wissenschaft* as the basic and overarching term for the philosophical and historical investigation of classical antiquity. He terms *Altertumskunde* a sectional discipline which deals with antiquities and archeological sources, but also notes that this doctrine still has undetermined and, depending on the nature of the articles, indeterminable boundaries.[15] *Alterthumskunde* is, in the definition offered in Johann Christoph Adelung's dictionary of 1810, the study and knowledge of antiquities, and more precisely of Greek and Roman antiquities.[16] The pedagogical intention that was inherent in the various -*kunde* subjects led in the nineteenth century to a split between -*wissenschaft* and -*kunde* subjects, which was powerfully supported by such influential works as Karl Müllenhoff's *Germanische Altertumskunde*.[17] *Altertumswissenschaft* became the preserve of classical philology, while *Altertumskunde* dealt with domestic history, its investigation and dissemination. Although people were agreed in their aims, the realization of these ideas was controversial. Two distinct approaches can be identified as far as *Altertumskunde* is concerned: the one integrative, the other interdisciplinary.

The debate about the concept of integrative *Altertumskunde* goes back to the beginnings of the nineteenth century. The statement attributed to Friedrich Hegel on philology, that he considered it not a science but just a collection of individual sciences, an aggregate of disciplines, was probably aimed at the 1807 work of Friedrich August Wolf cited already, namely his *Darstellung der Altertumswissenschaft*. That people were endeavoring at this time to establish a concept of philology and *Altertumskunde* that would transcend the isolation of individual subject-areas is also documented in the lectures of the classical philologist August Boeckh, which were delivered at the University of Berlin from 1809 over a number of decades. They were published under the title *Encyklopädie und Methodologie der philologischen Wissenschaften*.[18] The task of philology (or of *Altertumslehre*) was, he said, to present a cultural history of antiquity. In order to pursue this, one had to tear down the arbitrary boundaries that had been set around individual disciplines in a rough and incoherent process, and then reconstruct the disciplines based on a strict structure and dialectic and according to their principal elements. But a scientific basis will only be established when the individual details are brought together in some unity. He felt that a common element must be found that subsumes all the particular elements, namely that which the philosophers term the principle of a people or of an age, the innermost kernel of its being.[19] Elsewhere he maintained that the highest goal of *Altertums-wissenschaft* that any philologist must pursue who wishes to elevate himself to the pinnacle of his science is to subsume all the individual facts into the unified characteristic quality of antiquity, to observe that characteristic quality in the details, and to understand its spirit in all its contexts.[20] In this conception, an idea of *Altertumskunde* is urged that consistently integrates individual disciplines and directs them toward a common goal. In content, its aim is presented as the principle of one's own people and its cultural history.

If one reviews the rest of the nineteenth century, one finds a great variation in approaches that contributed to this idea of such an integrative *Altertumskunde*. Above all other, Jacob Grimm is the representative of a form of *Altertumskunde* that is based on the notion of the *Volksgeist*, the spirit of a people. With his works on law, mythology, language, and literature he sought to establish an overview of the German (that is, the Germanic) past. The integrative center of these phenomena he saw in a prevailing *Volksgeist* which suffused all these areas, and which had to be pinned down. Language, beliefs, and law were, to his mind, to be understood as emanations of this spirit — language, for him, was the most important, and capable of revealing unexpected information.[21] Grimm embraced this integrative approach by consciously avoiding physical facts — in other words: he put forward an expressly philological *Altertumskunde*. He states programmatically in the first chapter of his history of the German language that there is more vital evidence available about peoples than bones, weapons, and graves, and that this evidence is their languages.[22] This view can be traced in research down to more recent times, and, as long as the integrative approach retains "contents," then it cannot be refuted in principle.

The next integrative concept in *Altertumskunde* might be termed "comparative linguistics and pre-history" (taken from a title used by Schrader in 1883). The rise of comparative linguistics also promoted the interest in the culture and civilization of the Indo-European peoples. It was thought that by means of etymology one could trace a path back to the neolithic age.

After the philologist Adolphe Pictet (1799–1875), using only linguistic historical deductions, began to make discoveries about the natural environment and about the material, social, and intellectual culture of pre-history analyzing vocabulary and other linguistic data, and had adopted the term linguistic paleontology (*paléontologie linguestique*),[23] Schrader was able to declare that just as the archeologist turns up the earth with pick and shovel in order to reveal traces of the past in bones, fragments, and stones, so too the linguistic researcher has attempted to reproduce an image of pre-history from the remains of words from the remotest times that have been salvaged on the shores of tradition. There is, in other words, a linguistic paleontology.[24] Schrader does, however, urge the proper application of this method if it is to perform the best service. By proper application, he meant not only the use of linguistic historical arguments on a contemporary level, but that the appropriate consideration of pre-historic research was also part of this. He refers to Victor Hehn as the founder of Indo-European *Altertumswissenschaft*,[25] whose study of domestic plants and animals, *Kulturpflanzen und Haustiere in ihrem Übergang aus Asien nach Griechenland und Italien sowie in das übrige Europa* first appeared in 1870 and was part of the standard home library of German scientific literature.[26] In contrast to the hitherto one-sided linguistic construction of comparative linguistics in the area of Indo-European pre-history, Hehn, according to Schrader, had primarily taken up historical combinations: the tradition of classical antiquity, of the Celts, of the *Germani* and so on. Although the linguistic equations are of great significance, the argument must take care not to ascribe new meaning to old words or to interpret recent borrowings as ancient inheritance.[27] But he accepts Hehn's main thesis. The cultivation of plants together with the taming of domestic animals progressed from east to west and subsequently to the north, and in the process changed human beings and their activities. In keeping with this antiquarian interpretation, the sixth and subsequent editions of Hehn's work appeared with annotations by Schrader (and botanical specialists). That this *Altertumskunde* was of an integrative nature is attributable to the quality of Hehn's view. He overcomes the old romantic, popular natural perspective in favor of a concept of culture in which culture and nature are contrasting concepts.[28] Although Schrader, under the influence of Hehn's work, distances himself to some extent from linguistic paleontology in his other works, he does remain committed to the later development of linguistic comparison.[29] This open attitude toward pre-historic research he recognizes as progress in keeping with Hehn's view of *Altertumskunde,* which had already led the way in integrating the contribution of classical historians.

Linguistic paleontology, however, continued in an historically significant way, one which held Hehn's approach to be deficient and which was harshly critical of its methodology. In 1905 Johannes Hoops published *Waldbäume und Kulturpflanzen im germanischen Altertum.* In this work he stressed that all three relevant sciences — botany, archeology, and linguistics — were to be given equal weight.[30] In practice, however, it soon becomes clear that he had a hierarchical view of these subjects, which assigned to linguistics an expanding and a corrective function. This fusion of subjects became in practice a hierarchy of subjects. His significant contributions on woodland trees and cultivated plants (which were also included in the *Reallexikon* in abridged form) are based on the following precepts: the occurrence of a word in all dialects including Gothic leads to the unequivocal conclusion that the word and the thing verify a cultural state of the original Germanic people before its diffusion in the final centuries B.C. If a word is only attested in certain areas, then pre-historic archeological finds, literary evidence, or linguistic considerations of a general nature must support the argument.[31] A significant criterion in this thesis is the migration of the Angles and Saxons from the continent. If German and English, or German and Norse are in agreement on a name, he argues, we would have to conclude *a priori* that the plant in question was not yet or was no longer cultivated in the Nordic countries before the migration of the Anglo-Saxons.[32] Here too, the further considerations of occurrences in only certain areas were applied.

Not only Hoops's *Waldbäume und Kulturpflanzen* appeared in 1905 but also, with the same publisher, Herman Hirt's *Indogermanen.*[33] Hirt's work was of significance for the study of Germanic antiquity. Hirt agreed with Hoops's investigations[34] and was close to his view in the question of the Indo-European and Germanic homeland — in other words: they were also in agreement in their rejection of the Hehn-Schrader version of *Altertumskunde.* Schrader was criticized as having been under the influence of certain preconceived ideas about the culture of the Indo-Europeans.[35] Although Hirt concedes that properly employed linguistic science has some justification in the investigation of Indo-European culture (and constructs a cultural history on this), he qualifies this approach by arguing that priority must be given to what we know of the oldest living conditions of the individual peoples, then archeological evidence can be added, and only then, when we have considered these things, can language teach us anything, primarily whether the objective correspondences are coincidental or go back to some collectively experienced ancient past.[36] This procedure sounds at first quite reasonable, but when we take into account some of the Germanic aspects of particular interest here, it takes a new turn. The home of the Indo-Europeans and the *Germani* is assumed to be one and the same — and that is of decisive importance for the whole development of historical linguistics. He maintains that for centuries the *Germani* have dwelt on their ancient native soil, just as Tacitus presumed, and that this fact should also be evident in the language, which Hirt regards, in fact, as an *Ursprache,*[37] that is, as a language that goes back to pre-historic times.

If we take an overview of the comparative-linguistic variant of integrative *Altertumskunde,* we may distinguish two schools of thought: one linked with the names Hehn and Schrader (Hehn is recognized as the founder of this branch of the study) and the other represented in the works of Hoops and Hirt.[38]

There are objective, factual differences in their views — for example on the question of the original homeland of the Indo-Europeans (Europe or Asia) or the level of civilization of the Indo-Europeans (knowledge of agriculture and fixed dwelling-places, for example). There are also methodological differences. Hoops has the closest affinities with linguistic paleontology. From the integrative perspective, Hehn and Schrader agree in the assumption of a Germanic peripheral culture that is part of the flow of civilization spreading from the east in a westerly and northerly direction. Hoops and Hirt agree on the thesis of origins: a direct line (in a geographical and ethnic sense) leads from Indo-European to Germanic and finally to German. In other words: an integrative Germanic *Altertumskunde* is of itself a science that is oriented to contents and to the state of research at any one time.

The Germanist Friedrich Kauffmann attempted an integrative approach that would avoid the dangers of a non-empirically based approach, and his *Deutsche Altertumskunde* appeared in two volumes in 1913 and 1923. Beginning with the precept that "spirit" (*Geist*) is "form," he concludes that the German spirit, like everything human, was subject to change over the course of time, and could be most readily recognized from the changing styles of the German way of life.[39] The stylistic laws of popular creativity are, he maintains, no less characteristic in language and poetry than in social, economic and commercial products, though in the latter they are clearer, and their essential features are therefore much easier to comprehend. Archeology must become the prime mediator if we link language and literature with all other, naïve or artistic, forms of German life through the concept of style, and wish to describe the changing styles according to the only possible procedure of scientific discovery, namely by means of comparison.

If one reduces this argument to the concept of style, then Kauffmann can rely on an established tradition. When Friedrich Schiller writes of style that it is nothing more than the highest form of representation, free from all subjective and also contingent objective determinants, then style is obviously an individual and ethno-specific formal quality of a characteristic kind.

Kauffmann was not one of the collaborators on the *Reallexikon* — in which there is no article on style in general (only artistic styles were briefly dealt with, as in A. Haupt's article on *Stilarten*). The criticism that was leveled at Kauffmann was directed, among other things, at the author's often unconventional views. It is obviously a general phenomenon that the integrative approaches in *Altertumskunde* appear to be realizable only in individual undertakings — but also that its demands can too easily exceed the individual's ability.

Germanische Altertumskunde has not been made into a university discipline. On the other hand, however, new subject areas have developed in recent times: paleo-botany, paleo-zoology, soil science, metallurgy and others, which all contribute to academic and scientific research into the *Germani*. A single-discipline approach brought about notable academic and scientific results, but the inherent need for specialization also had its shortcomings. The call for an interdisciplinary approach is an expression of this. If one takes an overview of Germanic *Altertumskunde,* one can observe the increasing participation of diverse disciplines. Initially, *Altertumskunde* was led by the philologists. As the next step, the study of specimens and objects found by antiquarians was added. At the end of the nineteenth century, pre-historic archeology entered in the guise of a new academic subject. The twentieth century was marked by the additional contribution of the natural sciences. While, on the one hand, the academic and scientific basis of Germanic *Altertumskunde* expanded, there arose, on the other, the problem of how to combine these disciplines into a unified concept. The question arises whether, with the structuring of academic science by disciplines, as has happened over the past century of university history, an era of cultural history could be described in a comprehensive manner. As early as the first edition of the *Reallexikon,* Hoops referred to the establishing of closer contact between the different branches of Germanic cultural history that have in recent decades become more and more estranged as a consequence of the increasing specialization of research as a main objective of his undertaking. In particular, the establishing of links between pre-history and history and between archeology and linguistics was one of his goals. In the second edition (begun in 1973) Hoops's concerns were taken fully into consideration.[40] Beyond the *Reallexikon* too, voices were heard calling for close contact between disciplines. In 1967 the highly respected study-group in Constance, the *Arbeitskreis für mittelalterliche Geschichte,* published an article by Ernst Schwarz with the significant title "Germanische Stammeskunde zwischen den Wissenschaften" (Studies of Germanic Antiquity Between the Disciplines). The author urged a closer link as necessary between academic disciplines.[41] The goal of closer contact is a relative notion, as a cursory glance at the present eighteen volumes of the *Reallexikon* demonstrates. If there are archeological, historical, and philological contributions to an article, contact will lead to mutual stimulation, to possible changes, and to the raising of new questions. But mutually conflicting views may also remain, in which case the editors see their role not as trying to harmonize the state of research, but to document it.

What did not appear to be a problem in the 1960s, when the new edition of the *Reallexikon der Germanischen Altertumskunde* was being discussed, has turned out in recent decades to be a burdensome handicap:

"Germanic" is, to many scholars today, just as problematic as *Altertums-kunde*. We may ask, then, what concept might serve in today's view to cover the representation of central and northern European history in the period of the last millennium B.C. and the first millennium A.D.? The historical conditionality of the terms "Germanic" and *"Altertumskunde"* has become a burden in recent decades, and scholars are well aware of this. Those now undertaking projects like the revision of the *Reallexikon* are inclined to understand *Altertumskunde* in the sense of cultural studies (*Kulturwissenschaft*), and to replace the idea of "Germanic" by a broad geographical concept that could be described as pertaining to central and northern Europe.

Translated by Malcolm Read

Notes

[1] Eduard Norden, *Die germanische Urgeschichte in Tacitus' Germania* (5th ed., Stuttgart and Leipzig: Teubner, 1974).

[2] Jacob Grimm, *Geschichte der Deutschen Sprache* (Leipzig: Weidmann, 1848), IV–VI. A politicized nationalistic approach could, of course, become dangerously distorted, and did so between the First and Second World Wars in the lead-up to and during National Socialism, also in some major scholarly undertakings, although individual contributors to such projects did not always share the political direction of their editors.

[3] Grimm, *Geschichte*, 828.

[4] Grimm, *Geschichte*, 437–38.

[5] Jacob Grimm, *Deutsche Mythologie*, 4th ed. by Elard Hugo Meyer, 1875–78 (repr. Darmstadt: WBG, 1965), III.

[6] Victor Hehn, *Kulturpflanzen und Haustiere in ihrem Übergang aus Asien nach Griechenland und Italien sowie in das übrige Europa: Historisch-linguistische Skizzen,* 8th ed. by O. Schrader (Berlin: Borntraeger, 1911, repr. 1963), 635.

[7] O. Schrader, *Sprachvergleichung und Urgeschichte* (Jena: Costenoble, 3rd ed., 1907), IX.

[8] Kossinna was appointed in 1902 to the first chair of archeology. He is considered to be the founder of the settlement archeological method, the main principle of which is that "sharply delineated cultural provinces coincide in all periods with quite distinct peoples or tribes." Among his widely published works, see *Die deutsche Vorgeschichte eine hervorragend nationale Wissenschaft* [1912] (7/8th ed., Leipzig: Barth, 1941); *Altgermanische Kulturhöhe* [1927] (5th ed., Leipzig: Kabitsch, 1935); *Germanische Kultur im 1. Jahrtausend n. Chr.* [1932] (2nd ed., Leipzig: Barth, 1939).

[9] Cf. also Schrader's critique of Hoops in his *Sprachvergleichung*, 459–83.

[10] Much, "Germanen" in Johannes Hoops, ed., *Reallexikon der germanischen Altertumskunde* (Strasbourg: Trübner, 1911–19), II, 174–83. The second edition of

this work — discussed later in this article — is edited by H. Beck and others (Berlin and New York: de Gruyter, 1973–). Unless otherwise stated, reference here is to the original edition.

[11] This thesis was advanced by Carl Penka in several works, including *O. Schraders Hypothese von der südrussischen Urheimat der Indogermanen* (n.p., n.pub., 1908). See also, Hoops, *Reallexikon*, I, VII.

[12] Much, "Germanen," 175.

[13] Oscar Montelius, *Sveriges historia från äldsta tid till våra dagar I: Sveriges hednatid, samt medeltid, förra skedet, från år 1060 till år 1350* (Stockholm: Linnström, 1877), 70.

[14] Franz Dornseiff, "List und Kunst," *Deutsche Vierteljahresschrift für Literaturwissenschaft und Geistesgeschichte* 22 (1944): 231–36.

[15] Friedrich August Wolf, *Darstellung der Altertumswissenschaft nach Begriff, Umfang, Zweck und Wert* (Berlin: Realschulbuchhandlung, 1807, repr. Berlin: Akademie, 1985), 54.

[16] Johann Christoph Adelung, *Grammatisch-kritisches Wörterbuch der hochdeutschen Mundart, mit beständiger Vergleichung der übrigen Mundarten, besonders aber der Oberdeutschen* (2nd ed., Vienna: Bauer, 1811), I, 240.

[17] Karl Müllenhoff, *Deutsche Altertumskunde* ([1870–1900]; 2nd ed., Berlin: Weidmann, 1890–1929).

[18] August Boeckh, *Encyklopädie und Methodologie der philologischen Wissenschaften*, ed. E. Bratuscheck, 2nd ed. by R. Klussmann (Leipzig: Teubner, 1886).

[19] Boeckh, *Encyclopädie*, 57.

[20] Boeckh, *Encyclopädie*, 308.

[21] Grimm, *Geschichte*, 7.

[22] Grimm, *Geschichte*, 7.

[23] Adolphe Pictet, *Les origines Indo-européennes ou les Aryas primitifs, essai de paléontologie linguistique* ([1859–63]; 2nd ed., Paris: J. Cherbuliez, 1877).

[24] Schrader, *Sprachvergleichung*, III.

[25] Hehn, *Kulturpflanzen*, XX.

[26] Hehn, *Kulturpflanzen*, XXI.

[27] Hehn, *Kulturpflanzen*, XX.

[28] Klaus von See, "Victor Hehns Kulturtheorie," *Studi Tedeschi* 33 (1990): 39–74.

[29] See Herman Hirt, *Indogermanica: Forschungen über Sprache und Geschichte Alteuropas,* ed. by Helmut Arntz (Halle/Saale: Niemeyer, 1940), 42–50.

[30] Johannes Hoops, *Waldbäume und Kulturpflanzen im germanischen Altertum* (Strasbourg: Trübner, 1905), VI.

[31] Hoops, *Waldbäume*, 457.

[32] Hoops, *Waldbäume*, 457–58.

[33] Herman Hirt, *Die Indogermanen: Ihre Verbreitung, ihre Urheimat und ihre Kultur I* (Strasbourg: Trübner, 1905).

[34] Hirt, *Indogermanen*, 189.

[35] Hirt, *Indogermanen,* 241.

[36] Hirt, *Indogermanen,* 242.

[37] Herman Hirt, *Geschichte der deutschen Sprache* (Munich: Beck, 1919), 21.

[38] Hirt, *Indogermanica,* 51.

[39] Friedrich Kauffmann, *Deutsche Altertumskunde I* (Munich: Beck, 1913), IX.

[40] *Reallexikon* (2nd ed. 1973ff.) I, V–VII.

[41] Ernst Schwarz, *Germanische Stammeskunde zwischen den Wissenschaften* (Constance and Stuttgart: Thorbecke, 1967), 7.

Origo Gentis:
The Literature of Germanic Origins

Herwig Wolfram

T HE *ORIGO GENTIS* THEME — the literary examination of the origins of a given people, which in the Germanic context is the theme of this chapter — does not constitute a literary genre in its own right,[1] but is found in connection with various different genres to produce what is in fact a *genus mixtum,* which conveys details of the origins of a particular people by using various narrative patterns. Examples of the *origo gentis* may be found in heroic epics, may introduce or form part of ethnographic works, chronicles, biographies and legends, or may even be used in official writings either as justificatory support[2] or as a learned excursus or digression.[3] An *origo gentis* will often introduce the *historia,* a genre developed in particular by the Christian historian Paulus Orosius in the early fifth century, and characterized as "an exemplary Christian history of kings and institutions."[4] The models are the Old Testament and classical ethnographical writings.[5] The story of Noah and his three sons, who represent the three continents, and their seventy-two descendants[6] is particularly popular, as are Caesar's ethnographical discussions, the *Germania* and the *Agricola* of Tacitus, and indeed also Virgil's *Aeneid,* whose hero is the son-in-law of Priam, who had fifty sons and fifty daughters. The few members of the family who survived the capture of Troy were forced to travel the world and found new cities and peoples everywhere. Why should there not be a Franco, the father of the Franks, among them, if there was certainly an Aeneas, the founder of Rome.

The *origo gentis* is concerned with [*gentis*] *nobilitas et virorum fortium facta,* "the nobility of the people and the deeds of mighty men,"[7] and accordingly all Roman historians, most notably Sallust in the first century B.C., Valerius Maximus a century later, and also (on methodological grounds) the fifth-century Christian Orosius are potential models. Between A.D. 500 and 1200 it is essentially Latin writers, and only rarely vernacular writers, who describe the origins of a people within a universal history which extends down to their present, and who give that people a Roman and therefore a Christian identity.[8] In 533 Cassiodorus produced a history of the Goths (*Getica*) with a title which echoed Tacitus: *origo actusque Getarum,* "the origin and deeds of the Goths," and this was reworked by Jordanes in 551 to provide the version that survives. Gregory of Tours (who died in 593 or 594) wrote ten books of Frankish history. Isidore of Seville wrote in 625 his history of the Goths, Vandals and Suevi, or more specifically of their kings, based on classical sources, with an introductory *origo* of the Goths which is exclusively etymological.[9] In the seventh century there followed the so-called Fredegar chronicles, and the first written version of the Lombardic (Langobardic) tradition with which Paul the Deacon introduced his history of the Lombards just before 800. Bede used myths of origin to preface his history of the Anglo-Saxon Church in 731, and Celtic material appeared in Britain, too, with Gildas in the sixth, and with the *Historia Brittonum* (British History) ascribed to Nennius in the ninth century.[10] In the tenth century Widukind of Corvey dealt with Old Saxon origins, again using earlier material such as the *Translatio sancti Alexandri* and Cosmas of Prague and the Gallus Anonymus began their respective histories of the Czechs and the Poles at the start of the twelfth century with an *origo gentis.* Elements are found preserved in vernacular works, too, such as the Anglo-Saxon poems of *Widsith, Deor* and indeed of *Beowulf,* and also in the Old Russian chronicle of Nestor of Kiev. This sequence of *origo gentis* writings, which rework pre-ethnographic, orally transmitted data into ethnographic facts, concludes with the Danish history by Saxo Grammaticus around 1200.[11] Of primary importance was the presentation of as continuous as possible a royal line: a *gens* achieved the status of a civilized people, according to Hippocrates, only under the rule of kings, who in their turn guaranteed the continued existence of the people.[12] Thus the biblical Book of Judges ends with the treachery of the Benjamites and the sentence: "In those days there was no king in Israel: every man did that which was right in his own eyes" (Authorized Version Judges 21, 25 = Vulgate 21, 24). Only a royal succession can give structure to human time (*tempus est actus humani,* "time is human deeds") and make it into history (*actus humani memoria digni,* "human acts worthy of memory," or *virorum fortium facta,* "deeds of great men").[13] The parameters of the *Getica* are *"ab olim usque nunc per generationes regesque"* (*Getica* 1), "from former times to the present through the generations and the kings," although it is admitted that there are gaps in the succession. Gregory of Tours knows of times without a king, too, as do Isidore and Paul the Deacon in their histories.

The *Germania* of Tacitus follows a tripartite pattern that became a model for other writings.[14] It contains first the origin of a people, an *origo* (as a *pars pro toto* in the *Getica* 9 and 315). In contrast with the notion of a beginning sprung from the word, the *logos* of John's Gospel, the "mythical" beginning of an *origo gentis* is subordinated to the concept of eternal return, and always takes as read any earlier beginnings. Thus the *origo Amalorum,* the origins of the Gothic Amal dynasty in the *Getica* begins in the middle of the genealogy of the A(n)ses. The Lombards have a Scandinavian prehistory (Paul the Deacon, I, 7–9). The Bohemian House of Premysl are the inheritors of Libussa, who had two elder sisters and a father named Crocco (Cosmas, I, 3).

Second, attention is paid to customs and deeds: *mores, actus, facta.* Here the language is naturally of interest, but even more so the capacity for civilization and how a people can be integrated into the Roman army.[15] Furthermore, is a particular people, depending upon their customs and on fortune (*mores and fortuna*) capable of some day assuming world rule (*imperium*)? Seneca and Tacitus felt that Sallust's speculations on this score were an unlikely possibility as far as their realization was concerned,[16] but the idea did seem to become more concrete when in 414 we hear that Romania, that is the Western Roman Empire, might conceivably be replaced by a Gothia, when the Visigothic king Athaulf wanted to be to a forthcoming Gothic empire what Augustus had been to Rome.[17] A thousand years after Sallust, Widukind (I, 25) cited that classical historian in support of the transfer of imperial power from the Frankish to the Saxon line. The classical and biblical notions of *translatio,* of transference of power, are combined when a given people is presented as the chosen one. Like the Jews in the desert, the migrating Goths were tested by God for forty years.[18]

Third, attention is paid to writers' geographical position (*loca, situs, status*), in which *status* also means the political order and standing of a given people. This comprises both the people and the royal or ruling families (*nobilitas*), and an equation is also made between the people and the army.[19] *Status* as a geographical determinative locates a people within the classical world. Both the Sclavinia of Adam of Bremen and the Bohemia of Cosmas of Prague are located within Germania, in one of the four basic lands of ancient Europe. The term *status* is used by Widukind (II preface: *de origine statuque gentis*) and also by Adam of Bremen.[20] Both the *Getica* and Cosmas's Bohemian chronicle begin with a description of the world as divided into three parts, and on the edge is that most important island of Skandza, "workshop of peoples and the mother of tribes" (*Getica* 25), from which both the Goths and Lombards and other peoples trace their origins.[21]

Tacitus offers us examples of orally transmitted myths containing vernacular names; at the same time he attempts to explain these foreign concepts on the basis of his own experience, and tries to match them up, or, if possible, to translate them (*Germania* 2–4, and see 42). Cassiodorus followed the *interpretatio Romana,* the matching-up technique of Tacitus more closely than do later *origo gentis* writings,[22] and he, too, offers untranslatable names from the pre-ethnographic transmission of Gothic material. But when he uses data of this sort to provide him with facts for his history, he almost invariably turns them into a Latin ethnography. Autochthony and migration are important themes in these Roman interpretations. Mostly the migrations take place by ship; the value of native-born origins is frequently overestimated.[23] The Romans understood themselves to be descended from Aeneas and his Trojans, who intermarried in Latium with the indigenous population, as in Livy's *History of Rome from its Foundation* (*Ab urbe condita* 1, 1), and this model was followed by many others.[24] However, some peoples, such as the Sciri, the Juthungi and the Rugians made a distinction between themselves as being of pure race and those of mixed race, and did not allow intermarriage.[25] According to Tacitus, the *Germani* were not a mixed race because no one from the Mediterranean would move up to their lands of fog, woods, and swamps, and in addition because once a regular migration had been by sea, while "the ocean" had hindered this for Germania. Since the North Sea and the Baltic were reckoned to be navigable, immigrants were permitted to come, if not from Spain (as the Irish do according to the *Historia Brittonum*), then at least from Scandinavia (seen in any case as overpopulated), onto the continent (Goths, Lombards) or into Britain (Angles and Saxons).[26]

Old Testament and ethnographic models are used when an *origo gentis* is committed to writing, as are rationalizing explanations of myth as history, as well as classical etymology and word similarity,[27] in all of which the names of those individuals, places, or rivers that provide identities are seen as reality. Among the *Germani, origo gentis* writings that preserve pre-ethnographic data (*vera et antiqua nomina,* old and true names, says Tacitus in the *Germania* 2) are found only for those peoples mentioned by classical writers up to about A.D. 150 whose names are linked with the base word **theod*- "people" (as in *Gútthiuda, Saexthéod, Svithiod;* the asterisk indicates an assumed but not attested word), and whose tragic royal traditions were taken up in the Germanic heroic epic.[28] However, the non-Germanic chronicle of Bohemia treats its pre-ethnographic portions in the same way (Cosmas, I, 3–7). A limitation to Germanic content is not therefore the only possibility in an *origo gentis* description. Etymological constructs are also used together with pre-ethnographic "original" data. Like the Alamans, the equally kingless Bavarians sing of the Lombard Alboin, a foreign tragic-heroic king (Paul the Deacon I, 27). Their own history of origins, which arose only in the high Middle Ages, constructs on etymological grounds a Norix, son of Hercules as the ancestor of the Norican-Bavarians, who had come back to their ancestral homeland, Noricum.[29] A writer as early as Cassiodorus wonders whether Ostrogotha was named after his people, or whether the Ostrogoths were named after the king. The Lombard transmission leaves it open whether

Wodan-Longbeard named the Lombards after himself or whether he was the Lombardic god named after them.[30] Cosmas of Prague historicized pre-ethnographic data, but added to them the etymologically derived eponymic Bohemian hero Boemus. In one passage, Saxo Grammaticus etymologizes the Danes from Dan and the Angles from Angul[31] and describes them both as sons of Humblus-Hulmul, who is found in second place in the genealogy of the Amal dynasty in the *Getica* 79, immediately after Gaut, and therefore was plainly not simply invented around 1200.[32]

A people exists when the literate world takes notice of it. The writers, however, use their information without taking into account possible developments and changes in time and space, since the barbarians, devoid of history, are in any case unchanging.[33] Exceptions to this are provided by Tacitus, who does note the rise and the fall of the Cherusci (*Germania* 36), or Ammianus Marcellinus, who describes the Quadi (Suevi) in his own period as harmless in comparison with the danger that they once were.[34]

An *origo gentis* text is written with a purpose: Caesar's *Gallic Wars* (VI) makes a distinction between the *mores* of the Gauls and the *Germani*, distinguishing between the desert lands inhabited by grotesque creatures from the realms of fable on the right of the Rhine, and the fruitful and civilized land on the left, in order to make clear to the Romans that an attempt at the conquest of Germania in contrast to Gaul would not be worthwhile.[35] The *origo gentis* does, however, provide identities. Just as Tacitus identifies the *Germani*, Cassiodorus constructs a Gothic unity. Tacitus wrote the *Germania* as an historical memorandum, and Cassiodorus did diverge from time to time from the historical approach, referring occasionally to things happening "even nowadays." But with his expressed aim of turning "the Gothic tale of origins into Roman history" (*Variae* IX, 25, 5) he does indicate change, and a development which is both historical-political and concerned with the history of salvation. He also considers the possibility of providing a biblical origin for the Goths, from one of the descendants of Noah (Magog in *Getica* 29). The *origo Gothorum* of Isidore also restricts itself to this kind of origin (Isidore 1 and 66). A Noachite origin crops up for the Anglo-Saxons, and it is also found in the Bohemian chronicle.[36] The Old Testament, the model of Tacitus, etymology as an auxiliary aid, and an Augustinian myth-from-reality approach all serve to interpret pre-ethnographic data in order to construct an ethnographic identity out of barbaric origins, and to integrate that identity into the classical-Christian discourse and make it part of the general history of the Roman empire.

Origo/historia Gothica

The *origo gentis* of the Goths provides an early and full illustration which is both exemplary and relevant to many other early Germanic groups. In 238 the Goths made an incursion in the lower Danube area into imperial Roman territory. This event marks the beginning of their *historia,* their history as recorded by classical writers.[37] The Gothic history by Cassiodorus/ Jordanes, however, takes the beginnings of the Goths back much further than their known origins in eastern Europe. Depending upon whether it is centered upon the origin of the Goths, or on contemporary history as seen from the point of view of the classical writers, this history of origins can be seen either as an *origo gentis* or an *historia,* and it is indeed described in various ways, as "origin and deeds of the Goths," "the origin of the Goths," "their origin, places and customs," "the Gothic origin," or alternatively as *Getarum* or *Gothorum historia, historia Gothica* ("history of the Goths," "Gothic history").[38] This Gothic history was composed by Cassiodorus at the behest of Theoderic the Great, who died in 526. His *Getica* was completed in 533 in Ravenna, obviously after Queen Amalasuintha had defeated their opponents, and was reworked in Constantinople in 550–51. Jordanes, a Catholic Goth, gave it at this stage the form in which it has survived, since the more extensive twelve-volume original was no longer up to date. Jordanes changed little of the text and nothing of the outline provided by Cassiodorus.[39] The latter had begun his history of the Goths with a king, Berig, who had led them from Scandinavia to what is now the Pomeranian or West-Prussian coast. This had happened "about 1490 years before the birth of Christ" (*Getica* 313), that is, long before the Trojan War and the origin of the Romans. After "about" five generations, the Goths, it is claimed, migrated further under King Filimer, son of Gadarig the Great (or the Elder) to Scythia, that is, the modern Ukraine.[40]

Cassiodorus took Tacitus as his principal methodological model, but he also cites him directly. His official letter to the Aestii, that is, the peoples of the Baltic, refers to *Germania* 45. In classical writings the Swedes are referred to only in *Getica* 22 and *Germania* 44. The same section of Tacitus also treats the *Gutones* (*Gotones, Gothones*), taking them together, in fact, with the Rugians, and Cassiodorus does the same, with the difference only that he refers to *Goths* rather than *Gutones.*[41] Was Cassiodorus the sole classical author who knew about Tacitus's *Gutones* and equated them with the Goths, whom he then linked with the orally transmitted royal names Berig, Filimer and Gadarig? What value did he assign to pre-ethnographic data, and how did he convert them into ethnographic facts? Following earlier models, Cassiodorus understood the Goths to be the same as the Getae.[42] The *historia* of the Getae — known to classical antiquity since Herodotus, together with their Dacian and Scythian neighbors — was Gothicized. Cassiodorus's grouping of the Getae and the Scythians provided the written ethnographic context which would both elevate and preserve the Gothic *origo gentis*.

As a parallel, in 625 Isidore of Seville composed a history of the Gothic kings, beginning with Athanaric, but without any pre-ethnographic data, and using only written sources. His introduction is limited to a Scythian *origo*, in order to derive the Goths etymologically from Magog, the son of Japhet. Cassiodorus also considered the descent of the Goths from Magog, not because of any etymological connection, but rather because he thought of them both as Scythian.[43] Equally he made the Scythian Amazons into Gothic warrior-women, upon one of whom Hercules begat a son, whom he left behind as king of the Goths.[44] These warrior-women set themselves up against the Athenian hero-king Theseus, almost conquered Troy,[45] built the temple of Diana at Ephesus, and ruled for about a hundred years over Asia (*Getica* 49). In fact, they are so fierce that the *Getica*, in defiance of grammar, affords them the masculine gender. Meanwhile the male Goths conquer the Egyptians and Persians, at which the Macedonians seek their friendship, and Philip, the father of Alexander the Great, marries the daughter of the Gothic king Gudila; later on, Ermanaric is compared with Alexander the Great.[46]

Next, Burebista, king of the Dacians, and the princes Dekaineos and Dorpaneos of the Getae are made into Goths. Cassiodorus places the first war between the Goths and the Romans in their time, and follows the first Gothic victory with a seventeen-name genealogy which is not, however, as might have been expected, a Dacian-Getaean royal dynasty; nor does it even contain the genuinely Gothic name Gudila. Rather it presents the family tree of the Amal Goths (linked with the A[n]ses, the gods). These Gothic names are turned, in the spirit of Tacitus and his *interpretatio Romana,* from untranslatable pre-ethnographic data into ethnographic facts. The victory-bringing charisma of the Amal dynasty is described by the writer as *quasi fortuna*, rather than with a Gothic word. These men are not wholly human but are demigods and heroes. The background against which they prove themselves is an ethnographic event, though, not a Gothic victory but rather a victory of the Getae over one of the generals of the emperor Domitian (81–96).[47] The family tree of the Amal Goths is also presented ethnographically: following the pattern of the biblical *liber generationum*, "the book of the generations of . . . ," the author names sixteen of the forebears of Athalaric, maternal grandson of Theoderic the Great, and puts him accordingly in the seventeenth place. The names are Gothic. However, the form imposed on them is Cassiodorus's own, and that seventeen generations of Gothic kings (a point stressed elsewhere by Cassiodorus, *Variae* IX, 25, 5–6) are listed is an ethnographic tradition; but Cassiodorus has set up a genealogy of Gothic material which contains contradictions and inventions, and which only becomes indisputably historical in the generation immediately before Theoderic.[48]

The number of kings between Aeneas and Romulus was never established as a definite canon, and only a late classical manuscript counts Romulus as the seventeenth king after Aeneas, the progenitor of the Julian clan. Cassiodorus used this recently adapted example as the criterion for his own selection of seventeen names. Romanized and therefore made acceptable for the Roman ruling class, the dynasty of the Amals is presented as a second Julian family, which is intended to justify once again their rule over the Goths and the Italian people.[49] The Bible gives further support to the significant symbolic value of the number seventeen and of seventeen-member genealogies, as in I Esdras (Ezra), 7.

In the same way Cassiodorus constructs the story of the Gothic witches, "women who deal magically with the regions of the dead." Filimer, he says, drove them out of the tribe in Scythian Oium, after which they formed a liaison with the spirits of the Steppes, and became the mothers of the Huns. Originally located temporally in the second century, this tale was renewed repeatedly, and extended with different time frames into the fifth century. When Cassiodorus wrote it down he once again used the Old Testament as a supplementary model. Like Oium, however, the word he uses for the Gothic witches, *haliurun(n)ae* — the latter with a Latin ending — is Gothic. Beside the worship of the Amals as A(n)ses,[50] Cassiodorus also mentions pre-Amal heroic songs, panegyrics for the dead Visigothic king Theoderid, further Gothic genealogies and some rudiments of what would appear in the later Norse *Hamðismál*,[51] all of which provide pre-ethnographic data. Beyond this, we are given, beside some institutional terms,[52] only more or less Latinized Gothic place, national and personal names.

Amending Ptolemy's *Geography*, Cassiodorus gives us the names of numerous Scandinavian "Gothic peoples," including that of *Gauthigoth* (*Getica* 19–24). From the first century onward, continental *Gutones* and Scandinavian *Gutar* and *Gautar* (Old Norse *Gautar* = Old English *Geatas*) were known, and we must accept a connection between the last-named and the modern *Götar*. The island of Gotland is also claimed frequently as the original homeland of the Goths. Accounts from the High Middle Ages tell of how, because of overpopulation, some people had to leave the island, this being decided by the casting of lots. Against this, coastal Pomeranian legends relate how the story passed from father to son of how their ancestors once came across the sea in three ships.[53] The Gothic *origo gentis* contains the same legend, as does that of the Anglo-Saxons, while the three groups of the Lombards managed without ships.[54]

Cassiodorus's three ships stand for the three branches of the Goths, the Ostrogoths, the Visigoths and the "remainder," the Gepids.[55]

Modern onomastic philology, rather than ancient etymology, derives the names Goth (*Gutans, Gút-thiuda),[56] Gutar, Gutones, Gautar, Götar, all from the word *gautaz, meaning "out-pourer." Pliny the Elder lists what he saw as the most celebrated rivers that flow into "Ocean": the Guthalus, the Vistula, the Elbe, the Weser, the Ems, the Rhine, and the Meuse. This list runs from East to West, so that the Guthalus must have been to the East of the Vistula; but since the Oder is not mentioned, possibly the Oder was confused with the Vistula, and might itself have been the river of the Guti.[57] The Gutones were in any case originally localized around and to the east of the Oder. The word-form Guthalus is matched in the Swedish Götaälv, "River of the Götar." Later folk names appear (as spontaneous parallels?) in connection with a river, an "out-pourer," that is, both on the continent and in Scandinavia. Gutar, Gautar, Götar, Gutones and Goths might themselves all have been seen as "out-pourers," in this case of seed, the progenitors, the men. It has rightly been asked how they might then have been differentiated from non-Gothic men. But ethnocentric appellations claim a monopoly of human attributes for the greater glory of their own race. Outsiders may repay like with like by turning this ethnic self-glorification around, to make the Gothic men into "stallions" or even claim of their origo that the whole Gothic people has as much value as a single nag, a solitary "out-pourer of seed."[58]

There are many further examples.[59] Gothiscandza represents Gothic Scandia, or the Gothic coast on the southern shores of the Baltic; the dative plural Oium means "in the fruitful fields," or "on a fruitful island," and Geped-oios is the island of the Gepids in the estuary of the Vistula. A river serving as a border between the Goths and the Gepids is called Auha, "river or brook." Tacitus names the Rugians, and they appear in the Gothic tradition as Elm- or Island-Rugians. Cassiodorus knew the Amals as a Germanic royal dynasty of the first rank, and described them retrospectively as more noble than Attila, whom they served.[60] He took the equation between them and the A(n)ses, the gods, from the Gothic mythological tales. It was certainly unknown to him and his informants that both names seem originally to have meant the same thing, i.e., pillar-idols.

Amongst the dynastic families, the Visigothic Balts took second rank. Contemporary history taught Cassiodorus this, but from pre-ethnographic sources he knew that they were also, etymologically, "the bold ones." The same pattern is seen in the family tree of Berig and his descendants, that of the hero-king Geberic, and with the list of peoples who belong to the empire of Ermanaric.[61] The history of Alaric I and that of Attila contain similarities and comparisons, but hardly any pre-ethnographic material. Alaric was a Balt (Getica 146). The fifth-century diplomat and historian Priscus had already set down details of Attila in his (lost) Byzantine history, which was used by Cassiodorus for details of the Huns, although it is not clear whether or not he mentioned the (possibly) Gothic *strawa,* "pyre" on Attila's grave mound.

Once their origins had been committed to writing, the Goths acquired an ethnographic identity (*Getica* 40). Cassiodorus has King Athalaric told that this was not known (we might add "of course") even to the Gothic elders (*Variae* IX 25, 4). As a prerequisite for his Gothic ethnography, the author insists upon the credibility of his pre-ethnographic data. For Cassiodorus there was, as an alternative to these tales, the reality reported by contemporaries (*historia*), the possibility of historical speculation (*argumentum*), and the "tale against nature" *fabula contra naturam* (Isidore, *Etymologiae* I, 45). A *fabula* is, to be sure, something invented and thus "against all natural and reasonable experience," but it does have a deeper meaning. Thus Cassiodorus cites Gothic myths as evidence of the semi-divine and heroic origins of the Amal dynasty,[62] even though such a pagan concept was of course "against nature" for a sixth-century Christian. Cassiodorus adapts the Gothic origins and their pre-ethnographic details through their historicization in a dialectic sense: *originem Gothicam historiam fecit esse Romanam,* "he turned the Gothic tale of origins into a Roman history" (*Variae* IX 25 5). To this end the *Getika,* the lost history of the Getae composed by the Greek orator Dio Chrysostom (Cocceianus) in the first century A.D. was of primary use to him. However, the historicization of Gothic origins was already well prepared; they were always ruled by kings.[63] Moreover, their history ends with the collapse of the Amal house, the *regnum Amalorum.* Cassiodorus can say of Queen Amalasuintha that she had as many kings as she had ancestors, *tot reges quot parentes.* Thus their pre-ethnographic details contained historical elements, since the Goths' "old songs were close to history" in form. The story of Gothic origins, turned now into Roman history, was intended to confirm for the Goths their "primeval" rights of homeland within the ancient world.[64] The *Getica* cites a Gothic historian called Ablabius, who is still one of the great unknowns, although in the *Getica* he is given as an authority for oral traditions.[65]

Through the Amal dynasty, the Gaut-Anse tradition passed onto the Eastern Goths, at the head of which stands the third of the tribal progenitors, Ostrogotha (*Getica* 82, 98), and whose historicity has to be taken in conjunction with that of King Kniva (ca. 250–71) and with the pre-Amal history of the Goths, or perhaps only of those in the east. According to the *Getica,* Ermanaric is the most important of the Amals and an ancestor of Eutharic, although Cassiodorus does not include the great Ostrogoth king in his ten-member genealogy, and in the sagas he dies without issue.[66]

Contradictions like these are common, but can hardly be resolved. However, the question does arise of whether Scandinavia was not the ancestral home of the Goths but of the Gaut-Amal dynasty? At all events, in about 500 a Scandinavian-Gaut Roduulf "gave up his own kingdom (traveled down to Ravenna), and put himself under the protection of Theoderic, King of the Goths, and gained thus what he desired" (*Getica* 24). Cassiodorus may have learned details of current Scandinavian Gautar and Gothic peoples through him. Even the story of Berig, which follows immediately after the mention of Roduulf, might have been told to him by the latter in Ravenna. If this is the case, then pre-ethnographic details in the *Getica* do not come from a continental Gothic, but rather from a Scandinavian oral tradition that did not reach the Ostrogoths until around 500. This cannot apply, of course, to details relating to Eastern Europe, but a Scandinavian origin was in any case quite simply a prestigious one to have. Not only the Goths, but every other group which spoke a *lingua Theotisca* wanted to have been Scandinavian at one stage.[67]

That nations and royal dynasties derive their origins from Scandinavia is clear from name traditions, but it is systematized in classical and early medieval ethnography. There is a nice explanation given for this and it is reflected once again in the *Getica*. Scandinavia was a typical base for emigration. The cold climate extended the procreativity of men and women. The extremely long winter nights encouraged an imagined procreative urge among the inhabitants. It is for that reason that we find in *Getica* 25 the famous description of the "Island of Scandza as the workshop of peoples or the mother of the tribes." This notion of Scandinavian overpopulation is not historical. One reason for the preference for Scandinavia as a land of origin could lie in the long genealogies which form part of the tradition there. Greatly ramified (or probably better extended) genealogies provide the respectability of age and therefore precedence among peoples.[68] Long family trees and lists of dynastic names correspond to the conservatism of an island culture. On the other hand, they are found only to a far smaller extent on the continent. Early medieval sources know the Vandal house of Hasding and the Frankish Merovingians, the Gothic Amals and Balts, and also the names of Lombard-Bavarian noble and royal families. The names of the last three groups draw entirely or partly upon Scandinavian origins.[69] In the eastern part of the continent these traditions were used right at the end of the classical world to encourage special respect, to ensure belonging (*Variae* VIII, 2, 3). The Frankish king Clovis, on the other hand, is afforded only a genealogy in which he appears already as the fourth in line (Fredegar, III, 9–12). Genealogies were part of the essence of a people, and family trees were the basis for the sense of solidarity among early medieval elite groups and thus for the development of larger political units.[70] Without the bonding agency of a Roman *historia* which embraced the Christian history of salvation, and without the ethnographic identities provided in the service of kings and queens and which as simple "ethnographical ideologies" would have been quite ineffective,[71] the individual traditions would not have survived even in fragmentary form, and would not have permitted this of the Roman world.

Translated by Brian Murdoch

Notes

[1] Contrary to the arguments of Elias J. Bickermann, "Origines gentium," *Classical Philology* 47 (1952): 65–81. Herbert Grundmann, *Geschichtsschreibung im Mittelalter* (Göttingen: Vandenhoeck and Ruprecht, 1965). Herwig Wolfram, *The Roman Empire and its Germanic Peoples* (London, Berkeley, Los Angeles: U of California P, 1997), 31 and *Einleitung oder Überlegungen zur Origo gentis: Typen der Ethnogenese,* ed. Herwig Wolfram and Walter Pohl (Vienna: Akademie der Wissenschaften, 1990), 19–31, see 20 plus note 10; see Hans Hubert Anton, "*Origo gentis* — Volksgeschichte. Zur Auseinandersetzung mit Walter Goffarts Werk (The Narrators of Barbarian History)," in *Historiographie im frühen Mittelalter,* ed. Anton Scharer and Georg Scheibelreiter (Vienna: Akademie der Wissenschaften, 1994), 262–307, esp. 270 and 272–73.

[2] Joachim Herrmann, *Griechische und Lateinische Quellen zur Frühgeschichte Mitteleuropas* (Berlin: Akademie, 1988–92 = Schriften und Quellen der Alten Welt 37, 1–4), 3, 19.

[3] Herwig Wolfram, "*Origo et Religio*. Ethnic Traditions and Literature in Early Medieval Texts," *Early Medieval Europe* 3 (1994): 19–38, esp. 31–32.

[4] Anton, "*Origo gentis*," 262 and 303; quotation on 304.

[5] Herrmann, *Quellen,* 3, 19 and note 22.

[6] Genesis 10, and see Arno Borst, *Der Turmbau von Babel: Geschichte und Meinungen über Ursprung und Vielfalt der Sprachen und Völker* (Stuttgart: Hiersemann, 1957–63) and Herwig Wolfram, *History of the Goths* (Berkeley, Los Angeles, London: U of California P, 1988, paperback 1990), 19.

[7] Details of the editions (cited in the body of the text in parentheses) are as follows: Cassiodorus/Jordanes, *Getica* (discussed in detail below) = Jordanes, *Romana et Getica,* ed. Theodor Mommsen (Hanover: MGH, 1882, repr. Munich, 1982 = MGH AA 5/i), with *Getica* 315 cited here; in the body of this chapter, not every specific reference to the *Getica* will be given, but the work is the principal source for the study of the origins of the Goths, Cassiodorus, *Variae epistolae,* ed. Theodor Mommsen (Berlin: MGH, 1894, Nachdruck Munich, 1981 = MGH AA 12); ed. Åke J. Fridh (Turnhout: Brepols, 1973 = Corpus Christianorum, Series Latina 96); Tacitus, [*Germania* etc.], ed. Michael Winterbottom (Cambridge, MA: Harvard UP; London: Heinemann, 1970). On Caesar, see Gerhard Dobesch, "Caesar, Commentarii über den gallischen Krieg, Buch 1, Kapitel 1 — eine Sensation," *Wiener Humanistische Blätter* 42 (2000): 5–43.

THE LITERATURE OF GERMANIC ORIGINS

[8] *Getica* 316, *Variae* IX, 25, 5; see Herwig Wolfram, "Einleitung oder Überlegungen zur *Origo gentis*," in *Typen der Ethnogenese,* ed. Herwig Wolfram and Walter Pohl (Vienna: Akademie der Wissenschaften, 1990), 19–31, esp. 21.

[9] See *Getica* 1 and Herrmann, *Quellen* 3, 80 and 126. Isidore of Seville, *Historia vel Origo Gothorum,* ed. Theodor Mommsen (Berlin: MGH, 1894, repr. Munich, 1981 = MGH AA 11) — references are to this text unless otherwise stated, and see below for details of an edition of the *Etymologies;* Gregory of Tours, *Historia Francorum,* ed Bruno Krusch and Wilhelm Levison (2nd ed., Hanover: MGH, 1951, repr. Hanover 1992 = MGH SS rerum Merovingicarum 1/i) and ed. Rudolf Buchner (Darmstadt: WBG, 1959 = Ausgewählte Quellen zur deutschen Geschichte des Mittelalters 2 and 3).

[10] Fredegar, *Chronicae,* ed. Bruno Krusch (Hanover: MGH, 1888), repr. Stuttgart, 1984 = MGH SS rerum Merovingicarum 2), 1–168), and ed. Andreas Kusternig (2nd ed., Darmstadt: WBG, 1994 = Ausgewählte Quellen zur deutschen Geschichte des Mittelalters 4a), 3–271; Paulus Diaconus, *Historia Langobardorum,* ed. Georg Waitz (Hanover: MGH, 1878, repr. Hanover, 1988 = MGH SS rerum Langobardicarum), 12–187; Bede, *Historia ecclesiastica gentis Anglorum I–V,* ed. Charles Plummer (Oxford: Clarendon, 1956), on which see Anton, "*Origo gentis,*" 305; Gildas, *The Ruin of Britain,* ed. trans. Michael Winterbottom (Chichester: Phillimore, 1978); *Historia Brittonum,* ed. Theodor Mommsen (Berlin: MGH, 1898, repr. Munich, 1981 = MGH AA 13), 147–201.

[11] Widukind, *Res gestae Saxonicae,* ed. Paul Hirsch (5th ed., Hanover: MGH, 1935; repr. Hanover, 1989 = MGH SS rerum Germanicarum), and ed. Albert Bauer and Reinhold Rau (4th ed., Darmstadt: WBG, 1992 = Ausgewählte Quellen zur deutschen Geschichte des Mittelalters 8), 1–183; Cosmas of Prague, *Chronik der Böhmen,* ed. Berthold Bretholz (Berlin: MGH, 1923, repr. Munich 1980 = MGH Scriptores rerum Germanicarum, NS 2); Gallus Anonymus, *Chronicon et gesta ducum sive principum Polonorum,* ed. Karol Malezynski and Rudolf Köpke (Hannover: MGH, 1851, repr. Stuttgart 1983 = MGH SS 9), 418–78; Saxo Grammaticus, *Gesta Danorum,* ed. J. Olrik and H. Raeder (2nd ed., Copenhagen: Levin and Munksgaard, 1931). For the Anglo-Saxon poems see *Widsith,* ed. R. W. Chambers (Cambridge: CUP, 1912); *Deor,* ed. Kemp Malone (London: Methuen, 1933) and *Beowulf,* ed. Friedrich Klaeber (Boston: Heath, 3rd ed., 1950). On Nestor's redaction of the "Tale of Bygone Years," see Christian Hannick, "*Povest' vremennych let,*" in *Lexikon des Mittelalters* (Munich: Artemis, 1991) VII, col. 137 f.

[12] Wolfram, "Überlegungen zur Origo gentis," 21 and 24; see Reinhard Wenskus, *Stammesbildung und Verfassung: Das Werden der frühmittelalterlichen gentes* (Cologne and Graz: Böhlau, 1961, repr. 1977), 56–57 and 66–67, and Georg Scheibelreiter, "Vom Mythos zur Geschichte. Überlegungen zu den Formen der Bewahrung von Vergangenheit im Frühmittelalter," in *Historiographie im frühen Mittelalter,* ed. Scharer and Scheibelreiter, 26–40, see 27 and note 26.

[13] Isidore of Seville, *Etymologiarum sive originum libri XX,* ed. Wallace Martin Lindsay (Oxford: Clarendon, 1911), V, 31, 9–10; *Getica* 315.

[14] Herrmann, *Quellen,* 3, 126.

[15] *Getica* 118 and see 261–62, Wenskus, *Stammesbildung und Verfassung*, 96–97, and Wolfram, *Goths*, 6. See Caesar, *De bello Gallico* VI, 21–22.

[16] Sallust, *De Catilinae coniuratione*, ed. Rudolf Dietsch (Leipzig: Teubner, 1859 and reprints), chapter 2. See Herrmann, *Quellen*, 3, 14 and esp. 26.

[17] Wolfram, Goths, 163.

[18] Wolfram, Goths, 9 and Werner Goez, *Translatio imperii: Ein Beitrag zur Geschichte des Geschichtsdenkens und der politischen Theorien im Mittelalter und der frühen Neuzeit* (Tübingen: Mohr, 1958).

[19] Alfred Dove, "Studien zur Vorgeschichte des deutschen Volksnamens," *Sitzungberichte der Akademie der Wissenschaften, Heidelberg* 8 (1916): 25, note 3 and 82, note 2. See Wolfram, "*Origo et religio*," 20–21.

[20] Adam of Bremen, *Gesta Hammaburgensis ecclesiae pontificum*, ed. Bernhard Schmeidler (3rd ed., Hanover, 1917, repr. Hanover: MGH, 1993), I, 1 and IV, 1.

[21] Wolfram, "Überlegungen zur *Origo gentis*," 27 and note 61.

[22] Herrmann, *Quellen*, 3, 52–53.

[23] As Wenskus, *Stammesbildung und Verfassung*, 57–58.

[24] Livy, *Ab urbe condita*, ed. W. Weissenbronn, M. Müller (Stuttgart: Teubner 1959–). Wenskus, *Stammesbildung und Verfassung*, 58–59, 20–21, 32–34 and 483–84, Wolfram, Goths, 300 and note 260.

[25] Wenskus, *Stammesbildung und Verfassung*, 57–58.

[26] *Getica* 25; see Wolfram, Goths, 36 as well as 604.

[27] Wolfram, Goths, 28.

[28] Wolfram, Goths, 324.

[29] Johann Weissensteiner, *Tegernsee, die Bayern und Österreich* (Vienna: Akademie der Wissenschaften, 1983).

[30] Ulrich Müller, "Langobardische Sagen," in *Reallexikon der Germanischen Altertumskunde* 18 (2nd ed., Berlin: de Gruyter, 2001) 93–103.

[31] I, 10,27–11,18. See Ludwig Schmidt, *Die Ostgermanen* (2nd ed., Munich: Beck, 1941, repr. 1969).

[32] Helmut Birkhan, *Germanen und Kelten bis zum Ausgang der Römerzeit* (Vienna: Akademie der Wissenschaften, 1970), 342.

[33] Wolfram, Goths, 11 and note 77.

[34] Ammianus Marcellinus, *Rerum gestarum libri XXXI*, ed. Wolfgang Seyfahrt (Leipzig: Teubner, 1978), XXIX, 6, 1.

[35] Caesar, *De bello gallico libri VII*, ed. Otto Seel (3rd ed., Leipzig: Teubner, 1977), VI, 11–12. See Wolfram, *Empire and Germanic Peoples*, 5–6.

[36] Wolfram, Goths, 28.

[37] Wolfram, Goths, 44.

[38] See Anton, "*Origo gentis*," 265–72 and Johann Weißensteiner, "Cassiodor/Jordanes als Geschichtsschreiber," in *Historiographie im frühen Mittelalter*, ed. Scharer and Scheibelreiter, 308–25, esp. 316 and note 42f. Text references are respectively to *Getica* 1 and 315 (and see Jordanes. *Romana* 4); *Getica* 245; *An-*

ecdoton Holderii, ed. Hermann Usener (Bonn: Georgi, 1877); *Variae* IX, 25, 5 and see *Getica* 9; *Variae,* pref. 11; *Anecdoton; Variae* XII, 20, 4.

[39] See *Getica* 1. See also Weißensteiner, "Cassiodor/Jordanes," 308–9, 317 and 324–25 and the same author's "Cassiodors Gotengeschichte bei Gregor von Tours und Paulus Diaconus? Eine Spurensuche," in *Ethnogenese und Über-lieferung,* ed. Karl Brunner and Brigitte Merta (Vienna: Akademie der Wissen-schaften, 1994), 123–28, as well as Wolfram, *Goths,* 3 and note 18, 335–36 and notes 540 and 549.

[40] Wolfram, "Überlegungen zur *Origo gentis,*" 26–27 and *Goths,* 38. See *Getica* 25–28 as well as 9 and 16. Ptolemy, *Geographica,* ed. C. F. A. Nobbe ([1843–45] repr. Hildesheim: Olms, 1966) = *Geographica* II, 11, 33–35.

[41] Herrmann, *Quellen,* 3, 14–15 and 126–27; Weißensteiner, "Cassiodor/Jordanes," 316; Wolfram, Goths, 35–36. See also Schmidt, *Ostgermanen,* 118–19.

[42] *Getica* 58 follows Orosius I, 16. Wolfram, *Goths,* 28. Other classical writers do similar things, such as linking (as does Diodorus Siculus) the Cimbri and Cimme-rians (the Homeric *Kimmerioi*), taking them both as Celts. The complexity of the problem is illustrated by the fact that there is still no complete agreement: see Nora Chadwick, *The Celts* (Harmondsworth: Penguin, 1970), 52–53.

[43] See Wolfram, *Goths,* 28–29 on these points. See Isidore, *Historia* 1–2 and 66 on Magog and *Getica* 29.

[44] Scheibelreiter, "Vom Mythos zur Geschichte," 27, note 6.

[45] On the connection between Troy and Theoderic the Great (*Getica* 58–60), see Anton, "*Origo gentis.*"

[46] See Weißensteiner, "Cassiodor/Jordanes," 316.

[47] *Getica* 78, and see Wolfram, "*Origo et Religio,*" 30–31, Walter Goffart, *The Narrators of Barbarian History (A.D. 550–800). Jordanes, Gregory of Tours, Bede and Paul the Deacon* (Princeton: Princeton UP, 1988), 78 and note 280.

[48] Wolfram, "*Origo et religio,*" 31 and *Goths,* 257.

[49] *Codices Latini antiquiores* II, ed. Elias Avery Lowe (Oxford: Clarendon, 1972), n. 233a. See Wolfram, *Goths,* 324.

[50] Wolfram, *Goths,* 114–15 and 250; "*Origo et religio,*" 23–24 and 30–31; *Das Reich und die Germanen* (Berlin: Siedler 1990), 54.

[51] Wolfram, *Goths,* 34. and see the chapters in the present volume by Theodor Andersson (Old Norse) and Brian Murdoch (Gothic) on the *Hamðismál.*

[52] Anton, "*Origo gentis,*" 303–4.

[53] Wolfram, *Goths,* 20., 36; Wenskus, *Stammesbildung und Verfassung,* 464–65; Ulrich Jahn, *Volkssagen aus Pommern und Rügen* [Stettin: 1886], new ed. by Siegfried Neumann and Karl-Ewald Tietz (Bremen/Rostock: Tennen, 1999), 376, n. 662.

[54] *Getica* 25 and 94–95; Gildas, *Ruin,* 23, 3; Bede, I, 15; Paul the Deacon I, 2. See Weißensteiner, "Cassiodors Gotengeschichte," 125.

[55] *Getica* 82, 95–98, 130–31, 133, 246, 260–64; Wolfram, *Goths,* 26 and 590 sub voce.

[56] Wolfram, *Goths,* 21.

[57] Pliny the Elder, *Natural History,* ed., trans. H. Rackham et al. (Cambridge, MA: Harvard UP; London: Heinemann, 1949–52): IV, 100. Herrmann, *Quellen,* 1, 571; Wolfram, *Goths,* 12, 21, and 385, note 21 as well as Tacitus, *Germania* 44.

[58] *Getica* 38; Weißensteiner, "Cassiodor/Jordanes," 311 note 20; Wolfram, *Goths,* 21–22.

[59] See Heinz Löwe, "Vermeintlich gotische Überlieferungsreste bei Cassiodor und Jordanes," in *Ex ipsis rerum documentis: Festschrift Harald Zimmermann,* ed. Klaus Herbers, et al. (Sigmaringen: Thorbecke, 1991), 17–30, esp. 24–26. The term *belagines* in *Getica* 69 corresponds probably to the ancient, orally transmitted customs of the Goths, even though Cassiodorus understood it differently.

[60] *Variae* IV, 1, 1f., 39, 1f. V, 43, 1, IX, 1, 2 and 25, 4–5. *Getica* 199. Herwig Wolfram, *Splendor Imperii* (Vienna: Akademie der Wissenschaften, 1963), 108–9.

[61] Wolfram, *Goths,* 34–35 and 86–87.

[62] Scheibelreiter, "Vom Mythos zur Geschichte," 27.

[63] Wolfram, *Goths,* 12, 41 and note 37–38.

[64] Variae IV, 39, 1; VIII, 2, 1–2; XI, 1, 10 and 19–20. Wolfram, *Splendor,* 108–9.

[65] *Getica* 28; Weißensteiner, "Cassiodor/Jordanes," 308.

[66] Wolfram, "*Origo et religio,*" 24; *Goths,* 24–25, 31–32, 37–38, 42–43, 86–87, and 114.

[67] Wolfram, *Goths,* 326–27 and "Überlegungen zur *Origo gentis,*" 27.

[68] Wolfram "*Origo et religio,*" 32–33 and Adam of Bremen, IV, 22.

[69] Wolfram "*Origo et religio,*" 32.

[70] Wolfram "*Origo et religio,*" 34.

[71] Patrick Amory, *People and Identity in Ostrogothic Italy, 489–544* (Cambridge: CUP, 1997).

Germania Romana

Adrian Murdoch

IN A.D. 15 the Roman general Germanicus, adopted son of the emperor Tiberius, crossed the Rhine at the head of eight infantry divisions of the Roman army. His mission was to avenge Rome's most humiliating defeat, a battle that had taken place six years previously that wiped out three of Rome's elite legions, possibly as many as twenty thousand men. The effects of that massacre are in some respect still being felt today. What had happened? Over a period of three days the new governor of Germania, three legions, and three cavalry units were massacred in the Teutoburg Forest. The battle is known today as the *Varusschlacht*, named after the hapless governor and commander of the legions. Publius Quintilius Varus was, nominally at least, a comparatively experienced governor, if not much of a military man. The first-century Roman historian Velleius Paterculus, in his compendium of Roman history, dismisses Varus as "more accustomed to ease in a camp than to action in the field."[1] Long groomed for high office, he had already held positions in Syria. His rule, however, was characterized by tactlessness and stupidity, and according to another historian, Cassius Dio, "he not only gave orders to the Germans as if they were actual slaves of the Romans, but also levied money from them as if they were subject nations. These were demands they would not tolerate."[2]

The opposing Germanic leader was a barbarian only in name. Trained in the Roman army, Arminius, the son of Segimer, had not only received Roman citizenship, but had risen to the middle classes with the rank of *eques* or knight. He knew how the Romans thought, and Varus's oppression was the catalyst for his revolt. The headquarters of that revolt were naturally around the tribe of which Arminius was head, the Cherusci, who occupied the land around the modern town of Hanover, and they were soon joined by two other tribes, the Chaucii and the Marsii.

Their plan was always to ambush the Roman army, to trick them out from behind their walls and ramparts. Their plan was to send a false report of a revolt north of the Rhine, then a stepping stone rather than the watery barrier it was to become. The route north, for the Romans, led from Haltern on the river Lippe — the home of the Nineteenth Legion — through the Teutoburg Forest, roughly between Osnabrück and Paderborn. It was a difficult march, and the topography was against the Romans. "The shape of mountains in this region was irregular, their slopes being deeply cleft by ravines, while the trees grew closely together to a great height. In consequence the Romans, even before the enemy fell upon them, were hard pressed by the necessity of felling trees, clearing the tracks and bridging the difficult stretches wherever necessary on their line of march."[3] It was a perfect spot for an ambush: between the foot of the Kalkriese hills and the marshland, the six-kilometer path was narrow, forcing the Roman army to stretch out along ten to twelve kilometers. The German tribes had prepared ramparts, traces of which can still be seen, and the Romans had no idea they were going to be attacked. They were not only slowed down by as many as ten thousand camp followers, but were hardly traveling light: a fragment of ivory veneer from a decorated couch and floral bone carvings that once decorated beds have been found.

The signal came from the gods. When the heavens opened in an almighty storm, the ground turned to mud and the tops of trees began to break off, creating confusion. Then the Germans attacked. It was not a textbook battle with neat formations and tidy squares marching and wheeling. It was a messy, dirty fight at close quarters. Somehow the Romans broke free, found open ground and set up a camp. We have no idea what it was like; no reports from soldiers have survived, but parallels with the experience of infantry fighting in the jungle in Vietnam are neither unfair nor far-fetched. As the Romans waited for dawn, Varus had to decide what to do, whether to head back to civilization or to carry on north. After a night of constant harassment, he chose the latter. The Germans refused to oblige the Roman desire for a pitched battle, so the Roman army trudged on with growing gloom through the muddy forest, providing easy targets for guerrilla attacks. It was apparent that it was useless to continue; before they found camp for the second night, Varus had made the decision to retreat. On the next day, though, came the *coup de grâce*. As the frightened and diminished Roman forces prepared to make a run for it, Arminius and his troops found their ranks swollen by other Germanic tribes rallying to his banner. The *Germani* allowed the Romans to leave the safety of their camp and advance as far as a wooden barricade that Arminius had had constructed, and then it was soon all over. Varus ordered his soldiers to construct some form of defense, but they were overrun. A wounded Varus died by his own hand; one of his deputies fought to the death, while another surrendered. The cavalry units tried to desert but they were cut down to a man. The unlucky survivors of the pitched battle were burned alive or nailed to trees. The rest were simply left to die. The humiliation was complete. The territory north of the Rhine was to remain German. Only a handful of Varus's men ever made it back to Rome and the numbers of the three disgraced legions — the Seventeenth, Eighteenth and Nineteenth — were never used again. When news reached Rome, Suetonius shows us an unshaven Augustus beating his head against the doorpost near to madness and crying: "O, Quintilius Varus! Give me back my legions."[4]

Six years later, Germanicus found the site of the battle and the remains of the soldiers who had died that day under the leadership of Varus. The description of the battlefield by the historian Tacitus still sends a chill. "In the centre of the field were the whitening bones of men, as they had fled, or stood their ground, strewn everywhere or piled in heaps. Near, lay fragments of weapons and limbs of horses, and also human heads, prominently nailed to trunks of trees. In the adjacent groves were the barbarous altars, on which they had immolated tribunes and first-rank centurions."[5] Survivors of the disaster and those who had escaped German captivity were on hand to guide Germanicus and his troops. They showed him where officers fell; re-enacted how the Roman standards, the eagles, had been captured; pointed out the spot where the German chieftain Arminius had stood as he gloried over the defeated; and finally where the wounded Varus fell on his sword. There was little that Germanicus could do. In grief and anger his soldiers buried the bones of the legions, as Tacitus says (*Annales* 1, 62): "not a soldier knowing whether he was interring the relics of a relative or a stranger, but looking on all as kinsfolk and of their own blood, while their wrath rose higher than ever against the foe."

Like the battle of Poitiers in 732, or the siege of Stalingrad in the Second World War, the Kalkriese massacre is one of the defining moments in European history; but until recently it was also one of the most mysterious, as its location was for centuries simply not known. Over the past 200 years some 700 different sites have been suggested for the battle, but it was not until 1987 that Tony Clunn, an off-duty British army officer with a metal detector, finally identified the site beyond all reasonable doubt through the discovery of coins bearing precise dates.[6]

But why is this battle so important? First, it was the first crack in Rome's imperial armor. The loss of their presumed military infallibility affected the Roman psyche deeply. At a geopolitical level, Rome gave up any thoughts of the Elbe as the imperial boundary and retreated to the Rhine. Until the end of the Roman empire, Germany, on the wrong side of the Rhine, would continue to make the Romans very nervous.

It was fear of a repeat of the *Varusschlacht* that gave the impetus for the construction of one of the longest frontier defense systems in history, the so-called Limes ("boundary," "frontier") line, that ran from the lower Rhine, across the Taunus in Hessia, then south into the Main valley and across the Neckar plain. The Limes survived well into the third century, defining Roman Germania.[7] At its simplest, it was a cleared strip of no-man's land punctuated by timber observation posts, and supported by forts such as the one reconstructed at Saalburg, and it is reminiscent of nothing so much as the frontier between East and West Germany during the Cold War. This was not just a military barrier, like Hadrian's Wall, or the Great Walls of Constantinople; it was the physical expression of where civilization stopped and barbarism began.

But the battle had a far deeper impact. A. A. Gill has commented: "The slaughter in the Teutoburg Forest divided Europe into the warm south, who forever saw forests as dreadful places to be avoided and cleared, homes to dragons and trolls, antitheses of the civilized city, and the north, who understood them to be healing, protecting, mystical, spiritual places. How you feel about a silent birch forest at twilight says more about your blood and your kin than your passport."[8] The later Roman emperor Julian the Apostate (331–63), on campaign in Germany in the mid-fourth century, exhibited this fear all too well. In a fragment probably from his own account of his campaigns, he describes marching through the Hercynian forest — then used as a blanket term for all forests along the Rhine. "We hurried to the Hercynian Forest and it was a strange and monstrous thing that I beheld. At any rate I do not hesitate to engage that nothing of the sort has ever been seen in the Roman Empire, at least as far as we know. But if anyone considers Thessalian Tempe or Thermopylae or the great and far flung Taurus to be impassable, let me tell him that for difficulty of approach they are trivial indeed compared to the Hercynian Forest."[9]

But most significant of all, the battle of the Teutoburg Forest shaped the way that Germany has regarded itself. The massacre is one of the most politicized battles in history.[10] After the emergence of German nationalism following the uprisings in 1848, any discussion of a Germanic past took on political overtones. The corresponding Celtic heritage was a rather more *sotto voce* affair in the rest of western Europe. In France, Vercinge-torix, the king of the Arvani who held the fortress of Gergovia against Julius Caesar in 52 B.C., became a symbol of resistance and is, it is true, still seen as a figurehead, for example in the Asterix comics and in the 2001 eponymous film directed by Jacques Dorfmann. In Britain there was a lively interest in early leaders such as Caractacus and Boudicca (Boadicea), but it was expressed in idealized form by artists such as Laurence Alma-Tadema, whose 1865 painting *Gallo-Roman Women* epitomizes simultaneously the best and worst of this Victorian idealization of all things Celtic. In Germany, though, the equivalent concept of *Germanentum* was whipped into the intellectual mix that included the Grimms' children's stories and the myths of the Nibelungen. Naturally the myth of Arminius — or Hermann, his Germanic name — formed part of this. The physical expression was the *Hermannsdenkmal,* a twenty-six-meter high copper monument near Detmold, begun in 1838, which became a symbol of racial purity, unity and national freedom.[11] Only a few years later and with his tongue rather in his cheek, Heine wrote with what might be called accurate irreverence

> Das ist der Teutoburger Wald,
> Den Tacitus beschrieben,
> Das ist der klassische Morast,
> Wo Varus steckengeblieben.
>
> Hier schlug ihn der Cheruskerfürst,
> Der Hermann, der edle Recke;
> Die deutsche Nationalität,
> Die siegte in diesem Drecke.
>
> Wenn Hermann nicht die Schlacht gewann,
> Mit seinen blonden Horden,
> So gäb es deutsche Freiheit nicht mehr,
> Wir wären römisch geworden!
>
> In unserm Vaterland herrschten jetzt
> Nur römische Sprache und Sitten,
> Vestalen gäb es in München sogar,
> Die Schwaben hießen Quiriten![12]

[This is the Teutoburg Forest as described by Tacitus, and this is the classical swamp where Varus got himself stuck. It was here that the leader of the Cherusci, Hermann, the noble thane, defeated him, and German nationality was victorious in all this mud. If Hermann and his blond hordes had not won the battle, there would be no more freedom and we should all be Romans. In our fatherland there would only be Roman customs and language; there would even be Vestal Virgins in Munich, and the Swabians would be called Quirites.]

But national pride was eventually to develop a more sinister tinge. Comments by Tacitus that Germans "never contaminated themselves by intermarriage with foreigners but remained of pure blood, distinct and unlike any other nation,"[13] were seized upon by historians in the Third Reich. "Die Schlacht im Teutoburger Wald . . . ist eine der Schicksalsschlachten der Weltgeschichte. In ihr triumphiert der Freiheitswille der Germanen über die Machtmittel eines Reiches, das bis dahin nur in der Unwegsamkeit und Unüberwindlichkeit der Natur seine Schranken gefunden hat. Es ist der erste entscheidende Schlachtensieg der Deutschen"[14] (The battle in the Teutoburg Forest is one of the determining battles of world history.

In this battle the will for freedom felt by the *Germani* triumphed over the forces of an empire that thus far had been limited only by the stubbornness and invincibility of the natural world. It is the first decisive German victory in battle). This type of chauvinism received an even more popular expression in the 1936 propaganda film *Ewiger Wald* (*Eternal Forest*), directed by Hans Springer.

The kaleidoscope of impressions of Germania in Roman times makes it difficult to establish what it was actually like, but some judgments are possible. First and foremost the question must be asked, though, who the *Germani* actually were. The less than helpful answer is that in the classical period, and certainly for classical writers, there was no such people. Although the Greeks in the fifth century B.C. were aware of major groups of people in the general area that we now call Germany, Austria, and Switzerland, all of them were lumped together under the title *Keltoi,* and little other than fragments of gossip is recorded about them until the second century B.C.

Even the origins of the name "*Germani*" are uncertain. Our main source for this, as for so much about Germany at this period, is Tacitus, whose *Germania,* subtitled *On the Origin and Geography of Germany* (*De origine et situ Germanorum*) was completed toward the end of the first century. He suggests that the name is a modern invention. "It comes from the fact," he tells us in the second chapter of the *Germania,* "that the tribes which first crossed the Rhine and drove out the Gauls, and are now called Tungrians, were then called Germans. Thus what was the name of a tribe, and not of a race, gradually prevailed, till all called themselves by this self-invented name of Germans, which the conquerors had first employed to inspire terror." It is as plausible an explanation as any, but not only is there no evidence to back it up, we cannot identify the linguistic origins of the name for certain. By the third century, the name Alemanni (with spelling variations such as Alamanni and Almanni), began to be used as a general term for the Germanic tribes, and it is of course still in use today in some European languages as the name for the modern state, as with *Allemagne* in French; but again this seems to have been the case of the Romans lumping together various tribes under one name.

Throughout the Roman period, the area that we now call Germany was occupied by Gauls or Celts, Germans, and Romans, as well as the results of intermarriage between these groups. It was during the first Roman forays across the Rhine that Julius Caesar (fairly arbitrarily, it must be admitted), divided the ethnoi of northwest Europe into two: the Celts (if you spoke Greek) or Gauls (if you spoke Latin) on the one hand, and the *Germani* on the other. The implication is that Celts were potentially civilized; the Germans were out-and-out savages. It does not help matters that the Romans only had a hazy idea of how to distinguish the two.

Initial impressions, certainly from the Roman side, were not exactly favorable. As with many of the people who were not blessed enough to be citizens, the Romans dismissed the *Germani* as out-and-out barbarians. Julius Caesar, commenting on the ones who lived by the Rhine, patronizingly writes: "Caesar thought the condition of the Germans, and who are somewhat more refined than those of the same race and the rest [of the Germans], and that because they border on the Rhine, and are much resorted to by merchants, and are accustomed to the manners of the Gauls, by reason of their proximity to them."[15]

However far the *pax Romana* spread, the Romans were never able to shake off the belief in their innate superiority. As late as the fourth century, Julian the Apostate, in revolt against the emperor Constantius II, wrote a letter to the Roman senate justifying his actions, and at the same time named his cavalry commander, Nevitta, as consul for 362. The Roman senate was beside itself, and Julian's letter was heckled in the senate. The Roman senate could forgive anything, even a usurper, but they could not forgive Nevitta: the man was an uneducated boor and worst of all, he was a German. Even the comparatively open-minded historian Ammianus Marcellinus refers to him as a "barbarian."[16]

If this sounds confusing, it is made doubly so by the fact that neither the Celts nor the Germanic tribes thought of themselves as in any sense unified. For much of the Roman period, the people in question certainly do not appear to have had a concrete idea of themselves as anything as unified as a nation — they belonged to their tribe. Given this confusion, and to impose some consistency, we may use "Gauls" and "Celts" interchangeably, and refer to "the *Germani*," just as the Romans did, referring to individual tribes by name when required. Tempting as it is to speak of "Germans," using the equally vague Roman name at least preserves some distance. Germania, similarly, refers to the actual Roman provinces of Germania Inferior and Germania Superior, with Cologne and Mainz as the respective capitals, while "Germany" may serve only as a blanket term for the land mass that occupies the modern German-speaking area. As far as close contact between the *Germani* and Rome is concerned, both within Germania Romana and outside, three areas are of special interest: warfare, trade (which in spite of the proverb "Trade follows the flag," both *precedes* and follows the flag), and society as a whole. The evidence, of course, is provided to a large extent by Roman sources, which will always give a bias; but archeological finds may provide supportive evidence, in the absence of any written Germanic sources at this stage.

Warfare

By far the greatest amount of information we have about Germanic society throughout the Roman period is to do with warfare, not only because it was for the most part a militaristic society, but more prosaically because it was the battlefield where Germanic and Roman men came into contact. As might be expected in such a society, real power and status in any tribe rested with soldiers who were attached to a chief who, in turn, was elected for the duration of the war. Success on the battlefield conveyed status, and for the chieftain, loyalty was based on, and grew or declined in relation to success in battle. As Tacitus succinctly points out: "The chiefs fight for victory, the companions for their chief. The Germans have no taste for peace; renown is easier won among perils and you cannot maintain a large body of companies except by violence and war."

Warfare was primarily an infantry affair. Not only was cavalry warfare limited to few tribes, but the use of chariots, most infamously (from the point of view of the Roman world) deployed by the Trinovantes and Iceni under Boudicca in Britain, never caught on in Germany. Even by the fourth century it is noticeable that the last great Roman historian, Ammianus Marcellinus, who served several tours of duty in Gaul and Germany, is not only dismissive of Germanic cavalry, but preserves the telling anecdote that the Germanic soldiers were not entirely comfortable with horses either.[17] At the beginning of the Battle of Strasbourg — one of Rome's last great defeats of the *Germani* in A.D. 357 by Julian the Apostate — the rank and file demanded that their leaders should dismount and join the fray on foot. That way, they would be less tempted to run away if the battle did not go their way. The few items that indicate familiarity with horses in Germanic graves suggest that their use was more ceremonial and concerned with status than active or general, and it is not until the time of the Ostrogoth Emperor Theoderic in the sixth century that we see a genuine Germanic cavalry, and this was largely the result of contact with tribes on the western steppe.

Military equipment used by Germanic tribes changed little throughout the period of the Roman occupation and contact. Tacitus's detailed description will have been as terrifyingly familiar for a soldier in Julius Caesar's army as for Ammianus and his colleagues in the fourth century. "Only very few [soldiers] use swords or lances. The spears that they carry have short and narrow heads, but are so sharp and easy to handle that the same weapon serves at need for close or distant fighting. The infantry have also javelins to shower, several per man, and can hurl them to a great distance; for they are either naked or only lightly clad in their cloaks" (*Germania* 6).

Physical evidence from graves as well as pictorial evidence from reliefs support this description. The failure to mention swords is not an oversight on Tacitus's part; expensive and rare as they were, it is not until the second century that they were available in great number. Intriguingly, despite a ban on the export of arms from Rome, then as now, evidence from makers' stamps on swords found in Germanic graves shows that unethical entrepreneurs had little time for trade bans. Of the one hundred swords found recently in a grave in Illerup in Denmark, more than half had square or rounded stamps which clearly marked them as Roman.[18]

Despite the remains of a few workshops, German smiths appear to have been slow to copy swords, and spears remained the norm. In the best weapon cache, dating from the fourth century in Jutland, we see sixty swords and 200 javelins and 190 spears.[19] Similarly telling is the lack of mention of armor. Reliefs invariably show the Germans fighting either naked or wearing trousers and a cloak. It is not until the fifth century that we find evidence for what is normally called the *Spangenhelm* — a conical armored helmet often with hinged cheek pieces and a nose guard.

Tactics and strategy are a different matter. "The love of liberty and the lack of discipline of the Germans," was as much a recognized literary theme as the "docility and tameness of the Syrians" for the Emperor Julian (*Against the Galileans,* 138B). It came through in the tactics of the Germanic warriors. "The Germans rushed forward with more haste than caution, brandishing their weapons and throwing themselves on our squadrons of horses with horrible grinding of teeth and more than their usual fury. Their hair streamed behind them and a kind of madness flashed from their eyes. Our men faced them stubbornly, protecting their heads with their shields and trying to strike fear into the foe with drawn swords or the deadly javelins they brandished." This is Ammianus's description (Ammianus 16.12), and although to some extent it rests upon a literary topos, most commentators agree on the lack of discipline of the Germanic charge.[20]

In terms of strategy, one of the peculiarities of the Germanic excursions into Roman territory is that although they were often destructive, they rarely attacked towns. This is partly due to the fact that the Germans never developed effective siege weaponry. Some efforts were made to learn about siege equipment from deserters and prisoners of war, but it was regarded as a novelty.[21] There was also a cultural issue: warriors had to be convinced that it was worth the effort. The power of the chief rested on the example he set, rather than an ability to give orders. One of the few occasions when the *Germani* did lay siege to a city was in 357, when the Emperor Julian was trapped in the city of Sens for thirty days, but this was an exceptional case; spies from the Alemanni had found out that Julian had been left relatively unguarded. But the siege failed, and the *Germani* withdrew.[22]

More than this, there appears to have been some nervousness of towns — indeed, there were few attempts at major settlements — and in fact the German tribes seem actively to have avoided occupying cities, believing that they were "tombs surrounded by nets" (Ammianus 16.2). Ever since Rome and Germany had first clashed, as Tacitus noted (*Germania* 16): "It is a well-known fact that the peoples of Germany never live in cities and will not even have their houses set close together."

Trade

The Emperor Vespasian (9–79, reigned 69–79) famously commented that money has no smell, and whatever the Romans thought of the Germans, personal distaste was not allowed to get in the way of profit. It is through trade that the Roman and Germanic worlds first met. Caesar writes that before his Gallic Wars, Roman merchants traveled across the Alps to trade at great potential danger and personal cost. The danger of such undertakings is not to be underestimated. The Germanic tribes had a direct way of making their disapproval felt and, a good thirty years after Caesar's comments, during the reign of his successor Augustus, the Romans were forced to take revenge on some Germans who had arrested and then executed Roman merchants who entered their country to trade with them (Cassius Dio, 53.26). Nonetheless the pay-off must have been considerable.

To start with, the trade was to a great extent one-way. The Germanic tribes allowed the Romans merchants in, not to buy from them, but to exchange war booty. The price of free movement was clearly the giving of elaborate gifts. Items such the wonderfully ornate seventy-piece silver dinner service known as the Hildesheim treasure,[23] and now in the Altes Museum in Berlin, are most likely to have been diplomatic gifts. Demand then began to grow for Roman luxuries. Large numbers of bronze vessels, silver tableware, brooches, wine vessels and even statues have all been found in the graves of German chieftains; the breadth of finds — from Holland, across northern Germany and Scandinavia, into the heart of western Russia — is remarkable.[24]

Tacitus mentions (*Germania* 23) that the tribes along the Rhine bought wine, and the wine trade was important from the first century B.C. on. Both wine and wine drinking sets were hugely popular and have been found as far afield as northern Poland and Denmark. By the second century, Gaulish manufactured sets began to find their way north, and we may refer to a distinctive type of wine bucket called the Hemmoor bucket, made in Aachen. Linguistic evidence too points to the importance of viticulture. The Old High German word *choufo* or *koufa,* "trader," derives from the Latin *caupo,* with the specialized sense of "wine merchant."[25]

If trade was initially one-way, this did not last long. Before too long, the Germanic tribes were trading in their own rights and we begin to see a shift away from barter toward monetarization. Tacitus specifically mentions (*Germania* 5) that the border population "value gold and silver for their commercial utility, and are familiar with, and show preference for, some of our coins." Even though we should not place too much emphasis on a monetary economy, by A.D. 18–19 there was a Roman community deep in German territory in Bohemia, living off the earnings of trade and money-lending, sign of a healthy import/export market (Tacitus, *Annals* 2.62).

The Herminduri, who occupied the land to the north of the Danube as far as Thuringia, showed an admirable early entrepreneurial zeal. "They are the only Germans who trade with us not only on the river bank, but deep inside our lines in the brilliant colony that is the capital of Rhaetia [Augsburg]," writes Tacitus (*Germania* 41). It is hard to believe that they were the only ones. Additional impetus will have been provided by the fact that trade appears to have remained unregulated, and that it was not until the uprisings in the latter half of the second century under Marcus Aurelius that specific places and days for trading were established.[26] The remains of a large and well-preserved trading house — a structure forty by fourteen meters — are preserved in southwest Germany. The site, now protected as the Römerhaus Walheim in the town of Walheim in Baden-Württemberg, dates from the second and third centuries A.D. and gives at least some physical idea of the importance of trade.[27]

What did the *Germani* have to offer Rome? Perhaps the best-known and earliest trade is in amber. The discovery of large numbers of Roman coins close to the Samland area in East Prussia suggests that it was a center. Pliny the Elder gives us our first insight into one of the Roman *negotiatores,* traders. It is a telling story of an agent for Julianus, Nero's manager of gladiatorial shows, who visited trading posts along the main amber route, from northern Italy via Moravia and the Vistula to the Baltic. "From Carnuntum in Pannonia to the coasts of Germany from which the amber is brought is a distance of about 600 miles, a fact which has only recently been ascertained," Pliny writes. "Traversing the coasts of that country and visiting the various markets there, [the agent] brought back amber in such vast quantities that that the nets which are used to protect the podium [in the circus] against the wild beasts, are studded with amber."[28] It requires little reading between the lines to guess that up until now the amber trade had been a Germanic monopoly and that Julianus's agent was reconnoitering the area for future trade. Beside classical-textual and archeological evidence, the importance of the amber trade may be seen (along with indications of other trade) in the philological evidence of Germanic loan words in Latin. *Glaesum, ganta* and *sapo* — amber, geese and hair-dye — were all highly regarded in Roman society. It is plausible that agricultural produce, animals, hides and meat were also staples, but they leave no remains.[29]

But the item which, in many ways, can be said to have a done the most to open up German society was slaves. The use by German tribes of slaves is itself well known (Tacitus, *Germania*, 24) and a flourishing trade with the Roman empire emerged. For the Germans this killed two birds with one stone: in the beginning it allowed them to gain valuable Roman possessions while getting rid of prisoners at the same time. The deleterious effect was that in the long term, raids would occur specifically to gain the prisoners to sell; much in the same way that we see the growth of raids in West Africa following the arrival of the Europeans seeking slaves in the seventeenth century.

By the later Roman period the Germans had learned so well, that they were exporting products that had previously been imported. From the second century on, the Treveri, who lived round what is now the city of Trier, began not only to dominate the local market in wine, but began to export as far afield as Lyon and Milan. The fourth-century Latin poet Ausonius, in a long paean to the Moselle River, writes lyrically about the swelling grapes beside that river,[30] and the remains of two huge warehouses called *horrea* by the Romans by the Roman port on the Moselle are testament to the importance of the trade in Trier. A wonderful carving on the Roman tomb of a wine merchant from Neumagen (now in the Landesmuseum Trier) shows the crew and a distinctly inebriated pilot steering a ship carrying four wine barrels.

Society

It is again from Caesar that we have the first glimpses of Germanic life, though it must be emphasized that all the tribes with which he came into contact lived within striking distance of the Rhine. He has nothing to say about the interior of Germany. Thus, although we may make judgments on the outline of German society, much of the detail is shadowy, and it must be recalled that our written sources are Roman, and the writers need have had only a vague and imperfect understanding of Germanic society.

The fluidity of Germanic society has not helped. What we may be tempted to think of as a fixed group of "Germans," was no more than a confederacy of tribes held together by a common goal. The Battle of Strasbourg in 357 offers an illustration. Under the leadership of Chondomar (Chonodomarius), up to seven of the Germanic tribes had united to march on Strasbourg, but it was always a loose affair. At the end of the second century, too, when Marcus Aurelius had negotiated peace with the Germanic tribes, it is significant that he did so on a tribe by tribe basis.[31]

With archeological help is possible to build a picture of what typical Gaulish life might have been like. One of the most extensive excavations that has been carried out at Feddersen Wierde, near Bremerhaven, excavated in the late 1950s and early 1960s, and a similar picture is painted at other sites like Peeloo and Fochteloo in the Netherlands.[32] Much of Feddersen Wierde's importance comes from the fact that it was continuously occupied for around 500 years — from the first century B.C. until the fourth century A.D. In the beginning, society is clearly basic, a simple grouping of rectangular timber houses in a style normally called "long houses." By the first century A.D., the community began to develop. We begin to see more of a structure to the society and the site is now dominated by a single larger house, its importance emphasized by a palisade, while we see a growth in structures which are clearly craftsmen's workshops. Work was obviously diverse and evidence of wood, leather, bone and iron were all worked here. While Feddersen Wierde was clearly home to one — if extended — family, larger communities have also been found. Most famous is Wijster, again in the Netherlands,[33] which evolved from the first century A.D. until it was eventually home to possibly as many as sixty families in the later third century. A degree of planning can be seen in the regular alignment of the long houses. It was also clearly a rich community, and in this case profits undoubtedly came from garrisons on the lower Rhine. As elsewhere, it went into a decline after the collapse after Roman power along the Rhine in the early fifth century.

Most Germans lived agriculturally. They were famed for their green fingers and their animal husbandry, practicing techniques such as crop rotation and fertilization. Pliny writes admiringly that "the tribe of the Ubii are the only race known to us who, while cultivating extremely fertile land, enrich it by digging up any sort of earth below three feet and throwing it on the land in the layer a foot thick. The tribes of the Aedui and Pictones have made their arable land extremely fertile by means of chalk which is indeed also found most useful for olives and vines"(*Natural History* 17.4.47).

Here literary evidence is backed up by archeo-zoological and archeo-botanical evidence. The huge numbers of animal bones found in domestic settlements (at Feddersen Wierde they account for half of the animal remains), point specifically to a dependence on cattle not just for meat and milk, but also for agricultural work, with some reliance on pigs and sheep, while fowl were also popular in Germania. Analysis of grains from pollen spectra gives evidence that the diet of the *Germani* had a clear emphasis on barley, oats and some strains of wheat, while favorite vegetables were predominately peas, beans and lentils. It is an unresolved curiosity that while Roman settlers grew fruits and spices, there is little evidence of these in German sites. We simply do not know if Germans did not want them, or if they were unable to maintain them.

Conclusion

We can see from excavations at Feddersen Wierde and Wijster that most domestic sites throughout Germany end simultaneously toward the end of the fourth century. The answer lies in the huge disruption caused by the tribes coming into Germania Romana from the east. By the mid-fourth century the comparatively peaceful stalemate of the reign of Marcus Aurelius was long forgotten, and such Germanic incursions became a more regular occurrence, so that by 357 the Romans had in effect lost Germany. The future emperor Julian, then military commander, working from Gaul, gives us a snapshot of the state of the country before he set out on campaign in late summer. "A great number of Germans had settled themselves with impunity near the towns they had sacked in Gaul. Now the number of towns whose walls had been dismantled was about forty-five — not counting citadels and smaller forts. The barbarians then controlled on our side of the Rhine the whole country that extends from its sources to the ocean. Moreover, those who were settled nearest to us were as much as thirty-five miles from the banks of the Rhine and an area three times as broad as that had been left a desert by the raids so that the locals could not even pasture their cattle there. Then too there were certain cities deserted by their inhabitants, near which the barbarians were not yet encamped" (*Letter to the Athenians*, 279A–B). Julian managed to hold the frontier, but it was like sticking a plaster on a deep wound. His restoration of civilization was merely a pause, and by the beginning of the fifth century, Roman Germany began to unravel for the last time. At the end of 406, the dam holding back the barrier burst, and with it Rome's most important frontier, as a mixed group of various Germanic tribes crossed the Rhine and occupied Roman Germania and then Gaul, plundering settlements like Mainz and Trier. In tones like those of Augustine lamenting the burning of Rome only four years later at the hand of Alaric the Visigoth, Jerome wrote: "Savage tribes in countless numbers have overrun all parts of Gaul. The whole country between the Alps and the Pyrenees, between the Rhine and the ocean, has been laid waste [. . .] The once noble city of Mainz has been captured and destroyed. In its church many thousands have been massacred. The people of Worms after withstanding a long siege have been extirpated [. . .] And those which the sword spares without, famine ravages within."[34] The civilization of Germania Romana was at an end. The Dark Ages were about to begin.

Notes

¹ Velleius Paterculus, *Historia Romana,* 2.177. There is an edition by C. Stegmann de Pritzwald, *C. Vellei Paterculi ex Historiae romanae libris duobus quae supersunt* (Leipzig: Teubner, 1968) and see http://www.thelatinlibrary.com. See also the German text by Marion Giebel (Stuttgart: Reclam, 1989) and the Loeb text by F. W. Shipley (Cambridge, MA: Harvard UP; London: Heinemann, 1924).

² Cassius Dio, *Roman History,* 56.18. The text is edited and translated by Earnest Cary (Cambridge, MA: Harvard UP; London: Heinemann, 1914–27).

³ Cassius Dio, *Roman History* 56.20.

⁴ *"Quintili Vare, legiones redde!"* Suetonius, *Augustus,* 1.23. It is a scene that was unforgettably brought to life in the BBC dramatization of Robert Graves's *I Claudius.* Suetonius is edited and translated by J. C. Rolfe (Cambridge, MA: Harvard UP; London: Heinemann, 1914).

⁵ Tacitus, *Annales,* 1.61. Trans. Michael Grant, *Tacitus: the Annals of Imperial* (Harmondsworth: Penguin, 1956). The Loeb Tacitus, ed. and trans. M. Hutton et al., contains the *Annales* in volumes III–V (Cambridge, MA: Harvard UP; London: Heinemann, 1914–37).

⁶ For a considered overview on the archeological evidence, see Wolfgang Schlüter "The Battle of the Teutoburg Forest: Archaeological Research at Kalkriese near Osnabrück," in *Roman Germany, Studies in Cultural Interaction,* ed. J. D. Creighton and R. J. A. Wilson (Portsmouth, RI: Journal of Roman Archaeology, 1999 = JRA Supplementary Series 32, 1999), 125–60. The most comprehensive volume, however, is that edited by Wolfgang Schlüter and Rainer Wiegels, *Rom, Germanien und die Ausgrabungen von Kalkriese* (Osnabrück: Rasch, 1999). The story of the discovery by Tony Clunn and his metal detector has been told in a variety of television programs in the United Kingdom and Germany.

⁷ The most useful starting points are Hans Schönberger, "The Roman Frontier in Germany: an Archaeological Survey," *Journal of Roman Studies* 59 (1969): 144–97 and H. von Petrikovits, "Fortifications in the North-Western Roman Empire from the Third to Fifth centuries A.D.," *Journal of Roman Studies* 61 (1971): 178–218. More detailed overviews are those by Dietwulf Baatz, *Der Römische Limes* (4th ed., Berlin: Mann, 2000) and Dietwulf Baatz and Fritz-Rudolf Herrmann, *Die Römer in Hessen* (2nd ed., Stuttgart: Theiss, 1989). Dietwulf Baatz has also produced the useful guide to the reconstructed Limes-fort at Saalburg: *Limeskastell Saalburg* (8th ed., Bad Homburg: Saalburgmuseum, 1984).

⁸ A. A. Gill, *A. A. Gill is Away* (London: Cassell, 2002), 179.

⁹ Julian, *Shorter Fragments,* 2. There is a readily accessible edition of Julian's works ed. and trans. by Wilmer Cave Wright (Cambridge, MA: Harvard UP; London: Heinemann, 1930), but there is a better edition with a French translation by J. Bidez, Gabriel Rochefort, and Christian Lacombrade, *L'Empereur Julien: Oeuvres complètes* (Paris: Belles Lettres, 1924–63).

¹⁰ Dieter Timpe, "Die Schlacht im Teutoburger Wald: Geschichte, Tradition, Mythos," in Wolfgang Schlüter and Rainer Wiegels (eds.), *Rom, Germanien und die Ausgrabungen von Kalkriese* (Osnabrück: Rasch, 1999), 717–37.

[11] See Joachim von Elbe, *Roman Germany: A Guide to Sites and Museums* (Mainz: von Zabern, 1977), 148–51.

[12] *Deutschland: Ein Wintermärchen,* Caput 11, cited from the edition by Barker Fairley, *Heinrich Heine: Atta Troll, Deutschland* (London: OUP, 1966), 152. Of the monument, Heine, ends his passage "hab selber subskribieret" (I contributed to it myself). On the jokes in this famous passage, see S. S. Prawer, *Heine: The Tragic Satirist* (Cambridge: CUP, 1961), 116–17.

[13] Tacitus, *Germania,* 4: *Cornelii Taciti Opera Minora,* ed. Henry Furneaux and J. G. C. Anderson (Oxford: Clarendon, 1900, repr. 1962); *Tacitus on Britain and Germany,* trans. H. Mattingley (Harmondsworth: Penguin, 1948), 103–4.

[14] Richard Suchenwirth, *Deutsche Geschichte: Von der germanischen Vorzeit bis zur Gegenwart* (Leipzig: Dollheimer, 1935), 29.

[15] Caesar, *De Bello Gallico,* 4.3, trans. S. A. Handford, *Caesar: The Conquest of Gaul* (Harmondsworth: Penguin, 1951).

[16] Ammianus 21.10.8. Ammianus is ed. and trans. by J. C. Rolfe (Cambridge, MA: Harvard UP; London: Heinemann, 1935–40) and translated by Walter Hamilton with an introduction by Andrew Wallace-Hadrill, *Ammianus Marcellinus: The Later Roman Empire* (Harmondsworth: Penguin, 1986).

[17] Ammianus 16.12 and Adrian Murdoch, *The Last Pagan* (Stroud: Sutton, 2003), chapter 3.

[18] Jørgen Ilkjaer and Jørn Lønstrup, "Der Moorfund im Tal der Illerup-Å bei Skanderborg in Ostjütland (Dänemark)," *Germania* 61 (1983): 95–116.

[19] M. Orsnes, "The Weapon-Find in Ejsbøl Mose at Haderslev," *Acta Archaeologica,* 34 (1963): 232.

[20] A particularly vivid evocation of Germanic battle tactics is seen in the opening sequence of Ridley Scott's 2000 film *Gladiator,* set during Marcus Aurelius's campaigns in the latter half of the second century.

[21] Tacitus, *Historiae,* 4.23.3. See the Loeb text and the translation by K. Wellesley (Harmondsworth: Penguin, 1972).

[22] See E. A. Thompson, *The Early Germans* (Oxford: Clarendon, 1965), 135 n. 5 for the comments by Ammianus.

[23] *Der Hildesheimer Silberfund: Original und Nachbildung: vom Römerschatz zum Bürgerstolz,* ed. Manfred Boetzkes and Helga Stein, with Christian Weisker (Hildesheim: Gerstenberg, 1997).

[24] For further details see Jürgen Kunow, *Der römische Import in der Germania libera bis zu den Marcomannenkriegen* (Neumünster: Wachholtz, 1983) and Ulla Lund-Hansen, *Römischer Import im Norden* (Copenhagen: Nordiske Fortidsminder, 1987).

[25] For a detailed explanation of the linguistic evidence, see D. H. Green, *Language and History in the Early Germanic World* (Cambridge: CUP, 1998), chapter 12, esp. 224–26.

[26] Following the uprising of the Marcomanni in A.D. 173. Cassius Dio 72.15.

[27] Klaus Kortüm, "Auswahlverfahren bei der Auswertung und Bearbeitung großer Ausgrabungsvorhaben der Landesarchäologie: Der römische Vicus von Walheim (Kr. Ludwigsburg)," *Archäologisches Nachrichtenblatt* 6 (2001): 201 11.

[28] Pliny, *Natural History,* 37.11. Pliny the Elder is edited and translated by H. Rackham, W. H. S. Jones and D. E. Eichholz (Cambridge, MA: Harvard UP; London: Heinemann, 1950–62).

[29] See Werner König, *dtv-Atlas zur deutschen Sprache* (Munich: dtv, 1978), 47 and Green, *Language and History,* 182–200.

[30] There is a translation of the poem (much of which, be it admitted, is about types of fish) in Harold Isbell, *The Last Poets of Imperial Rome* (Harmondsworth: Penguin, 1971), 52–64. Ausonius came from Bordeaux, and makes favorable comparisons.

[31] Cassius Dio 71.11. See Thompson, *Early Germans,* 40 on the Battle of Strasbourg.

[32] For full details, see Todd, *Early Germans,* 64–66; W. Haarnagel, *Feddersen Wierde: Die Ergebnisse der Ausgrabung der vorgeschichtlichen Wurt Feddersen Wierde* (Wiesbaden: Steiner, 1979).

[33] W. A. van Es, "Wijster: a Native Village beyond the Imperial Frontier," *Palaeohistoria* 11 (1965).

[34] St. Jerome, Ep 123.16. See the 1893 text by W. H. Fremantle, G. Lewis and W. G. Martley of Jerome's *Letters and Select Works* (repr. Grand Rapids, MI: Eerdmans, 1979) See Michael Grant, *The Fall of the Roman Empire* (rev. ed., London: Weidenfeld and Nicolson, 1990), 11–12. For some indication of the situation later on in archeological terms, see Harald von Petrikovits, *Die römischen Provinzen am Rhein und an der oberen und mittleren Donau im 5. Jahrhundert n. Chr.* (Heidelberg: Winter, 1983).

Germanic Religion and the Conversion to Christianity

Rudolf Simek

O F ALL THE FIELDS of early Germanic culture and literature, none has been as badly marred by ideological controversies as the study of the pre-Christian heathen Germanic religion. The great interest taken by the political and cultural leaders of the Third Reich in this field was unfortunately shared by many university teachers at the time. They saw this interest as a unique chance to promote their fields and themselves. This led to a nearly total lapse of interest after 1945. For almost thirty years after the Second World War, work in this field restricted itself either to minor studies or to the reprinting of the old handbooks with only cosmetic changes to hide the political flaws. There were, of course, exceptions too: the studies by Walter Baetke in the former GDR, by several Scandinavian scholars, or the excellent, if now outdated handbook by Derolez.[1] But both among the public and the academic world, early Germanic religion was not a popular topic of study.

In the last quarter of the twentieth century, this situation changed dramatically, and for the better. One reason for the renewed interest in this neglected area of research is the general fascination with non-Christian mythologies, whether of living religions or dead ones, particularly in the western world, and another may be the distinct upsurge in so-called new pagan religions. A more important factor may be that many aspects of the predominant religion of northwestern Europe for at least the whole first millennium A.D. are still unknown to a wider public or as yet unsolved altogether. Such aspects include the resistance of the old religion toward advancing Christianity, the role of heathendom for the early Germanic literatures, or even the question of continuity versus change within the pre-Christian Germanic society.

It is impossible in a single essay to provide a full picture of the research on a religion which, at least in northern Europe, had a longer history than Christianity and which, during the period of folk migrations extended into most areas of the European continent with the sole exception of the Peloponnese, and even there Viking travelers left their traces. The reason for this broad spread of Germanic religion — compared with the Celtic or Slavonic religions — even though it was neither a codified religion nor the official religion of an empire, must mainly be seen in the movement of Germanic tribes during the migrations (*Völkerwanderungen*) right up to the last and best known of these tribal migrations originating in Scandinavia, namely the Viking expansion from the eighth century on until the twelfth.

Germanic Religions

An important notion we have to come to accept in recent decades is that there was no single Germanic religion. It is obvious that it was a non-codified religion, since it was the religion of a predominantly orally transmitted culture, but it was also a religion with strong regional variations, and one with distinct and noticeable development in its long history. It would therefore be more appropriate to refer to the Germanic *religions* of the first millennium which had certain unifying traits, rather than to a single religion. Our modern concept of religion, modeled on the so-called high religions, and only to be applied for the Germanic beliefs in the widest sense of the word, causes further problems. There is, for example, little evidence before the last quarter of the first millennium of a detailed personalized inventory of a polytheistic pantheon. Even at the very end of the heathen period the Scandinavians preferred to call their conversion to Christianity a *siðaskipti,* change of customs, rather than of beliefs.[2] This linguistic fact highlights the function of pagan religion as a set of social conventions, hallowed by age and derived from mythical antecedents. It would be wrong to understand it in terms of singular devotion to particular gods. Our understanding of religion in these terms derives from our experience of the great monotheistic religions of Judaism, Christianity, and Islam.

It should also be stressed that pre-Christian Germanic religion cannot be viewed without reference to its contemporary setting: it should be seen in terms of its historical, geographical, and social background, with special consideration to contemporary influences. No religion can remain static, but will respond at least in part to the needs of its society. Thus, Iron Age Germanic religion had much in common with certain traits of Roman religion and with the Celtic religion of Gallia. It may surprise us to realize, too, that the heathen religion of the Viking age was influenced by early medieval Christianity, just as modern Germanic heathendom is by other New Age sects.

Religion, Literature, and Archeology

A further caveat that cannot be sufficiently stressed is the secondary status of literature for the study of heathen religion. Medieval Icelandic and Norwegian literature, the Eddic poems as well as the sagas, have in the past been used as the predominant foundation on which to base the study of such religion. Today we know that the poetic texts are of extremely variable value for the history of religion and frequently tell us more about the social, psychological, or intellectual situation of a medieval Christian author than about pre-Christian beliefs. Similarly, the sagas, although frequently preserving themes and stories from the Viking period, can be dangerously deceptive when used as source material for heathen customs and practices.

For the most part, until recently, archeology had been used only to attempt to substantiate theories arrived at by the study of literary sources. Now, however, this method may be reversed, to exploit the rich archeological finds from the first millennium, including a wealth of iconographic matter; secondary sources are resorted to only where archeology and contemporary sources corroborate these findings. Thus we arrive at a somewhat more complex, more sober and less romantic, but certainly less fanciful picture of the pre-Christian religion of the Germanic tribes.

The Earliest Stages

It is impossible to mark the beginnings of Germanic religion. There are continuities, but also distinct changes, in the religious beliefs between the Bronze Age and the Iron Age, as well as from the neolithic period to the Bronze Age. No scholar today, however, is prepared to talk of a Germanic ethnicity in the population of northwestern Europe before the beginnings of the Iron Age, which may be dated to 400 B.C. for southern Scandinavia. Beyond that, we may only talk of a prehistory of the northern European religion, but we cannot seriously establish the ethnicity of the tribes in question. Our knowledge of this prehistoric religion is mainly confined to the beliefs and customs regarding death and the after-world, and to scenes depicted in the rock carvings, which become particularly enigmatic in the southern Scandinavian Bronze Age, even though we can identify them as of religious relevance.

In the Iron Age, however, despite the paucity of grave goods in comparison with the Bronze Age, our knowledge of pagan religion becomes much more detailed, especially as far as the sacrificial customs are concerned, and in several cases we can, despite all the gaps in our knowledge, reconstruct ceremonies relatively well.

One of these Iron Age sacrifices happened sometime after A.D. 300 in southeastern Jutland, in Ejsbøl near Hadersleben. A foreign army, consisting of about nine well-equipped mounted warriors, sixty fighters fully armed with swords, daggers, spears, lances, and shields, and two hundred soldiers carrying lances and throwing spears as well as their shields, had been defeated by a local defense force. The whole booty of the defeated army, including all the weapons, saddles, bridles, and personal belongings were not taken by the victorious army, but carefully and deliberately destroyed: swords were twice bent double, the tips of spears and daggers were bent over, shield bosses were flattened and then the whole armament of the entire army was burned on a pyre, together with at least part of a boat, the iron rivets of which survived in the ashes. Sometime after the arms had been burned in this way, they were collected, sorted and tied into bundles, weighed down by stones, and thrown into a very confined area of a little lake, together with thousands of stones and cut or sharpened sticks, the function of which we cannot reconstruct. A century later, another, somewhat smaller army was dealt with in a similar way, and its weapons deposited close to the original site. Such destruction of valuable equipment can only be explained as a deliberate and ritual ceremony, one calculated to insure that nobody in this world would use these weapons again. The arms were committed instead to the powers or god(s) to whom they may have been promised before the battle should victory occur, and both sacrificial sites were marked by crudely carved, but quite large wooden idols. Such weapon-booty sacrifices were by no means rare in Iron Age Scandinavia. In Denmark we know of similar ritual depositions from Hjortspring in northern Jutland even as early as 400 B.C., from Illerup-Ådal and Nydam in southern Jutland, Thorsberg on the German side of Jutland, Illemose on Fyn in Denmark, Käringsjön and Hassle Bösarp in southern Sweden and Skedemosse on Öland. Despite the relatively limited area of these finds, their character varies widely. In Skedemosse and in Thorsberg the sacrificial lakes were used for a variety of sacrifices apart from the depositions of weapons (leaving them as an offering), and were in use for several centuries by the local community. As a result, certain physical changes were instituted to service both public and private sacrifices at the holy place. In Skedemosse this consisted of a wide, cobbled ritual road leading from the settlement on the ridge down to the lake; in Thorsberg a wooden jetty was erected that led out into the lake, where a special place was surrounded by a wooden fence within the lake. Here, weapons, jewelry, ceramic pots containing votive gifts, and animal bones constituting the remnants of sacrificial meals were deposited. In Illerup Ådal and Nydam, three or more weapon-booty sacrifices were deposited on the same spots in the course of some 300 years, but no other sacrifices. Despite all the details we know about the weapon-booty sacrifices, the way in which the burned weapons were either thrown from the shore or ferried into the lakes by boat, or the runic inscriptions carved on the ruined objects in Illerup Ådal, there is one important piece of information missing. We do not know what happened to the warriors of the defeated army, as none of the weapon booty sacrifices contained any human skeletal remains. We therefore do not know whether the dead and the prisoners were also burned, but in a different place, sacrificed in a different way, or whether they were not sacrificed at all.

Some late classical or Christian writers may give us a hint as to the fate of the invaders, as does Orosius in his fifth century *Historia adversus paganos* on the battle of Arausio (Orange) on the Rhône on October 6th, 105, in which the Cimbri and the Teutones destroyed everything they had conquered because of an extraordinary oath they had taken: "the clothes were rent and trodden into the mud, the gold and silver was thrown into the river, the armor was cut up, the decoration of the horses destroyed, the horses themselves drowned in the pools of the river, and the men were hanged by ropes in trees, so that the victors retained none of the immense booty" (V, 16). Of a battle in 405 he also reports that the Goths vowed to sacrifice all captured Romans (VII, 37). It is therefore conceivable that the prisoners of war in Iron Age Scandinavia were sacrificed in a similar way, but no archeological evidence for it has so far been unearthed.

The weapon-booty sacrifices were undoubtedly a form of public sacrifice, used in times of crisis and obviously only held at long intervals. However, public sacrifices were also held at regular intervals. The Iron Age bog finds do not tell us how often that was the case, and even such rare finds as around thirty-eight human skeletons among the 17,000 bones in the sacrificial lake at Skedemosse tell us little of how often such sacrificial feasts were held in the five centuries the lake was used, to about A.D. 477. Around that time much of Öland was suddenly deserted and sacrifices of a rich, cattle-farming population stopped forever. Other Danish and German bog finds speak of a far less varied use than we have in Thorsberg and Skedemosse. In Rislev on Zealand, in Kragehul on Fyn, and perhaps to a lesser extent also in Soest in northwest Germany, as well as in Donnstetten in southwest Germany,[3] bogs have yielded numerous examples of sacrificial animals, mainly horses, cattle, and sheep, all showing signs of ritual slaughtering. The remains of the horses in Rislev are limited to the skulls, the lower legs and the tails, a type of horse sacrifice also documented in settlements as in Vestervig (Jutland) and Sorte Muld (Bornholm).[4] It seems likely that in these cases most of the meat of the horse, ritually slaughtered with a blow of an axe against its forehead, was used for the communal meal, while the skin of the horse together with the skull and extremities were displayed as an outward sign of the sacrifice, before being consigned to the depths. Apart from the horses, cattle and sheep as well as goats and roosters were used for sacrifices, and in some instances the skin of an ox, together with the horns, seems to have been displayed in a similar fashion to that of the horses. However, despite a certain veneration of bulls shown by a number of miniature animals found in Germany and Sweden, it was mainly the horse that had a strong symbolic value for Germanic heathendom, both reflected in numerous missionary edicts banning the eating of horse meat for newly converted Christians, as well as the Icelander's publicly acknowledged exemption from this ban on their formal conversion in the year 1000.

Animal sacrifices, with or without a communal meal, were one form of public sacrifice in the Iron Age, but there were others too. Precious objects were deposited in bogs or even on the open heath. These could include precious loot from southeastern Europe such as the famous Gundestrup cauldron, golden ritual objects of local production such as the now lost Gallehus horn, the Trundholm sun wagon or even the 100 tiny gold boats from Nors on Jutland. But they could also consist of hoards of everyday but nonetheless valuable objects. Among these are the deposits of dozens of cartwheels, found especially in the Netherlands, but also in Germany or Denmark, where several wheels found would have been unusable, and had obviously been made for the sole purpose of the sacrifice. These may point to some sort of wheel god or goddess as we know them from the late stages of the Roman religion, but may also be seen in connection with cult carts such as found in Dejberg in Jutland, carrying a type of throne. They have also been brought into connection with a cult, as described by Tacitus (*Germania* 40), but without first-hand knowledge, of a goddess Nerthus somewhere on a Baltic island. The deposits of wheels may, however, also be seen in the light of other hoards, as of iron ingots, deposited as a gift to the powers or certain gods. There are numerous finds of anthropomorphic wooden figures made from forked branches, which may be anything from under one meter to over four meters high, as in Ejsbøl on Jutland. Unfortunately, this latter figure does not reveal its gender, but was found in the context of the large weapon-booty sacrifices and may well have symbolized the god to whom these sacrifices were offered. In the case of the sacrificial bog in Oberdorla in Thuringia, several crude wooden gods were found, some apparently designed to depict a female goddess, just as in the case of the three-meter-long figure from Forlev Nymølle on Jutland, no more than a forked branch crudely marked as female with a cut in the fork to represent the vulva. No less obviously male is another figure from Broddenbjerg on Jutland, where a fourth branch forms an enormous erect penis on this figure. In two examples, wooden pole gods turn up in couples, as in the tall and well carved figures from Braak near Eutin in Schleswig-Holstein (dating back to the early Iron Age or even late Bronze Age) or several much more symbolic carved gods from Wittenmoor in Lower Saxony. The former couple stood on a sacrificial site marked by many fires and Iron Age pottery, the latter protected a wooden causeway through a bog.[5] Some of these wooden idols seem to have been dressed in rich cloaks (Nydam; Rebild), and may have been painted as well, so that we get the impression of wooden statues of gods, which were only rarely shaped in any detail, but impressed by their size or decoration. We can therefore safely reject the statement made by Tacitus that the Germanic tribes did not think it proper to shape their gods in any human form: the poles may be fairly symbolic (especially by Roman standards) but they are nevertheless distinctly anthropomorphic.

Private Sacrifices

Private Iron Age sacrifices differed considerably from the public ones. It is quite likely that they consisted mainly of objects thrown into bogs, springs, and even rivers, although the latter is by nature more difficult to prove. In the case of bog offerings, such objects were frequently ceramic vessels filled with food, animal fats or even flax or hair, which were then deposited in the marshy ground in such a way that they were protected from theft. Occasionally, more valuable personal items like brooches (fibulae), gold and silver rings, or the occasional single sword were added to the sacrificial collection in the depths, but more usually the sacrifices were consistent with the objects found in a farming community and are evidence of their produce and domestic usage.

Although some of the sacrificial places in bogs are distinguished by both these personal gifts to the gods as well as weapon-booty sacrifices (as is the case in Thorsberg), personal offerings such as these were frequently deposited in springs. As opposed to the Celtic spring cult, however, we have no finds of pictures of gods or goddesses in Germanic areas. On the other hand, animal sacrifices seem to have been dedicated to the springs and their deities, as is shown by the remnants of horses, dogs, cattle, and sheep found in the spring basins. The Germanic habit of venerating springs was also mentioned by classical and early medieval authors, and eighth-century writings condemn the "abominable" veneration of springs by the only recently Christianized Saxons.[6] To some extent, the ancient European veneration of wells is still found in the proliferation of wishing wells even now.

*Guldgubber from Sorte Muld, Bornholm,
Denmark (seventh century).*

*Left: Grumpan bracteate, Skaraborgs län, Sweden, sixth century;
right: Vadstena bracteate, Östergötland, Sweden, sixth century*

The Veneration of Gods and Goddesses

Around the middle of the first millennium, sacrificial customs started to change. Undoubtedly, animal sacrifices and communal meals were still held, but the booty sacrifices of the Iron Age stopped, and so did the custom of burying ceramic vessels with offers of food or other agricultural products. In the centers of secular and religious power these spring and bog sacrifices became obsolete in the sixth and seventh centuries and were apparently replaced with more sophisticated forms of veneration of gods and goddesses. The latter are reflected in pictures of gods used as amulets in the gold bracteates or the tiny gold-foil figures, depicting gods and goddesses, priest-kings or noble ancestors and used either as a type of sacrificial money or else as commemorative plaques for important religious events or important dynastic weddings. Again, we are unable to link the gods on the little gold-foil figures known in Danish as *guldgubber* (in Swedish *gullgubbar,* "old men of gold") with any specific deities of the Germanic pantheon, and it may well be the case that they reflect a large number of local or regional semi-deities. Only the dominant figure on gold bracteates (thin, single-sided coins or medallions) of a particular type, which is always shown in conjunction with a horse, has been successfully identified as the god Wodan/Odin, in his function as the divine healer. The Old High German Second Merseburg Charm, not contemporary with the bracteates but written down in the tenth century, allows us to interpret these bracteates as showing Wodan healing a horse with a broken limb. The magic words on the bracteates may also point to a protective and healing function of these golden discs. The bracteates only show women as a rare exception[7] and may thus refer to a predominantly male cult, but among the *guldgubber* more than twenty percent show a couple, and just under fifteen percent show women alone.[8]

We know, however, that the Germanic tribes in the first half of the first millennium venerated a large number of local female deities, which in the Germanic areas conquered by the Roman army led to a Roman style cult of these Germanic (and similarly Celtic) goddesses. These *matres* or *matronae* were approached by partly Romanized members of early Germanic tribes such as the Ubians or the Frisians for personal or familiar needs, vows made to them, and after the fulfillment of the vow, a stone altar with an inscription and frequently a picture of three seated women in relief was set up. The prayers thus fulfilled could concern matters as varied as the health of the family, the desire for offspring, or even promotion within the Roman civil service. The over one hundred different names for mother-goddesses that are considered unquestionably Germanic on the grounds of their Germanic morphology or etymology can refer to Germanic tribes, like the dedication to *Matribus Frisiavis paternis* ("the paternal Frisian mothers"), to places and towns, like the Mahlinehae (to Mahlinium, today's Mecheln), or to their generosity (such as Gabiae, Friagabiae, Arvagastiae) or even to their role as goddesses of springs and rivers (Aumenahenae, Nersihenae, Vacallinehae). Some of these names are only recorded once, but others indicate cult centers by being named over 130 times on votive stones. The cult of some of these mother-goddesses, like the Matrones Aufaniae, of which nearly ninety instances are known in Bonn, prompted the replacement of their cult center there with an early Christian minster. The triads of holy women survived even the process of Christianization, as church dedications to three female saints or to Fides, Spes, and Caritas occur exactly in those areas left of the lower Rhine that had been central for the cult of the matrons earlier on.[9]

Other deities known only from contemporary Latin writers, principally Tacitus and Caesar, or from votive altars of the Roman type, include first those gods only named by their Latin equivalents by Tacitus, who claims that the highest god among the Germanic tribes was Mercury, followed by Hercules and Mars. Only one of these identifications in Tacitus's *interpretatio romana* can be corroborated by the *interpretatio germanica* found in the third- or fourth-century translations of the Roman weekday names, namely Mercury as Wodan/Odin. Mars might have been equated with Týr, but the west and south Germanic weekday names Tuesday/Dienstag cause etymological problems if derived directly from Týr, as opposed to Norwegian or Danish Tirsdag. In the case of Hercules, however, the Roman interpretation must have meant Thor, who in the Germanic interpretation was, however, translated as Jupiter. This does not necessarily imply that Thor was the main Germanic god in the third century, but rather that his weapon, the hammer, had similar attributes in evoking thunder and lightning as Jupiter's lightning bolt.

The altars and votive stones of the second and third century repeatedly name Mercury, Mars, and even Hercules in conjunction with Germanic epithets, thus giving the Roman interpretation some foundation, but the Roman provinces of Germania and Gallia also had around 800 Jupiter columns. These cult monuments, showing a mounted Jupiter figure riding down a snake-like giant, are between four and nine meters high. Although it is more likely that these columns relate to a Celtic version of Jupiter, it cannot be ruled out that the Germanic population, too, saw Donar/Thor in this monster-defeating god, thus furthering the equation of Donar/Thor and Jupiter to be found in the weekday names Thursday/Donnerstag/Torsdag for Latin *dies Jovi*. Although hardly any names of gods can be found in the elder runic script, one fibula of the early seventh century names Wodan, but otherwise the earliest vernacular sources are the Saxon baptismal vow and the Second Merseburg Charm (ninth and tenth century, respectively). English place names containing

Woden,[10] several genealogies of Anglo-Saxon royal houses, as well as a couple of charms, also testify to the veneration of this god in Britain in the pre-Viking period.

Late Roman inscriptions on votive altars tell us, however, even apart from the above named *matronae,* about several gods venerated from the second to the fourth centuries, although they may not be known from later sources. These include the goddess Nehalennia, known from twenty-eight votive altars on the Rhine island of Walcheren (in the Netherlands), a similar number from the island of Noord-Beveland and two more from Cologne. The goddess is depicted with her attributes, mostly baskets of fruit, a dog, or the prow of a ship or an oar. Despite various attempts, the meaning of her name remains obscure, and so is the question whether she could possibly related to a Germanic Isis or to Nerthus as mentioned by Tacitus. Anyway, she was obviously an important goddess of shipping and trade.[11]

A well-documented goddess of the second and third centuries is Hludana, who is known from five inscriptions along the Lower Rhine and Frisia. Her name cannot be fully explained, but it has an Old Norse cognate in Hlóðyn, the mother of Thor, who is also known as "the son of the earth" (*Jarðar burr*), making Hlóðyn/Hludana a chtonic goddess. This may be supported by the etymology of the name if it is indeed cognate with Anglo-Saxon or Old High German *helan,* to hide, which may be the root behind other enigmatic mythological women such as Hel, Nehalennia, Huld, and Frau Holle (Mother Winter) of Grimm's fairy tale fame.[12]

Otherwise, the only other divine beings we are aware of in the Germanic pantheon of the Roman period are the mythical pair of brothers, the Alci, and a mythical ancestor by the name of Tuisto, both named by Tacitus. Early medieval Christian sources name additionally Balder, Folla and Frija (in the Second Merseburg charm), as well as Saxnot, who is the third god named together with Wodan and Donar in the Saxon baptismal vow. Saxnot must be a local Saxon god ("the companion of the Saxons"), and Balder, Folla and Frija all have counterparts in the Norse pantheon (Baldr, Fulla, Frigg). Thus it seems that by the ninth or tenth century, a common, personalized Germanic pantheon had been developed and widely accepted in all the Germanic areas.

Despite a late development toward more widely accepted and commonly venerated deities, the Germanic religion never developed into a codified religion, nor did it ever possess a dogmatic set of rules or even truths to be accepted by every believer; the whole concept of membership in a religion was apparently foreign to it. Rather, religion was seen as a traditional set of customs, beliefs, and perhaps a fund of mythological stories with only limited claim to universality. This may be illustrated by the burial customs of the Germanic tribes. It is well known that at least in Scandinavia in the later Bronze Age a change took place from burial in graves, characteristic for the early Bronze Age, to cremation, which rapidly became widespread. By the Roman Iron Age inhumation graves began to spread from south to north. These became the norm first among the Goths in southeastern Europe, while Tacitus in the first century is still only aware of cremation among the south Germanic tribes. From the post-Roman Iron Age to the end of the pagan era both cremation and inhumation burials can be found side by side among the western and northern Germanic peoples. In the south Christianization accelerated the transition to inhumation, which was only accepted slowly in Scandinavia, while cremation continued to be the standard form of burial among Saxons and Frisians until the eighth century, when they accepted Christianity and its burial form.

In continental Germanic areas, cremation graves mainly took the shape of level graves with house or face urns, although in Scandinavia the barrow continued right to the end of the heathen era. In the British Isles, it declined during the Roman Iron Age, but asserted itself again during the Viking Age areas of Scandinavian settlement and served as a sign of the social standing of the deceased. As such, it was mainly used for warriors and chieftains. Both in barrows and flat graves, boat burials were extremely common from the beginning of the Migration Age with a wide variety of both cremation and inhumation being practiced. It has been disputed whether buried boats or the custom of boat-shaped stone settings can actually reflect the belief in a sea journey to the other world, rather than the social status, possession or even abode of the chieftain thus buried, but several descriptions (the most detailed being the contemporary account by the Arabian traveler Ibn Fadlan to Russia in 922) of boat cremations certainly point toward an other-world journey by ship.

Surprisingly, we know less of the Viking Age heathen cult than of Iron Age or cults of the time of the *Völkerwanderungen,* which is a consequence of changes in public and private cult practices. It seems that the remnants of sacrificial meals were no longer carefully disposed of, and private offerings in bogs, springs, and rivers declined sharply. Runestones inform us that in southern Scandinavia, the god Thor was invoked, and also that his attribute, the lightning weapon in the shape of a hammer called Mjöllnir, became the pagan answer to the Christian symbol of the cross. It can be found in great numbers as decorations on neck rings, as amulet hammers in every mode of artistic form and in base or precious metals. It also served, with or without the naming of Thor, as a symbol of heathendom on gravestones and other runic monuments; its distinct meaning is given on several rune-stones as "Thor bless these runes!"

Germanic Temples

Adam of Bremen, writing in the 1070s, gives a description of Uppsala in his *Gesta Hammaburgensis Ecclesiae Pontificum* (IV, 26): "There is a very famous temple in Uppsala, which does not lie very far from Sigtuna. In this temple, which is made entirely of gold, the people worship the statues of three gods. Thor, as the mightiest of them, has his seat in the middle of the room and the places to the left and right of him are taken by Wodan and Fricco." He later (or a later scribe) comments on this: "The temple is encircled by a golden chain which hangs down from the gable of the house and shines from afar to the people arriving, for the shrine which lies in the valley is surrounded all the way round by mountains, like an amphitheatre." In analyzing Adam's description, it is obvious that at least the golden decoration of the temple, the chain from its gable-ends, and its position among mountains are inaccurate, and thus the remaining items are not necessarily trustworthy either. It has been suggested that Adam, for lack of other information, was actually describing an early medieval house-shaped reliquary, which would certainly fit the description better than any type of Scandinavian cult building. Archeological investigations in 1926 discovered post-holes underneath the church at Gamla Uppsala in the penultimate layer which could possibly be connected to result in (incomplete) concentric rectangles. As a result of this discovery, there have been various widely differing attempts at reconstruction, most of which were influenced by the form of Norwegian stave churches. The investigator of the excavations later changed his mind and attributed the postholes to the earliest church. However, the monumental grave mounds, the several hints toward the role of Uppsala as a cult center, and finally the large royal halls discovered more recently, all point toward Uppsala as a religious center, even if the notion of a massive temple may no longer be entertained.

The problem is that Old Norse *hof* seems to be a homonym, denoting on the one hand simply farm, on the other a cult building, and it has in the latter sense usually been translated as "temple," following the use of early medieval Christian authors, who glossed it with *templum, fanum*. However, recent excavations all over Scandinavia have shown that this distinction between a secular and religious meaning of the word — and the type of building — may be inaccurate. Archeological excavations of huge halls have indeed established them as being an integral part of major farms, but they were clearly used for cult purposes, too. None of these halls is likely to have been used exclusively for religious ceremonies, as far as we can see, although some have an apparent lack of the usual settlement debris. However, it is clear from finds of *guldgubber*, the gold foil figures mentioned above, as well as large quantities of expensive imported glass and a few other objects of high social prestige, that some form of religious ceremonies were indeed conducted there.

Such halls have been discovered in Borg on the Lofoten islands (74 meters long), in Gudme on Fyn and at Lejre on Zealand (both 47 meters), on Helgö (40 meters) and also in Uppsala in central Sweden (north of the church), as well as in Slöinge in Halland (30 meters) and in Hofstaðir in Iceland (45 meters). Halls between thirty and forty meters in length were, despite their apparently large size, mainly used as simple farm halls (large Iron Age farm halls could be up to twenty-seven meters long even in small settlements, such as in Dankirke in southern Jutland),[13] but could also serve a substantial community as a feast hall at sacrificial times. The aforementioned hall in Gudme, which was nearly totally devoid of normal settlement finds, might point to a more specialized use of such halls in certain affluent centers. This may also have been the case on Helgö, but there is little that points toward a type of building reserved exclusively for religious ceremonies. We should rather see the *hof* as a large farm hall of a local or regional chieftain, which was utilized as a feast hall for the ceremonial meal and drinking at special feast days. Just how impressive some of these buildings were may be gleaned from the sheer dimensions of the two rows of wooden posts holding up the roof, which were up to fifty centimeters in diameter in Gudme. Such halls were used for communal sacrificial feasts from the third to the tenth century, and the examples found so far are surely only a small proportion of those that existed. These great halls make the need to find Germanic "temples" in the narrow sense of the word obsolete.

Christian authors writing in the earlier centuries of the first millennium may well have thought of something quite different when they referred to Germanic temples. In the Roman provinces of both Germania and of Britannia, the German population in the pay of the Roman Empire adapted Roman forms of veneration to the cult of their own religion, and thus the veneration of local gods and female deities, such as the *matronae,* was conducted in sanctuaries modeled on the Roman temples. In the areas to the west of the Lower Rhine we know of extensive temple districts dedicated to the matrons, which were eventually destroyed during the Christianization of the fourth and fifth centuries. In Britain, however, the missionaries were exhorted at least in one letter by Pope Gregory to Abbot Melitus[14] not to destroy the temples of the heathen, but to utilize their buildings, their feast times, and even their customs of slaughtering animals. The buildings which were reused in this way were most likely stone temples of the Roman kind, which were then used by Christians in a manner similar to the way Roman temples were reused by Christians in the Mediterranean. In Germanic areas that did not come under the influence of Rome, no need seems to have been felt to venerate deities in any form of covered building. The halls served the people for the communal feasts, the deities required no roof.

A typical Germanic sanctuary, such as that found in Thorsberg in southern Jutland or at Oberdorla and Possendorf in Thuringia, is more likely to have consisted of a wooden jetty leading out into a little lake in a bog, where a post-and-wattle fence surrounded the actual sanctuary in one part of the lake. In some cases these places were adorned with carved wooden gods. The objects to be sacrificed would be either thrown into the water or else taken out by boat to be sunk into the depths. The remnants of the sacrificial animals — either the skin of a horse with the skull attached or the skin of cattle with its horns on (as found in Rislev) — may have been displayed on poles in the vicinity, while the actual sacrificial meal was held on a farm somewhere nearby.

Ceremonies

It is clear from our evidence that the Germanic people had certain times of the year for recurrent sacrifices, although not all information we have tallies. Tacitus, as mentioned earlier, suggested that the sacrifice to the goddess Tanfana took place in autumn, Bede mentions the *modraniht, id est matrem noctem* (night of the mothers) in early February (*De temporum ratione* 13), and the Swedish Disting (which acquired its name as it coincided with a sacrifice to the *dísir,* and is still reflected in place names like Disathing/Uppland), was held at the same time. We know, for example, that in 1219 it fell on February 2. Otherwise, only the widely testified Yule feast, which coincided with the later date of Christmas, can be dated with any certainty. When Snorri Sturluson gives the dates for pre-Christian Scandinavian sacrifices (in his *Ynglinga saga* 8), he mentions one at the beginning of winter for a good harvest, one at midwinter for fertility (presumably the Yule-feast), and one at the beginning of summer for victory. Snorri's remarks must be treated with caution, as the midwinter sacrifice was more likely one to honor the dead ancestors, with the spring sacrifice that for fertility. The sacrifice he refers to at the beginning of summer is not mentioned anywhere else. A notice in the late twelfth-century Icelandic chronicle compilation, *Ágrip af Nóregs konunga sögum* (Summary of the History of the Kings of Norway) regarding King Olaf Tryggvason (994/95–999/1000) should also be mentioned here; he banned heathen sacrifices but allowed special beer to be brewed in their stead at Christmas, Easter, St. John's day, and in autumn, thus arriving at a regular division of the year by sacrifices. Here again, we do not know how much the Christian writer of *Ágrip* had projected back from the feast days of his own days into the tenth century.

The Families of Gods

Sometime between the Iron Age and the Viking age, Germanic beliefs seem to have changed from a general belief in holy places, in the powers and in the Aesir generally (in the sense of the gods), some of which, like Odin or Thor, must have stood out early on, in favor of a more personalized pantheon. This pantheon consisted of a number of gods and even two major families of gods, but these gods were of very different importance. Some of the gods were indeed venerated in certain areas and in specific circumstances in the sense of high gods, but several others are no more than pale figures originating from mythological stories, in which they played minor roles. Other gods and goddesses, whose names are preserved in high medieval mythography, such as the gods Víðarr, Váli, Ullr, Hoenir and Forseti, and the goddesses Sigyn, Fulla, Nanna, Eir, Sjöfn, Lofn, Vár, Vör, Syn, Hlín, Snotra, and Gná, remain obscure. Only in a few cases can we assume that these gods were older, possibly regional semi-deities (Fulla-Folla, Hludana-Hloðyn), whereas in the case of others we are probably looking at young mythographical or possibly even literary creations.

In dealing with the North Germanic gods, the distinction between the two families of gods found in late literary sources, namely between the Aesir and the Vanir, is frequently given inordinate emphasis. It is unlikely that the religious reality of pre-Christian times reflected this literary distinction. While most gods listed by Snorri belong, he claims, to the Aesir, a small group, namely Njörðr and his children, Freyr and Freyja, as well as possibly Ullr, are considered to belong to a distinct family, the Vanir, who once waged war with the Aesir during the Vanir Wars. However, the story of this war is constructed by Snorri on the basis of only two stanzas of the Eddic poem *Völuspá* which are by no means clear, and thus it is safest to view the Vanir War as a mythological story which enabled Snorri to connect several smaller, older, but possibly unconnected myths.[15]

This change in attitude may be best exemplified on the figure of the god Freyr. Together with Odin and Thor, he is certainly the most prominent god of the Viking age and was without doubt specially venerated among the Yngling-dynasty in Sweden, who counted him and his father, Njörðr, among their divine ancestors. Traditional research has mainly stressed his virility (symbolized by his main iconographic attribute, a prominent phallus) in conjunction with his ability to bestow fertility and riches on his followers and has thus seen him as the main god of fertility among the Norse gods.[16] This supposition, however, rests on the principle assumption that an agricultural society necessarily needed such a god of fertility[17] and on the exclusion of other traits of Freyr, obvious from a close study of the sources, such as his military prowess (underlined by some of his attributes, such as the sword, the boar and the ship) and his wealth, which he is able to confer on his followers. It therefore seems that he is not the fertility god of a farming population, but that he has all the necessary requisites of an ideal king: virility (to ensure dynastic succession), wealth (to keep a large following) and military prowess. To these one may add the ability to guarantee the fertility of the land, an important feature of early Scandinavian kingship.

Other gods, too, do not easily fall within the categories provided by the divine functions of power, war, and fertility, and even Georges Dumézil, who made this distinction, was himself forced to note a certain shift of his system within the Old Norse pantheon. This resulted in Odin — originally king of the gods — increasingly taking over aspects of the second function, war, while Thor, originally a god of war (through his symbol, the hammer), becomes increasingly associated with fertility. This supposed shift, although neatly explaining the differences between Norse mythology and a supposed Indo-European system, fails to take into consideration some of the more important aspects of these two gods. Odin, as we have seen from migration age iconographic evidence, was taken as the supreme god, as well as the healer. He was also important as the god of magic, prophecy, poetry and subsequently runes, all of which tally with his function as a healer and may ultimately be traced back to a shamanistic aspect of Odin's character. Despite these many and ambivalent functions, he was still considered to be the most important god in the Viking age and he was described in similar terms to those used by the Christians for their one god (Hár "The High One": *Hávamál*; *Gylfaginning* 1; Alföðr "All-father": *Gylfaginning* 19). Whole Germanic tribes traced their ancestry to him, and he and his wife Frigg could make or unmake the destiny of nations.

Týr, who only plays a very minor roles in Viking age Scandinavian mythology, seems to be the oldest of the Norse gods etymologically speaking, as his name (< **T-iwaz*, cf. Old High German *Ziu*) is cognate with Old Indian *Dyaus*, Greek *Zeus*, Latin *Jupiter,* as well as Old Indian *deva,* Old Irish *día,* Latin *dei,* Old Norse *tívar* (a plural of Týr), all meaning "gods." His importance had apparently waned considerably in the second half of the first millennium, and we hear little more about him than that he was a god of war and had lost his right arm in the fettering of the wolf Fenrir, which has parallels in other Indo-European religions. His role as a god of war seems to be confirmed by the name of the rune, Norse *týr,* Anglo-Saxon *ti,* Gothic *tyz,* which was used in migration-age rune-magic as a rune for victory.

Baldr was one of the most important Germanic gods and also known from Anglo-Saxon and Old High German sources (as Balder), and the protagonist of the myth of Baldr's death. In his full and very literary account of Baldr's funeral, Snorri could follow the poem *Húsdrápa* (composed around 983 by the Icelandic skald [= poet] Ulfr Uggason), which describes the wooden carvings in an Icelandic festive hall, but Baldr's death is also mentioned in several Eddic lays (*Baldrs draumar, Völuspá, Lokasenna*). In *Völuspá*, Baldr's death is one of the events leading up to the Ragnarök, the twilight of the gods. The extensive (and different) treatment by the Danish writer of the late twelfth century known as Saxo Grammaticus of Baldr suggests among other things that he was possibly the mythical ancestor of the Danish royal family. The central elements of the Icelandic version of the myth about Baldr's death, namely by mistletoe, Odin's handing over of the ring Draupnir, and Baldr's arrival at Hel have been identified on a group of migration-age bracteates, the so-called three-god-amulets.[18]

All the other gods play a far less important part in Viking age mythology, and some are simply literary, but not necessarily post-conversion, creations, like Bragi, the deified skald (poet) of the ninth century, who obviously had made it to the status of (literary?) semi-deity by the end of the heathen age. Others, like Heimdallr, must have had a relatively important function in some myths, but he has rightly been called an enigmatic god,[19] and this could also be said of Ullr, whose importance was once considered to be high according to the many southern Swedish and Norwegian place-names formed with his name, which have been found in areas similar to those formed with the names of Freyr and Freyja,[20] but the correct derivation of these names has been seriously doubted more recently.[21]

The situation with the goddesses is not dissimilar; the only main goddess who can be traced to a pre-Viking period is Frigg, the wife of Odin, and although one critic has even recently tried to see the many female deities as no more than emanations of Freya, who would as such be the great goddess, this has little basis in our sources.[22] Rather, these goddesses should be seen as a variety of female deities, answering the multifaceted religious needs of mankind, and, like the Roman Age *matronae*, partly reflecting their functions in their names. As in the case of the older *matronae* with the word for "giving" in their names, such as Gabiae, Alagabiae and Friagabiae, the name of Gefjon may reflect such a giving deity, who later became associated with a legend of Swedish origin. Gerðr, like Skaði, who are both actually giantesses, are probably only counted among the *ásynjur* (female Aesir) because of their role in some late mythological stories in which they became associated with certain gods.

Cosmologies

Numerous attempts have been made to establish, within the framework of the pre-Christian religion, a heathen cosmology[23] as a sort of physical and historical *Weltbild*, but it is worth noting that the whole view of the world changed when the religious system in Scandinavia changed fundamentally around the beginning of the eleventh century, and therefore the main sources for the pagan *Weltbild,* namely Snorri's works and a few mythological lays of the Poetic Edda, only go to prove how little we actually know about how the West Germanic peoples envisaged the origin and the form of the world. Writing about the beliefs on origins, Tacitus, in his *Germania,* merely recorded the worship of a god called Tuisto, who is descended from earth itself, and whose son Mannus is the forefather of the three Germanic tribes, Ingaevones, Herminones, and Istaevones. Tuisto is etymologically connected to the number "two," and might possibly have been a hermaphrodite being like the Nordic proto-giant Ymir who engenders children out of himself. *Völuspá* (stanza 17) says of Ymir that he was alive before the dawn of time, when neither the heavens nor the earth existed (*iörð fannz aeva né upphiminn*), when there was only the chasm Ginnungagap (in the later Middle Ages this became a name for the northwest passage of the Atlantic). This alliterative formula of the north Germanic source is not only found in the Old High German *Wessobrunn Prayer* in the ninth century, but also in a variant form in the Old Saxon *Heliand,* in Anglo-Saxon texts, on a Swedish runestone and also on the late medieval Danish rune stick from Ribe. Despite the frequent usage in Christian contexts the formula appears to go back to an ancient common Germanic cosmological formula. According to the Codex Regius and the *Hauksbók,* the first line of the *Völuspá* 17 reads "In olden days when Ymir lived" (*Ar var alda, þat er Ymir bygði*); the version in the *Snorra Edda* reads, however, "when nothing was" (*þat er ecci var*). Snorri's version has been generally considered as the more original, even though it is distinctly reminiscent of Genesis 1,2 (*terra . . . erat . . . vacua,* "and the world was void"). Another mythological poem of the Edda-collection in the Codex Regius, the *Vafþrúðnismál* 29,30 refers to another proto-giant, Aurgelmir, whom Snorri (*Gylfaginning* 4) identifies as being the frost-giants' name for Ymir. According to Snorri, there were two opposing poles even before the creation of the world: icy Niflheim and fiery Muspell. The rivers Élivágar subsequently fill Ginnungagap with poisonous frozen mist. The heat from Muspell, which meets the rime, causes it to melt and leads to the genesis of Ymir, an idea which Snorri appears to have taken from *Vafþrúðnismál* 31. Ymir is fed by the cow, Auðhumla, which itself feeds on the frost, thus licking Buri, the forefather of the gods, free from the ice. Buri is the father of Burr who, together with the giant-daughter Bestla, begets the gods Odin, Vili and Vé, who then kill Ymir and create the earth from his flesh (*Vafþrúðnismál* 21, *Grímnismál* 40; *Gylfaginning* 7): from his bones they make the mountains, the sky from his skull, the seas from his blood. The entire giant tribe drowns in Ymir's blood, apart from Bergelmir. In the creation of the world from Ymir's body, we have one of the obvious cases of Christian syncretism in Snorri's description. He seems to have taken this concept of the creation of the world from the body of a proto-being from the microcosm-macrocosm comparison in a well-known handbook on Christian teachings from the twelfth century, namely the *Elucidarius,* where the elements of the physical world are all likened to the parts of the human body.

When the three gods had created the world from Ymir's body, they took two tree-trunks from which they created the first human couple, Ask and Embla. Although different and older traditions have been merged in both the *Völuspá* as well as in Snorri's *Edda,* Buri is inconceivable as the human ancestor of the gods. Therefore, the concept of the creation of man from tree-trunks has to be separated from the divergent tradition of the genealogy Buri-Burr-divine triad (compare the Tuisto-Mannus triad of the tribes in Tacitus). This genealogical descent of man from the gods manifests itself in ethnographies of Germanic tribes as well as the gene-alogies of kings. There may also have been yet another — parallel or later — concept of the origin of the first human couple by a divine triad: Snorri tells how Odin, Vili and Vé create the first human couple, but in *Völuspá* 18 the divine triad is Odin, Hönir and Loðurr; Odin gives man the breath of life, Hönir the soul, Loðurr the warmth of life. In *Vafþrúðnismál* 45, too, a human couple, Lif and Lifþrasir, survive the end of the world in a tree and then become the progenitors of a new human race. Although primary sources are sparse, Germanic cosmogony has nu-merous equivalents in other cultures: the parallelism between the her-maphrodite figures Tuisto/Ymir and the Indian forefather (Sanskrit Yama, Avestic Yima) has repeatedly been pointed out, but correlation to the three generation succession of the protoplasts (Buri-Burr-Odin) with the killing of the forefathers can also be found in Greek, Phoenician, Ira-nian and Babylonian mythologies.[24] Even the creation of the world from the body of a proto-being finds worldwide equivalents.

The Physical Cosmos

Of the actual physical cosmos, not only Snorri but several Eddic poems agree that Midgard is the part of the world inhabited by men. The gods have their abodes a short distance away in Asgard. The known world of Midgard and Asgard is surrounded by a sea in which the Midgard serpent coils itself around the world, and this is a concept that was known in south Germanic areas as late as the Middle Ages, where the movement of the world serpent was considered to be responsible for earthquakes. Out-side the regions inhabited by men lies Utgard, where the demons live, and in the east, separated from Midgard by rivers, lies Jötunheim, giant-land. In the north and under Midgard is the realm of the dead, Hel, where the dead lead a shadow-like existence not unlike the Hades of Greek and Roman mythology.

The center of the cosmic system is the World Tree (called in medieval sources Yggdrasill, but this is probably not an old name) whose roots reach out to the ends of the inhabited world. In *Völuspá* 19, 47 and *Grímnismál* 35, 44 the World Tree is said to be an ash, but elsewhere it is thought to be an evergreen, which led some scholars to assume it was a yew tree (taxus baccata), whereas the expression barr used in *Fjöls-vinnsmál* 20 suggests a conifer. It seems likely that there may well have been conceptual or specific differences between the image of the World Tree in central Europe and Iceland even in heathen times. Whatever kind of tree may have been considered central to the human universe one should not attribute too much importance to its function as a world-axis, a world-tree, a support of the skies, Odin's tree of sacrifice, since all these interpretations presuppose a type of allegorical thinking hardly inherent in Germanic heathendom.[25]

Just how mythological concepts developed over the centuries, how principle features of a primitive and archaic cosmology were embellished and decorated in the poems of the very late Viking age can be seen quite clearly on the example of Valhalla — in Old Norse Valhöll. Originally, the abode of the gods in Asgard was an abstract notion. Later in the Viking age it acquired the name Valhöll — modeled on the great feasting-halls of human rulers — and in the late tenth century the originally featureless elements of the cosmology begin to gain shape. In two skaldic poems, the *Eiríksmál* and the *Hákonarmál,* the poets began to draw Valhöll as a paradise for dead Vikings, with the Valkyries greeting the fallen warriors. But *Hákonarmál* also uses a backdrop of the confrontation of the Viking's religious world with the Christian, and with a certain pessimistic tone to it at that. The Fenris wolf is mentioned, who will break free at the Ragnarök, and it seems that the days of Asgard are numbered. In Snorri's high medieval mythography, finally, Valhöll is a conglomerate of these late Viking notions, combined with elements of Christianity and antiquity, to result in a description of a building very different from any Germanic notion of a home of the gods.

The Coming of Christianity

These late Viking-age poems may be counted as belonging to an age of syncretism, as they betray knowledge of the Christian faith, but they still hold onto the old values. Other poems, and not only poems, show how Christian teaching had already merged with heathen lore, for example in the *Völuspá,* where many elements are so typically un-pagan, but are either Christian or classical, that many scholars have tried to detect different layers of influences in the work. However many layers of influence there may be, nothing can detract from the way in which the author has successfully created a unified splendid poem.

The Christianization of the Germanic tribes took almost a millennium. The Goths in the Balkans first came into contact with Christianity around the middle of the third century, when they took Christian prisoners after defeating the emperor Decius in 251 and in Cappadocia, in Asia Minor soon after, but Sweden was not completely converted until well into the twelfth century. In the intervening centuries, the other tribes gradually converted to Christianity: the Visigoths in the fourth century, the Vandals, the Rugians and the Lombards in the fifth. The Anglo-Saxons (the Celtic Britons had already been Christianized once before, during the Roman Empire) were converted during the sixth and seventh centuries, the Franks early in the sixth century, and the Alemanni and Bavarians in the course of the seventh. The Saxons, despite early missions, only became finally converted by Charlemagne in the eighth century, as were the Frisians. In Scandinavia, most countries were converted during the Viking age, first of all Denmark in the middle of the tenth century, Norway and Iceland around 1000, and finally Sweden and Finland.

The process of Christianization was, however, rarely as straightforward as it may seem. Early missionaries (the two Ewalds and Lebuin among the Saxons, Bonifatius and Willibrord among the Frisians, Ansgar and Poppo among the Danes, Ansgar and Rimbert among the Swedes) were active even at the beginning of the Viking Age, and St. Ansgar, who tried to teach the Gospel first in Denmark and then in Sweden between 829 and 850, seems to have left at least a small Christian community behind when he left Sweden, and Poppo is credited with convincing the Danish King Harald Bluetooth by an ordeal by fire.

However, despite personal fortitude and repeated efforts, the first missionaries seem to have made little actual impact as seen against the whole history of conversion of the Germanic tribes. The conversion period can be conveniently subdivided into at least the following (the dates given are for Scandinavia):

Age of Paganism and Early Contacts with Christianity	–800
Age of Syncretism	800–950
Age of Conversion	950–1000/1050
Age of Christianization	1000/1050–1100
Age of Antiquarian Interest in Heathen Times	1100–1300

The actual act of conversion of any one of the Germanic peoples is, in the context of cultural studies, of less importance than the duration of exposure to the new religion. Thus, the conversion of Iceland in the year 1000 marks only the pivotal point of a long relationship between paganism and Christianity, which probably started with Christian Irish settlers among the first Icelanders in the ninth century, and only ended with the introduction of the church tithes in the late twelfth, finally making Christianity an economic, as well as a political and ideological reality.

Thus, a period of "pure" Germanic heathendom existed in theory alone because we may assume that at least to some extant even the North Germanic tribes came into contact with some forms of Christianity probably as early as the late Roman Iron Age, whereas in their various expansions the Angles and Saxons in Britain and the Goths as well as the Lombards in southern Europe came into immediate contact with areas of well established Christianity. Even in Scandinavia, Migration Age movements as well as established trade links (many of them going back to the Bronze Age) preceded the early Viking period, which brought larger numbers of Scandinavians into direct contact with the manifestations of the Christian church. Initially their interest was purely secular. It soon became obvious to them what lucrative targets churches and monasteries in Britain, Ireland, and France could be. In these places they found not only food and wine, but also precious metals, artistically used for reliquaries, crosses, liturgical vessels and books. However, the Viking expansion did not rest with isolated attacks on treasure-troves, and relatively soon after the first attacks, at the latest after the first winter camps had been erected in Britain and on the western shores of Europe, contacts with the native Christian populations entered a new phase. Settlement, intermarriage, female slaves — all these exposed the Scandinavian raiders to the stories of the Old and New Testament, the Apocrypha and the legends of the saints. Sections of these stories, many of them popular and widespread, were to some extant used as elements in the indigenous oral literature, from whence they infiltrated the mythological tales, where there were no limits to a wealth of traditions or stories posed by any books. Traces of Christian influences can be found even in the oldest Eddic poems, not least in *Völuspá* (probably composed late in the tenth century, even if written down only after 1270). Syncretism, however, left its mark also on the Christianity of the newly converted, although much less intensely. These examples are mainly taken from the visual arts, especially depictions of pagan mythological scenes on Christian crosses and grave slabs. Thus, the scene of Thor fishing for the Midgard serpent could be shown on a Christian cross (Gosforth, in England, tenth century) and was reinterpreted as Christ trying to bait the devil in the shape of Leviathan; similarly, the wolf Fenrir swallowing the sun at Ragnarök was interpreted as a symbol for the devil by Christians,[26] and when Mary was shown under the cross (also on the Gosforth Cross), she was depicted with the iconographic shape of a female northern deity, complete with Migration Age hair style and drinking horn.[27]

During this phase of syncretism, the understanding for each other's religion must have grown particularly in those areas of intensive cultural contact between local and Scandinavian population, as in the Danelaw of northern England, the Viking kingdom of Dublin or in Normandy. Here, it was probably not only the teachings of Christianity but also the fascinating Christian liturgy and church music, the impressive organizational abilities of the church (still based on the foundations of the Roman Empire) and most importantly, the higher social prestige of the new faith that made it attractive. In addition to this was the fact that there was neither an in-built interregional organization nor a distinct dogmatic system within the earlier religion, and this, too, made it vulnerable to the advances of Christianity.

Christianity in Scandinavia

In other areas of Europe, especially the northwestern continent and Scandinavia, the imperatives of politics played a much larger role in the conversion of the kings and chieftains than either the supremacy of the Christian teaching or the zeal of the missionaries. The first Scandinavian king to be baptized, a Danish king Harald Klak, did so in the face of the political pressure of the Carolingian empire, when he and his entourage accepted Christianity in Mainz as a result of his contacts with Louis the Pious in 826, but his political conversion had no impact yet for another generation. Similarly, after the death of Ansgar in 865 and his successor and biographer Rimbert in 888, their work in Sweden was completely abandoned and consequently Sweden was not fully Christianized for another two centuries.

The third phase, that of actual conversion of whole kingdoms to Christianity, which was completed in Britain within the seventh century and in Frisia and Saxony in the eighth, did not reach Scandinavia before the late tenth century. In 965–66 Harald Bluetooth was converted and this event was proudly documented on the Jelling runestone, which declared that he had made the Danes Christians. When his son Sweyn Forkbeard became King not only of Denmark but also of England in 1013, the process of Christianization was accelerated. The English influence on the Scandinavian church also increased, so that under the reign of Cnut (Canute) the Great (1014–35) hundreds of churches were built in Denmark, bishoprics established, and by the mid-eleventh century not only the conversion, but also the Christianization of Denmark was widely completed.

In Norway, the process was possibly faster, but more violent. Olaf Tryggvason, a member of the Norwegian royal family, had been baptized sometime during his Viking raids in England. When he claimed the throne of Norway in 995, he thought it politically expedient to emphasize his Christianity, not least to oppose openly the claims of the expressly pagan Jarl Hakon of Hlaðir. He landed in Norway with an army, but also a bishop and several priests, defeated his opponent, and set about Christianizing the country by force. However, when he died in a sea battle in the year 1000, Norway was divided politically between nominally Christian rulers, who did nothing to further the new faith and most of western Norway lapsed. Only another royal pretender, Olaf the Saint, took up Olaf Tryggvason's work in 1015 and seriously set about Christianizing Norway, among much opposition from the conservative farmers who adhered to the old customs. He had churches built, re-established the cult of St. Sunniva on the island of Selja, set himself up as a Christian king in Nidaros (now Trondheim) and set up a church organization with the help of his legislation. When he fell in the battle of Stiklastaðir against his own countrymen in 1030, his work seemed endangered, but, strangely enough, the unpopular king instantly became a popular saint and has remained so. The saintly martyr king posthumously caused Norway to become a Christian nation, gathered around his cult. Consequently by the mid-eleventh century Norway had a well-established monastic and church organization. Thus, despite the quasi-official conversions under the two Olafs, the actual Christianization of the Norwegian people occurred only after the death of the native Olaf.

In Sweden, the first Christian king was Erik the Victorious (*hin sigrsælli,* ca. 957–995), but he made little permanent impact. After a succession of Christian and non-Christian kings, however, it was not before Inge in 1083–84 that Christianity gained any stronger foothold, so that the Christianization of Sweden took well into the twelfth century.

Preserving the Pagan Past

Over the next few generations, the process of Christianization in Scandinavia led not only to the building of churches, the establishment of bishoprics, the foundation of monasteries, the education of priests of local stock and the teaching of the new faiths, but also to some literacy, at least in parts of the population. This occurred to a greater degree in Iceland and to a lesser degree in Sweden, but it meant that not only religious, administrative, legal and scholarly matters could be committed to parchment, but that also stories and poems from heathen times found their way into writing. This had happened in the eighth and ninth century on a small scale in Britain and Franconia, where a few magical charms had been adapted and noted down in the vernacular by monks on the empty space of Christian manuscripts. In Scandinavia, however, such an interest in old and heathen matters took a much more organized form. Because formally recited poetry was still practiced as an art form all through the Christian Middle Ages, a strong interest sprang up in preserving the form and the matter of older poems, both for their intrinsic value and also as examples to younger poets. At the same time, new poems were composed, using mythological matter, parallel to the composition of a rich Christian poetry. It is therefore difficult to establish the age of most of these anonymous poems written in the Eddic meters, as they could have been composed late in the heathen period, even if they show Christian influences (such as the greatest of Old Norse mythological poems, the *Völuspá*). However, some were no doubt composed in the eleventh or early twelfth century and collected and written down somewhat later (as may have been the case with *Hávamál*), whereas others only originated in the great age of Icelandic learning and literature, the later twelfth and the thirteenth centuries, like *Alvíssmál* or *Vafþrúðnismál,* when Iceland had long become a Christian country.

This period of learning was also the heyday of an antiquarian, scholarly interest in the pagan past. The history of the people and the old religion were studied, poems and stanzas as well as anecdotes collected and woven, for the first time in history, into a systematic concept of the heathen religion, notwithstanding the fact that such an organized system of heathen mythology had not actually existed in pre-Christian times. There seems to have been a desire by the Icelandic scholars to create a canon of the old religion in much the same way that there was a canon for the new. The two main protagonists of this scholarly interest in the heathen religion were Saxo Grammaticus (ca. 1150–1220), who wrote his Latin *Gesta Danorum* (History of the Danes) in Lund, and Snorri Sturluson (1179–1241) in Iceland. Saxo's work, which records Danish history from the beginnings to 1202, is of particular value not only because of his detailed retelling of old legends and myths but also because he used Icelandic informants and sources, thus giving us a large number of Old Norse mythological and heroic tales which we would otherwise no longer have any access to today, even despite the fact that he dealt with his sources fairly freely.[28]

Of even more importance is Snorri Sturluson, the Icelandic scholar and politician, who did our knowledge of heathen religion such good service, especially in his *Heimskringla* (literally World-Circle, a history of the Norwegian kings from mythical beginnings to 1177), and his *Edda,* a didactic handbook for skalds.[29] In the first part, *Gylfaginning,* he offers a scholarly portrayal of Old Norse mythology, which is admittedly heavily influenced by his Christian education and classical education, but remains nonetheless our most important medieval source for North Germanic mythology. However brilliant a re-teller of old myths and thus preserver of old poems he is, we must not make the mistake that some scholars do (or rather, once did) to see in him a primary source for the actual religion of pre-Viking Age northern Europe. It is at times abundantly clear that in some cases Snorri had no more knowledge about some of the mythological figures whose names he found in old poems than we have. While in the rest of Europe the heathen religion was gradually forgotten in the course of the Christian Middle Ages, save for a few "survivals" in folk beliefs, proverbs, and folk literature, in Iceland, mythological matters continued to be used as a literary framework for new poetry even in the thirteenth and fourteenth centuries (for example, *Hyndluljóð, Svipdagsmál*), to some extent even in the Rímur-poetry of the late Middle Ages (for instance *Lokrur, Thrymlur*). Again, we must not make the mistake of confusing this poetical reception of Germanic mythology with genuine sources for our knowledge of the pre-Christian religion.

Notes

[1] R. L. M. Derolez, *Götter und Mythen der Germanen*, trans. Julie von Wattenwyl (Zurich and Cologne: Benziger, 1968).

[2] Gerd Wolfgang Weber. "Siðaskipti. Das religionsgeschichtliche Modell Snorri Sturlusons in Edda und Heimskringla," in *Sagnaskemmtun: Studies in Honour of Hermann Pálsson*, ed. Rudolf Simek, Jonas Kristjansson and Hans Bekker-Nielsen (Vienna: Böhlau, 1986), 309–29.

[3] W. Haio Zimmermann, "Urgeschichtliche Opferfunde aus Flüssen, Mooren, Quellen und Brunnen Südwestdeutschlands," *Neue Ausgrabungen und Forschungen in Niedersachsen* 6 (1970): 53–92, esp. 74–75.

[4] Michael Müller-Wille, *Opferkulte der Germanen und Slawen* (Stuttgart: Theiss, 1999), 32–33.

[5] Torsten Capelle, *Anthropomorphe Holzidole in Mittel und Nordeuropa* (Stockholm: Almquist and Wiksell, 1995).

[6] Holger Hohmann, "Indiculus superstitionum et paganiarum," in J. Hoops, *Reallexikon der germanischen Altertumskunde*, ed. H. Beck (2nd ed., Berlin, New York: de Gruyter, 2000), XV, 369–79.

[7] Alexandra Pesch, "Frauen und Brakteaten — eine Skizze," in *Mythological Women: Studies in Memory of Lotte Motz*, ed. Wilhelm Heitzmann and Rudolf Simek (Vienna: Fassbaender, 2002).

[8] Margarete Watt, "Kings or Gods? Iconographic Evidence from Scandinavian Gold Foil Figures," in *The Making of Kingdoms*, ed. Tania Dickinson and David Griffiths (Oxford: Oxford University Committee for Archaeology, 1999), 173–83.

[9] K.-E. Westergaard, "Die vergessenen Göttinnen der Fruchtbarkeit," in *Frauen und Frauenbilder dokumentiert durch 2000 Jahre* (Oslo: Germanist. Inst., U of

Oslo, 1983), 203–26; Rudolf Simek, *Dictionary of Northern Mythology* (Wood-bridge: D. S. Brewer, 1982).

[10] Margaret Gelling, *Signposts to the Past* (London: Dent, 1978; 3rd ed., Chiches-ter: Phillimore, 1997).

[11] Sigfrid J. de Laet, "Nehalennia, déesse germanique ou celtique?" *Helinium* 11 (1971): 154–61; Elisabeth Cramer-Peters, "Zur Deutung des Namens Nehalen-nia," and "Frija-Isis-Nehalennia," *ABäG* 3 (1972): 1–14 and 15–24. The goddess Nerthus is more obscure: see Lotte Motz, "The Goddess Nerthus: A New Ap-proach," *ABäG* 36 (1992): 1–19, Jan de Vries, *Altgermanische Religionsgeschichte* (2nd ed., Berlin: de Gruyter, 1957), II, 164–65, and Lotte Motz, *The King, the Champion and the Sorcerer* (Vienna: Fassbaender, 1996), 116.

[12] Karl Helm, "Hluðana," *PBB* 37 (1912): 337–38; L. Motz, "Gerðr," *Maal og Minne* (1981): 121–36. Two more goddesses, Baduhenna and Tamfana, are only mentioned by Tacitus (*Annales* 4.73 and 1.51) who writes that a grove in Frisia was dedicated to Baduhenna, and that 900 Roman soldiers were slaughtered near this grove in A.D. 28. The name is clearly Germanic, the first part may be cognate with *badwa-* "battle," and the second part is frequently found as *-henae* in *ma-tronae* names. It is quite possible that in this case Tacitus may be transmitting genuine information about a goddess of war, even though we have no other source to indicate her veneration. He writes of Tamfana that a temple dedicated to her was destroyed somewhere between the rivers Lippe and Ruhr during a sac-rifice held there in the autumn of A.D. 4.

[13] E. Thorvildsen, "Dankirke," in Hoops, *Reallexikon,* VI, 248–49.

[14] Dated 601 and quoted by Bede, *A History of the English Church and People,* I, 30.

[15] Motz, *King,* 103–24.

[16] For example E. O. G. Turville-Petre, *Myth and Religion of the North* (London: Weidenfeld and Nicolson, 1964), 175.

[17] Georges Dumézil, *Gods of the Ancient Northmen,* trans. Einar Haugen (Berke-ley: U of California P, 1977).

[18] K. Hauck, *Goldbrakteaten aus Sievern* (Munich: Fink, 1970); Dumézil, *Gods;* Lotte Motz, "The Conquest of Death: the Myth of Baldr and its Middle Eastern Counterparts," *Collegium Medievale* 4 (1991): 99–116.

[19] Jan de Vries, "Heimdallr, dieu énigmatique," *Études Germaniques* 10 (1955), 257–68.

[20] de Vries, *Altgermanische Religionsgeschichte,* II, 153–63.

[21] B. Falck-Kjällquist, "Namnet Ullerö," *Namn och Bygd* 71 (1983): 152–56.

[22] Britt-Mari Näsström, *Freyja — the Great Goddess of the North* (Lund: University of Lund Dept. of History of Religions, 1995).

[23] F. R. Schröder, "Germanische Schöpfungsmythen," *GRM* 19 (1931): 1–26 and 81–99; Kurt Schier, "Die Erdschöpfung aus dem Urmeer," in *Märchen: Festschrift für Friedrich von der Leyen,* ed. Hugo Kuhn and Kurt Schier (Munich: Beck, 1963), 303–34; J. S. Martin "Ár vas alda," in *Speculum Norrænum: Studies in Honour of E. O. G. Turville-Petre* (Odense: Odense UP, 1981), 357–69; L. Lönnroth, "Iörð

fannz æva né upphiminn," in *Speculum Norrænum,* 310–27; G. Steinsland, "Antropogonimyten i Völuspá," *Arkiv för nordisk filologi* 98 (1983): 80–107.

[24] G. S. Littleton, "The 'Kingship in Heaven' Theme," in *Myth and Law among the Indo-Europeans,* ed. Joan Puhvel (Berkeley: U of California P, 1970), 83–121.

[25] See Gro Steinsland "Treet i Völuspá," *Arkiv för nordisk filologi* 94 (1979): 120–50.

[26] Otto Gschwantler, "Christus, Thor und die Midgardschlange," in *Festschrift für Otto Höfler 1,* ed. Helmut Birkhahn and Otto Gschwantler (Vienna: Notring, 1968), 145–68; Otto Gschwantler, "Die Überwindung des Fenriswolfs und ihr christliches Gegenstück bei Frau Ava," in *Poetry in the Scandinavian Middle Ages, Spoleto, 4–10 Sept. 1988 (= Atti del 12° Congresso Internazionale di Studi sull' Alto Medioevo,* Spoleto, 1990), 1–26.

[27] Rudolf Simek, "The Image of the Female Deity in Migration Age and Viking Age Scandinavia," in *Mythological Women: Studies in Memory of Lotte Motz,* ed. Heitzmann and Simek.

[28] See Saxo Grammaticus, *The History of the Danes,* trans. Peter Fisher and ed. Hilda Ellis Davidson (Cambridge: Brewer, 1979).

[29] This is not to be confused with the earlier poetic *Edda,* containing the poems discussed already.

Orality

R. Graeme Dunphy

Oral Traditions

IN THE CONTEXT OF LITERARY HISTORY, "orality" refers to traditions of oral performance of works which may also be literary works, or which may resemble literature. The widely used tag "oral literature" is a contradiction in terms, and is in several respects too problematic to be helpful. It is better to speak of oral verse, oral narrative traditions, oral epic and so forth. However, in a literary history which looks back to the beginnings one must take into consideration the production of literature before it took on written form. Long before the advent of writing, the careful assembly of words into sophisticated verbal productions was an art form that shaped and reflected the cultures in which it emerged, and in these oral poetic and narrative traditions we seek the origins of our literatures. And even in a highly literate society such as that in which we live today, many forms we might bracket as literature are written for oral performance, or indeed need not be written at all: obvious examples are public speaking, drama, storytelling, and various forms of poetry and song. Thanks to its permanence, the written word lends itself readily to analysis, and in literary studies we tend therefore to think of it as the norm, oral forms being a sub-category, variant or even a poor imitation. In reality the opposite is true. Human language evolved solely to meet the needs of oral communication, and writing, even formal and highly stylized writing, imitates speech. The poetic muse arose in the earliest cultures as a result of the fascination with the possibilities of the spoken word, and the modern reader processes literature using cerebral faculties developed for the reception of speech. Oral performance and literature are the two sides of linguistic art, but orality has both a historical and a logical priority.

It follows that an appreciation of oral dynamics is necessary for an understanding of both the origins and the functionality of literature. In the medieval context we are interested here in three main areas of investigation. First, in the nature of pre-literature, of ancient oral verse, narrative and performance, and the way in which it shaped the character also of the earliest vernacular writings. Second, in the polarization between written and spoken art in a partially literate medieval society, with the concomitant implications for social groupings and power structures. And third, in the performance aspect of medieval literature and in the various ways in which the differing needs of listeners and readers might take precedence, depending on the form of delivery and the author's intended recipients.[1]

Primary Orality and Germanic Pre-Literacy

The term "primary orality" is a useful designation for the orality of a culture that has never had any contact with writing. Primary oral cultures are by definition pre-historic, since by the time a society begins to write its history, its primary oral phase must be past. Southern Europe ceased to have a primary oral culture at the latest by the fifth century B.C., northern Europe perhaps a millennium later, though regional variation is considerable.

The twenty-first century knows only very few pockets of residual primary orality, but scholars of the earlier twentieth century had opportunities to study orality in Africa and elsewhere, and much can be learned about the nature of European pre-literacy by studying the culture of illiterate peasant populations who maintained elements of primary orality well into the twentieth century, though they were certainly not uninfluenced by the parallel culture of educated European society. It can be difficult — perhaps in the end it is impossible — for those of us with the literary competence to read a book such as this one to think our way into the mindset of a primarily oral world. Although the poetry of such a society may appear to bear formal similarities to ours, psychological differences make its organization and functionality fundamentally different. Poetry, and indeed knowledge of any sort, exists in a primarily oral society only as the potential of individuals to give utterance to it. Knowledge can only be maintained by constant repetition, and only what is actively cultivated can remain in the tradition. Techniques of memorization are therefore particularly important, and it may be that verse first arose for mnemonic purposes.

In a society without writing, words are events and cannot be visualized spatially. The poet may arrange words in lines, but has no clear concept of a "word" and none at all of a "line" — language can only be linear when it is written. Without a system of writing, poetry is performance and cannot be pinned down to a permanent state in which it can be analyzed. Our concept of "text" as a fixed corpus of words makes no sense in an oral culture, since there is no way to check whether two recitations are identical; if the same narrative is twice told using the same poetic art, the two performances are thought of as the "same" poem, though the wording will certainly be substantially different. It must be different, as memory also operates orally: without a fixed point of reference (a book) there is no way to memorize more than a few lines by rote. It is therefore not possible to learn a longer poem "by heart" in the modern sense. Nevertheless, singers accomplish amazing feats of memory, precisely because they are not caught up in concerns about exact wordings. They memorize a basic narrative framework and turn it into poetry as required, the poem having a new crystallization with every performance. As there can be no canonical version of any text, there must be a flexible approach to such questions as truth and fictionality. Consequently, the development of writing was more than just a useful adjunct to orality: it heralded an alteration of human consciousness so radical that the old and new thought-processes could not exist side-by-side. The world of primary orality is as closed to the competent reader as the world of books is to the illiterate.[2]

Probably the most sophisticated form in pre-literary oral art, certainly that which had the most profound impact on the development of fine literature, is the oral epic poem, which can be demonstrated to lie behind the earliest epic literature in many European cultures. The nature of this art form only became clear in the 1930s as a result of Milman Parry's work on Homer (continued after Parry's early death by Albert Lord). Parry recognized that the frequent repetition of fixed phrases in the *Odyssey* and the *Iliad* which had been regarded variously as genius or as an aesthetic flaw were in fact neither; they were characteristics of oral production. In order to prove that Homer was originally an oral poet whose composition was subsequently committed to writing, he began the examination of the narrative performance of illiterate Yugoslav singer-storytellers, his extensive fieldwork ultimately producing the Parry collection of over twelve thousand recordings and transcriptions of oral epic and lyric poetry, now in Harvard University Library. The result of his analysis was the development of Oral Formulaic Theory, also known as the Parry-Lord Theory, which finds its classic expression in Lord's book *The Singer of Tales*.[3] This theory describes the method by which a narrative singer operates, the way in which a young performer can learn the art and how the skilled executant is able to reproduce a poem many thousands of lines in length after only a single hearing, and that to a high degree of artistry. The singer's real skill lies less in powers of memory than in the ability to compose elegantly and fluently at performance speed, well enough to satisfy the rigorous demands of music and meter. The mechanism that makes this possible is the use of set pieces that can easily be assembled like building blocks. Here Parry distinguishes between "formulae" and "themes." A formula is a linguistic set piece, the familiar collocation of words ready-made to fit the meter under given conditions, sometimes as little as a standard adjective which combines with a personal name to provide the required rhythmic pattern, sometimes larger, even several lines in length, providing perhaps a convenient narrative link that can be used at various places in different stories. A theme is a larger narrative block which has its own conventions and formulae and which again can be inserted at appropriate moments in any epic tale; examples are the arming of the warrior, the sending out of the messenger, the gathering of the clans. By means of these techniques, it is possible for one motif to flow automatically into another, chains of associated formulae and groups of related themes embellishing the narrative and pushing it forward. While a mediocre singer may use this mechanically — even that is a considerable achievement — the truly talented performer can make of it a thing of great beauty. Lord records:

> When Parry was working with the most talented Yugoslav singer in our experience, Avdo Međedović in Bijelo Polje, he tried the following experiment. Avdo had been singing and dictating for several weeks; he had shown his worth and was aware that we valued him highly. Another singer came to us, Mumin Vlahovljak from Plevlje. He seemed to be a good singer, and he had in his repertory a song that Parry discovered was not known to Avdo; Avdo said he had never heard it before. Without telling Avdo that he would be asked to sing the song himself when Mumin had finished it, Parry set Mumin to singing, but he made sure that Avdo was in the room and listening. When the song came to an end, Avdo was asked his opinion of it and whether he could now sing it himself. He replied that it was a good song and that Mumin had sung it well, but that he thought that he might sing it better. The song was a long one of several thousand lines. Avdo began and as he sang, the song lengthened, the ornamentation and richness accumulated, and the human touches of character, touches that distinguished Avdo from other singers, imparted a depth of feeling that had been missing in Mumin's version.[4]

This art, while certainly demanding great skill and accomplishment, does not require unique genius. Every generation produces enough gifted singers to keep the songs alive. In a world without electronic media this requires the presence of a singer in every larger village, though singers can also be itinerant. While the number of themes and formulae is large, it is not an insuperable task to learn them. There is a formula to meet every regularly occurring metrical and narrative need, but interestingly, there is only one — Parry's so-called principle of thrift, an economy of expression that is necessary to make the system manageable. It is this principle that results in the high degree of repetition that Parry had first noticed in Homer. According to some studies, as many as ninety-eight percent of words in a given poem may belong to phrases that occur more than once in the local corpus.[5]

A comparison of the earliest epic literature demonstrates not only Parry's thesis, that the Greek verse of Homer is formulaic in character, but also that the same is true of other literatures all over Europe, including the Germanic tradition of alliterative heroic verse, which is represented in Old English by *Beowulf, The Battle of Maldon* and other works, in Scandinavia by the Norse sagas, and in early German most obviously by the *Hildebrandlied*. These poems give us a window on what must have been a rich tradition of Germanic verse stretching back in a continuous if constantly evolving tradition far beyond the times of the folk migrations. In classical times this tradition of orality was known by the Romans to be part of the Germanic culture, as is noted by Tacitus in the *Germania*. One can imagine the warriors sitting around a fire in the chieftain's longhouse, a scene reminiscent of Hrothgar's mead-hall in *Beowulf,* there to be entertained and inspired by the singer of battles past. It seems likely that an important element in the warrior ethos of the Germanic peoples was the ambition to immortalize oneself through heroism worthy of a place in the songs of future generations. This culture is lost to us, because orality itself leaves no records, but it does leave its mark on the literate culture that succeeds it. In this way the earliest written poetry testifies to its own prehistory.[6]

Conversely, an awareness of the oral background gives us a key without which we cannot rightly understand heroic verse. The modern awareness of formulaic art in European pre-literature has changed the way we read the epics. If we understand that a standard epithet is applied to a personal name for metrical reasons, we will be less inclined to set great importance on the potential implications of the epithet for the characterization of a protagonist in a particular narrative context; by contrast, when we read a modern novel, where the author chooses epithets freely for their effect in the specific context, we would pay close attention to them. In this way oral-formulaic theory helps us in an author-based interpretation, understanding the author's intentions in the context of the limitations of the mode of composition. It can also help in a reader-based interpretation: if we imagine the reader as a listener we may come closer to a true sense of the effect of the literature on the contemporary recipient. The fact that a heroic epic imitates orality does not mean that it could not nevertheless have been composed in the scriptorium with all the laborious care, the drafting and redrafting, and above all the fixed-text mentality that this involves. And even if a poem really was composed orally and then dictated, it can be affected in subtle ways by the process of writing. When oral-formulaic poetry is recorded in a precise transcription such as those of Parry, we may speak of the written form faithfully preserving the oral tradition, but such a careful record will only result when the scribe has the modern scholar's interest in orality. Since every retelling of an oral poem is different, it would never have occurred to the medieval scribe that there might be any obligation to fix the last oral version unchanged. We must assume that early amanuenses taking down oral verse would allow themselves the same freedoms that copyists generally did with written sources, which is entirely legitimate given their intentions. Thus, while the influence of formulaic thinking on the earliest Germanic literature has been established beyond doubt, the relationship of these works to the oral tradition *per se* is still keenly debated, and the truth of the matter may well be that the polarization "orality versus literacy" is too simplistic a model for understanding a complex period of transition. Whereas the first adherents of Parry-Lord noticed only the formulae which they sought in alliterative verse, the next generation realized that a work may display features characteristic of both orality and writing. For example, a heroic epic may contain formulaic composition, but have sufficient variation of expression that the principle of thrift is not obviously in operation. Given that scribal work in the early period was conducted almost exclusively by monks, whereas the warrior tradition was pre-Christian, we may regard Christian elements in early alliterative verse as a sure sign that these passages could not have arisen in their present form in a context of primary orality. Both *Beowulf* and the *Hildebrandlied* appear to show some Christian influence. A particularly striking instance is the Old Saxon *Heliand,* where the Christian elements cannot be secondary as the narrative itself is a heroic presentation of the life of Christ. Here we have a work deliberately composed — presumably for propaganda purposes — in the style of local oral poetry, yet none of the material is received tradition: this is the original composition of a highly literate poet. As the centuries went on, the balance gradually shifted, narrative literature becoming less formulaic. Whereas the *Hildebrandlied,* which survives in a ninth-century manuscript, appears to be a typically oral work but with some influence of chirographic culture in its surviving written form, the early thirteenth-century *Nibelungenlied* is a good example of a heroic epic that still retains a little of the flavor of its oral predecessors, but is in every respect the composition of a writer.[7]

The application of oral-formulaic theory to Germanic literatures has been controversial, and a number of criticisms have been leveled at it. In part, these revolve around difficulties in the analogy between the Balkans and Germany. Why should different cultural groups, speaking only distantly related languages, composing poetry using different metrical and alliterative principles, recorded more than a millennium apart, operate in precisely the same way? The Parry-Lord Theory deals with the way in which a culture can overcome the limitations of human memory, but although these limitations are universals, the strategies for dealing with them need not be. As a result, there has been much discussion of whether the definition of "formula" which was worked out to describe south Slavic phenomena must be adapted for the Germanic context. Other objections, as we have seen, relate to questions of whether the surviving texts fulfill the Parry-Lord criteria. A weakness of many of the arguments is their failure to differentiate between two different phases: we are interested on the one hand in the consequences of formulaic elements in early works for our understanding of the oral-formulaic pre-history of these works, and on the other hand, in the consequences for our reception of the works themselves. It seems that a majority opinion today affirms Parry-Lord on the former question, but shows reservations on the latter: the prehistory of these poems is certainly in some sense oral-formulaic, but the surviving texts may be several steps away from the oral tradition.[8]

The oral-formulaic theory describes the "high" culture of pre-literate society. However, there are other forms of oral transmission that do not require the skills of the singer of tales. Simply to tell a story without any pretensions to poetic art, but with the sense of continuing an ancient tradition, is presumably an activity in which every member of a primarily oral community can participate. Fairy tales (*Märchen*) and other forms of traditional lore generally have been regarded as the province of anthropological and folklore studies rather than literary science, but it is worth remembering that the most famous collectors of German folk tales, the Brothers Grimm, were also the leading scholars of their generation in Germanic philology. Germanic folk tales have only been collected in any number since the late eighteenth century, and it is difficult to assess how old they might be, but some have parallels in Celtic, Slavic, and Indian folk cultures. This wide distribution would suggest a very great age.[9] Equally important are folk songs, cradle songs, nonsense rhymes, sayings and proverbs, jokes, and riddles, magic charms and spells, and any study of such popular lore must also take consideration of children's oral culture, which develops historically in parallel with that of adults.[10] Here again, it can be difficult to know what elements of modern culture have their roots in the native orality of pre-literate Germanic culture, and what has developed in the popular orality of relatively recent times. The tendency among folklorists is to look with healthy skepticism at exaggerated claims of antiquity, but even if the specific proverbs and rhymes we know today are only a few centuries old, the forms themselves will be far older. Occasionally, and sometimes in the corners of manuscripts from the early Middle Ages, a little gem is recorded in one of the early Germanic languages which testifies to the existence in prehistory of one or other of these smaller forms of oral art. For example, the Old High German *Merseburger Sprüche,* two magic charms which are certainly pre-Christian, or in Old English, the *Exeter Riddles,* are the only proof we have that ancient Germanic societies entertained themselves with puzzles not so very different from those we might pose today.

Secondary Orality and the Subculture of Literacy

Primary orality may be contrasted with "secondary orality," orality within a chirographic or even a typographic society — that is, a society which knows handwriting or print respectively. Secondary orality ranges from the illiterate person influenced indirectly by a literate environment to, at the other extreme, the oral practice of a highly literate individual; it may therefore retain many of the characteristics of primary orality, or only very little. But the evidence suggests that even a limited exposure to literacy affects the psychodynamics of orality. The adoption of literacy by a society marks an important turning point for the whole of that society, including those who do not embrace it. But clearly, this transition will not normally be abrupt, and different degrees and varieties of literacy will exist side by side. One of the main desiderata of recent scholarship on orality has been to bring differentiation to the older view of monolithic literate or illiterate societies and social groupings in medieval Europe.[11]

The beginnings of literacy in the Germanic world are difficult to define because we still know all too little about the origins and social functions of runes. It seems likely that knowledge of this script was limited to a small circle of "rune-masters"; thus, even in ancient Germanic society, literacy was a factor in elitism and power. However, it appears that in the runic period the Germanic communities never developed the possibilities literacy offered for communication and the organization of society, for the keeping of records or the preservation of poetic art, since the surviving inscriptions appear limited to certain ritual functions. Contacts with the Roman world, especially with the Roman army, may have made the inhabitants of both Germany and England aware of the potential of writing, but no attempt was made at that stage to bring Roman methods to bear on communication in any Germanic language. As a result, the Germanic world remained a primary oral world until the spread of Christian missions. With the rise of the monasteries as centers of learning and culture, however, and at the latest with the new status of literacy at the court of Charlemagne, a constellation emerged in which the written form became associated with both intellectual and political authority and thus became normative for the whole of society, though even basic literacy skills remained the monopoly of an elite.[12]

For any understanding of medieval German society it is important to be aware of who could read, and when. From the earliest stages of established Christianity, from the fourth century onward, the Christian establishment was almost fully literate, mainly because of the centrality of the word in Christianity as opposed to classical religions; monasteries were therefore the focal point of early literary production. Writing soon became important for secular administration and for the functioning of the law courts, but here the ruling houses were dependent on clerics in secular service, and to some extent continued to be so until the late Middle Ages. At the turn of the ninth century, Charlemagne made the first serious attempt to foster literacy at the imperial court, but his successors were less enthusiastic in this regard, and it was only gradually in the course of the tenth to twelfth centuries that literacy became the norm among the nobility. From the thirteenth century on, writing skills become important for trade, and one finds the first urban schools springing up to cater to the highest patrician classes. The peasantry and the urban lower classes remained illiterate well into modern times. The spread of literacy among women followed the same sequence, but generally with some delay. Thus, we must divide medieval society into literate and oral subcultures, a division complicated by the fact that the boundary between these groups was gradually changing, and that this boundary was in any case never clear cut; for there are many degrees of exposure to education. But always, the boundary reflects broader social divisions, for in any partially literate society, literacy is power.[13]

We find, then, that at the beginning of the secondary oral period in German history, there was an educated society cultivating the first flowering of Germany's Latin and vernacular literature, innovative and resourceful in the pioneering of new written forms, but in keeping with what we have said about the psychodynamics of orality, was neglecting its oral heritage. Literate people can be carriers of oral tradition in the sense that they may continue to sing the old songs, but they preserve it as a dead thing, a relic, because their text-based thinking — although it opens whole new worlds of literary production to them — tends to close for them the possibility that they can be part of an oral tradition that is still evolving as it did in pre-literate society. Parallel to this we find an illiterate society that is aware of writing, which is influenced by it without having access to it — a Marxist analysis might say: which is oppressed by it — and which maintains its own subculture by purely oral techniques resembling those of pre-literate Germanic society. Evidence from the Middle High German *Spielmannsepik*, the pre-courtly so-called "minstrel epics," suggests that long after courtly literature had lost its formulaic character, oral-formulaic narrative verse was still being sung in other circles.[14] Where the one group was inclined to cultivate literature but to "fix" oral tradition, the other group continued to "live" oral tradition.

We might also note the way in which church art, frescos and plastics, could function as a kind of alternative writing, depicting Bible stories in a form which the illiterate could "read." To be sure, these also existed in book form, the so-called *Biblia pauperum* (Bible of the poor), which showed a series of pictures of Biblical scenes, with Old and New Testament events grouped according to typological patterns. But *Biblia pauperum* is a misnomer, for in the days before printing the poor could never have afforded these opulent volumes; the intended recipients would be the non-literate members of the court or convent. In this visual sphere, too, literate thinking left its impact in the oral world.[15]

Literature in its Oral Context

So far we have been considering oral culture mainly in opposition to literary culture, be it diachronically (pre-literate primary orality) or synchronically (the secondary orality of the illiterate classes of medieval society). But literature itself has an oral dynamic. We can see this at the point of composition, where it is known that many medieval writers dictated their work to a scribe, as was common already in classical literature. And we can see it in the "oral tone" of many of the texts. As Old and Middle High German had not yet developed a formal style for written prose, medieval prose works mimic orality far more closely than is the case with most modern authors. Obviously, this does not apply in the same way to verse, nor to many translations, which mimic instead the linguistic structures of the Latin, but here we might legitimately ask whether it was precisely an awareness of orality that motivated these choices; if for example a chronicle writer used verse in German where the corresponding works in Latin used prose, the reason may well be that a lack of dignity was perceived in the use of language which smacked of the every-day spoken register. Similarly, the absence of a standard language meant that not only the dialect but also the personal quirks of an author or scribe were reflected on paper, and this applies to verse and prose in equal measure: the written form reflected personal pronunciation, so that the voice of the writer is present in a way that a modern typographic culture does not allow. All writing involves a flow of oral consciousness into the channel of writing, but perhaps this was more obviously so before the advent of print gave us a more distanced attitude to the written word.

However, the oral dynamic of writing becomes most important at the point of delivery. In the medieval world, as in the classical period, reading often meant reading aloud, and many of the recipients of a text may have been listeners rather than readers. We might say it was the combination of private reading and public listening that characterized the literary scene.

This is in part to be explained by the high level of illiteracy even in the upper levels of medieval society, and in part by the great expense involved in book production, both factors which militated against a culture of private reading. But it is also an ideal in its own right, and one that is inherited from classical culture. The first-century historian Pliny, one of the most highly literate men in his generation, is on record as preferring the public mode of reading, as it is more pleasant to be read to. Reading as performance is well attested as an important form of entertainment at the medieval court and in the salons of the patrician houses of the late medieval towns. In the monasteries, the reading of theological texts for the edification of the listening monastic community was a spiritual discipline, practiced for example in the refectory during meals. And of course, scripture was read in worship, the one context in which even the peasantry would regularly be recipients of written texts. The culture of public reading fulfilled several important purposes. At court it had an important political dynamic, too. We might remember that influential rulers were often commissioners of literary works, in which they were generally praised, their values were represented, and their political legitimacy was proclaimed. It would be naïve to imagine them as altruistic patrons of the arts, ordering manuscripts for their own private reading and deriving quiet satisfaction when they found themselves praised in the texts. Rather, these works were utilized as elements in planned events such as banquets, weddings, state occasions and festivities, as demonstrations of the power and wealth of the ruler. Entertaining texts may also have been read in more informal settings, and here the dynamic of building group cohesion will have been very important. For the patricians too, there is evidence that public readings were intended to foster a sense of community and define group identity.

Of course, private reading and study was also practiced in the Middle Ages. One of the interesting questions here is whether it is possible to determine how far any given author intended the reception of a work to be by reading or by listening, or indeed both, for a dual-level mode of reception seems to apply to some works which were sometimes read privately, sometimes in public. Although the actual use of a text was in practice not necessarily that which the author planned, the relationship of a writer to the patron, to the immediate audience and to contemporary society will be better understood if the intended modality of the text can be ascertained. Recent research has sought to produce effective criteria by which such a judgment can be made. Lexical evidence can take us part of the way. When authors use such words as *lesen, hoeren, sprechen, sagen, singen* when addressing their public, this may indicate the intended mode of reception. But these must be handled with some care. *Lesen*, which appears to focus on a reader, could still refer to the process of reading aloud, while *hoeren,* at first glance a clear sign of a listening audience, was also used metaphorically in the sense of "pay attention" or "learn from the text." Nevertheless, the frequently used formula *lesen unde hoeren* does seem to suggest an anticipated dual reception. Other indicators can point to the oral reception of a work, such as the author's request for silence as a key passage approaches, or a hint that certain delicate matters should not be elaborated on in case there are ladies present.[16]

A sure sign of oral reception is any evidence of musical performance. The neumes that appear with the text in some manuscripts may originally have been a kind of punctuation to give shape to dramatic reading, but they are most familiar as musical symbols indicating the structure of plainsong; in either case, presentation to an audience is presupposed. It is interesting that these appear also in one manuscript of the *Heliand,* which tallies with the many accounts of Germanic alliterative verse being performed — intoned perhaps, rather than sung — to stringed instruments. Songs in our modern sense, short strophic pieces with melodies, were sung both by and to the assembled company at court, at weddings, at religious festivals, on journeys, and no doubt in many other settings of which we have no record. The love lyrics of the *Minne* tradition were certainly intended to be sung, and occasionally they have been preserved with their original melodies. Taken at face value, these songs appear to be directed toward a lady whom the singer wishes to woo, and possibly they really were used in romantic situations, but like modern pop songs, which can have similar thematics, their principal function was the entertainment of an assembled public. Other lyric works by the *Minnesänger* include political verse, praise of the patron, comment on social affairs and gnomic pieces, and these too appear to have been sung: lyrics of this kind used to be referred to as *Sprüche,* but the tendency in recent literature has been to expand this misleading term to *Sangspruchdichtung,* which emphasizes the mode of performance. The *Minne* cult is a specifically courtly tradition, but we also have songs from other social levels. The *Carmina Burana,* lively and sometimes bawdy songs in Latin and German, can be imagined sung in the market place. Some songs were specifically dance songs, others were processionals. The early Middle High German *Ezzolied* (later eleventh century) was probably intended to be sung on a pilgrimage.

The evidence relating to the courtly novel suggests that both private reading and reading at court was intended. Those works written in short lines were presumably simply read aloud, but in the case of the heroic epics, composed in the forms known as the *Nibelungenstrophe* or the *Kudrunstrophe,* a highly rhythmical reading or possibly a musical rendition must be assumed. Many of these works assumed vast lengths and must have been performed in installments. The divisions of the heroic narratives into *aventiuren* or of Wolfram's romances into books may have been intended to facilitate manageable blocks for public performance. The Dresden manuscript of *Wolfdietrich A* has been shortened from 700 to 333 stanzas with the specific stated purpose of allowing performance from beginning to end at a single sitting. Performance in installments means that a work need not be completed on paper before it is begun in performance. This explains how it is possible that audience reaction to a passage early in a work might be taken into account in a later passage. The most celebrated example of this is Wolfram's two references to the neutral angels guarding the grail; at first he suggests they may be saved, but later recants, apparently because members of his audience objected that this was theologically unorthodox.

Some works are obviously designed for oral use because of the nature of the form. Unequivocal examples are prayers and magic spells, which have power only when the user claims them by the process of enunciation. Likewise, drama as a form only makes sense in the context of oral performance. Medieval drama was a relatively late phenomenon, and began as an embellishment of certain festivals of the Christian year, especially Easter and Corpus Christi. These religious dramas were not written for a theater as such, but rather were produced in the street or market place, or in front of the church. In some cases there is evidence that the congregation processed around the town, visiting a series of stations where different scenes were performed. Sometimes the actors speak, in which case they must have memorized their lines. In other plays, the actors mime while a presenter describes what is happening, and here the text may be read rather than recited. Although drama is not a significant component of German literature much before the fourteenth century, it is in a sense the epitome of an orality arising out of literary creation.

Finally, a form that is clearly literary in its conception but oral in its reception is the sermon. Many medieval German sermons are recorded, offering a fruitful object of study. While the mass was conducted in Latin to emphasize its mystery, the vernacular sermon was extremely important as a means of instilling Christian ideas into the population. Of course, the manuscript collections of sermons that have come down to us were not the medieval equivalent of the script a modern preacher might take into the pulpit. Quite in the tradition of classical rhetoric, medieval sermons were prepared in the scriptorium, but in all probability were then held freely, not read. Rather, the vast corpus of written sermons is to be understood either as records of the work of such famous preachers as Berthold von Regensburg, or as textbook anthologies from which young clerics were to learn their trade. In either case, they are one step removed from the orality of the original preaching situation. Nevertheless, they do reflect actual practice in the preaching of the Gospels and may be thought of as an idealized form of what was one of the most important formalized oral-communicative procedures in the medieval world.

Notes

[1] A vast amount of literature on orality generally has appeared in recent years. In particular, the series *ScriptOralia* (Tübingen: Narr, 1987–) should be noted, which by July 2002 had produced almost 130 volumes of monographs and collections of essays on literacy and orality in various cultures. The Center for Studies in the Oral Tradition (CSOT) at the University of Missouri Columbia produces the journal *Oral Tradition*.

[2] An excellent first introduction to the nature of primary oral societies is Walter J. Ong, *Orality and Literacy: The Technologizing of the Word* (London and New York: Methuen, 1984). The terms "primary" and "secondary orality" were coined by Ong. There are interesting general essays in David R. Olson and Nancy Torrance, eds., *Literacy and Orality* (Cambridge: CUP, 1991).

[3] Albert B. Lord, *The Singer of Tales* (Cambridge, MA: Harvard UP, 1960).

[4] Lord, *Singer of Tales*, 78.

[5] For literature on the Parry-Lord Theory in general, Lord's *Singer of Tales* is the student's first port of call. For Parry's work, see *The Making of Homeric Verse: The Collected Papers of Milman Parry,* ed. Adam Parry (Oxford: Clarendon, 1971). A collection of reprints of milestone essays on oral-formulaic theory will be found in John Miles Foley, ed., *Oral-Formulaic Theory: A Folklore Casebook* (New York and London: Garland, 1990). See also Edward R. Haymes, *A Bibliography of Studies Relating to Parry's and Lord's Oral Theory* (Cambridge, MA: Harvard UP, 1972). Rosalind Thomas, *Literacy and Orality in Ancient Greece* (Cambridge: CUP, 1992) has a useful "bibliographical essay" (171–75); John Miles Foley, *The Singer of Tales in Performance* (Bloomington and Indianapolis: Indiana UP, 1995).

[6] Literature on the application of the Parry-Lord Theory to Germanic literature: Robert L. Kellogg, "The South Germanic Oral Tradition," in *Franciplegius: Medieval and Linguistic Studies in Honor of Francis Peabody Magoun,* ed. Jess B. Bessinger and Robert P. Creed (New York: New York UP; London: Allen and Unwin, 1965), 66–74; Michael Curschmann, "Oral Poetry in Medieval English, French and German Literature: Some Notes on Recent Research," *Speculum* 43 (1967): 36–53; Arthur T. Hatto, "Germanic and Kirgiz Heroic Poetry: Some Comparisons and Contrasts," in Brigitte Schludermann et al. (eds.), *Deutung und Bedeutung: Studies in German and Comparative Literature Presented to Karl-Werner Maurer* (The Hague: Mouton, 1973), 19–33; Hans Dieter Lutz, "Zur Formelhaftigkeit mittelhochdeutscher Texte und zur 'theory of oral-formulaic composition,'" *Deutsche Vierteljahresschrift,* 48 (1974): 432–47; Ruth R. H. Firestone, *Elements of Traditional Structure in the Couplet Epics of the Late Middle High German Dietrich Cycle* (Göppingen: Kümmerle, 1975); Teresa Paroli, *Sull'elemento formulare nella poesia Germanica antica* (Rome: Istituto di Glottologia, 1975); Edward R. Haymes, "Oral Composition in Middle High German Epic Poetry," in John Miles Foley (ed.), *Oral Traditional Literature: A*

Festschrift for Albert Bates Lord (Columbus, OH: Slavica, 1980), 341–46; Franz
Bäuml, "The Oral Tradition and Middle High German Literature," *Oral Tradition* 1 (1986) 398–445; on Old English, Francis P. Magoun, Jr., "The Oral-
Formulaic Character of Anglo-Saxon Narrative Poetry," *Speculum* 28 (1953):
446–67; Katherine O'Brien O'Keeffe, "Diction, Variation, the Formula" in
Robert E. Bjork and John D. Niles (eds.), *A Beowulf Handbook* (Lincoln, NE: U
of Nebraska P, 1996), 85–104.

[7] On the *Hildebrandlied* as an adaptation of an oral work, see: Siegfried Gutenbrunner, *Von Hildebrand und Hadubrand* (Heidelberg: Winter, 1976); Ralph
W. V. Elliott. "Byrhtnoth and Hildebrand: A Study in Heroic Technique," *Comparative Literature* 14 (1962): 53–70; Alain Renoir, "The Armor of the *Hildebrandslied: An Oral-Formulaic Point of View,*" *Neuphilologische Mitteilungen* 78
(1977): 389–95; Alain Renoir, "Fragment: An Oral-Formulaic Non-definition,"
New York Literary Forum 8–9 (1981): 39–50; on the gradual transition away
from formulaic literature, see the literary histories, especially: Joachim Heinzle et
al, *Geschichte der deutschen Literatur von den Anfängen bis zum Beginn der
Neuzeit,* vol. 2/ii: *Wandlungen und Neuansätze im 13. Jahrhundert (1220/30–
1280/90)* (Königstein: Athenäum 1984); Ursula Liebertz-Grün, *Aus der Münd-
lichkeit in die Schriftlichkeit: Höfische und andere Literatur 750–1320* (Reinbek bei
Hamburg: Rowohlt, 1988); on formulaic elements in the *Nibelungenlied,* see
Arthur T. Hatto, "Medieval German," in Arthur T. Hatto, ed., *Traditions of He-
roic and Epic Poetry* 1: *The Traditions* (London: Modern Humanities Research
Association, 1980), 165–95; Edward R. Haymes, "Chevalerie und alte maeren:
Zum Gattungshorizont des 'Nibelungenliedes,'" *GRM* 34 (1984): 369–84; Alois
Wolf, *Heldensage und Epos: Zur Konstituierung einer mittelalterlichen volks-
sprachlichen Gattung im Spannungsfeld von Mündlichkeit und Schriftlichkeit)*
(Tübingen: Narr, 1995), especially section V.

[8] On reservations about the applicability of the theory, see: Jeff Opland, *Anglo-
Saxon Oral Poetry: A Study of the Traditions* (New Haven and London: Yale UP,
1980); Michael Curschmann, "The Concept of the Oral Formula as an Impediment to our Understanding of Medieval Oral Poetry," *Medievalia et Humanistica*
NS 8 (1977): 63–76.

[9] An indispensable tool for studying motifs from folk culture is the Stith Thompson index and its analogues: Stith Thompson, *Motif-Index of Folk Literature: A
Classification of Narrative Elements in Folktales, Ballads, Myths, Fables, Medieval
Romances, Exempla, Fabliaux, Jest-Books and Local Legends,* rev. ed. (Blooming-
ton: Indiana UP, and Copenhagen: Rosenkilde and Bagger, 1955–58). Stith
Thompson catalogues European folk motifs according to types, and other indices
to folk tales from other parts of the world use his system, so that cross-referencing
is easy. See also Antti Aarne, *Verzeichnis der Märchentypen* (1910), translated by
Stith Thompson as *The Types of the Folk-Tale* (2nd rev. ed., Helsinki: Suomalainen
Tiedeakatemia, 1964); János Honti, *Studies in Oral Epic Tradition* (Budapest:
Akadémiai Kiadó, 1975); Leander Petzoldt and Siegfried de Rachewiltz, eds.,
*Studien zur Volkserzählung: Berichte und Referate des ersten und zweiten Sympo-
sions zur Volkserzählung Brunnenburg/Südtirol 1984/85* (Frankfurt am Main:
Lang, 1987); Rosmarie Thee Morewedge, "Orality, Literacy, and the Medieval

Folktale," in Ursula Schaefer and Edda Spielmann, eds., *Varieties and Conse-quences of Literacy and Orality /Formen und Folgen von Schriftlichkeit und Mundlichkeit: Franz H. Bäuml zum 75. Geburtstag* (Tübingen: Narr, 2001), 85–106.

[10] On these minor forms, see for example: Flemming G. Andersen, Otto Hol-zapfel, and Thomas Pettitt. *The Ballad as Narrative: Studies in the Ballad Tradi-tions of England, Scotland, Germany, and Denmark* (Odense: Odense UP, 1982); F. H. Whitman, *Old English Riddles* (Ottawa: Canadian Federation for the Hu-manities, 1982); Peter and Iona Opie, *The Lore and Language of Schoolchildren* (Oxford: OUP, 1959).

[11] Franz Bäuml, "Varieties and Consequences of Medieval Literacy and Illiteracy," *Speculum* 55 (1980): 237–65.

[12] On the transition to literacy, see: Dennis H. Green, "The Beginnings of Liter-acy in the Early Germanic World," in Schaefer and Spielmann, *Varieties and Con-sequences of Literacy and Orality,* 185–98. On the impact of literacy on medieval society, see for example the essays in Ursula Schaefer, *Schriftlichkeit im frühen Mittelalter* (Tübingen: Narr, 1993); Werner Röcke and Ursula Schaefer, eds., *Mündlichkeit — Schriftlichkeit — Weltbildwandel: Literarische Kommunikation und Deutungsschemata von Wirklichkeit in der Literatur des Mittelalters und der frühen Neuzeit* (Tübingen: Gunter Narr, 1996); Will Erzgräber and Sabine Volk, eds., *Mündlichkeit und Schriftlichkeit im englischen Mittelalter* (Tübingen: Narr, 1988). See also the chapter on runes, below.

[13] On literacy as a criterion for categories in medieval society, see Michael Richter, "Kommunikationsprobleme im lateinischen Mittelalter," *Historische Zeitschrift* 222 (1976): 43–80.

[14] Armin Wishard, *Oral Formulaic Composition in the Spielmannsepik: An Analysis of Salman and Morolf* (Göppingen: Kümmerle, 1984).

[15] On pictures see: Michael Curschmann, "*Pictura laicorum litteratura?* Über-legungen zum Verhältnis von Bild und volkssprachlicher Schriflichkeit im Hoch- und Spätmittelalter bis zum Codex Manesse," in H. Keller, K. Grubmüller and N. Staubach, eds., *Pragmatische Schriftlichkeit im Mittelalter: Erscheinungsformen und Entwicklungsstufen* (Munich: Fink, 1992), 211–29.

[16] On the orality of medieval German literature: Manfred Günter Scholz, *Hören und Lesen: Studien zur primären Rezeption der Literatur im 12. und 13. Jahrhun-dert* (Wiesbaden: Steiner, 1980) and D. H. Green, *Medieval Listening and Read-ing: The Primary Reception of German Literature 800–1300* (Cambridge: CUP, 1994). "Primary reception" is Scholz's term, meaning the form of reception in-tended by the author at the time of composition.

Kylver rune-stone, Gotland, Sweden, fifth century

Noleby Stone, Skaraborgs län, Sweden, sixth century

Runic

Klaus Düwel

RUNES ARE THE NAME given to the earliest Germanic written characters, characters that differ from any modern alphabet. Their precise origin remains unknown, though it is assumed that they were based on a Mediterranean alphabet (Greek, Latin, or Northern Italic), Latin because of the great impact of Roman culture on Northern Europe being the most probable. In any case, the several related Northern Italic alphabets used in inscriptions found in the Alps from the fourth to the first century B.C. demonstrate the most obvious parallels to runic shapes. The earliest extant runes can be dated archeologically to the second century A.D., but it is assumed that the use of runes predates this period.

The term rune is documented in various individual Germanic languages (for example Gothic *rūna* Old High German *rūna(stab)*, Old English *rūn*, Old Norse *rún*) and means primarily "secret." According to epigraphic and literary evidence they are considered to be "descended from the gods" (as recorded on the sixth-century Noleby stone in southern Sweden). Other sources suggest the god Odin invented or discovered them (thus the Norse poem known as "The Words of the High One," *Hávamál* stanza 138–39). The myth that a god created the script is widespread and is the basis of the idea of the "power of writing in belief and superstition."[1] Runic writing is, like any other script, a means of communication that can be used for profane and sacred as well as magical purposes.

The usual arrangement of the twenty-four runes does not follow a formal alphabet, but represents an independent and characteristic sequence that, taken from the sound value of its first six characters, is called the *futhark:*

ᚠ	ᚢ	ᚦ	ᚨ	ᚱ	ᚲ	ᚷ	ᚹ
f	u	þ (th)	a	r	k	g	w (ƿ)

ᚺ	ᚾ	ᛁ	ᛃ	ᛇ	ᛈ	ᛉ	ᛋ
h	n	i	j	ï	p	z (R)	s

ᛏ	ᛒ	ᛖ	ᛗ	ᛚ	ᛜ	ᛞ	ᛟ
t	b	e	m	l	ŋ (ng)	d	o

A *futhark* that corresponds essentially to these letters is present, alone or together with other runic inscriptions, on a total of nine monuments from the fifth and sixth centuries, among them the Kylver stone and the bracteates (thin, round, uniface gold medallions which were worn as amulets), from Vadstena and Grumpan in Sweden. The bracteate tradition shows the *futhark* divided into three groups (each of eight runes) or genders (ON *ætt,* pl. *ættir*). This makes it possible to use them as a secret script, in a variety of graphic ways, by indicating firstly the group and then the position within the group.[2] But the cryptographic use is for the older runes only uncertainly attested.

The graphic features of the runes are stave, twig, and hook, which can appear in pairs and be combined in different ways, with the exception of the twig-hook combination. A twig cannot stand alone, though a hook can. In inscriptions there is the tendency to raise the "smaller" runes to the height of the others, which explains some of the variants. There was at first no rule governing the direction of the inscription, although the bidirectional form known as *boustrophedon* was seldom used. The twigs and hooks attached to the left or right-hand side of a stave determined the direction in which the inscription was written. Runes that stand opposite to the direction of the inscription are called reversed runes; runes which are turned upside down are called inverted runes. As in Roman epigraphy, runic script also has ligatures, known as bind-runes.[3] Conventionally the standardized runic forms of the *futhark* are given in an angular form. The reason for this is the assumption that runes were originally conceived to be incised into wooden objects that have not been preserved. This is contradicted on the one hand by the early survival of wooden objects bearing runic inscriptions (the wooden plane from Illerup on the Jutland peninsula, ca. A.D. 200) and on the other by the contemporaneous rounded forms found on metal objects (ᛟ ᛃ on shield-mount 2 from Illerup). Angular and rounded forms could be peculiarities of particular runic writers, but they appear to be determined primarily by the nature of the material on which they were inscribed, as there are runic inscriptions on such different materials as stone, metal, wood, bone, and leather. Associated terminology[4] appears in the Germanic *wrītan (Eng. write, Germ. reißen) to suggest inscription on metal while *faihian "to color, to paint" indicates the painting-in of (stone) inscriptions.

Each grapheme (single character) corresponds to a phoneme (single sound). This precise reproduction of the Germanic phonemic system by the *futhark* is commonly stressed, namely "that there was a near-perfect fit between the twenty-four runes of the older *futhark* and the distinctive speech sounds of the language or languages of the runic inscriptions that predate ca. A.D. 550–650."[5] The conversion of a runic character into a Latin letter is called transliteration, and such transliterations are printed in bold type. In addition to its sound value, each rune also represents a *Begriffswert* (semantic value)[6] which is identical to the name of the individual rune, for example **f** = Germanic *fehu* (cattle, property), **u** = *ūruz* (aurochs, the now extinct wild ox), **o** = *ōþalan/ōþilan* (inherited property). Clear evidence of the epigraphic use of *Begriffsrunen* (ideographic runes, where the rune-name rather than the rune's sound value is to be read) is present in the line "Haduwolf gave **j**," the last rune meaning "a (good) year" (Stentoften stone, southern Sweden, seventh century). One assumes that the rune-names had always been associated with the runes even though these names are only documented in manuscripts from the eighth century. The relevant main sources are medieval runic poems with a mnemonic function. The reconstruction of the rune-names in the earliest Germanic form is disputed. In the following table[7] entries with a question-mark are speculative.

f	*fehu*	cattle, (movable) property
u	*ūruz*	aurochs (manly strength?)
þ	*þurisaz*	Thurse, giant (terrible, pernicious force)
a	*ansuz*	the deity Anse, Ase
r	*raidō*	journey, riding, carriage
k	*kaunan* (?)	ulcer, illness
g	*gebō*	gift
w	*wunjō* (?)	joy
h	*haglaz* masc./*haglan* neut.	hail (sudden ruin)
n	*naudiz*	need, necessity, constraint of fortune
i	*īsaz* masc./*īsan* neut.	ice
j	*jēran*	(good) year
ï	*īwaz*	yew-tree
p	*perþō* (?)	a fruit-tree?
z/R	*algiz*	elk (defence, protection?)

s	*sōwilō*	sun
t	*tīwaz*	Tyr (the old sky-god)
b	*berkanan*	birch-twig
e	*ehwaz*	horse
m	*mannaz*	man
l	*laguz*	water
ŋ	*ingwaz*	god of the fertile year
d	*dagaz*	day
o	*ōþalan/ōþilan*	inherited property

The sequence of the runes in the *futhark,* which deviates from the "alphabetical" order found elsewhere, may result from the rearrangement for mystical purposes of pairs of letters in a pre-existing alphabet upon which it was modeled.[8]

Runic script has been in use continuously from the numerous inscribed objects found in bog-lands (Illerup, Thorsberg, Nydam on the Jutland peninsula) dating from around A.D. 200 until well into the modern era, in certain regions of Scandinavia even as late as the nineteenth century. Given this unbroken continuity, it was not necessary to decipher the runic script as laboriously as was the case with other ancient writing systems. Furthermore, since the sixteenth century, studies and collections have been made by antiquarian scholars. Johan Göransson's *Bautil* of 1750[9] with its illustrations of around 1200 Swedish rune-stones is still of significance. For the original of the now lost golden Gallehus horn, eighteenth-century engravings are our only source. Pre-academic study was elevated primarily by Wimmer[10] in the nineteenth century to a scientific level that remains to a large extent determinative to the present day. Wimmer recognized the correct chronological sequence from the older to the younger *futhark.* Wilhelm Grimm[11] deduced as early as 1821 that there must have been German runic monuments; these were then later discovered. At the end of the nineteenth century, national editions of runic inscriptions were begun in Scandinavia[12] of which the Swedish one[13] is not yet complete, while the less substantial Danish corpus[14] will soon reach its third edition. The history of research shows that runic script and monuments have been used for ideological and political purposes, in the seventeenth century by Sweden and Denmark, and in the twentieth by Germany, the use of runic signs for the SS being the most familiar.[15] In the second half of the twentieth century, runic research increased greatly, and international symposia and the academic journal *Nytt om runer* (University of Oslo, Norway) which has appeared annually with a bibliography since 1986, attest to the variety of research interests and activities. Runology, although it is not an established university discipline as such, has developed into a wide-ranging subject area.

From a period of approximately 1500 years, through the times of the migration period, the Vikings, and the Middle Ages — each with its own particular modification of the runes — around 6500 runic monuments have been preserved. They are to be found from Greenland in the north to Byzantium and Piraeus in the south, from Greenland in the west to Lake Lagoda and the Dnieper estuary in the east. The main area of concentration is Scandinavia: Sweden has 3600 examples (of these 2400 are rune-stones, 1200 of these in Uppland alone, the area with the greatest density of runes), Norway approximately 1600, Denmark about 850, Greenland over 100, and 96 in Iceland. These are followed by England, with around 90 (discounting runic coins) from the period of the fifth to the eleventh centuries, and Germany with around 80 from the Merovingian period (predominantly sixth century). The number of Scandinavian inscriptions on the British Isles is in excess of 100, with 17 in Ireland. The Frisian corpus is quite modest at 20. There has been no authenticated find of a runic inscription in North America, despite strenuous efforts to find them. The case of the spurious inscription on the Kensington stone is rather alarming,[16] and reports of runes in South America[17] are unequivocally the stuff of legend. Striking are new runic inscriptions by Anglo-Saxon pilgrims in Italy and of Nordic origin in the Hagia Sophia in Istanbul.

Details of the numbers of runes are usually approximations, and it is not always possible to distinguish beyond doubt between runes, rune-like symbols, and non-runes.[18] Sometimes inscriptions that are held by some to be forgeries are included, and sometimes omitted. In Scandinavia, the total numbers depend on whether one does or does not include the post-Reformation runic inscriptions (around 350 of them in the Dalarna region alone). In England and Denmark there are coins with runic legends that may be listed in the runic corpus or treated as a separate group. Where multiple examples are made from a single die-stamp, one might take the number of die-stamps or the number of impressions made with them. This is true of bracteates and for runic die-stamps in general, as are known on pottery (Spong Hill, fifth century) and on weapons (Illerup spearhead, ca. A.D. 200).[19]

The runic period that covers inscriptions in the older *futhark* extends from around A.D. 200–700, and from these five hundred years, at least 350 inscriptions have thus far been discovered. This figure is reached only if one includes around 150 bracteates with purely runic inscriptions. Derolez has asked "what fraction of the total number of inscriptions actually carved over five centuries has survived?,"[20] and he estimates the losses at 25,000.[21] On the other hand, finds of third-century lance- and spearheads demonstrate that only a small percentage of the thousands known are decorated with runes, often with silver inlays. These take the form of poetic and magical names such as **raunijaʀ** (tester) (Øvre Stabu), **tilarids** (goal pursuer) (Kowel), **ranja** (attacker, router) (Dahmsdorf) or **wagnijo** (the runner) (Illerup, Vimose), which put the function of the weapon, namely to test the opposing weapons and thereby test and attack the enemy, into words. One can well imagine such ceremonial weapons being used for the ritual of opening of battle by hurling a spear over or into the enemy's army, a ritual based upon the example of the god, Odin (*Vǫluspá*, stanza 24; *Hlǫðskviða*, stanza 27f.).[22]

Among artifacts recovered from the older runic period, several complexes of finds may be distinguished:

1. **Bog finds**. In the bogs of southern Scandinavia and northern Germany (Illerup, Vimose, Thorsberg, Nydam) numerous objects, among them some bearing runes, have been found.[23] They date from around A.D. 200. According to current views, these objects deposited in the bog were votive offerings of war booty that the native defenders had taken from the defeated invaders. However, it is equally imaginable that the invaders were victorious and made a sacrificial offering of the spoils of war captured from the defenders in some existing holy place or shrine.[24] This question is of significance since all speculation about the origins of runic script begins with geographical location of the earliest recorded items.

2. **Grave finds**. Six fibulae from around A.D. 200, with personal names or the name of a rune-master, as well as roughly scratched inscriptions, have been recovered from the graves of women from the social elite class.[25]

3. **Bracteates**. The more than 900 golden bracteates[26] of the migration period form a separate and specific group. These may be grouped typologically according to ornamentation: A = man's head in profile; B = full-length figure or group of figures; C = man's head in profile above a quadruped; D = stylized representation of monsters; F = quadrupeds. Runes can be found on A-, B-, C-, and F-types, but predominantly on C-types. According to Hauck's iconographic research (most recently 2002)[27] the figure portrayed is that of Wodan/Odin who appears in various roles (Mars, divine physician) and is depicted on the A-bracteates, in imitation of the imperial image on gold medallions, as a divine prince. On the C-bracteates he is portrayed as divine healer of Balder's fallen foal, aided by animal-like helpers. This act is invoked in mythical analogy to the second Merseburg Charm, discussed elsewhere in this volume.

For the interpretation of the inscriptions on bracteates there is (and this is unique to the older runic period), a frame of reference in late classical magical practice as recorded in Egyptian magical papyri of the third to the sixth century. From this the significance of the true, secret name of a spirit is vital for the success of the magical process. The language of "the gods and the spirits"[28] exhibits expressions and names which, even though they may appear meaningless or incomprehensible to humans, "all, without exception, have their meaning and significance, but naturally only for the gods."[29] The spirits, beings that stand midway between the humans and the gods, use this code in speech and writing.[30] Many of the bracteate inscriptions that remain incomprehensible to humans are to be placed and "understood" in this communicative sense.[31]

4. **Individual finds** such as the Kowel spearhead already referred to represent a problematic category. In this group are such familiar pieces as the golden neck-ring from Pietroassa (now Pietroasele in Romania).[32] The standard interpretation of the runes on this ring, which was cut in pieces after a robbery, is: *Gutanī ō[þal] wī[h] hailag* (property of the Gothic people, sacred [and] inviolate), or alternatively *Gutan[ī] Iowi hailag* (consecrated to Jupiter of the Goths). This cannot be maintained after a close examination of the part of the ring which was cut, where only a **j**-rune ❖ or possibly a **ŋ**-rune ◇ can have stood. A **j**-rune can be interpreted as a *Begriffsrune,* an ideographic rune to be read as the rune-name, but it is still unclear what "(good) year of the Goths, sacred and inviolate" might have meant.[33]

The most important individual find among the older runic inscriptions is the golden horn of Gallehus. The carefully engraved inscription on the brim states: *ek HléwagastiR hóltijaR hórna táwido* "I, Leugast (Greek *Kleoxenos*) son/descendant of Holt (or: wood/forest dweller) made the horn." Efforts to interpret this verse inscription in perfect *Stabreim* on the precious, richly decorated horn as anything other than a maker's formula inscription have been futile.

5. **Stones**. The runic inscriptions on stones form a larger group with various sub-divisions: loose, transportable stones, stone slabs, pictorial or decorated stones, or fixed bauta-stones (cf. *Hávamál* stanza 72), which are found predominantly in Norway.[34] From the fourth century such bauta-stones can be found with runic inscriptions, and are often linked with grave-sites. The stone and inscription are a memorial to the dead, and additionally are to ensure the peace of the grave, and to protect the grave from intruders and against possible revenants by confining the dead person to the grave.[35] Individually, the interpretations of some inscriptions are controversial, for example, **alu** which appears alone on the Elgesem stone (it was found during the excavation of a grave mound). According to the interpretation of **alu**, it might be a protective formula to preserve the peace of the grave and the dead, or, if **alu** refers to a state of ecstasy, it may have been placed upon the stone "as a symbol of a cult-place."[36] There is hardly a single inscription of the older runic period that has an agreed reading, let alone an agreed interpretation. This uncertainty is true, for example, for one of the longest runic inscriptions on the Norwegian Tune stone dating from around A.D. 400. It runs vertically in two rows on the front side (A) and in three rows on the back (B). With the exception of only a few runes, the actual reading is fairly clear:

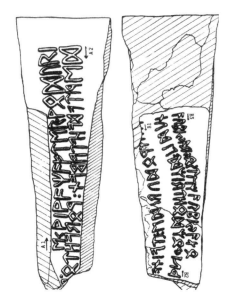

The Tune rune-stone (above)

The Gallehus horn decorations and runic inscription (left)

A   I   **ekwiwaʀafter • woduri**
    II   **dewitadah͡alaiban : worahto • ?** (break)
B   I   (break) **ʀwoduride : staina •**
    II   **þrijoʀdohtriʀd͡alidun**
    III   **arbija̱r[** or **si]josteʀarbijano**

The wide range of possible *interpretations,* however, may be illustrated by
the following two: "I Wiw after Wodurid, the bread keeper, wrought [the
runes]. For me(?), Wodurid, three daughters prepared the stone, the inheritance (but) the most distinguished of heirs."[37] And: "I Wiw composed
according to Wodurid, he who supplied the bread; I intended the stone
for Wodurid. Three daughters prepared a pleasant inheritance, the most
favored among the heirs."[38] Grønvik later amended the latter with the
following change: "I Wiw after Wodurid, who provided the bread,
'wrought the rune[s],' intended the stone for Wodurid."[39]

How, then, can such widely varied interpretations (to which others
could be added) come about?

     a.   Different readings determine different interpretations (**arjosteʀ**
or **asijosteʀ**).

     b.   The substitution of the missing part of the inscription at the top
of the stone permits various possibilities.

     c.   Following on from this, the researchers come to differing starting
points for their interpretations (**worahto,** preterite of **wurkian* "to make,
prepare, work, preterite: wrought" or "to compose (in verse)").

     d.   Syntactical breaks are made at differing positions in the inscrip-
tion (AI, II or AI, II, BI).

     e.   Understandings of the cultic and inheritance aspects of burial and
death rites, which can be reconstructed in different ways, distinguish the
individual interpretative approaches.

These problems can be illustrated even more markedly by a second example. The Eggja stone (West Norway, archeological dating ca. A.D. 700)
originally lay with the inscribed side facing down, as the covering stone on a
flat grave. It cannot be ascertained whether this grave had been occupied
and robbed or whether it was a cenotaph, an empty grave as a memorial to
a dead person. Between two long rows of runes running left to right (I +
II) there is the incomplete outline of a horse, the connection of which with
the inscription is questionable. An inverted short third line of runes running
right to left (III) is placed after the horse's tail, between I and II. The inscription in itself is already difficult to read and additionally there are illegi-
ble sections which have been variously amended, leading to a correspondingly diverse dozen or more attempted interpretations since 1919 (among
them several monographs).[40] Individual researchers have offered several at-

tempts at interpretations. Here, two translations may again be used to demonstrate the differences; the first is by Wolfgang Krause:

"I It is not struck by the sun nor is the stone cut with an (iron) knife.
   One shall not *lay* (it) bare, when the waning moon wanders (across the sky).
   May misled men not lay (the stone) *aside*!

II This (stone) (the) man (= the rune-magician) covered with 'corpse-sea' (= blood), smeared with it (= with the blood?) the rowlocks (?) in the 'bore-tired' boat (?).
   As who (= in what form) has the army-Ase (= Odin?) (or: who as a warrior has) come here to the land of warriors (or: of horses)?
   Fish, swimming from the *terrible* river, bird, shrieking *into the enemy host.*

III Protection (**alu**) against the evil-doer!"[41]

We may compare the interpretation by Grønvik,[42] in which the sections are taken in the order II, III, I:

"II The household is shrinking
   over the remainder wīlR casts the wave of death:
   the rowlocks were ground off them
   on the point of the mast weakened by the/in the bore-hole:
   Who led the army
   across into that country?
   The man-fish
   from the current-furrows by Firnøy,
   swimming in the foam,
   from the land with the glowing meadows.
   (May I) always (receive) help when I compose my verse!
   Not by daylight and not with the sword
   shall the carved stone be visited;
   nor shall the man
   who calls the naked corpse
   (and) nor shall confused men visit this resting place!"

Once again, Grønvik[43] made changes, to the beginning of II ("Over my dear ones cast itself the wave of death") and to line III ("[he] who brought prosperity and happiness"). As with the Tune inscription, these very varied interpretations depend on equally varied assumptions and presuppositions:

   a)   Whether it is a grave or a cenotaph.
   b)   The arrangement of the lines of the runes.

c) Deviant reading of not clearly recognizable runes.

d) Varying completion of lacunae in the inscription.

e) Differing division of words/units in the continuously carved inscription.

f) Deviant transcription of individual sequences of runes.

g) Differing approaches to the interpretation of words.

h) Alternative understanding of words as *nomen appellativum* (generic name) or *nomen proprium* (proper name).

i) Alternative interpretation of a sequence as a compound or as a kenning.

j) Varying syntactical divisions

k) Assumptions about magic and cultic, ritual activities surrounding a burial as protection against desecration of the grave or against the return from the grave of the dead person as a revenant.

l) Differing religio-historical and religio-psychological starting points.

While there is agreement that line 1 refers to a ritual act to protect the stone and the grave, yet again a whole range of very different procedures and intentions are assumed for an understanding of line 2:

a) Consecration of the runes and the gravestone by covering them with blood.

b) Burial of a chieftain with a blood sacrifice and consecration of the boat on which he was carried.

c) Inscription on a cenotaph designed to stop a criminal, who was sunk on a ship in the fjord, from returning as a ghost.

d) The rune-master's call to the god Odin to come to Eggja to accompany the dead warrior to Hel.

e) An act of remembrance for a dead man who has vanquished naval warriors, spilt their blood, and sunk their ship.

f) Burial in the presence of the dead man's household retinue of someone who, while travelling by ship, had suffered a broken mast.[44]

Thus the enigma of the Eggja inscription, despite all the efforts of leading runologists (Magnus Olsen, Lis Jacobsen, Arthur Nordén, Gerd Høst, Wolfgang Krause, Niels Åge Nielsen, Ottar Grønvik), is still unsolved and will probably remain so.

A general characterization of the inscriptions in the older *futhark* by highlighting their magic, and in some cases cultic, aspect or by stressing the profane content of their message is difficult to establish. On the one hand, one has to consider the nature of the object that bears the inscription since the inscription on a bracteate worn as an amulet and promising the wearer protection (for example, Raum Køge, IK 98: *gibu auja* [I grant protection]) is to be assessed differently to a commemorative inscription on a rune-stone (Bø stone: "Hnabud's Grave"). On the other, the corresponding interpretation also depends upon the understanding, perhaps even the preconception, of the runologist making the interpretation. Our restricted knowledge of the peculiarities of an earlier culture, about which, apart from the limited runic self-documentation, we may make judgments only based on reports from outside the culture, is a problem. Insofar as relatively plausible interpretation attempts have been made, older runic remains comprise primarily the recording of names (often as a statement of ownership), makers' inscriptions, magical inscriptions on amulets, cultic and ritual acts, memorials to the dead, and inscriptions in which a mastery of the skill of writing runes as such is expressed. Only a few people were familiar with this art. Among these, the *erila*ᴿ is particularly prominent. On the Bratsberg buckle of around A.D. 500 there is the single inscription e͡kerila͡ᴿ, and the formula *ek erila*ᴿ is to be found on a total of eight monuments, all of them from the sixth century. Whether *erila*ᴿ is linked with the name of a people, the (H)erulians (protogermanic **erulaz*), is disputed. *erila*ᴿ is not the name of a tribe, but a designation of some rank or title. It refers to an elevated man who has knowledge of the runic art (rune-master) and may have the function of a priest. In later times this may have become a secular office, corresponding to ON *jarl,* although the transition from *erila*ᴿ to *jarl* is difficult to accept on phonological grounds.

The difficulty, frequently referred to, of reaching any interpretation, let alone a generally acceptable one can be illustrated once more with a methodologically instructive case, but this may be prefaced with a few words on the runologist's working methods. New runic inscriptions are usually chance finds, and these are almost exclusively loose objects. At the excavation site or later in the museum the discovered objects are cleaned. Since this cannot always be done immediately, runes are sometimes not discovered on objects in museums until years or even decades later. If, during cleaning, script-like symbols appear, the piece is handed to an expert to determine whether they are runes or just rune-like symbols. If they are runes, then they are carefully examined on the original piece (the technical term for which is "autopsy") and the characters identified. The form of the runes allows a rough chronological classification. To establish an exact dating, the runologist works together with an archeologist. After the reading has been determined, the philological part of the work begins. Especially on monuments from the older runic period, word-dividers are often not present in the text. Consequently, the division into individual words of a continuous inscription (*scriptio continua*) can be a difficult task. According to the location of the find, the attempt will be made, on the basis of the familiar runic vocabulary from that area and using dictionaries and onomastic reference texts, together with literary sources, to make some overall sense of the words discovered. In the course of this, new difficulties can arise if unknown forms of names or grammatical features should appear, or a word is used for the first time.

In the linguistic, philological analysis, runic inscriptions should be analyzed synchronously as textual evidence from a certain period. They have a specific (denotative) function, and only on another level do they have other linguistic and textual functions, such as magic or number symbolism. They follow rules of a universal, typological nature, as well as the rules of an individual language, rules that can be determined for any text from a language, including inscriptions.[45] The epigraphic context is of primary importance, and the aim is a linguistic structure that is convincing in itself. If possible, the communicative situation of an inscribed text should also be investigated: in addition to communication between human beings, there is also the question of communication with supernatural beings.[46]

However, the extra-graphical context is also of importance for analysis and for interpretation. This includes, on the one hand, the relationship between the inscription and the object that bears it: are the runes on the object itself or on a repaired part, are they on the obverse or reverse? Were the runes placed on the object as part of the manufacturing process or in the course of the use of an inscribed object? On the other, the relationship between the object bearing the rune and the contemporary cultural milieu needs to be elucidated. With loose objects: provenance, routing (imported or exported article), usage, nature of the deposition, whether accidental or intentional (funerary gifts, deposition in a bog, store), nature of the find (*in situ* or in a disturbed site, completely or partly plundered), belonging to a cremation or inhumation grave. With runic standing stones: original location, possible change of location, original position (standing or lying), an individual stone or part of an arrangement of stones, the natural features of the location, any link with a grave (flat or mound grave) or a grave field, any link with special categories of find (such as hoards) in the vicinity.[47]

In addition one must always take into account the fact that certain pre-suppositions of the runologists play a role, suppositions that can lead to different, not to say sometimes contradictory interpretations. These can be characterized by such contrastive pairs as "skeptical — imaginative," "mundane — magical," "profane — sacred" and so on.[48] It makes a difference whether a runic inscription is processed by somebody with linguistic, paleographic, cultural-historical, or religious-historical interests without clearly expressing this interest.

A bronze fragment of a shield-boss recovered from the Thorsberg bog (Schleswig, ca. A.D. 200) shows on the reverse side of the rim six runes **aisgRh** running from right to left. These cannot be interpreted, and are therefore now considered to be a non-linguistic, meaningless sequence of runes. This is, it is true, a modern view; it is unknown what understanding of runes or what "message" (and to whom it was directed) this runic engraving is based upon. At one level, Antonsen[49] understands *aisk-z* as "challenger," reads **h** as an ideographic *Begriffsrune* "hail" in the sense of "a hail of spears and arrows" and thereby establishes a weapon name that puts into words the significance of the shield. On a second level, the attempt has been made to create, by the insertion of vowels into the sequence of consonants, a comprehensible word: *ais(i)g(a)R* "the raging, furious one" to which is added the abbreviated *h(aitē)* (= "I am called") or the ideographic "hail" rune, again resulting in the name of a weapon. Other scholars, meanwhile, read the runes as an owner's inscription or as the name of a rune-master. All these attempts work with suppositions that cannot be demonstrated unequivocally. Taking an archeological approach, it has been deduced from the regularity particularly of the **a**-rune on the distorted upper part, that the shield-boss was engraved with runes after it had become distorted and before it was deposited in the bog. If this is the case, one can discount the interpretations that saw here an owner's or weapon name. At the same time, it could still be the name of a rune-master. With regard to the overall interpretation of bog deposits as votive offerings to the gods, the inscription could be linked to the one god that corresponds to the concept of rage, wrath, namely Wodan/Odin (from **wōþ-* "raging anger," cf. German *Wut*). In the first of these cases the shield would have been engraved in the area of origin of the peoples who were defeated when invading the place where the deposition was made. In the second case, by contrast, it would have been engraved later by victorious local people who had captured the weapons from the invaders. None of the theories about the deposition in the bog and the possible interpretation of the inscription can be demonstrated with any certainty.[50] Interestingly, a Roman shield-boss with the punch-marked inscription AEL[IVS] AELIANVS was also recovered from the Thorsberg bog. Although at first the possibility was considered that the Roman custom of inscribing a name had been adopted in the runic examples,[51] further attempts at interpretation indicate essential differences between these two written cultures.

This is confirmed by a comparison between the approximately eighty inscriptions making up a continental (southern Germanic) corpus from the older runic period, and the roughly contemporary, though not so extensive group of Latin inscriptions from the same area.[52] Runic monuments from the fifth century and especially after the first third of the sixth century in the southwestern area (Alemannia) differ from the Scandinavian examples previously characterized. There are hardly any magical inscriptions among them, apart from one obvious instance of alphabet magic to prevent a return from the dead by a female revenant on the Beuchte fibula.[53] There have, however, been more recent discussion of the "runes of the Merovingian period as a source for the survival of late classical Christian and non-Christian script-magic."[54] In the main these involve the inscription of personal names with attached wishes and formulaic blessings referring to human relationships of various kinds. The move toward Christianity and the acceptance of the new creed are documented, according to one of the new interpretations, by the inscriptions from Nordendorf I, the demonization of the old gods Wodan and Donar, as well as the condemnation of the stag-dance rituals on the Pforzen buckle, and especially the wish "God for you, Theophilus" expressed on the Osthofen disc-fibula. The belt buckle (second half of the sixth century) recovered from a man's grave in Pforzen in 1992 is in this connection of particular interest, offering as it does the longest inscription and the first well-rendered line in alliterative verse in continental runic inscriptions: *Áigil andi Áilrun élahu[n] gasókun* (Aigil and Ailrun have condemned the deer [the deer costume of the *cervulum facere*]). The second half-line has **ltahu** of which ᛁᛏ was possibly intended as the bind rune **el͡**.[55] Overall, it seems reasonable to say that Alemannic runic culture was associated with women.

The golden disc brooch from Chéhéry, which has Latin and runic inscriptions (not bilingually matched, however) is unique. Although its poor state of preservation, particularly of the runes on the reverse side, does not permit an interpretation, this brooch is important because, as part of a richly equipped grave, it documents a knowledge of Latin and runic script among those close to a woman of high social rank.[56] Summarizing the runic and Latin epigraphic finds, the following contrasts emerge:

Latin Inscriptions
- Status symbols in graves of the upper class
- on objects belonging to men and women
- on the front
- mostly inscribed during production
- of a public, representative character
- formed an essential part of the inscribed object

Runic Inscriptions
- Status symbols in graves of the middle class
- predominantly on women's objects
- on the back
- mostly inscribed after the production of the object
- concealed, intended as a private communication
- of incidental nature

– often show some relationship to the object	– do not demonstrate any recognizable relationship to the object
– have the character of a communicative message	– show names, which are not unequivocally linked to the object's maker, giver, owner, or the inscriber of the runes
– record the making, the nature, and the function of the object	– sometimes stress the ability to make inscriptions
– mostly document the acceptance of Christianity	– document the move toward the new religion (linked with syncretism)

"What kind of science is runology?" asks Antonsen provocatively.[57] One answer is: "Runology is paleography, linguistics, archeology, and mythology,"[58] but paleographic (today one would term it graphemic) analysis take precedence, before linguists and religious specialists process the inscriptions. Antonsen, who put the question, clearly considers "the linguist to be the primary actor in deciphering and interpreting runic inscriptions."[59] A little earlier, in 1994, Barnes in his "On Types of Argumentation in Runic Studies"[60] passed a similar judgment. His various subheadings criticize some of the more common shortcomings in runological studies: "unsubstantiated claims and assertions — ignorance of other disciplines and lack of intellectual rigor — conjecture quoted as fact — reliance on unestablished or questionable principles." A little later, Braunmüller too called for "a consistently synchronic linguistic analysis of runic inscriptions."[61] There is criticism of the lack of any methodological basis, lack of terminological precision and (therefore) an arbitrary interpretative approach.[62] Does the solution really lie in the strict observation of linguistic principles? Is there an expectation which is typical for that of the neogrammarians? Precise, unambiguous linguistic terminology certainly aids understanding. It is necessary to follow these steps in sequence: transliteration, phonetic and phonemic transcription, production of text with reference to a linguistic status, linking to familiar lexemes from an individual language, possibly etymological recovery, all leading to an interpretation which considers the supralinguistic context. However, one must bear in mind that the older runic inscriptions stem from an archaic, oral culture whose writing habits are only partially known. Linguistic processes of change are only sketchily apparent, and this across wide geographical areas in which there will have been regional differences.[63] The paucity of recovered finds often only offers names which are not easily susceptible to linguistic analysis. There seem to be contradictory linguistic forms. In essence, one must ask whether modern linguistic procedures are exclusively appropriate for the understanding of archaic inscriptions. The impression sometimes arises that linguistic analyses strain the linguistic record and become an artistic game. Linguistic argumentation leads to improbability when the phonemic system that the oldest *futhark* inscriptions are based upon is traced back to the middle of the first millennium B.C., thereby establishing the origin of runic writing in a pre-classical Greek alphabet.[64]

The question of the origin of runic writing was already being debated during the first, pre-academic phase of runic research. From the late nineteenth century on, theories have been voiced that have again occasioned heated debate over the last decade. There are three basic principles at issue. First, that runic writing neither arose *ex nihilo* nor from purely Germanic conditions. Second, that the stimulus or model was a Mediterranean alphabet. And third, that the starting point for all considerations has to be the geographical area and chronological setting of the oldest runic remains. Assuming that some alphabet was taken as a model, various aspects are stressed: the cultural-historical (the cultural status); the formal (matching the inventory of symbols); the linguistic (phonemic correspondences); the (comprehensive) alphabet-historical (considering the direction of the script, writing of double sounds, ligatures, word division etc.). In all authoritative works on the subjects, the following five questions emerge about why the runic script was created:

1. Which alphabet was taken as a model, and from where?
2. At what time was this done?
3. In which area?
4. By what person/people or ethnos?
5. For what purpose?

Some answers have been suggested:

1. The following have been suggested as a model for the runic alphabet: first, Latin capitals (later also perhaps cursive).[65] "The Latin theory is supported by the oldest concentration of runic memorials, the powerful Roman cultural influence, as well as the obvious similarity to corresponding Latin letters, above all the runes for **f**, **r**, **b**, and **m**."[66] Second, the classical Greek alphabet or cursive script, and also, particularly in American research, an archaic Greek alphabet from the sixth century B.C.[67] A problem with this chronologically very early start for runic script is some explanation for the lack of any finds for a period covering at least 500 years. And, third, an origin from Northern Italic alphabets was first intensively investigated in the twentieth century. It is favored in Italian

research,[68] and has more recently been advanced by epigraphic scholars[69] and linguists.[70]

2.   Chronologically, the creation of runes pre-dates the oldest runic inscription, but which is the oldest — the Meldorf fibula (ca. A.D. 50), the Vimose comb (archeologically, ca. A.D. 160), or is it the Øvre Stabu spearhead (second half of the second century A.D.)? How far one can go back from there depends, on the one hand, upon an assumption of a "dark" age of fifty to one hundred years in which there are no recorded finds, and, on the other, upon the assumption that the runic script had, because of its lack of rounded forms, been created to be incised into wood, and that such perishable wood had not been preserved. This assumption cannot be confirmed because of the preservation of early inscriptions on wood in bogs.

3.   The geographical location for the origin of runes varies depending on the alphabetic model that one chooses. On a larger scale, only objects with Latin inscriptions can be demonstrated to have entered the Germanic *barbaricum* — therefore southern Scandinavia seems likely; the *Germani* could only have become familiar with other alphabets in the areas from whence they first spread.

4.   Whether a single individual or a group of people created runic script cannot be ascertained. Ethnically, depending on one's theory, it could have belonged to the Angles, Herulians, Marcomanni or — if attested — to ethnic groups who migrated further to the southeast, though for chronological reasons the Goths can be eliminated.

5.   On the question of the purpose for which runic script was invented, one can only speculate: as a cultic script or as a magic symbol, as a profane means of communication (above all in trade, in which context Moltke[71] hoped to find a consignment note written in runes on wood), or for divination. Here too it is a question of *quot capita tot sensus*. To offer here a personal view, the five aspects can plausibly be combined: runic script was created on the basis of a Mediterranean alphabet, most likely Latin, in the time from around the birth of Christ into the first century A.D., in the region of the western Baltic (perhaps with some impulse from the Rhine area) by one or more "intellectuals" as a means of communication for secular, but also for sacral and magic use.

In this context, one may ask which is the oldest runic inscription of all, and then one must preface any such speculation with the observation that all attempts to make datings runologically (by the form of the characters, phonological value, direction of the script, splitting of words, ligature, script conventions) or linguistically (phonological change, syncope etc.) can at best achieve only a relative chronology.[72] Archeological datings, which are, however, also susceptible to variation in the course of research, form a definite basis. The large numbers of objects recovered primarily from graves but also from bogs and hoards permits an adequately differentiated typology and, on the basis of this, a reliable chronology,[73] which is supported by specific investigative methods (radiocarbon-dating, dendrochronology — dating by the use of tree-rings). The attempted dating of standing stones and *in situ* rock carvings is problematic if these are not closely linked to a grave containing gifts or offerings. With archeological dating it must also be clear what is being dated: the date of production or of its deposition in the grave, perhaps even the period of time that an object was in use.[74] A runic inscription can be carved on an object at any time during its existence. Only in a few cases is there any clear evidence. Thus, for example, the runes **eho** inscribed on the Donzdorf fibula, and also the similar decorations on the reverse, were engraved during the production process,[75] while on the Beuchte fibula, which had been used for a long time and was very worn, the runes show hardly any signs of wear and were inscribed only shortly before the deposition as a grave offering/gift.[76] For the greater number of loose objects with runes, the inscription can have been made over a long period of use, in the case of inherited pieces as long as half a century. Similar considerations hold true for the early south Scandinavian runic finds from graves and bogs from the period around 200.[77]

The oldest definite inscription, with the runes **harja,** a masculine name-formation from *Hari* (German *Heer* [army])[78] is to be found on the Vimose comb, which Ilkjær[79] dates archeologically to around A.D. 160. Previously the Øvre Stabu lancehead with the magico-poetical spearname **raunijaR**, old Icelandic *reynir* "tester," was thought to be the oldest inscription, dating from the second half of the second century A.D.[80]

In 1979 the chance discovery of the Meldorf fibula was made, a piece that is dated to the first half of the first century A.D. Some consider the tremolo-style markings on the hasp to be ornamentation, others think they are written characters. But what characters? Epigraphers variously see them, depending on their own area of specialization, as runic, Roman majuscule, Greek, or Etruscan script. Since the first publication,[81] there are now different, conflicting views: Latin capitals (or an imitation) versus runes (perhaps proto-runes). The four characters were, correspondingly, read either from left to right or from right to left. The characters IDIN, in Latin, could mean "for Ida" (female) or "for Iddo" (male).[82] The runic reading **hiwi** could be understood as an inscribed dedication to a woman, "for Hiwi," whose function as head of the family (*mater familias*) is possibly alluded to.[83] These and other attempted interpretations are open to question, particularly the most recent suggestion, **irįlį** (for the [rune-]master).[84]

Runology is not at present a formal and independent academic discipline, unlike, for example, epigraphy at some universities. With a few exceptions, runologists are philologists whose specialization in teaching and research is one of the older Germanic languages, or Indo-European philology in general. In this case other individual languages such as Celtic can also play a central role. In the broadest sense, runology is part of the study of Germanic antiquity, though this is no longer an independent subject area in Germany, and it is evident that an exhaustive study of the place and role of runic monuments will only be achieved through interdisciplinary cooperation.[85]

Among runologists a distinction is made between field runologists and desk runologists. Field runologists work primarily on the original objects, especially when, as in Scandinavia with its numerous rune-stones, these are scattered about the countryside. But desk runologists should also examine the originals of the inscriptions they are processing. The findings made in this way can be of great significance for their conclusions. They may, for example, come to a new reading that might provide the basis for a new interpretation. The desk runologists will sometimes discover that a fresh, untreated inscription on a freshly excavated and cautiously cleaned object will be clearer and more definite than after conservation. After decades of being kept in a museum, the legibility of runes, which were readily identifiable at the time when they were discovered, can be severely reduced. It can sometimes even happen that in the course of study a rune can become lost which is then only rediscovered through a new autopsy.[86] And such a direct viewing of the rune is, after all, necessary to demonstrate perhaps that an inscription taken to be genuine is in fact a falsification.[87] But the reverse can also happen, as with the Weser runic bones, which for a long time were suspected to be forgeries but were, with the help of scientific and forensic investigative methods, demonstrated to be genuine.[88]

To return to Antonsen's question, then: what kind of science is runology? The answer is that it is a difficult but rewarding activity in which precision and experience on a solid philological and linguistic basis works in cooperation with the relevant related sciences requiring imagination and deductive powers but also rational, critical control, in order to offer a plausible explanation for the meaning, role, and importance of an inscription and the object that bears the runes. As is so often the case, for the runologist as for other scholars, the best questions often come from outside.

> An archeologist's questions to the runologist:
> Why did anyone write in an illiterate society like the Germanic?
> Why this native alphabet?
> Who wrote? Surely not everybody. Some did, but who?
> Who was able to read the runes?

Did it matter to the magic function that runes were not common
knowledge as long as there was someone around to interpret?
Was the act of writing the prime object of the exercise?
How reliable are the sources?
How can we make them more reliable?
Why were only specific types of objects inscribed? Why spear-/
lanceheads instead of swords? Surely swords were the more
prestigious weapons and there does not seem to be any rule
as to which spearheads got inscriptions. It was not only silver inlaid masterpieces which were inscribed. Why a plane
and not the gold rings (like Pietroasa in the south)?
Is it symptomatic of the social situation that there is something
wrong in practically every inscription written in the old futhark? Does that reflect a still experimenting milieu?[89]

Runologists will hardly be able answer a single one of these questions
with any degree of certainty, but they can, for their part, pose further questions. For example, one might speculate as to how runic writing was
learned and how it was passed on, and what people of what social rank par-
ticipated in this. Further, one needs to explain the relatively standardized
set of symbols which is remarkable given the large geographical area from
which runic monuments originate.[90] Two further questions are whether
there is an acceptable explanation for the fact that the sequence of the runes
in the *futhark* deviates so obviously from sequence of the alphabet and
what function has an inscription consisting only of this *futhark*?

We should not leave the impression that runology is not at all scientific, even though certain work by outsiders might give this impression.[91]
It must not be forgotten that runology belongs to those human sciences
whose aim, within the hermeneutic process, can be of value on an interdisciplinary basis as long as its initial premises are clear and it can present a
transparent working method. Given such a basis, then it is rewarding to
pursue the study of these autochthonous memorials of early writing, these
original and unique documents from an age which is otherwise known to
us only from outside (and almost always partisan) sources.

Translated by Malcolm Read

Notes

[1] Alfred Bertholet, *Die Macht der Schrift in Glauben und Aberglauben* (Berlin:
Akademie-Verlag, 1949).

[2] Wolfgang Krause, *Die Runeninschriften im älteren Futhark* (Göttingen: Vandenhoeck and Ruprecht, 1966), I, 10–29; Klaus Düwel, *Runenkunde*, 3rd ed. (Stutt-

gart and Weimar: Metzler, 2001), 183–88; Raymond I. Page, *An Introduction to English Runes*, 2nd ed. (Woodbridge: Boydell, 1999), 80–88.

[3] Mindy MacLeod, *Bind-Runes: An Investigation of Ligatures in Runic Epigraphy* (Uppsala: Uppsala universitet. Institutionen för nordiska språk, 2001).

[4] Else Ebel, *Die Terminologie der Runentechnik* (Göttingen: E. Ebel, 1963); Rune Palm, *Runor och regionalitet: studier av variation i de nordiska minnesinskrifterna* (Uppsala: Uppsala Universitet, Institution för nordiska språk, 1992).

[5] Michael P. Barnes, "On Types of Argumentation in Runic Studies," in J. E. Knirk (ed.) *Proceedings of the Third International Symposium on Runes and Runic Inscriptions* (Uppsala: Uppsala universitet. Institutionen för nordiska språk, 1994): 11–29, esp. 21; René Dèrolez, "On the 'Otherness' of the Anglo-Saxon Runes and the 'Perfect Fit' of the Fuþark," in *Runeninschriften als Quellen interdisziplinärer Forschung*, ed. K. Düwel (Berlin and New York: de Gruyter, 1998), 103–26, esp. 110–26.

[6] See K. Düwel, "Begriffsrunen," in *RGA*, vol. 2, 150–53.

[7] Adapted from W. Krause, *Die Runeninschriften im älteren Futhark*, I, 4. Cf. K. Düwel, *Runenkunde*, 198–99; R. I. Page, *English Runes*, 63–79. Robert Nedoma, "Runennamen," in *RGA*, vol. 25, 556–62.

[8] Elmar Seebold, "Was haben die Germanen mit den Runen gemacht? Und wieviel haben sie davon von ihren antiken Vorbildern gelernt?" in *Germanic Dialects: Linguistic and Philological Investigations,* ed. B. Brogyanyi and T. Krömmelbein (Amsterdam: Benjamins, 1986), 525–83; E. Seebold, "Fuþark, Beith-Luis-Nion, He-Lamedh, Abǧad und Alphabet. Über die Systematik der Zeichenaufzählung bei Buchstaben-Schriften," in *Sprachen und Schriften des antiken Mittelmeerraums: Festschrift für Jürgen Untermann*, ed. F. Heidermanns, H. Rix and E. Seebold (Innsbruck: Institut für Sprachwissenschaft der Universität Innsbruck, 1993): 411–44.

[9] Johan Göransson, *Bautil* (Stockholm: Salvius, 1750).

[10] Ludvig F. A. Wimmer, *Runeskriftens Oprindelse og Udvikling i Norden* (Copenhagen: V. Priors boghandel, 1874); L. F. A. Wimmer, *Die Runenschrift* translated by F. Holthausen (Berlin: Weidmann, 1887).

[11] Wilhelm C. Grimm, *Über deutsche Runen* (Göttingen: Dieterich, 1821).

[12] *Norges Indskrifter med de ældre Runer,* edited by Sophus Bugge and Magnus B. Olsen (Christiania: Brøgger, 1891–1924); L. F. A. Wimmer, *De danske runemindesmærker,* 4 vols. (Copenhagen: Gyldendal, 1893–1908).

[13] *Sveriges Runinskrifter* published for the Kungliga Vitterhets, Historie och Antikvitets Akademien, vol. I– (Stockholm: Almqvist & Wiksell, 1900–).

[14] *Danmarks Runeindskrifter,* ed. Lis Jacobsen and Erik Moltke (Copenhagen: Munksgaard, 1941–42).

[15] Ulrich Hunger, *Die Runenkunde im Dritten Reich* (Frankfurt am Main: Lang, 1984).

[16] Hertha Marquardt, *Bibliographie der Runeninschriften nach Fundorten,* vol. I (Göttingen: Vandenhoeck and Ruprecht, 1961); see Robert A. Hall Jr., *The Kensington Runestone, Authentic and Important. A Critical Edition* (Lake Bluff, IL: Jupiter Press, 1994): R. Nielsen, R. A. Hall Jr. and J. E. Knirk, "Forum: The Kensington Rune-

stone," *Epigraphic Society Occasional Publications* 23 (1998): 187–265. Cf. J. E. Knirk, review of Hall, *The Kensington Runestone, skandinavistik* 26 (1996): 45–47.

[17] See for example Jacques de Mahieu, ed., *Les inscriptions Runiques Précolombiennes du Paraguay* (Buenos Aires: Instituto de Ciencia del Hombre, 1972).

[18] R. I. Page, *Runes and Runic Inscriptions* (Woodbridge: Boydell, 1995; paperback ed. with new material, 1999), 161–79.

[19] Peter Pieper, "Der Runenstempel von Spong Hill. Pseudorunen oder Runenformel?" *Neue Ausgrabungen und Forschungen in Niedersachsen* 17 (1986): 181–200; and P. Pieper, "Spiegelrunen," in *Runor och runinskrifter* (Stockholm: Almquist & Wiksell, 1987), 67–72.

[20] R. Derolez, "The Origin of the Runes: an Alternative Approach," *Academiae Analecta — Klasse der Letteren* 60 (Brussels: Koninklijke Academie voor Wetenschappen, Letteren en Schone Kunsten van België, 1998), 5.

[21] Personal communication. See on the Anglo-Saxon corpus, R. Derolez, "Runic Literacy among the Anglo-Saxons," in Alfred Bammesberger, ed., *Britain 400–600: Language and History* (Heidelberg: Winter, 1990), 397–436, esp. 400–01.

[22] K. Düwel, "Runeninschriften auf Waffen," in *Wörter und Sachen im Lichte der Bezeichnungsforschung*, ed. Ruth Schmidt-Wiegand (Berlin and New York: de Gruyter, 1981), 128–67.

[23] Marie Stoklund, "Die Runen der römischen Kaiserzeit," in Ulla Lund Hansen, *Himlingøje — Seeland — Europa* (Copenhagen: Det Kongelige Nordiske Oldskriftselskab, 1995), 317–46.

[24] Jan Bemmann, and Güde Hahne, "Ältereisenzeitliche Heiligtümer im nördlichen Europa nach den archäologischen Quellen," in *Germanische Religionsgeschichte — Quellen und Quellenprobleme*, ed. Heinrich Beck, D. Ellmers, and K. Schier (Berlin and New York: de Gruyter, 1992), 29–69, esp. 66–69.

[25] M. Stoklund, "Die Runen der römischen Kaiserzeit," 317–46.

[26] Morten Axboe, Urs Clavadetscher, K. Düwel, Karl Hauck, and Lutz von Padberg, *Die Goldbrakteaten der Völkerwanderungszeit: Ikonographischer Katalog* (IK Einleitung, vols. 1–3 Text und Tafelbände; Munich: Fink, 1985–89).

[27] K. Hauck, "Zur religionsgeschichtlichen Auswertung von Bildchiffren und Runen der völkerwanderungszeitlichen Goldbrakteaten" (Zur Ikonologie der Goldbrakteaten, LVI), in *Runeninschriften*, ed. K. Düwel, 298–353. See also his "Die runenkundigen Erfinder von den Bildchiffren der Goldbrakteaten" (Zur Ikonologie der Goldbrakteaten, LVII), *Frühmittelalterliche Studien* 32 (1998): 28–56 and pl. XI. Finally, see H. Beck and K. Hauck, "Zur philologischen und historischen Auswertung eines neuen Drei-Götter-Brakteaten aus Sorte Muld, Bornholm, Dänemark," *Frühmittelalterliche Studien* 36 (2002): 51–94 and pl. I, II.

[28] Hermann Güntert, *Von der Sprache der Götter und Geister* (Halle: Niemeyer, 1921).

[29] Jamblichos, *De Mysteriis*, cf. K. Düwel, "Buchstabenmagie und Alphabetzauber. Zu den Inschriften der Goldbrakteaten und ihrer Funktion als Amulette," *Frühmittelalterliche Studien* 22 (1988): 70–110, esp. 102.

[30] Augustine, *De civitate Dei* IX, 1.

[31] K. Düwel, "Buchstabenmagie und Alphabetzauber," 93.

[32] It is part of a hoard that was earlier thought to be linked to the Visigothic king Athanarich (fourth century) but which is now ascribed to an Ostrogoth from the first half of the fifth century. See Dorina Tomescu, "Der Schatzfund von Pietroasa," in *Katalog: Goldhelm, Schwert und Silberschätze* (Frankfut/M.: Stadt Frankfurt am Main, 1994), 230–35.

[33] Hermann Reichert, "GUTANI? WI HAILAG," *Die Sprache: Zeitschrift für Sprachwissenschaft* 35 (1991–93): 235–47; R. Marhiou, P. Pieper and R. Nedoma, "Pietroassa," in *RGA*, vol. 23, 147–58.

[34] W. Krause, *Die Runeninschriften im älteren Futhark*, I, nr. 53–102.

[35] See K. Düwel, *Runenkunde*, 35, 98–99. See further A.-S. Gräslund and K. Düwel, "Runensteine," in *RGA*, vol. 25, 585–96; K. Düwel, "Runen und Runendenkmäler," in *RGA*, vol. 25, 499–512; and his "Runeninschriften," in *RGA*, vol. 25, 525–37.

[36] Elmer H. Antonsen, "Die Darstellung des heidnischen Altars auf gotländischen Bildsteinen und der Runenstein von Elgesem," *Frühmittelalterliche Studien* 18 (1984): 334–35. Cf. E. H. Antonsen, *Runes and Germanic Linguistics* (Berlin and New York: Mouton de Gruyter, 2002), 196–200.

[37] W. Krause, *Die Runeninschriften im älteren Futhark*, I, 166.

[38] Ottar Grønvik, *Runene på Tunesteinen: Alfabet — språkform — budskap* (Oslo, Bergen, Tromsö: Universitetsforlaget, 1981), 162–63.

[39] O. Grønvik, "Enda en gang om Tuneinnskriften," *Maal og Minne* 1998, 35–40.

[40] See P. Fett and Gerd Høst, "Eggja," in *RGA*, vol. 6, 460–66; and Thomas Birkmann, *Von Ågedal bis Malt: Die skandinavischen Runeninschriften vom Ende des 5. bis Ende des 9. Jahrhunderts*, Ergänzungsbände zum Reallexikon der Germanischen Altertumskunde 12 (Berlin and New York: de Gruyter, 1995): 100–101.

[41] W. Krause, *Die Runeninschriften im älteren Futhark*, I, 232. Italics indicate words surmised for defective parts of the inscription.

[42] O. Grønvik, *Runene på Eggjasteinen: En hedensk gravinnskrift fra slutten av 600-tallet* (Oslo: Universitetsforlaget, 1985).

[43] O. Grønvik, "Om Eggjainnskriften," *Arkiv för nordisk filologi* 103 (1988): 36–47.

[44] For individual points, cf. T. Birkmann, *Von Ågedal bis Malt*, 103ff.

[45] Kurt Braunmüller, "Methodische Probleme in der Runologie — einige Überlegungen aus linguistischer Sicht," in *Runeninschriften*, ed. K. Düwel, 3–23, esp. 16ff.

[46] K. Düwel, "Buchstabenmagie und Alphabetzauber," 101–2; K. Düwel, "Zur Auswertung der Brakteateninschriften. Runenkenntnis und Runeninschriften als Oberschichten-Merkmale," in *Der historische Horizont der Götterbilder-Amulette aus der Übergangsepoche von der Spätantike zum Frühmittelalter*, ed. K. Hauck (Göttingen: Vandenhoeck & Ruprecht, 1992), 32–39, esp. 36ff.

[47] K. Düwel, "Runeninschriften als Quellen der germanischen Religionsgeschichte," in *Germanische Religionsgeschichte*, ed. Beck, Ellmers and Schier, 336–64, esp. 345–46.

[48] R. I. Page, *English Runes* 13.

[49] E. H. Antonsen, *A Concise Grammar of the Older Runic Inscriptions* (Tübingen: Niemeyer, 1975), nr. 3.

[50] K. Düwel, "Runeninschriften als Quellen der germanischen Religionsgeschichte," 346ff. and n. 13.

[51] Joachim Werner, *Das Aufkommen von Bild und Schrift in Nordeuropa* (Munich: Bayerische Akademie der Wissenschaften, 1966), 32–33.

[52] K. Düwel, "Runische und lateinische Epigraphik im süddeutschen Raum zur Merowingerzeit," in *Runische Schriftkultur in kontinental-skandinavischer und angelsächsischer Wechselbeziehung,* ed. K. Düwel (Berlin and New York: de Gruyter, 1994), 229–308.

[53] K. Düwel, "Runeninschriften als Quellen der germanischen Religionsgeschichte," 353–54.

[54] Ute Schwab, "Runen der Merowingerzeit als Quelle für das Weiterleben der spätantiken christlichen und nichtchristlichen Schriftmagie?" in *Runeninschriften,* ed. K. Düwel, 376–433.

[55] K. Düwel, "Die Runenschnalle von Pforzen (Allgäu) — Aspekte der Deutung: 3. Lesung und Deutung," in *Pforzen und Bergakker: Neue Untersuchungen zu Runeninschriften,* ed. A. Bammesberger (Göttingen: Vandenhoeck and Ruprecht, 1999), 36–54. This volume also contains interpretations by Ute Schwab, Robert Nedoma, Norbert Wagner, and Elmar Seebold. Cf. further V. Babucke and K. Düwel, "Pforzen," in *RGA,* vol. 23, 114–18. On the metrical character of the inscription see H.-P. Naumann, "Runendichtung," in *RGA,* vol. 25, 512–18, esp. 514–15.

[56] K. Düwel, "Runische und lateinische Epigraphik," 235–36.

[57] E. H. Antonsen, "What Kind of Science is Runology?" *Det Kongelike Norske Videnskabers Selskabs Forhandlingar* (1995): 125–39; cf. L. Peterson, "Runologi: Försök till ett aktuellt signalement," *Saga och sed: Kungliga Gustav Adolfs Akademiens årsbok* 1995 (publ. 1996): 39–54, esp. 39.

[58] Carl J. S. Marstrander, "Opedalstenen," *Norsk tidsskrift for sprogvidenskap* 3 (1929): 158–96. For a variation on and a history of this dictum see L. Peterson, "Runologi," 39.

[59] E. H. Antonsen, "What Kind of Science is Runology?" 137.

[60] M. Barnes, "On Types of Argumentation in Runic Studies," 11–29.

[61] K. Braunmüller, "Methodische Probleme in der Runologie — einige Überlegungen aus linguistischer Sicht," in *Runeninschriften,* ed. K. Düwel, 3–23, esp. 20.

[62] See L. Peterson, "Runologi" and also his "Tolkaren och texten, texten och tolkaren," in *Runor och ABC: Elva föreläsningar från ett symposium i Stockholm våren 1995,* ed. S. Nyström (Stockholm: Sällskapet Runica et Mediævalia; Riksantikvarieämbetet, Stockholms Medeltidsmuseum, 1997), 141–48.

[63] Palm, *Runor och regionalitet.*

[64] Richard L. Morris, *Runic and Mediterranean Epigraphy* (Odense: Odense UP, 1988).

[65] See most recently Henrik Williams, "The Origin of the Runes," in *Frisian Runes and Neighbouring Traditions,* ed. T. Looijenga and A. Quak = *ABäG* 45 (1996): 211–18; A. Quak, "Noch einmal die Lateinthese," *ibid.,* 171–79; H. Williams,

"The Romans and the Runes — Uses of Writing in Germania," in *Runor och ABC*, ed. Nyström, 177–92; and K. Düwel, *Runenkunde*, 175–81 (= K. Düwel, "Runenschrift," in *RGA*, vol. 25, 571–85, esp. 579–85).

[66] W. Krause, *Die Runeninschriften im älteren Futhark*, I, 7.

[67] Most recently, E. H. Antonsen, "Runes and Romans on the Rhine," in *Frisian Runes and Neighbouring Traditions,* ed. Looijenga and Quak, 5–13; Morris, *Runic and Mediterranean Epigraphy.*

[68] Piergiuseppe Scardigli, *Der Weg zur deutschen Sprache* (Bern: Lang, 1994), 175.

[69] Helmut Rix, "Thesen zum Ursprung der Runenschrift," in *Etrusker nördlich von Etrurien: Etruskische Präsenz in Norditalien und nördlich der Alpen sowie ihre Einflüsse auf die einheimischen Kulturen: Akten des Symposions von Wien — Schloß Neuwaldegg 2.-5. Oktober 1989,* ed. L. Aigner-Foresti (Vienna: Österreichische Akademie der Wissenschaften, 1992): 411–41.

[70] T. L. Markey, "Studies in Runic Origins 1: Germanic *maþl-/*mahl- and Etruscan **meθlum**," *American Journal of Germanic Linguistics and Literatures* 10 (1998): 153–200; his "Studies in Runic Origins II: From Gods to Men," *American Journal of Germanic Linguistics and Literatures* 11 (1999): 131–203; and B. Mees, "The North Etruscan Thesis of the Origin of the Runes," *Arkiv før nordisk filologi* 115 (2000): 33–82.

[71] Erik Moltke, *Runes and their Origin: Denmark and Elsewhere* (Copenhagen: National Museum of Denmark, 1985), 69.

[72] E. H. Antonsen, "On Runological and Linguistic Evidence for Dating Runic Inscriptions," in *Runeninschriften,* ed. K. Düwel, 150–59.

[73] On the gold bracteates see for example M. Axboe, "Die innere Chronologie der A-C-Brakteaten und ihrer Inschriften," in *Runeninschriften,* ed. K. Düwel, 231–52.

[74] Heiko Steuer, "Datierungsprobleme in der Archäologie," in *Runeninschriften,* ed. K. Düwel, 129–49.

[75] K. Düwel and Helmut Roth, "Die Runenfibel von Donzdorf," *Frühmittelalterliche Studien* 11 (1977): 409–13.

[76] K. Düwel, "Runeninschriften als Quellen der germanischen Religionsgeschichte," 353ff.

[77] For a summary, see U. Lund Hansen, "Zur Ausstattung und sozialen Stellung runenführender Gräber der Kaiserzeit in Südskandinavien," in *Runeninschriften,* ed. K. Düwel, 160–79.

[78] W. Krause, *Die Runeninschriften im älteren Futhark*, I, nr. 26.

[79] Jørgen Ilkjær, "Runeindskrifter fra mosefund i Danmark — kontekst og oprindelse," in *Frisian Runes and Neighbouring Traditions,* ed. Looijenga and Quak, 63–76, esp. 73–74.

[80] W. Krause, *Runeninschriften*, I, 76; and E. H. Antonsen, *A Concise Grammar,* nr. 1.

[81] K. Düwel, "The Meldorf Fibula and the Origin of Writing," *Michigan Germanic Studies* 7 (1981): 8–18; K. Düwel, and M. Gebühr, "Die Fibel von Meldorf und die Anfänge der Runenschrift," *Zeitschrift für deutsches Altertum* 110 (1981): 159–76.

[82] Bengt Odenstedt, "The Inscription on the Meldorf Fibula," *Zeitschrift für deutsches Altertum* 112 (1983): 153–61; and "Further Reflections on the Meldorf Inscription," *Zeitschrift für deutsches Altertum* 118 (1989): 77–85.

[83] K. Düwel, "The Meldorf Fibula," 12; K. Düwel and M. Gebühr, "Die Fibel von Meldorf," 171–72, and "Meldorf," in *RGA*, vol. 19, 520–22.

[84] B. Mees, "A New Interpretation of the Meldorf Fibula Inscription," *Zeitschrift für deutsches Altertum* 126 (1997): 131–39.

[85] See K. Düwel, ed., *Runeninschriften*.

[86] K. Düwel, "Die 15. Rune auf dem Brakteaten von Nebenstedt I," in *Studien zur Sachsenforschung*, ed. H. J. Häßler (Hildesheim: Laux, 1977), 90–96; and M. Axboe and K. Düwel, "Nebenstedt," in *RGA*, vol. 21, 31–33.

[87] See K. Düwel and W.-D. Tempel, "Knochenkämme mit Runeninschriften aus Friesland," *Palaeohistoria* 14 (1968/70): 353–91, esp. 377–78 on the Jouswier bone plate.

[88] See P. Pieper, *Die Weser-Runenknochen* (Oldenburg: Isensee, 1989).

[89] Henrik Thrane, "An Archaeologist's View of Runes," in *Runeninschriften,* ed. K. Düwel, 219–27, esp. 224–25.

[90] On this, see Otto Höfler, "Herkunft und Ausbreitung der Runen," in his *Kleine Schriften,* ed. Helmut Birkhan (Hamburg: Buske, 1992, originally in *Die Sprache* 17, 1971, 134–56), 285–307.

[91] K. Braunmüller, "Methodische Probleme in der Runologie — einige Überlegungen aus linguistischer Sicht," in *Runeninschriften,* ed. K. Düwel, 3–23, esp. 14–16.

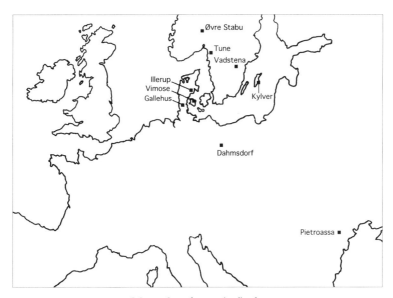

Map of early runic finds

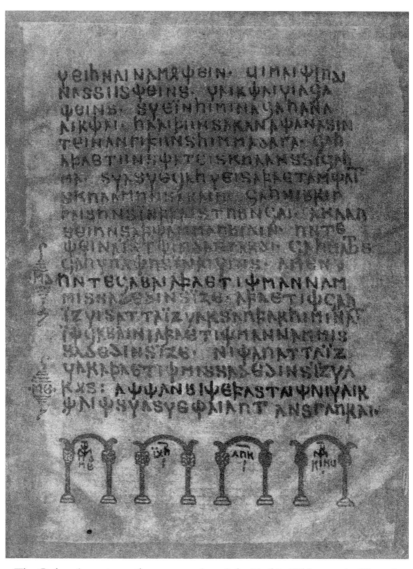

The Codex Argenteus, the manuscript of the Gothic Bible now in Uppsala

Gothic

Brian Murdoch

GOTHIC IS THE EARLIEST GERMANIC LANGUAGE to be written down
in full form in manuscript — other than isolated Germanic words
recorded by Roman writers. Written Gothic dates from the fourth century, several centuries before the ancestor of modern German was committed to writing for the first time. Nevertheless, titles like *Gotische Literaturdenkmäler* found in the secondary literature are at best optimistic,
since most of what we have in the written Gothic language (for the most
part Visigothic) are translations of parts of the Greek Bible. Such non-
biblical fragments as survive are small indeed: a fragment of a biblical
commentary, which may or may not be a translation; a calendar fragment;
a few isolated words (some in a Latin epigram); two subscriptions in legal
documents, and, as the last flicker of the Gothic language, a list of words
recorded in the Crimea in the seventeenth century.[1]

Allusions in Latin writings about the Goths, and references to Gothic
historical figures in works which have survived in other languages lead us
to suppose that, as with other early languages, there was an oral tradition
of poetry in the vernacular. These may well have been heroic epics associated with the aristocratic warrior classes, but these works have not survived in written form. Elfriede Stutz points out on the first page of her
bibliographical handbook that we do not have a single line of Gothic poetry.[2] The fact that what we refer to as Gothic literature means, effectively,
an incomplete Bible translation, determines the approach to Gothic. The
antiquity of the language and thus the relative closeness to the primitive
Germanic ancestor which it, as an East Germanic language, shared with
the West Germanic languages (represented now by English and German),
and with the Northern group of early and modern Scandinavian languages, make it of great interest to philology. Gothic is associated with
other so-called East Germanic languages spoken by tribes such as the
Burgundians, the Vandals and the Gepids (classical historians group them
with the Goths), the Herulians, and the Rugians.[3] For other languages in
that group, such as Burgundian or Rugian, we must rely on place names
and personal names for philological evidence, but with Gothic, sufficient
material has survived to provide for a solid corpus, even if not every para-

digm can be completed from the written material, so that the precise form and gender of some words remain unclear and, of course, much vocabulary is wanting.

In literary terms, however, our interest is more restricted. Translations depend upon an original, and in the case of the Bible we are faced also with a sacred text and the explicit or implicit reluctance to diverge too greatly from the letter of the original, quite apart from the skill of the translation, which is accordingly very difficult to assess. In simplest terms, the apparently literal translation of (in this case) a Greek idiom may or may not be idiomatic or possibly even acceptable in Gothic. Nor is it possible to call in this case upon modern *Sprachgefühl*, certainly not of modern German.[4] The situation is similar with later biblical translations, of course, such as the Old High German version of Tatian's Gospel Harmony four centuries later. There is an additional problem with the Gothic Bible in determining the precise text from which it has been translated, so that an examination of the text requires some knowledge of early and medieval biblical versions as such, both in Greek and in Latin.

Who, then, were the Goths?[5] As shown in an earlier essay in this volume, in which the origins of the Goths are discussed as an example of the literature of Germanic origins, the earliest written records we have are in the writings of Greek and Roman historians, and early tribal names when recorded by classical authors are always confused and confusing. The most substantial early records of Gothic history are found in the writings of the Roman historian Ammianus Marcellinus in the fourth century and in the *Getica*, which has come down to us under the name of the historian Jordanes, who was himself a Goth. The *Getica*, however, was written in the middle of the sixth century, in 551, and is an abbreviation of the much larger, but now lost Gothic history written between 526 and 533 by Cassiodorus the Senator, a Roman aristocrat who had served under Theoderic when the latter was ruler of Italy (493–526). Although Jordanes and Cassiodorus via Jordanes offer a wealth of material and clearly knew the traditions, the work is still many centuries away from the beginnings of the Goths, and not everything can be supported. Nor, of course, is archeological evidence always easy to assess, especially since early cultures did not always correspond to what would be seen now as ethnic groupings. In the *Getica* it is claimed that the groups who made up the Goths originated in southern Scandinavia, which may or may not be the case. From the ninth century onward an association is made between Scandinavia and the Goths in that in Old Norse poetry Gunnar is referred to as the king of the Goths, and very much later, in Britain in the *Annales Cambriae* (The Welsh Annals) for 1066, Haraldr harðráði, King of Norway is described as *rex Gothorum,* king of the Goths.[6]

Leaving the Scandinavian tradition aside, the Goths more certainly moved south from the first century A.D. on, through Poland to the Black Sea, where they existed as separate kingdoms. This folk migration is, of course, not to be "regarded in terms of an advancing army. Rather was it the intermittent and partial thrusting of droves, sometimes larger, sometimes smaller, from an inchoate mass of tribes and septs vaguely coordinated as 'Goths,' but dependent largely on the accidents of individual leadership."[7] Archeological evidence for this movement is always hard to link with an identifiable group, but an association has been made between the early Goths and the Wielbark and Przeworsk cultures found in what is now Poland (distinguished, for example, by practices, unusual elsewhere, such as not burying weapons in male graves) and the later Tchernjachov culture close to the Black Sea, the principal area of Gothic settlement in the first Christian centuries. The spread and date of these cultures from the Baltic to the Black Sea coincides more or less with what is known from written sources of groups calling themselves Goths. Whether the origin some Gothic groups was genuinely in Scandinavia, as in the tradition known to the *Getica*, remains a matter of speculation, in spite of place name evidence that seems to support it (Götland in Sweden and the Baltic island of Gotland). Tracing their path backward from known sites by the Black Sea, however, Peter Heather (who begins his history by the Vistula early in the first century A.D.) notes that "the trail of physical remains fizzles out in northern Poland."[8] There is no question of literacy for the first three centuries of our era, apart from a few disputed and difficult runic inscriptions.[9] There are possibly Gothic-runic inscriptions on two spearheads perhaps of the third century, and another on a gold neckring of the fourth. Of the two spearheads, the word *tilariþs* or *tilarids* is on that found in Suszczyno, Volhynia, in the Ukraine, and this may mean "attacker." The word *ranja*, perhaps "runner," "swift one" as a personal or weapon name, found on a spearhead from Dahmsdorf, in Brandenburg in northern Germany has also been seen as Burgundian. The inscription on the neckring from Pietroassa in Wallachia, Pietroasele in modern Romania seems to read: *gutaniowihailag*, and this inscription is even more unclear, but perhaps — it has been much discussed — means "the holy inheritance of the Goths," although different interpretations of the ring inscription, taking it as "dedicated to the Jupiter of the Goths" have been offered. At least the first part seems to be the ethnic name and the last part the word for holy. These artifacts have been lost and found more than once. An inscription on plaster discovered in Brunshausen, near Gandersheim in Lower Saxony in 1965, written in the ninth century, and headed *runica*, but still in Latin script, contains the word *uaiþia*, which may be a Gothic word for hunter, although linking this with a possible lost Gothic version of Genesis, as has been done, is tenuous in the extreme, in spite of the presence of Nimrod the mighty hunter in Genesis. Some runic inscriptions in Scandinavia, finally, have been interpreted from time to time as Gothic.

By the third century, relevant groups were established along the north of the Black Sea as far as the Crimea, and Ammianus Marcellinus talks about the Goths occupying territory from the Danube to the Don. They came into conflict with the Roman Empire and their territories along the Danube frontier, and were defeated in A.D. 269 at the battle of Naissus (modern Niš in Serbia), from which the Emperor Claudius II gained the title "Gothicus." The Goths were still in a number of discrete political units, and various tribal names are relevant here for groups that would eventually be susceptible of a clearer division into Visigoths and Ostrogoths, even though these names are used at an early stage. While Ostrogoth seems actually to mean "East Goth," Visigoth, although interpreted as "West Goth," may originally have meant something like "noble Goth."[10]

The Tervingi, some of the Greuthungi, and those Goths led by Radagaisus seem to have joined together in the fourth and fifth centuries, eventually forming the major sub-group known as the Visigoths. Under pressure from the Huns as they moved in from the east, these moved along the Danube and across into the Roman Empire, and were also used as *foederati,* associates, often in the pay of Rome against other Germanic groups.[11] It is by no means clear when any of these groups first came into contact with Christianity, but it was in the fourth century that a Christian Gothic missionary bishop born in the early years of that century first translated the Bible into Gothic and thus gave the Gothic language its first written form, and did much to establish Christianity among the Goths.

When the Goths turned against Rome they were capable of inflicting much damage, most notably at the massively bloody battle of Adrianople (Edirne, now in Turkey) in August, 378 against the forces of the joint emperors, Valens and Gratian. Valens's successor, Theodosius the Great, made peace again, but relations between Rome and the Germanic tribes fluctuated, and were never easy. By the first years of the fifth century the Visigoths under Alaric, elected king in Thrace in 395, were attacking Italy. The commander of the army of the Western Roman Empire, Stilicho the Vandal, held them back, but after his murder in 408, Alaric and the Visigoths famously sacked Rome in 410, "although the actual sack was mild and almost respectful."[12] But Alaric died within a year, and his successor, Athaulf took the Visigoths further on, into Roman Gaul, establishing what would become an extensive Visigoth kingdom within the empire in modern Aquitaine, with a capital at Toulouse, from which they later moved across the Pyrenees into Spain. With the Visigoths technically still allied to Rome as *foederati* — Athaulf married Gallia Placidia, daughter of the Emperor Theodosius — the Visigoth kingdom in the west under

Athaulf and his able successors, Walja (Wallia, Vallia, possibly the model for the heroic figure of Waltharius) and then Theoderic I, who ruled for more than thirty years, covered at its high point Aquitaine, Gascony, Narbonne, Provence and most of Spain. In fact, Visigothic laws maintained for a long time the initial legal separation of Roman and Visigoth within their kingdom, and intermarriage was actually forbidden for a long period. One of the most powerful Visigoth kings in the West, Euric (466–84) caused to be written in the latter part of the fifth century the so-called *Code of Euric,* which shows considerable influence of Roman law, and Alaric II, Euric's son, produced in the *Lex Romana Visigothorum* a legal code for the Roman subjects.[13]

The use of the Visigothic language gradually declined in favor of local Latin and its Romance successors. Later, under pressure from a West Germanic tribe, the Franks, who defeated the Visigoths at Vouillé in 507, they were pushed down toward Spain, and eventually established there a Visigothic kingdom with its capital at Toledo in the sixth century that would last for two more centuries, until it fell to the forces of Islam with the establishment of the Caliphate of Cordoba at the start of the eighth century, during which, incidentally, the Gothic-Christian church was well tolerated. Even after the last king, Roderic or Rodrigo, fell in 711, his viceroy Theudemer established a short-lived Gothic kingdom of Murcia. But the Goths did not leave Spain, and Henry Bradley, in his history commented in 1888 that "to this day the noble families of Spain boast, if not always with reason, of the purity of their Gothic blood."[14] As far as the victorious Franks were concerned, the Visigothic kingdom in Spain provided the ruling Merovingian family with one great queen in the later part of the sixth century, the formidable Brunichildis,[15] and the Visigoth Theodulf would compose Latin verse and hymns at the court of an even later Frankish ruler, Charlemagne.

In the fifth century, meanwhile, those groups of Goths that had remained in the Black Sea area came with other peoples under the domination of the Huns. Only after the death of Attila in 453 and the collapse of the Hun empire was there a reassertion of Gothic independence and the formation of the Ostrogoths under the rule of the Amal dynasty. The next signal event was toward the end of the fifth century with the Ostrogoth king Theoderic, known as the Great. Negotiating with the Eastern Roman, the Byzantine emperor, Zeno, and ostensibly working with him, Theoderic led his armies into the Balkans and then on into Italy, by now ruled by a presumably Germanic king, Odoacer,[16] a former leader of the Germanic *foederati* in Italy, who had deposed the last emperor, Romulus Augustulus in 476. In 493, after several battles, Theoderic first agreed to share power with Odoacer, then murdered him at Alaric's old capital, Ravenna. Theoderic then set up an Ostrogothic kingdom in Italy, ruling it

until his death in 526 and coming close to declaring himself Roman emperor. Not many years after his death, however, and in spite of the efforts
of the last effective Ostrogoth leader Totila, who fell in 554, Italy was re-
taken by the Byzantine (Eastern Roman) emperor Justinian and his military leaders Narses and Belisarius, and the Ostrogoth kingdom there was
eradicated, as many emigrated and others simply merged with the local
population. The still readable, entertaining and instructive lectures originally given at Cambridge in the 1860s by the writer Charles Kingsley, tell
how Narses "let [the Goths] go, like a wounded lion crawling away from
the hunter, up through Italy and over the Po, to vanish. They and their
name became absorbed in other nations, and history knows the East
Goths no more."[17] After a period of Byzantine rule of less than twenty
years, Italy was taken in 568 by another Germanic group, the West Germanic Lombards under their leader Alboin, who imposed their identity
upon the country far more indelibly than did the Goths, and there is little
evidence left of Theoderic's kingdom.

As far as the Black Sea territories are concerned, an Ostrogoth residue
seems to have remained in the area around the Crimea, still speaking the
language, although this Ostrogoth dialect would not be written down for
many centuries, and then only as a handful of words. *Goti*, Goths, are mentioned as living in the Crimea in different writings at various points from
the ninth century to the sixteenth, and occasionally there are tantalizing
references to songs in the Germanic language of that area. In 1562, however, a Flemish traveler and diplomat called Ogier Ghiselin de Busbecq
(1522–92) met during a mission to Constantinople a Crimean Goth, and
took down from him sixty-eight words, which he published in 1589. It is
difficult to interpret some of the words, as not all of them are Gothic in
origin, but philologically the differences between the language as represented so late and biblical Visigothic is interesting.[18] Whether or not another Crimean Goth turned up in the mid-eighteenth century is not clear,
but the Greek church referred until that time to the Crimea as Gothia.
However, Busbecq's vocabulary is the last recorded native Gothic.[19]

It is not clear when the Goths first began to be converted to Christianity, but their conversion, when it came, was not to Catholic or Ortho-
dox Christianity, but to Arianism. The followers of the theologian Arius
of Alexandria (ca. 250–ca. 336), the Arians held the view that Christ was
not God by nature, but was made by the Father and effected the creation
of the world. It has been suggested that the apparent superiority of the
Father over the Son implied in this doctrine appealed to the paternal-
hierarchical structure of Gothic society, and also that the adherence to
Arianism for such a long time in fact preserved Gothic independence and
prevented an integration with Rome.[20] In any event, Arianism contradicted the Catholic doctrine defined later as *homoousios,* the consubstan-

tiality of the Father and the Son. The Arian doctrine was declared a heresy at the Council of Nicaea in 325 under the Emperor Constantine the Great, but Arius's views were reinstated and the conflict continued until the Catholic view was established as orthodoxy in the Roman Empire at the Council of Constantinople in 381. Adopted by the Goths, Arianism is of considerable importance to their history and to their role in Europe. The Visigothic adherence to the doctrine was strong, and they converted other Germanic tribes to Arian Christianity. Indeed, among the first missionaries to southern Germany were Visigoths, whose language contributed a number of ecclesiastical terms (including *Pfaffe, Pfingsten, Samstag*) to the High German language. Friedrich Kluge's study of early Gothic influence begins with *Kirche* which represents Greek *kyriake (oikia)* or later *kyrikon*, "Lord's house," and is likely to have entered through Gothic as the principal route for Greek borrowings in this sphere. The phrase is not attested in written Gothic, which uses *aikklesjo*, representing Greek *ekklesia*, the Latin version of which has given the word for church to the Romance languages (*église, chiesa*).[21] Arianism persisted among the Germanic tribes, promoted to a large extent by the Visigoths, and only disappeared when Clovis, king of the Franks was converted to Catholicism at the end of the fifth century, and then defeated the Visigoths at Vouillé. Another Arian Germanic group, the Burgundians, moved to Catholic Christianity in 516, and so did the Visigoths themselves after the Council of Toledo in 589, when the Visigoth king of Spain, Reccared (586–601), finally renounced the Arian creed and brought the Visigoths into the Roman church, even though there were by now no other connections with the once great empire. The adoption of Latin Catholic Christianity put an end to the liturgical use of Gothic, something which had begun with the translation for church use of the Bible into Gothic in the fourth century, and was a considerable blow to the Gothic language.

Arianism was in the forefront of religious thought, however, when in about 340 or 341 Ulfila was consecrated in Constantinople by the moderate Arian Eusebius of Nicomedia as bishop with a mission to the Visigoths. He settled with the Visigoths in Moesia, along the Danube, now Serbia and Bulgaria, and there developed an alphabet and translated the Bible. The name of this highly significant figure exists in various forms, including Ulphila(s) and Ulfilas, but Ulfila is probably the most acceptable, although he is known also as Wulfila(s), which perhaps indicates more clearly the etymology as the diminutive of the Gothic word *wulfs* and thus meaning "little wolf." Born around 311, Ulfila earned by his works of conversion his title Apostle of the Goths, although there had been some Christianity among the Goths already. Quite a lot is known about him and his work from Greek and Latin ecclesiastical sources, as well as from Cassiodorus/Jordanes, and most fully from the determinedly Arian writings of his pupil, Auxentius, who praises his piety and his attacks on heresy. More interesting is another Arian, Philostorgius, whose Greek ecclesiastical history (surviving in an excerpted form) speaks of Ulfila's Cappadocian background, with his mother's family coming from Sadagolthina, near ancient Parnassus in Asia Minor, about fifty miles southeast of modern Ankara. He probably had a Gothic father, and a Christian Cappadocian mother or grandmother. The Goths had raided as far as Christian Cappadocian territories in Asia Minor, to the south of the Black Sea, in the late third century, so that Ulfila's grandparents on his mother's side presumably were taken at that time. It is Philostorgius who tells how he provided the Goths with a written language, and translated all the books of the Bible except the Books of Kings, because they are largely about war and the Goths were already too warlike. Other writings refer to Ulfila's conversion of large numbers of Goths, and to his translation work (this is mentioned in the *Getica*), and later ecclesiastical historical writers in the west, such as Isidore of Seville (ca. 560–636), note Ulfila's achievement in writing and translating, even if Isidore (who came from a pre-Visigoth noble family in Spain and was a principal defender of Catholicism against Arianism) condemned the long-held Arianism of the Goths and rejoiced in its demise.[22] Ulfila died probably in 381 or 382 at Constantinople, where he had gone to attend a synod.

To translate the Bible, Ulfila needed an alphabet, and several ancient sources are agreed that he invented an alphabet for the purpose himself, something which has to be seen as a signal achievement. Ulfila's Gothic alphabet is based largely upon Greek; most of the letters, and the order in which they come, derive from the Greek alphabet, and the letters also have numerical values, as they do in Greek. Gothic also uses some spellings that match Greek usage, such as the representation of the nasal guttural (*-ng-*, *-nk-*) as a double guttural (Greek *aggelos*, Gothic *aggilus*, "angel") or the use of the combination *ei* for long *i*. Not every Greek letter had the same sound-value as the original: the Greek *theta* was used for the single Gothic sound represented as a ligatured *hv;* he used the Greek *psi* for the unvoiced th (þ), and in his alphabet *theta* and *psi* change places in relation to the Greek. Some Greek letters (such as *xi* or *eta*, which looks like a Latin H) were not used at all, presumably since they were not needed, while the X-shaped Greek *chi-* appears rarely, and mainly in the name of Christ. Six letters are taken from the Latin alphabet: *h, g* (used for *j*), *r, s, f* and *u* (which is used for *q*, that is, *kw*). Possibly the Latin, rather than the Greek forms for *r* and *s* were chosen because their Greek equivalents might be confused with *p* and *c*. Two letters are probably runic: that for the short *u* (named **urus*, "aurochs, wild ox," in the Germanic runic system) and that for short *o* (the rune probably named *opal, "inherited property, land").[23] Finally, two Greek signs are used in Gothic only for the numbers 90 and 900. The runic alphabet, which was almost certainly known to the Goths, was designed for inscription rather than for script, and besides, probably carried with it overtones of pre-Christian magic.

We are told that Ulfila translated the entire Bible apart from the Books of Kings, although of the Old Testament we have only some fragments of the book of Nehemiah, which raises doubts about how much Ulfila actually *did* translate. Nor is it clear whether he alone translated what we have. What is particularly conspicuous is the absence of Genesis and of the Psalms, arguably the most important books of the Bible after the Gospels, even though it has been suggested that a version of Genesis once existed.[24] In the New Testament, the Gospels and Paul's letters were certainly all translated, apart from Hebrews, of which we have no trace, though all these books except II Corinthians are incomplete. Of the Gospels, Mark is the fullest. Acts, the minor epistles and the Apocalypse are not present.

The Gothic Bible is, because of its antiquity, of great interest to biblical studies as well as to Germanic philology, but questions of source are complex, since both Testaments existed in a variety of forms in this early period.[25] Ulfila's main sources were a Greek Old and New Testament each of the type current in the diocese of Constantinople in the fourth century, but he knew Latin, and there is some evidence that he also used an Old Latin text of the New Testament as well, one that preceded the standardized Vulgate. His Greek Old Testament source was probably the edition of the Septuagint (the Greek Old Testament) made by Lucian the Martyr, who died in 312, an Arian, although there is little in the Gothic Bible translation to suggest any Arian bias. Assessing the possible source of the New Testament raises further problems in that all the manuscripts in which the Gothic text has survived date from the fifth to the seventh centuries, and were written in Italy, so that it is not clear to what extent they represent Ulfila's text. There were differences between versions of the New Testament in the Greek *koine* (standardized) text as it circulated in the Byzantine world, and those known in the west, but with the manuscripts we have it is difficult to tell whether the "western" variations that crop up do go back to Ulfila's original translation (in which case they may have been influenced by an Old Latin version), or whether they are later changes to Ulfila's text that also conform to a Latin version.

The Gothic Bible has been preserved in several major manuscripts, mostly from upper Italy, written during the period of Ostrogothic rule.[26] The principal and best-known manuscript is the so-called Codex Argenteus, datable to the sixth century. It was written in silver and gold lettering on parchment that had been dyed purple, and originally contained 336 leaves, of which 187 survive. It contains the text of the Gospels, Matthew, and John by one scribe, Luke and Mark by another, in that order. It may have been written in Brescia (Brixen) in northern Italy because another very similar purple and silver manuscript containing only the Latin text of the Gospels comes from there.[27] The Gothic codex may have been taken from Italy in the late eighth century by Liudger, who was a pupil of Alcuin, when he founded the monastery of Werden, near Cologne. This is where the manuscript was housed in the sixteenth century, but by the early seventeenth it was in an imperial collection in Prague, and in 1648 was removed by the Swedes during the Thirty Years' War. In 1669, now bound in silver — although it seems to have been called *argenteus,* presumably from the lettering, already before the binding — it was placed in the University of Uppsala, where it remains. In 1970, a further leaf of this same manuscript was found in a reliquary in Speyer cathedral, containing the end of Mark's Gospel. The folium is slightly larger than the rest of the codex, which has clearly been trimmed.

A sixth-century parchment double folio of uncertain origin was discovered in Egypt and taken in 1907 to Giessen (the Codex Gissensis). It contained some of Luke's Gospel in a Latin-Gothic bilingual text. It was, however, destroyed in a flood in 1945. The other manuscripts and fragments are extremely difficult to read since they are palimpsests, texts that have been partly erased and then overwritten. The Codex Carolinus, once in Weissenburg and now in Wolfenbüttel, was another Gothic-Latin bilingual, and the four leaves that survive contain parts of Romans. The final biblical material survives in a series of fragmentary manuscripts, two of them substantial, two more of only a few leaves, known as the Codices Ambrosiani A–D, in the Biblioteca Ambrosiana in Milan (and a fifth fragment with some Gothic, Ambrose E, contains the *Skeireins,* which will be discussed later). A set of four badly damaged leaves now known as the Codex Taurinensis, in the Turin University Library, is in fact part of Ambrose A. Ambrose A (with the Turin codex) and B, the two major fragments, contain the Pauline letters apart from Hebrews, plus (at the end of A) a fragment of a Gothic ecclesiastical calendar. Ambrose C has some of Matthew, and Ambrose D the sole Old Testament survival, part of Nehemiah. All these are *codices rescripti,* and a glance at the photograph of Ambrose B in the Braune/Ebbinghaus *Grammatik* makes the problem clear. The manuscript has been turned upside down and a Latin text written over the Gothic original text, so that the Latin runs in the opposite direction.

Two further manuscripts with survivals related to the Gothic Bible may also be mentioned. First, a fifth or sixth century manuscript from Verona (and still there) of Latin homilies by Maximinus (who was an Arian Gothic bishop), contains some Gothic biblical citations, very difficult to read, mostly from the Gospels; they match the Codex Argenteus where

an overlap exists, and add two Luke passages not present in the large codex. Finally, the ninth- or tenth-century Salzburg-Vienna Alcuin manuscript in the Austrian National Library in Vienna, which contains two
versions of the Gothic alphabet and some Gothic numbers, also contains a
few sentences from Luke's Gospel, which in this case do not match those
in the Codex Argenteus, together with a phonetic version in Latin script.
It should be reiterated that no manuscript survival is from the time of
Ulfila, nor can we be sure to what extent they represent his translation,
however conservative religious texts usually are. Nor were any of these
manuscripts written in his Visigothic-Greek ecclesiastical orbit, but mostly
in the later Ostrogoth kingdom of Italy. Textually we are faced with the
familiar philological problem of a text made uncertain because of the distance from the original, compounded with problems of variation and indeed sometimes of legibility.

The Gothic text of the Bible was intended not for individual study,
but for liturgical usage, for reading aloud, and this will have affected the
literary fluency of the work, which is impressive. The fact that Ulfila's
work exits at all is perhaps its most significant feature, but in looking at
the translation as such, it must be borne in mind that the position of the
Bible as a sacred text demanded of the early medieval translator a respect
that can easily lead to an over-literal or wooden rendering. The faithful
translator aimed to stay as close to the original as possible, and this holds
true for the Gothic text. There is also much regularity in the rendering of
individual words, although some varied translations do occur. All these
features are useful for assessing the source. As a simple example, the title
for the Gospel of Mark reads *Aiwaggeljo þairh Marku anastodeiþ*, literally
"the Gospel of Mark begins." The usual Greek title *evangelion kata
Markon* does not have the verb, but the Old Latin texts do. The technique of close translation, however, is noticeable throughout. Thus the
opening of Mark, which in Greek could be translated literally as "Beginning of the Gospel of Jesus Christ son of God, as is written in Isaiah the
prophet . . ." may easily be recognized: "Anastodeins aiwaggeljons Iesuis
Xristaus sunaus guþs, swe gameliþ ist in Esaïin praufetau. . . ."[28] Thus,
too, Ulfila uses a plural for the first reference in the Lord's Prayer to
heaven, *in himinam* (Greek *en tois ouranois*, in the heavens) and, as with
the Greek, a singular in the following verse, *in himina*. The same closeness may be observed in some Old High German translations of the
prayer. Possible influences from Old Latin versions is evident, as indeed is
the assessment of variations within scribal forms, such as *praitoria* in John
18, 28 (and elsewhere) as against *praitauria* in John 18, 33 (praetorium,
judgment hall), where attention has to be paid to Ulfila's presumed original, to later pronunciation in Gothic Italy, and to the Greek or Latin
equivalents of the loan word.[29] On the other hand, the Gothic text can

also be distinctive, as in the careful use of the dual number, which is a feature of Gothic, but not of New Testament Greek or of Latin (though it was present in classical Greek): the first and second personal pronouns, for example, can take the form of *ik, þu* (singular: I, thou) and *weis, jus* (plural: we, you), but also *wit, *jut* (dual: we two, you two).[30]

Translating the Bible was a major achievement too, and Ulfila faced the same problems that later Old High German translators confronted when seeking the best version for words specifically linked with Christianity. Some of these have been noted already as having influenced the earliest stages of High German, and the same applies to words like *halja,* hell, which is used for the New Testament Greek term *Hades;* linked to the idea of concealment (as with modern German *hüllen*) it presumably uses an earlier term for the world of the dead, transferring into it the biblical meaning. Of particular interest are the loan words and loan translations, especially those in the theological context, such as *synagoge* for synagogue, or *sabbato* for Sabbath, or less usual words like *anakumbjan,* to lie down, from Latin *accumbere,* echoing the Roman idea of reclining at a meal. Loan translations include *armahairtei,* mercy, from Latin *misericordia,* or *piupiqiss,* translating Greek *eu-logia,* "good saying," blessing (compare Latin *bene-dictio*). Some of the theological terms will have predated Ulfila (*aiwaggeljo,* Gospel, *aipiskaupas,* bishop), of course. Other loan words in the Gothic language as attested in the Bible translation are often of some antiquity, and come from a variety of different sources. A celebrated example is *reiks,* ruler or king, related to Latin *rex* but from the Celtic form *rix* found in personal names such as *Vercingetorix.* Other words remain obscure, such as *ulbandus,* translating "camel" in the Gospels, and possibly, though by no means certainly, from *elephantus.* The Goths themselves, finally, are referred to as *Gutþiuda* in the Calendar text in Ambrose A, and the compound *þiudisko,* an adjective also based on the noun *þiuda,* people, is of some interest. It is used to render *ethnikos* in Galatians 2, 14, where it is means heathen or gentile, in contrast with Jewish. It is an attested early cognate of the much discussed word which appears in Latin documents as *theodisce* and was used by the Franks and others to mean "Germanic," and ultimately became *deutsch.*

The other Gothic texts are much more limited in literary value. A calendar page for some of October and November attached to Ambrose A is brief, but does give us some insights into liturgical customs and specifically Gothic feasts. It mentions not only the celebration of the Gothic martyrs on October 29, but also the town of Beroia (*Bairauja*), in Thrace (near the modern university town of Stara Zagora in Bulgaria), and thus localizes the document in what was then Visigoth territory. The feast days of St. Philip on November 14 (in the eastern church) and St. Andrew on November 30 (accepted also in the western church) are given as November 15 and 29 respectively; Dorotheos, listed here on November 6, was an Arian archbishop who died on that day in 407, reputedly at the age of 119, and November 3 is dedicated apparently to Constantine the Great (*Konstanteinus piudanis*). This should refer to his son, Constantius II (337–61), who died on November 3, and who is honored as a protector of the Goths and supporter of Arian Christianity.[31] The error of a single letter is an easy one, and the account of Gothic Christianity excerpted from Philostorgius makes the same mistake.

More substantial, however, and of considerably greater importance in spite of its present condition, is the fragmentary work known as *Skeireins*, which means "interpretation."[32] Eight leaves of a manuscript originally from Bobbio, in northern Italy five of which are now with the other Gothic manuscripts in the Biblioteca Ambrosiana in Milan (as Ambrose E), and three more in the Vatican, contain a commentary on parts of St. John's Gospel. The biblical quotations match Ulfila's text, but we cannot attribute or date this work in any satisfactory manner. It is written in a Greek style, and it may be a translation from an unknown source. But if it is an independent piece, it becomes the sole substantial relic of free-standing Gothic, and thus of the greatest interest in ascertaining Gothic syntax free of the structuring influence of a sacred source. It is also of interest in theological terms; here is a passage from the fifth leaf (in Milan):

> unte þata qiþano "ei allai sweraina sunu, swaswe swerand attan,"
> ni ibnon ak galaika sweriþa usgiban uns laiseiþ.[33]

The passage interprets John 5, 23, and may be translated as: "For where it is said that 'all men should honor the son even as they honor the father,' this teaches us to show similar and not the same honor." The Gothic *galeiks* and *ibna* form a contrast, and later on the same contrast is used in the form of *ibnaleiks*, which probably renders the Greek word *homoousios*, and *galeiks*, rejecting the former. This kind of contrast in the interpretation supports the Arian view of the Father and the Son.

Not much else remains of extant Gothic. Two Latin bills of land sale (in Gothic *frabauhtaboka*) exist with signatory affidavits in the Gothic language and script. One was written around 551 and was once in the archive of St. Anastasia in Ravenna (it is now in Naples). The other, which was once housed in the cathedral archive at Arezzo, has been lost, although a transcription was printed in 1731. The Naples document has a number of clerical signatories, mostly Latin, but with four in Gothic. Finally, a Latin verse criticizing the barbarians contains a few Gothic words. The text reads:

> Inter *eils* Goticum *scapiamatziiadrincan*
> non audet quisquam dignos educere versus.

The Gothic seems to be the equivalent of: *hails . . . skapjam matjan jah drigkan,* meaning "Greetings, let's get something to eat and drink."[34] Scattered through other Latin writings, including the *Getica,* are other words that may be Gothic, but even these rescued scraps are not quite the final sources for our knowledge of Gothic. The listing by Ogier de Busbeq of Crimean Gothic vocabulary has been mentioned already, and these are largely everyday words.[35] They are not of literary importance, but they bear witness to the survival of the spoken language, at least at a late stage. Additional sources from which we can assess Gothic vocabulary are first in the study of place and personal names, such as those recorded in association with the Visigothic church down to the fall of the Spanish kingdom and beyond, and indeed in place names and loan words in Romance languages, such as Spanish *alevosía,* treachery, from Gothic *lewjan,* to betray. Borrowings from Gothic in Baltic languages, like Finnish, of course, may help with the early history of the Goths.[36]

As with other early Germanic languages, it is likely that there was an oral tradition of secular poetry which in the case of Gothic was never committed to writing. Heroic songs are referred to in the *Getica,* and seem to have been known too at the court of the Visigoth king Theoderic II at Toulouse. More detailed evidence has to be sought, however, from existing sources outside Gothic, and links can sometimes be tenuous and remote. Thus the medieval Latin epic of Waltharius, probably written in Germany in the tenth century, has as its first theme the sending of hostages to the court of Attila the Hun by three Germanic tribes, the Franks, the Burgundians, and the people of Aquitaine. Prince Waltharius is the hostage sent by the people of Aquitaine, who are not named in the text. In the poem the various tribes mentioned are not necessarily placed in the "correct" historical location, and at the time of Attila, it was the Visigoths who ruled Aquitaine from their capital at Toulouse. There are some faint echoes of actual history in the Latin poem, but apart from Visigothic participation in what was technically the Roman army when Attila and the Huns were driven back in 451 from Orleans, their westernmost point of incursion, not much remains that is relevant. Only the hero's name, Waltharius, perhaps echoes, as indicated above, that of the Visigoth king Walja, the successor of Athaulf, who ruled for a few years (415–18) at the start of the fifth century; whether there was ever anything about him in Gothic is a matter of complete speculation.[37]

Attila the Hun appears again, though this time in combination with the Ostrogoths, in the poem preserved in a mixture of Old Low and Old High German (though this version was composed in the latter) known as the *Hildebrandlied.* Here we find references to Dietrich, the Ostrogoth king Theoderic the Great, fleeing to the court of Attila to escape from Odoacer, and then returning, presumably to fight Odoacer at Ravenna in 493. The history is again garbled — Theoderic was not born until after the death of Attila — but there are echoes here of the Hunnish domination of the Ostrogoths, and of the later establishment of the Ostrogoth kingdom of Italy under Theoderic after the death of Odoacer. A case has been made — partly on the basis of some of the other names in the work — for a Lombardic precursor to the Old High German text, but again, whether there were any Gothic antecedents is conjectural. The extensive role played in later German literature by Dietrich, though based on Theoderic, is a long way from the Gothic king himself, just as the literary Brünhilt is at some distance from the Visigothic princess Brunichildis.

Beside survivals in Latin and Old High German there is evidence at least of material relating to the Goths in several Old Norse poems, first in two works found in the oldest of the collections of verse, the poetic Edda, the *Hamðismál* and the *Guðrúnahvöt* (Lay of Hamdir, Incitement of Gudrun), perhaps of the ninth century. The key here is in the person of Jörmunrekkr, the equivalent of Ermanaric, king of the Goths. In the poems he plays a peripheral part, in that the essence is Guðrun's demand that her sons, Hamðir and Sörli avenge their sister Svanhildr, who has been killed by her husband, Jörmunrekkr. Ammianus Marcellinus talks of Ermanaric's suicide after an attack by the Huns, and Jordanes has a different tradition involving a feud between Ermanaric and a woman named Sunilda. Like Dietrich, Ermanaric survives as a figure in West Germanic literature for many centuries, and we may refer at least to a Low German poem surviving in a sixteenth-century form called *Koninc Ermenríkes dot*. Of interest too, finally, is a poem about a battle involving the Huns, attached to the thirteenth-century *Hervarar saga*, and based presumably on a battle in which the Goths defeated the Huns. Various names in the piece point to early Gothic history; Tyrfing and Grytingalidi match the Gothic tribal names Tervingi and Greutungi, and place names mentioned such as Dun (the Don) and Danpar (the Dnieper) give a location in the Gothic settlement to the north of the Black Sea.[38] Again the existence of Gothic allusions in Norse texts does not have to indicate lost Gothic works, but it does give a hint of Gothic history as the subject of heroic poems.

The word "Gothic" has undergone major changes in use over the centuries since the Goths and their writings effectively disappeared from view, Visigothic after the decline of Arianism after the Council of Toledo, and Ostrogothic after the fall of Totila. Although it has absolutely nothing to do with the Goths, Gothic came to be used in architectural vocabulary as a contrasting term to classical and is applied to what in English is known as the perpendicular style, seen as quintessentially medieval. For the same reason the word has become attached in printing to black-letter type, the forerunner of German *Fraktur,* also known as Gothic type, and in this case even more obviously unconnected with the

Goths themselves. Another later use is generally pejorative, linked again with the perception of the Germanic tribes as the destroyers (rather than as the inheritors) of the Roman Empire; in this respect the Vandals have probably suffered the greatest opprobrium, and the word "vandalism" dates back to the eighteenth century. But the Goths shared this linguistic fate; Dryden used the lines

> And reeking from the stews, adult'rers come
> Like Goths and Vandals to demolish Rome.

Later still comes the nineteenth-century misuse of the name Gothic (and of course nothing *but* the name) to describe a specific kind of novel involving the supernatural, the fantastic or the morbid. Presumably it derived from the use of Gothic almost as a synonym for medieval, and it had a final resonance in a type of youth fashion at the end of the twentieth century. But the road from Ulfila to Mary Shelley and beyond is a strange one.[39]

The Gothic language and writings proper were rediscovered in the sixteenth century, first with the finding (and shortly after the copying) of the Codex Argenteus at Werden in the middle of that century. It was first edited in the seventeenth century, after its move to Sweden, and the start of the nineteenth saw much interest and activity, notably with the production of editions and lexica. Clearly the language was of major interest to those German scholars engaged in establishing philology on a scientific basis, but it had its effect on literary critics and writers too. August Friedrich Christian Vilmar (1800–1868), whose *Geschichte der deutschen National-Litteratur* remained in print for the entire second half of the nineteenth century, found what he called this most completely preserved of the languages of their Germanic forefathers strange, but at the same time familiar and homely (fremd und doch zugleich heimisch und vertraut), while in Britain in the twentieth century, J. R. R. Tolkien's career as a philologist — which so much informed his creative writings — was given initial impetus when in his teens he acquired and reacted with great enthusiasm to a copy of Joseph Wright's Gothic *Primer* (the forerunner of Wright's *Grammar of the Gothic Language*). Tolkien sometimes wrote inscriptions in other books in his possession in what he later referred to as "a beautiful language, which reached the eminence of liturgical use, but failed owing to the tragic history of the Goths to become one of the liturgical languages of the west." The final word, however, may be given to Hans Ferdinand Massmann (1797–1874), who in 1857 edited all the Gothic material then known. When he edited the Old High and Low German Creeds in 1839 he dedicated that volume of the *Bibliothek der gesammten deutschen National-Literatur* to Jacob Grimm with a letter in Gothic, addressing him as *laisari sverista, frijond liubista,* "most honored teacher and dearest friend," and concluding, as may we, with the elegant salutation in what we might call modern Gothic:

Hails sijais jah hulths vis sinteino theinamma: "May you be healthy and may respect be forever yours."[40]

Notes

[1] Most of what survives in Gothic may be found in a single volume, *Die Gotische Bibel*, ed. Wilhelm Streitberg (5/6th ed., Heidelberg: Winter, 1920, repr. 1965, 7th ed. with new material by Piergiuseppe Scardigli, 2000), which contains the texts, principally the biblical texts and their Greek originals, with, as an appendix, the smaller survivals. The second part (2nd edition 1928, 6th ed. with new material by Scardigli, 2000) is a Gothic-Greek-German dictionary. The new edition takes account of recent finds with any evidence of Gothic. See also *Stamm-Heynes Ulfilas*, new ed. by Ferdinand Wrede (Paderborn: Schöningh, 1920), also with the smaller pieces. The survivals in Crimean Gothic can be found in Friedrich Kluge, *Die Elemente des Gotischen* (Strasbourg: Trübner, 1911), 110–14 and in Wilhelm Streitberg, *Gotisches Elementarbuch* (5/6th ed., Heidelberg: Winter, 1920), 280–84. The Latin epigram is in Wrede, for example, as well as Heinrich Hempel, *Gotisches Elementarbuch* (Berlin: de Gruyter, 1962, 5th ed. by Wolfgang Binnig, 1999), 158 and Wolfgang Krause, *Handbuch des Gotischen* (3rd ed., Munich: Beck, 1968), 21–22. For a bibliography of Gothic, including all the extremely numerous individual studies of linguistic points, see Fernand Mossé, "Bibliographica Gothica," *Medieval Studies* 12 (1950): 237–324, "First Supplement," in the same journal, 15 (1953): 169–83, the "Second Supplement" completed after his death by James W. Marchand in 19 (1957): 174–96 and the "Third Supplement" by Ernst Ebbinghaus, 29 (1967): 328–43; see finally the *Ausgewählte Bibliographie* in Wilhelm Braune, *Gotische Grammatik*, 18th ed. by Ernst Ebbinghaus (Tübingen: Niemeyer, 1973), 126–39, and Lehmann's dictionary (below, n. 4). Citation is from Streitberg, although in Greek borrowings, vocalic *y* is used rather than *w*. In some earlier transcriptions *v* is used in place of *w*. The Anglo-Saxon/Old Norse þ is used for *th*. Among the enormous and disparate bibliography of Gothic, attempts to link Gothic with Etruscan, for example, probably need not detain us.

[2] Elfriede Stutz, *Gotische Literaturdenkmäler* (Stuttgart: Metzler, 1966), 1.

[3] There are features that link the East Germanic languages more closely with the Norse group than with West Germanic: both kept a dental ending -*t* in the imperfect second person singular of strong verbs, which the West Germanic languages did not. Against this, the Germanic nominal masculine a-stem ending -*az*, which develops to -*(a)r* in Norse, as in Old Norse *dagr*, day, and which is lost in West Germanic, for example, becomes syncopated to a simple -*s* in East Germanic, to give us Gothic *dags* (it seems to have disappeared in late — Crimean — Ostrogothic *dag*). There are, further, a number of vocalic variations that distinguish the East Germanic group.

[4] The principal lexical aids for Gothic are: F. Holthausen, *Gotisches etymologisches Wörterbuch* (Heidelberg: Winter, 1934), Sigmund Feist, *Vergleichendes Wörterbuch der gotischen Sprache* (3rd ed., Leiden: Brill, 1939), adapted by Winfred P. Lehmann, *A Gothic Etymological Dictionary* (Leiden: Brill, 1986); this contains

(592–712) an extremely comprehensive alphabetically ordered bibliography by Helen-Jo J. Hewitt; Brian T. Regan, *Dictionary of the Biblical Gothic Language* (Phoenix, AZ: Wellspring, 1974); Felicien de Tollenaere and Randall L. Jones, *Word-Indices and Word-Lists to the Gothic Bible and Minor Fragments* (Leiden: Brill, 1976). See also the Gothic-Greek-German dictionary attached to Streitberg's Bible-edition. There is also a *Deutsch-gotisches Wörterbuch*, ed. O. Priese (3rd ed., Halle/S.: Niemeyer, 1933), with thematic word-lists and useful (and also familiar biblical) phrases. The older *Comparative Glossary of the Gothic Language* by Gerhard Hubert Balg (London: Truebner, 1887–89) is available online at http://onlinebooks.library.upenn.edu.

[5] The best modern general history in English is Peter Heather's *The Goths* (Oxford: Blackwell, 1996), replacing the pioneering one by Henry Bradley, *The Goths* (London: Fisher-Unwin, 1888). Heather's book has a full historical bibliography. The standard German text is Herwig Wolfram's *Die Goten* 4th ed. (Munich: Beck, 2001), translated from the second edition as *History of the Goths* by Thomas J. Dunlap (Berkeley: U of California P, 1987). See also Heather's other studies *Goths and Romans 332–489* (Oxford: Clarendon, 1991) and his book of sources (with J. F. Matthews) *The Goths in the Fourth Century* (Liverpool: Liverpool UP, 1991) and T. S. Burns, *A History of the Ostrogoths* (Bloomington: Indiana UP). See also D. H. Green, *Language and History in the Early Germanic World* (Cambridge: CUP, 1998).

[6] Ammianus Marcellinus is available in Latin and English translated and edited by J. C. Rolfe in the Loeb Classical Library (Cambridge, MA: Harvard UP; London: Heinemann, 1935–50); Jordanes, *Romana et Getica,* ed. Theodor Mommsen (Hanover: Monumenta Germaniae Historica, 1882 = MGH AA 5/i) and in English trans. Charles Christopher Mierow, *The Gothic History of Jordanes in English* (Princeton: Princeton UP, 1915; 2nd ed., Cambridge and New York: Barnes and Noble, 1966). Cassiodorus's letters and edicts written for the Gothic kings, his *Variae epistolae* are edited by Theodor Mommsen (Berlin: MGH, 1894, repr. Munich, 1981) and are also in J. P. Migne, *Patrologia Latina* (Paris, 1844–64), 69–70. There is a translation by Thomas Hodgkin of some of these: *The Letters of Cassiodorus* (London: Frowde, 1886).

[7] Mortimer Wheeler, *Rome Beyond the Imperial Frontiers* (Harmondsworth: Penguin, 1954), 43.

[8] Heather, *Goths,* 30–31.

[9] See Krause, *Handbuch,* 45, and Sigmund Feist, *Einführung in das Gotische* (Leipzig and Berlin: Teubner, 1922), 98. On the link with Genesis, see Krause, *Handbuch,* 22–23, and on the putative Scandinavian links, see Fernand Mossé, *Manuel de la langue Gothique* (2nd ed., Paris: Aubier, 1956), 30–31.

[10] See Krause, *Handbuch,* 10–16 on the names of the various Gothic groups and also on the forms of Ulfila's name.

[11] See beside Heather, *Goths,* and Wolfram, *History,* also Michael Grant, *The Fall of the Roman Empire* (London: Weidenfeld and Nicolson, new ed. 1990). There is a useful selection of translated sources in C. D. Gordon, *The Age of Attila* (Ann Arbor: U of Michigan P, 1960).

[12] Colin McEvedy, *The Penguin Atlas of Medieval History* (Harmondsworth: Penguin, 1961), 18. This work presents a graphic view of the movements of the various barbarian groups. Gibbon points out in the *Decline and Fall* that Alaric's actions were mild compared with later military ventures, and acceptably, but rather confusingly, he refers to Athaulf as Adolphus.

[13] Hermann Conrad, *Der deutsche Staat* (Frankfurt am Main: Ullstein, 1969), 14–15.

[14] Bradley, *Goths*, 363. There is a considerable bibliography on the Visigoths in Spain. See A. Ferreiro, *The Visigoths in Gaul and Spain*, A.D. *418–711* (Leiden: Brill, 1988), and as individual studies: J. M. Wallace-Hadrill, *The Barbarian West 400–1000* (revised ed., London: Hutchinson, 1967), 115–39; Edward James, *Visigothic Spain* (Oxford: Clarendon, 1980); Luis A. García Moreno, *Historia de España Visigoda* (Madrid: Cátedra, 1989); Peter Heather, *The Visigoths from the Migration Period to the Seventh Century* (Woodbridge: Boydell, 1999). See also A. T. Fear, *Lives of the Visigothic Fathers* (Liverpool: Liverpool UP, 1997). The fall of Rodrigo would later be celebrated (and historically revised) in ballads: see Ramon Menéndez Pidal, *El rey Rodrigo en la literatura española* (Madrid: Revista de archivos, bibliotecas y museos, 1924), with texts in his *Floresta de leyendas heroicas españolas: Rodrigo, el último Godo* [1925–27] (4th ed., Madrid: Espasa-Calpe, 1973).

[15] Brian Murdoch, "Politics in the *Nibelungenlied*," in *A Companion to the Nibelungenlied,* ed. Winder McConnell (Columbia, SC: Camden House, 1998), 229–50, compares the actual Brunichildis with her literary reflection, Brünhilt. Brunichildis was ultimately killed, but only after a forceful rule in which she outwitted and outlived many of her enemies.

[16] Odoacer (Odoaker, Odovacer) is usually presumed to be from an (East) Germanic group, and is described in reference works with equal confidence as a Herulian or Rugian; Gibbon (who rather approves of him) assumes in the *Decline and Fall* that he was a Goth, as is the case with some early chronicles. Occasionally he has been seen as Hun, and he is associated with the Sciri or Skiri in classical writings.

[17] Charles Kingsley, *The Roman and the Teuton* (London: Macmillan, 1864, with a new edition with an introduction by the philologist Max Müller published in 1889 after Kingsley's death, and reprinted many times), cited from the 1889 edition, 151; see especially the fourth, fifth and sixth, entitled "The Gothic Civiliser," "Dietrich's End" and "The Nemesis of the Goths." Modern studies include Chris Wickham, *Early Medieval Italy* (Totowa, NJ: Barnes and Noble, 1981), 9–27, and the substantial volume by Patrick Amory, *People and Identity in Ostrogothic Italy, 489–554* (Cambridge: CUP, 1997) on Christian community and Ostrogoth Arianism.

[18] See Krause, *Handbuch,* 36–38 on the dialects within Gothic.

[19] See on the background of Crimean Gothic Krause, *Handbuch,* 23–25 and A. A. Vasiliev, *The Goths in the Crimea* (Cambridge, MA: Medieval Academy of America, 1936). There is a full study by McDonald Stearns, *Crimean Gothic: Analysis and Etymology of the Corpus* (Stanford and Saratoga, CA: Anima Libri, 1978). On the putative eighteenth-century Crimean Goth, see Bradley, *Goths*, 363–64.

[20] Grant, *Fall of the Roman Empire,* 137–38. See also E. A. Thompson, *The Visigoths in the Time of Ulfila* (Oxford: Clarendon, 1966). For a full discussion of Arianism, see J. N. D. Kelly, *Early Christian Doctrines* (London: A. C. Black, 5th ed., 1977), 244–51 and for a succinct summary, Barrows Dunham, *The Heretics* (London: Eyre and Spottiswoode, 1963), 112–19. In view of the use by the Nazis of the image of the Goths, it is perhaps worthwhile nevertheless pointing out that to link Arianism with *Aryan* is a howler.

[21] See Green, *Language and History,* 308–24, and Theodor Frings, *Grundlegung einer Geschichte der deutschen Sprache* (3rd ed., Halle/S.: Niemeyer, 1957), 22. The extent of the loan words has been debated. See such early studies as Karl Helm, *Die gotische Sprache im Dienste des Kristenthums* (Halle: Waisenhaus, 1870) and most important Friedrich Kluge, "Gotische Lehnwörter im Althochdeutschen," *PBB* 35 (1909): 134–60 (see 124–26 on *Kirche*) and Hans Eggers, *Deutsche Sprachgeschichte I: Das Althochdeutsche* (Reinbek: Rowohlt, 1963), 148–54.

[22] The relevant passages of Auxentius (preserved in Latin) are in Streitberg, *Bibel,* xiii–xxv, with those in Greek from Philostorgius, and also the references from Catholic sources by Socrates Scholasticus, Sozomen, Theodoret of Cyrrhus, Jordanes, Isidore and writers as late as Walahfrid Strabo (ca. 809–49). They are usefully translated in Regan's *Dictionary of the Biblical Gothic Language,* 165–77. See also Isidore of Seville's *History of the Goths, Vandals and Suevi,* trans. G. Donini and G. B. Ford (2nd ed., Leiden: Brill, 1970), and in Kenneth Baxter Wolf, *Conquerors and Chroniclers of Early Medieval Spain* (Liverpool: Liverpool UP, 1999). Isidore's *Historia Gothorum* is a major source for Visigoth history. It might be noted that Eusebius of Nicomedia should not be confused with his contemporary Eusebius of Caesarea, the church historian, although both were involved with the Arian controversy, as indeed were at least two further clerics of the same name. On his consecration, see Wolfram, *History,* 77–79. Wolfram refers also to Eutyches of Cappadocia, possibly an older contemporary of Ulfila.

[23] Ralph W. V. Elliot, *Runes* (Manchester: Manchester UP, 1959), 34–35 discusses the two Gothic alphabets and letter names (which are probably not those of the fourth century), and also the runic ones in the ninth- or tenth-century Salzburg-Vienna Alcuin codex (Österreichische Nationalbibliothek Cod. 795); see 48–49 for a chart of the Germanic runes and the Gothic letters, and 4–5 for some comments on the complex views of the Goths and the invention of the runic alphabet. See also Klaus Düwel, *Runenkunde* (Stuttgart: Metzler, 1968) and his chapter in the present volume. Most of the standard grammars and handbooks of Gothic give the alphabet: see in addition to those already noted (Krause, Feist, Hempel, Braune/Ebbinghaus, Mossé) also M. H. Jellinek, *Geschichte der gotischen Sprache* (Berlin: de Gruyter, 1926); Joseph Wright, *Grammar of the Gothic Language,* 2nd edition by O. L. Sayce (Oxford: Clarendon, 1954); H. Krahe, *Historische Laut- und Formenlehre des Gotischen,* 2nd ed. by Elmar Seebold (Heidelberg: Winter, 1967) and W. H. Bennett, *An Introduction to the Gothic Language* (New York: MLA, 1980).

[24] In the Salzburg-Vienna Alcuin manuscript referred to in the previous note there are some numbers in Gothic form which seem to indicate life spans and which

have been linked with the genealogy in Genesis 5. Even this, however, does not provide firm evidence for a lost Genesis translation.

[25] See M. J. Hunter, "The Gothic Bible" in G. W. H. Lampe, *The Cambridge History of the Bible II: The West from the Fathers to the Reformation* (Cambridge: CUP, 1969), 338–62. The fullest studies are those by G. W. S. Friedrichsen, *The Gothic Version of the Gospels* (London: OUP, 1926) and *The Gothic Version of the Epistles* (London: OUP 1939), and his article "The Greek Text Underlying the Gothic Version of the New Testament. The Gospel of St. Luke" in *Mélanges de linguistique de philology: Fernand Mossé in memoriam* (Paris: Didier, 1959). See Friedrichsen's *Gothic Studies* (Oxford: Blackwell, 1961). On translation, see Werner Schwarz, *Schriften zur Bibelübersetzung und mittelalterlichen Übersetzungstheorie* (London: Institute of Germanic Studies, 1985). On the position of Hebrews within the Pauline letters, see Alexander Souter, *The Text and Canon of the New Testament,* rev. C. S. C. Williams (London: Duckworth, 1954), 174.

[26] See on the manuscripts Krause, *Handbuch,* 16–18; Hunter, "Gothic Bible," 340–41; and in most detail Stutz, *Denkmäler,* 16–27. These all predate the Speyer find, and Hunter does not mention the loss of the Giessen manuscript. See for the Speyer text Braune/Ebbinghaus, *Grammatik,* 4 (with bibliography); the new find provided evidence for several more words and forms in Gothic. See for illustrations of the manuscript (and of the land documents), plus the original papers by Franz Haffner and Piergiuseppe Scardigli, Scardigli's *Die Goten, Sprache und Kultur* (Munich: Beck, 1973); this is the translation by Benedikt Vollman of the new edition of Scardigli's *Lingua e Storia dei Goti* (Florence: Sansoni, 1964). For illustrations of the Codex Argenteus and of Ambrose B, see Braune/Ebbinghaus, but especially the facsimile editions: *Codex Argenteus Upsaliensis,* ed. O. von Friesen and A. Grape (Uppsala: Malmogiae, 1927) and *Wulfilae codices Ambrosiani rescripti,* ed. Jan de Vries (Turin: Molfese, 1936). On the Giessen text see Paul Glaue and Karl Helm, *Das gotisch-lateinische Bibelfragment der Universitätsbibliothek zu Giessen* (Giessen: Töpelmann, 1910), with illustrations. Since the discovery of the Speyer folio in 1971 have come that of a lead tablet with a Gothic Christian inscription from Hács-Béndekpuszta in Hungary in 1978 (the position of which may well be significant) and some smaller indications of Gothic in a ninth-century French manuscript in 1984: see Scardigli's new edition of Streitberg.

[27] On this important manuscript, see Stutz, *Denkmäler,* 39–43.

[28] Streitberg, 163.

[29] See the notes to the extracts in Mossé, *Manuel,* and Feist, *Einführung,* from which these examples are taken. On *praitauria* see Mossé, *Manuel,* 273 on John 18, 33.

[30] The second person dual nominative is not recorded, but can be deduced with some certainty; the other cases are all attested; see Braune/Ebbinghaus, *Grammatik,* 90, §150, Anm. 2.

[31] See the notes to Streitberg's edition of the text, as well as Heather, *Goths,* 60–61. Ulfila was consecrated under Constantius II.

[32] There is a text in Streitberg, *Bibel,* but see William Holmes Bennett, *The Gothic Commentary on the Gospel of St. John* (New York: MLA, 1960, repr. Kraus, 1966)

for a text and translation. Feist, *Einführung,* has a German translation of some of it, and Ernst A Kock, *Die Skeireins* (Lund: Gleerup, 1913) is full. There is a useful analysis with a sample in Stutz, *Denkmäler,* 64–69.

[33] Streitberg, *Bibel,* 465; Bennett, *Commentary,* 68–70.

[34] Krause, *Handbuch,* 21–22 discusses this verse. Several others are listed in Wrede, *Stamm-Heynes Ulfilas,* xvii–xix.

[35] Feist, *Einführung,* 94–98 offers a systematised selection with analysis, showing for example the loss of final *-s* in masculine a-stems (*tag, fisc* for older *tags, fisks,* day, fish), the loss of initial *h-* (*lachen* for *hlahjan*). Some words appear to be Persian or Turkish, and may or may not have been current in Crimean Gothic.

[36] See Green, *Language and History,* 164–81.

[37] See Henri Grégoire, "Le *Waltharius* et Strasbourg," *Bulletin de la Faculté des Lettres de Strasbourg* 14 (1936): 201–213, esp. 212–13 and Herfried Münkler, *Das Blickfeld des Helden* (Göppingen: Kümmerle, 1983), 46–56. See my translation: *Walthari* (Glasgow: Scottish Papers in Germanic Studies, 1989).

[38] See R. C. Boer, *Die Sagen von Ermanarich und Dietrich von Bern* (Halle/S.: Waisenhaus, 1910), 3–14; Heiko Uecker, *Germanische Heldensage* (Stuttgart: Metzler, 1972), 63–79 and the introduction by Egon Wamers, "Die Völkerwanderungszeit im Spiegel der germanischen Heldensagen," in the catalogue to the 1987/1988 exhibition *Germanen, Hunnen und Awaren* at the Germanisches Nationalmuseum in Nuremberg, and published there in 1988, 69–94. The two latter publications have full bibliographies.

[39] Dryden is cited in the useful survey by Josef Haslag, *"Gothic" im siebzehnten und achtzehnten Jahrhundert* (Cologne and Graz: Böhlau, 1963); Haslag's introductory chapter (3–36) on the Goths and the use of their name is relevant to the present study.

[40] A. F. C. Vilmar, *Geschichte der deutschen Nationallitteratur* (20th ed., Marburg and Leipzig: Elwert, 1881), 10. First published in 1845, the book had a 25th edition in 1901. Tolkien's letter to Zillah Sherring (20 July 1965) discusses his interest in Gothic, in *The Letters of J. R. R. Tolkien,* ed. Humphrey Carpenter and Christopher Tolkien (London: Allen and Unwin, 1981), 356–58 (letter 272, with a copy of one such inscription). Tolkien, a philologist to the last, took the opportunity of correcting a couple of errors in his own early Gothic. H. F. Massmann, *Die deutschen Abschwörungs-, Glaubens- Beicht- und Betformeln* (Quedlinburg and Leipzig: Basse, 1839).

Old Norse-Icelandic Literature

Theodore M. Andersson

T HE BODY OF OLD NORSE-ICELANDIC LITERATURE is larger, more varied, and of longer duration than the partially overlapping litera-tures of early medieval England and Germany. Old English literature dis-appeared from view for several centuries because of the linguistic transi-tion after the Norman Conquest, and Old High German and Old Saxon literature were not recovered until the early nineteenth century. Old Ice-landic literature, by contrast, was protected by a substantial linguistic con-tinuity in Iceland and never disappeared from circulation altogether, although, like Old English, it received a notable stimulus from the anti-quarian and national impulses of the Renaissance. In particular, the great manuscript collector Árni Magnússon (died 1730) was able to salvage a great deal of widely dispersed material that might otherwise have been lost. Most of it was recovered in Iceland, and although we routinely refer to "Old Norse-Icelandic" literature in order to account for a number of texts in Old Norwegian, it should be borne in mind that the great pre-ponderance of texts are Icelandic. For all practical purposes, therefore, this chapter deals with Old Icelandic literature.[1]

More than the other Old Germanic literatures, Old Icelandic has been bedeviled by genre boundaries. We do not write histories of the lit-erature as a whole but of distinct literary types, skaldic poetry, Eddic po-etry, kings' sagas, sagas about early Icelanders, sagas about twelfth- and thirteenth-century Icelanders, romances, legendary sagas, and so forth. The approach by genre is partly dictated by the difficulties that beset the dating of our texts. Some sagas can be dated, others only quite approxi-mately. The problems attendant on the dating of Eddic poetry are much greater, to the point that we seem to have entered a period of agnostic resignation. Skaldic poetry, on the other hand, constitutes the exception to the dating impasse because the skalds, unlike the usually anonymous saga writers and always anonymous Eddic poets, are named and associated with kings who can be located in time. Skaldic verse also has the advan-tage of envisaging the whole period of our concern from ca. 800 to ca. 1300.

Skaldic Verse

If skaldic verse is known at all, it is known for being "hard" or even "incomprehensible." By now there are enough aids and commentaries to make most of the material accessible with patient study, although, as in all archaic languages, many cruxes remain. The stanzas are difficult in part because the meters and poetic contrivances are intricate, in part because the mythological frame of reference is unfamiliar, and in part because normal syntax is fragmented and reordered in unexpected ways. A fluent reader of Old Icelandic prose can look at a skaldic stanza and at first recognize only the meaning of individual words. The extraction of overall meaning proceeds through the trial-and-error combination and recombination of lexical items into poetic metaphors and then into sentences.[2]

The first stumbling block is the *kenning,* a type of poetic circumlocution in which two nouns, a "base word" and a "key word," stand in for a single noun. Thus in *Beowulf* we find the circumlocution "whale's road," with the base word "road" and the key word "whale," keying us in to the idea that the sort of road being referred to is a road traveled by whales, that is, the sea. In Norse the substitutions become more elaborate. In the earliest skaldic poem the "sea" is rendered as "the land of Leifi." The listener/reader must know that Leifi is, by convention, a sea king and then deduce that the kind of land inhabited by a sea king is "the sea." In this instance, however, the metaphor is expanded. The poet extends the phrase to "the tree of the land of Leifi" and relies on the listener/reader's ability to extrapolate that an elongated wooden object in the sea should be identified as a "ship." The poet then goes a step further and adds a fourth noun in this accordion-like process, speaking of "the foliage of the tree of the land of Leifi" and inviting us to ponder what part of a ship is comparable in shape and appearance to a leaf on a tree. Guided chiefly by convention and experience, we will surmise that the leaves in question are the shields that line the gunwales of a Viking ship. Thus, the kenning "foliage of the tree of the land of Leifi" as a whole means simply "shield."

Sometimes such kennings seem purely conventional. For example, "tree of the sword" (an erect, roughly tree-shaped creature holding a sword = "warrior") and "goddess of the ale" or "goddess of the necklace" for "woman" have little pictorial appeal, but sometimes the images can be worked out with engaging novelty and appropriateness. A sea king can be visualized as operating on the sea just as an ordinary king operates on land. At one level trees really do grow on land, but on a secondary poetic level they can be fashioned into ships that float on the sea (albeit horizontally rather than vertically). Foliage literally grows on trees in a decorative way, but figuratively it may be compared to the painted shields that seem to sprout on the hull of a Viking ship. Part of skaldic art is the interplay of these images.

One of the mysteries of skaldic verse is that it appears full-blown in the ninth century, in the poem from which the example above is taken (Bragi Boddason's *Ragnarsdrápa*). In Bragi's poem the elaborate court meter (*dróttkvætt*) is fully, or almost fully, evolved — six-syllable lines, internal rhyme, strict rules for alliteration, trochaic cadence, syntactic independence of each half stanza in the eight-line stanza. With Bragi the meter is established once and for all. Whether he was the inventor (and hence gave his name to the god of poetry Bragi) and, if so, what his models may have been, is not known.

By far the largest volume of skaldic verse is composed in this court meter, about 85 percent according to Roberta Frank. The corpus comprises both longer poems, chiefly praise poems addressed to kings and other powerful men, and individual stanzas referred to as *lausavísur* (loose stanzas). The latter were composed on the spur of the moment and could be motivated by practically any occasion. A number of later anecdotes suggest that quick improvisation was a much admired skill. The longer praise poems are typically preserved in the sagas about Norwegian kings although they are rarely set down complete. The *lausavísur* are more commonly recorded in the sagas about individual Icelanders, who, after the ninth century, became the almost exclusive custodians of skaldic art. Since the kings' sagas are focused on the kings, rather than on the poets who celebrated them, we have relatively little information on the panegyric poets, even the most prolific (or at least the best preserved) among them, most prominently of all Saint Olaf's skald Sigvatr Þórðarson, of whom we possess some 150 stanzas. On the other hand, the fashioners of the lesser *lausavísur* are often well known to us because they became the protagonists of such "skald" sagas as *Bjarnar saga Hítdœlakappa*, *Hallfreðar saga*, *Kormáks saga*, *Fóstbrœðra saga*, and *Gunnlaugs saga*. In most cases the skalds were both praise poets and occasional poets. The most notable of these was Egill Skallagrímsson in the tenth century, whose saga records three long poems (a "head-ransom" poem addressed to King Erik Bloodax, a praise poem to his Norwegian friend Arinbjörn, and an elegy on his sons) as well as forty-six *lausavísur*. There are also shorter anecdotal stories about some of the skalds (the so-called *þættir*), to which we will refer below.

Where skalds are depicted in the sagas, we may have the illusion of knowing their personalities, but it is impossible to separate fact from fiction, to guess which scraps of information might be traditional or ultimately "true" and which scraps are the deductions of later storytellers. In most cases there are even questions about the authenticity of some of the verse, although it seems fairly certain that much of it was transmitted by memory more or less faithfully from the tenth and eleventh centuries down to the first half of the thirteenth century, when a concentrated effort seems to have been made by the authors of the kings' sagas and the sagas about early Icelanders to get as much poetic material as possible onto parchment. This harvest is printed in the first four hundred pages of the first volume of the edition by Finnur Jónsson (1894–1902), with prose resolutions and Danish translations at the foot of the page. The thematic range is considerable. At the end of his second volume Finnur Jónsson provides a topical index for the corpus as a whole; it includes elegies, erotic verse, riddles, genealogies, mythological verse, travel verse, religious verse, agonistic verse, and premonitions in verse. In her introduction to court meter Roberta Frank devotes chapters to "Poets on Poetry," "Celebrations and Denunciations," "War Poetry," "The Versified Travelogue," and "Men and Women."

Among these subtypes the battle celebrations are predominant, and carnage is the fundamental image. Such images once exercised a certain fascination, promoted perhaps by an earlier era's nostalgia for primitive reality. The popularity of Norse battle poetry was comparable to the popularity of *Brunnanburh* and *Maldon* in Old English and the *Ludwigslied* in Old High German, but the evolution of taste and sensibility has been such that in the most recent literary history to come out of Iceland the genre of battle poetry is illustrated with one of Goya's horrific war canvases.

At the opposite pole of our sentimental migration is an emerging interest in the love poetry attributed to a number of skalds, amounting to a corpus in the neighborhood of fifty stanzas. This poetic material has attracted attention not so much because of the intrinsic poetic qualities but because it is analogous to the medieval love poetry on the Continent. The Icelandic scholar Bjarni Einarsson in fact argued that the love poetry attributed to Kormákr Ögmundarson was contrived by a later poet under the influence of troubadour love poetry. Others have thought that the styles were merely analogous and that skaldic love poetry is an indigenous phenomenon. If they are right, love poetry affords an instructive measure of just how independent Icelandic literature is down to the time in the twelfth century when Christian literary modes spread in Iceland.

Although it is possible to establish a rough chronological order for skaldic poetry, it is by no means easy to write a history of the development. So much effort has gone into the decoding of the texts that larger critical issues have tended to suffer neglect. In addition, the formal complexities of the verse are apt to obscure the poetic perspectives. Add to this the confusion that arises from the portraits of certain skalds offered by the sagas contrasted to our own efforts to construct poetic personalities by inference from the verse alone. Whether we choose to accept the eccentricities attributed to the skalds by the sagas or arrive at our own conclusions, we remain under the spell of particular personalities, and clusions, we remain under the spell of particular personalities, and those personalities divert us from the task of outlining a historical evolution. We cannot tell whether a particular poetic feature is part of a literary flow over time or a personal idiosyncrasy.

The most influential events in the development of skaldic verse can be concisely stated: the transfer of skaldic art from Norway to Iceland in the tenth century; changes in diction brought about by Christianity around the year 1000; the gradual shift from a court venue in the early period to a more inclusive repertory promoted by the *lausavísur* in Iceland; the application of skaldic meters to religious topics beginning with Einarr Skúlason's celebration of Saint Olaf from 1153; and the scholarly treatment of skaldic diction by Snorri Sturluson in his *Prose Edda* (ca. 1220) and by Snorri's nephew Óláfr Þórðarson in the so-called *Third Grammatical Treatise* (ca. 1250). Perhaps this late academic retrospection conspired with certain linguistic developments that undermined skaldic phonology and brought the skaldic era to a close around 1300.

The watershed in the development of skaldic poetry was the advent of Christian ideology. The transition is illustrated by an oft-repeated anecdote in which King Olaf Tryggvason (died 1000), the first of two conversion kings, is celebrated by his skald Hallfreðr Óttarsson in a stanza laden with the customary pagan mythology. The king demands that Hallfreðr shed the remnants of his heathenish ways, and the anecdote goes on to relate how Hallfreðr does so only slowly and reluctantly. The story invites us to imagine how the new faith may have cramped the old poetics, and for a time at least there seems to have been a revision of the pagan ornaments found in the earlier skaldic verse. Around 1000 there is also a marked simplification of the syntax, especially in the poetry of Sigvatr Þórðarson, who was in the service of several kings, notably the second of the proselytizing Norwegian kings, Olaf Haraldsson (died 1030). The simplification allows for the unfolding of a wit and narrative verve that make Sigvatr more literarily accessible than his predecessors. It is possible that the pruning of the pagan framework and the normalization of syntax were allied developments and combined to adjust the skaldic style to more straightforward poetic models outside Scandinavia.

The next revolution dates from the middle of the twelfth century, when Einarr Skúlason composes a poem of seventy-one stanzas in commemoration of Saint Olaf and delivers it in Christ Church in Trondheim in 1153. The poem is usually referred to as "Geisli" ([Sun] Beam) and is remarkable for its incorporation of Christian imagery, Christ as "sol salutis" and "sol justitiae." It follows the convention of the older memorial panegyrics by rehearsing Olaf's life and deeds, but it goes on to recapitulate his afterlife and miracles as well.

From the same era there is preserved a *Plácítúsdrápa,* which recounts the life of the legendary Roman Placidus (or Saint Eustace) and the trials he endures with steadfast faith. In addition, we have a *Harmsól* by a canon named Gamli. The title is supplied in the poem and is a *kenning* conveying the idea that Christ is the "sun of sorrow," that is, he reprieves from the sorrows of this life. The poem is penitential in tone, looking ahead to the salvation earned by genuine devotion. Another anonymous poem titled *Leiðarvísan* (path pointer) gives guidance on the history and observance of Sunday. The body of religious verse in skaldic meters has been relatively neglected, although it provides a sometimes impressive demonstration of the tradition's capacity for growth and change.

The most encompassing attempt to evaluate skaldic verse in artistic terms is found in two papers by Hallvard Lie from 1952 and 1957. Lie rejected the derivation of court meter from Irish or other foreign models and considered it an indigenous form, most nearly comparable to the zoomorphic tradition in Scandinavian art. Basing himself on Bragi Boddason's "shield poem" (the description of four myths depicted on the four fields of an ornamental shield), Lie considered that the *dróttkvætt* stanza originated as a pictorial poem, that is, as a static, deliberately non-narrative, abstract, ornamental form most closely associated with the "Vestfold school" of Norwegian art brilliantly illustrated by the decorations in the Oseberg ship burial from the ninth century. Only gradually did both the native art form and skaldic style come under the influence of southern (in the first instance Carolingian) models and, in the process, become more realistic. Hence, the evolution from ornamental scrolls toward identifiable animals in monumental art and the evolution from fragmented syntax toward normal syntax in skaldic poetry, an evolution in which Lie points to Bragi Boddason, Egill Skallagrímsson, and Sigvatr Þórðarson as the symptomatic exponents. At the same time, the transition to Christianity also leaves its mark, facilitating the replacement of an older self-assertive bravura with a new sense of poetry as a vehicle for explication, in line with the enlightening mission of Christian literature. The original opacity of skaldic diction persisted down into the thirteenth century, but even in the antiquarian Snorri Sturluson Lie perceives an underlying tension between an older and a more modern esthetic. Lie's analysis operates largely with metaphors, but it remains the most broadly conceived and thought provoking we have.

Eddic Verse

In contrast to the fairly rich transmission of skaldic verse, found in many manuscripts, Eddic verse is known to us chiefly from one manuscript from around 1270. This manuscript is referred to as Codex Regius (2365 4°) because it was housed for three centuries in the royal collections in Copenhagen, from which it was transferred to the Arnamagnaean Manuscript Institute in Reykjavik in 1971. It contains thirty poems, with one or more poems missing in the lost fifth gathering. They are organized into a mythological section (eleven poems) and a heroic section (nineteen poems). The mythological section includes a complex of 164 stanzas of largely gnomic verse known as *Hávamál* (The Sayings of the High One [Odin]) as well as the borderline heroic-mythological poem about the legendary smith Wayland (*Völundarkviða*). Painstaking codicological analysis by Gustaf Lindblad suggests that this collection accrued from smaller collections dating back to the early thirteenth century.[3]

Partly because the heroic poems often deal with common Germanic legends, Eddic poetry was once considered very old. In the first large-scale literary history by Finnur Jónsson, the Eddic poems were in fact dealt with first, but there has been a steady trend toward later datings to the point where there is now considerable doubt whether any of the Eddic poetry that we have is older than the twelfth century. On the other hand, Bragi Boddason's shield poem from the ninth century shows knowledge of two stories represented in Codex Regius, one mythological (*Hymiskviða*) and one heroic (*Hamðismál*). It therefore seems likely that, even if these poems themselves are not old, there were at least early precursors presumably in verse form. "Eddic" poetry as such is probably not a late invention.

We may begin with the heroic group because it is illuminated by a larger context in the other Germanic literatures. Six of the Eddic poems (*Grípisspá, Reginsmál, Fáfnismál, Sigrdrífumál, Brot af Sigurðarkviðu, Sigurðarkviða in skamma* (and in addition a longer poem known as **Sigurðrkviða in meiri* but lost in the lacuna of Codex Regius and only hypothetically reconstructable from other texts) tell the same story, with notable deviations, as the first part of the German *Nibelungenlied*. They are generally referred to as the Sigurd poems, although Brynhild (German Brünhild) is the preeminent figure rather than Sigurd (German Siegfried). The tale is one of erotic betrayal: how Sigurd, duped by a potion of forgetfulness, jilts Brynhild and marries the sister of the Burgundian king Gunnarr (German Gunther) instead. The sister is named Guðrún in the Icelandic version rather than Kriemhild as in the *Nibelungenlied*. Sigurd, accused by Brynhild of having slept with her, is murdered by the Burgundian brothers. Overwhelmed by betrayal and sorrow, Brynhild dies in a grand Didoesque scene complete with sword and pyre. Guðrún, however, lives on to marry the Hunnish king Atli (the historical Attila, German Etzel). Her story is told in two further poems (*Atlakviða* and *Atlamál*) equivalent to the second part of the *Nibelungenlied*. In the Icelandic versions Atli invites the Burgundian brothers to a feast in a vain attempt to extract from them the secret of the treasure they have seized from Sigurd. Rebuffed, he kills the brothers and is in turn killed in bed by their sister Guðrún after she has served him a Thyestean meal of his sons.

These poems are remarkable for a lapidary intensity not found either in skaldic verse or in the surviving German analogues. They are not only more operatic, as any retelling will reveal, but are also emotionally complex and erotically haunting in a way that sets them apart from the rest of medieval love narrative. In Codex Regius we also find a final act not replicated elsewhere, although a passage in Jordanes's *Getica* (ca. 550) indicates that the story was pre-Icelandic. Guðrún lives to marry a third time and bear three children, a daughter Svanhildr and the sons Hamðir and Sörli. Svanhildr is married off to the Gothic king Jörmunrekkr (Ermanaric), who kills her on a suspicion of infidelity. Vengeance prevails once more; Guðrún incites Hamðir and Sörli against Jörmunrekkr and they succeed in maiming him, though they succumb in the mission. This story is told in the last two poems of Codex Regius, *Guðrúnarhvöt* and *Hamðismál.*

All these tales have deep roots on the Continent. The legend of Brynhild and Sigurd is attested in Germany not only by the *Nibelungenlied* but also by an amalgam of heroic legends centering on Dietrich von Bern and titled *Þiðreks saga,* because it is extant only in a Norse version. This collection is traditionally thought to be a Norwegian registration of German oral stories from ca. 1250, but it could equally well be the translation of a German book. If so, that book must predate the *Nibelungenlied,* of which it makes no use, and could have been written as early as the 1180s. The stories are, however, much older, and the protagonist Dietrich is referred to in the *Hildebrandlied* from the early ninth century.

The Continental matrix of the stories shows that they were ultimately brought to Scandinavia and Iceland from Germany. That supposition is supported by the form of the Norse poems. They are composed in the standard alliterative meter known from Old English, Old High German, and Old Saxon poetry, and they have the same dimensions as the *Hildebrandlied,* running from as few as thirty stanzas (*Hamðismál*) to as many as a hundred and five stanzas (*Atlamál*). The chief innovation is the stanzaic form, in opposition to the stychic form in the other Germanic languages. It is tempting to think that the stanzaic form was adopted by analogy to skaldic practice, but that leaves open the question of how the stanzaic form in skaldic verse originated. On the other hand, Eddic poetry is conservative in retaining the short form of the original heroic lay, provided we consider the short form to be original. Adherents of the oral-formulaic theory believe that the epic form is old and would therefore view the Icelandic short form as an innovation. In any event there is little evidence of an epic trend in Iceland parallel to the epic developments in verse elsewhere in the Germanic world. There is nothing analogous to *Beowulf,* the *Heliand,* or, much later, the *Nibelungenlied*. An epic impulse was reserved for the prose sagas.

An apparent innovation in the Eddic corpus is represented by a set of retrospective ruminations or laments attributed to the women of heroic legend (*Guðrúnarkviða* I, II, and III, *Helreið Brynhildar, Oddrúnar-grátr*). These poems have been classed as "elegies" and have most often been regarded as a late Icelandic form created under the influence of a nascent ballad literature on the Continent. Unlike the core poems about Brynhild and Sigurd they have no counterpart in the larger Germanic world, but it has recently been argued by Daniel Sävborg that the case for the late dating of the Eddic elegies is weak. Although the poems themselves are not paralleled elsewhere in Germanic, Joseph Harris has also argued that the elegiac form, for example in the so-called Old English elegies, is old. These doubts about the long-standing typology that posits a linear development from a short heroic poem (with common Germanic roots) to a somewhat more extended and sentimentalized heroic poem and finally to the excrescent elegies throw the standard literary-historical outline into disarray. It remains to be seen whether a relative chronology based on stylistic criteria can be rebuilt.

No such system can in any case be worked out for the mythological poems. They are fewer in number and have no context outside of Iceland. Nor are they comparable among themselves. The closest approach to an identifiable subgenre is the wisdom contest, in which a god and a human (or a supernatural creature) test each other with questions about cosmic or mythic phenomena. In *Vafþrúðnismál* a disguised Odin visits a giant and bests him with an impossible question. In *Grímnismál* Odin visits King Geirroðr, who has usurped the throne from his brother, is at first tormented between two fires, then gradually reveals his identity with arcane information. In *Alvíssmál* Thor has an encounter with a dwarf, who seeks the hand of his daughter in marriage, and tests his knowledge until sunrise, an hour that is fatal for dwarves. In each case the god triumphs and his antagonist succumbs: Vafþrúðnir alludes to his own death, Geirroðr accidentally falls on his sword, and Alvíss is turned to stone. All three poems have minimal dramatic frames and seem chiefly to serve the purpose of cataloguing mythological lore.

A lesser subtype is the flyting, or carefully crafted exchange of insults. In *Hárbarðsljóð* (Hárbarðr being one of the many pseudonyms for Odin) Odin and Thor meet on opposite banks of a river with Thor seeking passage and Odin playing the part of the ferryman. Each boasts of his own achievements and discredits those of his antagonist. In *Lokasenna* the trickster god Loki is barred from a feast of the gods but returns to upbraid them serially. The gods are found wanting in various respects, while the goddesses are accused somewhat monotonously of sexual misconduct. In these poems the information, much of it no doubt contrived for effect, is less tiresome than in the preceding quasi-didactic poems, and the bantering tone is more entertaining.

Two more poems are devoted to the adventures of Thor. In *Hymiskviða* he is delegated by the gods to fetch a kettle from the giant Hymir. In the course of the adventure he goes fishing with the giant and, not content with two whales, hooks the Miðgarðsormr (world serpent) as well. But the serpent sinks back into the sea, and, after further tests of strength, Thor obtains the kettle and completes his mission. Even more burlesque is *Þrymskviða*. Here the giant Þrymr has stolen Thor's hammer and demands the hand of the goddess Freyja in exchange for its return. The gods disguise Thor as the bride Freyja and present him to Þrymr, who is readily duped, though he is astonished by the bride's enormous appetite at the wedding feast and the flashing eyes revealed beneath her bridal veil. The hammer is duly produced, and, having repossessed it, Thor makes short work of Þrymr and eight other giants. *Þrymskviða* in particular has been suspected of being a late literary contrivance.

Whereas Odin and Thor figure in several poems, the fertility god Freyr figures at the center of only one, *För Skírnis* or *Skírnismál*. As if by way of compensation, this poem has been more intensely studied and more often interpreted than the aforementioned. It tells the story of how Freyr catches sight of the giant maiden Gerðr and dispatches his servant Skírnir as a delegate wooer. When honeyed words fail, Skírnir pronounces a curse to make the recalcitrant bride compliant. She must then agree to a marriage in nine days' time. In an earlier era this marriage was understood as a *hieros gamos,* with Freyr as the fertility god, his delegate Skírnir (the bright one) as the fructifying sun, and Gerðr (connected with *garðr* "cultivated yard") as the earth to be made fruitful. More recently interpretations by Lars Lönnroth and Margaret Clunies Ross have instead connected the plot with human marriage practices, taboos, and rules governing courtship and partner selection.

Easily the most impressive and frequently discussed of the mythological poems is *Völuspá* (The Prophecy of the Sybil). It is the lead poem in Codex Regius, almost certainly because it is synthetic, giving an account of the creation of the world, the gods, and the human race, a history of the gods down to *ragnarök* (the twilight of the gods), and suggesting the rise of a new world. The framework for the narrative is provided by the quizzing of a prophetess who sees into the future. Much is elliptical and allusive in the poem, which has therefore posed difficult problems for a succession of commentators, but the mantic style conforms to the prophetic content. Roughly speaking the poem might be divided into sections on cosmogony, the gods (Æsir), visual omens of doom, auditory omens of doom, *ragnarök*, and the rebirth of a new world. Because of the allusion to a better world and other reminiscences of Christianity *Völuspá* has customarily been dated around 1000, the time of the advent of Christianity in Iceland and the moment at which there would have been a dual consciousness of the heathen and Christian religions. But since all the other poems in the collection have been assigned, or have tacitly drifted down, to the twelfth century or later, *Völuspá* has become something of a chronological outlier.

Early Prose

Iceland was settled in the decades around 900 and converted to Christianity in the year 1000. As the Church and the prerequisite schools became established in the eleventh century, there must have been some glimmerings of literature, but the first literary names we encounter are from the period ca. 1120–30. These names are Sæmundr Sigfússon (died 1133), who, judging from later references to the lost book, must have written a little digest of the Norwegian kings, and Ari Þorgilsson (died 1148), by whom we have a miniature history of early Iceland (*Íslendingabók* or *Libellus Islandorum*) in the native tongue. Ari tells of the settlement of Iceland, the foundation of the state and the legal institutions, the conversion, and several other significant moments in Icelandic history. He also enumerates bishops and lawspeakers.

His sources were chiefly oral informants, whom he identifies, but he also mentions one book, a life of Saint Edmund by Abbo of Fleury. This life deviates from the general run of hagiography to the extent that the first two chapters provide information on the history and early settlement of England, specifically the nature of the land in East Anglia. That regional focus could have provided the point of departure for *Íslendingabók*. It has also been suggested that Ari was influenced by Bede's *Ecclesiastical History,* and the references to oral informants, the focus on settlement and conversion, and the alternating profiles of bishops and secular leaders is certainly reminiscent of Bede's history. The emergence of Icelandic literature might therefore be seen as a Bedan (or post-Bedan) moment, but the secular spark did not ignite until a century later.[4]

In the meantime, Icelandic literature was dominated by hagiographic writings as evidenced by a few twelfth-century manuscript fragments and a reference to *þýðingar helgar* (ecclesiastical translations) in the so-called *First Grammatical Treatise* from the second half of the twelfth century. Which of these writings are old and which are from a later period is hard to know unless they appear in early manuscripts, as only a very few do, but what they have in common is that they are notably non-Icelandic.

They include, as a small sample, the stories of the apostles, biographies of church fathers such as Ambrose and Augustine, the story of the desert father Anthony, the *Dialogues* of St. Gregory, the life of St. Martin, the life of St. Brendan, the *Visio Tnugdali* (Vision of Tundal), and an array of stories about early Christian martyrs. The ideology of this literature is without exception Christian and the scenes are remote, chiefly Mediterranean. Icelandic readers must have felt themselves transported to utterly foreign cultures and climates. Then, in a quite unmediated way, literary taste shifted to native and more strictly historical matters around 1190.

Ari had explained in the preface to *Íslendingabók* that the text in hand was a second edition, without the "genealogies" and "kings' lives" that had been included in the first edition. Given our lack of twelfth-century materials, these allusions are somewhat mysterious, but they point in the direction of the genealogies and kings' sagas that are very fully documented in the thirteenth century. The genealogies, in whatever form they originated, were compiled in an imposing book called *Landnámabók* (The Book of Settlement). It accounts for some four hundred original settlers and proceeds family by family around the island. We know that there were two major redactions in the thirteenth century, one by Styrmir Kárason (died 1245) and one by Sturla Þórðarson (died 1284). There were also later redactions from the fourteenth down to the seventeenth century. Whether Ari was responsible for some proto-redaction of this book or was merely an early figure in a long chain of contributors, it seems reasonable to assume that the genealogical material was already accruing in the twelfth century. A number of colonists and their progeny came to play important parts in the sagas about early Icelanders that emerge in the thirteenth century.

Ari's reference to "kings' lives" is more difficult to fathom because there is no intimation of a gradual accrual of kings' sagas in the twelfth century. The only exceptions are a lost saga about events in the middle of the twelfth century, called *Hryggjarstykki in later accounts, and some brief epitomes of kings' lives in Norway, a *Historia de Antiquitate Regum Norwagiensium* by a certain Theodoricus monachus (ca. 1180), an anonymous *Historia Norwegiae* of uncertain date, and a vernacular *Ágrip af Nóregs konunga sögum* (ca. 1190). These epitomes may be ultimately inspired by Sæmundr and Ari, but the evidence is tenuous. Taken together they provide at least a skeletal outline of Norwegian history from the middle of the ninth century to the middle of the twelfth century.

The literary scene changed dramatically around 1190. At first, activity was centered at the monastery at Þingeyrar in northwestern Iceland, whereas Sæmundr and Ari had written in the south. Þingeyrar fostered a series of considerably longer biographies of individual kings. The ruling Norwegian king, Sverrir Sigurðarson (died 1202), commissioned the abbot of Þingeyrar, Karl Jónsson, to write his biography around 1185, although the saga may not have been completed, perhaps by someone other than Karl, until after the king's death. One of the monks at Þingeyrar, Oddr Snorrason, composed a life of King Olaf Tryggvason (995–1000) in Latin around 1190. Three vernacular versions of the Latin original are extant. Another monk, Gunnlaugr Leifsson, also wrote a life of Olaf Tryggvason, but it survives only in the form of passages that were woven into later compilations. It is likely that around the same time a biography of King Olaf Haraldsson (1015–30), later Saint Olaf, was composed, whether at Þingeyrar or elsewhere is not known, but only six small fragments survive. Norway was, however, not the only focus of attention. In the same period, around 1200, histories of the Orkney Islands (*Orkneyinga saga*) and the Faeroe Islands (*Færeyinga saga*) were produced. In this case too we do not have the original texts but only disassembled sections or later amalgamated versions. The focus on the two Olafs in this early biographical phase may be accounted for by their status as conversion kings, Olaf Tryggvason in both Norway and Iceland and Olaf Haraldsson as the prosecutor of his predecessor's mission in Norway.[5]

Some years after the appearance of the individual biography as an established form the scene was set for full-scale historical compendia. The first of these, known by the name of the unique manuscript from ca. 1275, is called *Morkinskinna* (rotten parchment). Originally written around 1220, it covers Norwegian history from the death of Olaf Haraldsson (1030) down to 1157, where the manuscript breaks off. The full text may well have extended down to 1177 and may therefore have bridged the gap between the individual biographies of Olaf Haraldsson and Sverrir Sigurðarson. About half the text is devoted to Haraldr Sigurðarson, the half brother of Olaf Haraldsson, who ruled from 1047 to 1066, when he fell in a vain attempt to conquer England. Haraldr, known as harðráði (Hardrada, "hard-ruler"), was the most adventurous of all the Norwegian kings. He grew up in Russia after the death of his half brother, made his fortune in the service of the Byzantine emperor, returned to Norway, and campaigned tirelessly in Denmark before succumbing in England. There are textual difficulties connected with *Morkinskinna* as well as the earlier sagas because the manuscript of 1275 may not accurately represent the original of 1220, but the inclination now is to assume that the deviation is not great.

There are two noteworthy features of *Morkinskinna*. It is the first text to make extensive use of skaldic verse to underpin historical events. Second, it inserts numerous (as many as forty) episodic or anecdotal stories (so-called *þættir*) only loosely connected with the lives of the kings. The largest number of these stories are attached to the history of Haraldr harðráði, but they typically concern individual Icelanders and their signal success in dealing with the Norwegian monarchy. *Morkinskinna* thus not only marks a shift from biography to compendium but also alters the face of saga writing by emphasizing the Icelandic elements, the authenticating verse of Icelandic skalds and the experience of Icelanders in their interactions with Norway. The text thus tells us as much about Iceland as it does about Norway and therefore effectively refocuses away from the land of the royal patrons and toward the land of the literary executors. From this moment on the sagas become a more palpably Icelandic project.

Soon after the writing of *Morkinskinna* a second anonymous compendium was produced, this one also named after one of the manuscripts (*Fagrskinna* "fair parchment"). The coverage is much extended, from the mid-ninth century to 1177, but the narrative dimensions are also much reduced so that the book as a whole is smaller than *Morkinskinna* though the period of time covered is greater. The amount of skaldic verse is pruned and the anecdotal stories about Icelanders are systematically suppressed, thus curtailing the Icelandic emphases of *Morkinskinna* to the extent that *Fagrskinna* has raised the suspicion that it is a Norwegian composition. It seems more likely, however, that it too is Icelandic, though the work of a less discursive author with a stricter view of historical relevance.

The culmination of the historical compendium was *Heimskringla* (Circle of the World), commonly dated between 1225 and 1235. It was in all probability written in western Iceland by Snorri Sturluson (died 1241), although the evidence is inferential. Snorri was also the author of *Snorra Edda* (the so-called "Prose Edda"), a book about the practice and mythological foundations of skaldic verse and a capital source for our knowledge of these matters. Snorri belonged to the most powerful family of the thirteenth century in Iceland and is well known from contemporary sources. He was politically active, for example as lawspeaker, ambitious for wealth and power, and deeply engaged in the designs of King Hákon Hákonarson (died 1263) to extend Norwegian hegemony over Iceland, a plan that ultimately came to fruition in the years 1262–64. Unfortunately the sources tell us less about his literary activity; although we learn something of his poetic compositions, there is only one fleeting reference to his saga writing.

Snorri's *Heimskringla* is the fullest and most ambitious of the historical surveys. He prefaces Norwegian history with a legendary prehistory of Sweden (*Ynglinga saga*) and devotes particularly full coverage to the life of Olaf Haraldsson. In his capacity as a keen student of skaldic poetry, he makes disciplined use of his verse sources, including no fewer than 583 stanzas (or partial stanzas) in his book. But like the author of *Fagrskinna* he makes it a rule to exclude the anecdotal stories about Icelanders. With the completion of *Heimskringla* the creative era of kings' saga writing was essentially over. A history of the Danish kings (*Knýtlinga saga*) was added in the middle of the thirteenth century, and Snorri Sturluson's nephew Sturla Þórðarson (died 1284) wrote a biography of the reigning monarch Hákon Hákonarson (1217–63) from contemporary reports and documents around 1260, but there was no strikingly new historical impulse after Snorri, merely supplemented and expanded versions in compilations of the fourteenth and fifteenth centuries.

The decade 1220–30 was a real turning point in Icelandic letters. Not only did it see the culmination of kings' saga writing but probably also the first stages of the writing about Icelanders of the Saga Age (ca. 930–1030) and the first sagas about the twelfth century, later collected in the early fourteenth century in the compendium known as *Sturlunga saga*. But before turning to these matters, we must cast a glance at those works that ushered out the twelfth century and persisted into the thirteenth. They are works that have been somewhat neglected because they stand in the shadow of the Norwegian kings and illustrious Icelanders who came to dominate Icelandic literature after 1220, but they too have a literary tale to tell.

We have seen that the twelfth century was largely devoted to religious literature, providing what the Icelanders may have thought of as a narrative of the early Church's heroic age. As the century advances, there is a tendency to secularize this perspective on foreign literature and to adopt the humanistic impulses seen elsewhere in Europe during the Renaissance of the twelfth century. In the 1150s the monastery at Munkaþverá in the north produces a little guidebook (*Leiðarvísir* or "Road Guide") to the Holy Land, outlining the pilgrim routes from Iceland to Jerusalem. The fabled seat of Christendom thus becomes a tourist site. There are other fragments of geographical and encyclopedic lore, some of which must go back to this period and which have been conveniently assembled by Rudolf Simek. They presumably served to make the far reaches of the world less unfamiliar to the remote Icelanders. These exotic extravagations even took the form of sagas, as early as the 1190s when the same Oddr Snorrason who wrote a life of Olaf Tryggvason appears to have written *Yngvars saga víðförla*, the fabulous tale of a northern exploration into Russia in the early eleventh century. Ultimately this taste for exploration culminated in two sagas about the discovery of Vinland, *Eiríks saga rauða* and *Grænlendinga saga,* perhaps written in the 1220s.

The fascination with foreign shores also brought with it a modest rediscovery of classical literature. Around 1180, or possibly earlier, an unknown writer put together a book titled *Rómverja saga* (History of the Romans), a conflation of Sallust's *Jugurthine Wars* and Lucan's account of the civil wars in his *Pharsalia*. The setting in North Africa is hardly less exotic than the remote regions of Russia and America, or the Byzantine and African scenes of Haraldr harðráði's early adventures. It bespeaks a similarly imaginative appropriation of the larger world. A short time later ca. 1190 a little text known as *Veraldar saga* (History of the World), perhaps from the pen of Gizurr Hallsson (died 1206), extends the historical parameters further. It is a capsule epitome of universal history, devoted about half to biblical history and half to the kingdoms of classical antiquity and the early Middle Ages down to the days of Frederick Barbarossa.

Sometime in the 1190s it can be surmised that there was an Icelandic redaction of Dares Phrygius's *De excidio Trojae* known as *Trójumanna saga,* though it is only preserved in much later versions. The Icelanders therefore had some notion of the Trojan War, although there is hardly a trace of Virgil's great epic that had had wide currency in the rest of Europe for several centuries. Around 1200, again only by surmise, the Trojan diaspora was brought closer to home in an Icelandic reworking of Geoffrey of Monmouth's *Historia Regum Britanniae,* part of which ("The Prophecies of Merlin") was translated by Gunnlaugr Leifsson at Þingeyrar. The dating of these texts has been much disputed, with proposals ranging from 1200 to 1250, but the most recent study by Stefanie Würth opts for the earlier date. They may well have been significant for the emergence of Icelandic literature because they involve a historical discovery of self elsewhere in Europe, not unlike the self-discovery that was soon to preoccupy Icelandic writers. The most elegant rendering of a pseudo-historical text, however, came half a century later in Bishop Brandr Jónsson's *Alexanders saga,* a translation of Walter of Châtillon's epic version of the life of Alexander the Great (*Alexandreis*).

The twelfth-century literary scene is dominated by hagiography and Christian biographies, with a growing interest in classical history and medieval pseudo-history toward the end of the century, followed by an evolving preoccupation with the lives of Norwegian kings and the tributary islands of Norway (Orkney and the Faeroes) starting around 1190. The only native text, apart from Ari's *Íslendingabók* and perhaps some lost redactions of *Landnámabók,* is Eríkr Oddsson's lost *Hryggjarstykki from the middle of the century, but, as Bjarni Guðnason has argued, that text too seems to have been cast in the dominant hagiographic mold, with the protagonist, the pretender Sigurðr slembir, concluding his life as a martyr. Around 1200 Icelanders became distinctly more interested in their native history. The shift began with the lives of native Icelandic bishops, but the focus soon came to embrace secular figures as well.

The best text to illustrate this transition in Icelandic literary taste is a little epitome of Icelandic bishops entitled *Hungrvaka* (appetizer, that is, an invitation to more reading) from the first decade of the thirteenth century. Ari had already made prominent mention of early bishops, but *Hungrvaka* provides thumbnail sketches notably of Ísleifr Gizurarson

(1056–80), Gizurr Ísleifsson (1082–1118), Þorlákr Rúnólfsson (1118–33), Magnús Einarsson (1133–48), and Klængr Þorsteinsson (1152–76). At about the same time there were full-scale biographies of Bishop Jón Ögmundarson (1106–21) by Gunnlaugr Leifsson and Bishop Þorlákr Þórhallsson (1178–93). The bishop who was literarily most celebrated, but also most controversial, was Guðmundr Arason, who presided over the northern see at Hólar from 1203 to 1237 and was politically very active. A number of sagas were devoted to him, the first relating his life only down to his consecration in 1203 and three more covering his whole life, but not written until the fourteenth century. There are other bishops' sagas as well, and although this class of sagas are decidedly less compelling than the kings' sagas and the sagas about early Icelanders, they do offer interesting insights into life and politics in medieval Iceland.

The first decade of the thirteenth century may also have produced the earliest sagas proper, sagas about the chieftains of twelfth-century Iceland, in chronological order *Sturlu saga* and *Guðmundar saga dýra*. The first tells the story of Sturla Þórðarson, the progenitor of the great Sturlung family, which produced such literary figures as Snorri Sturluson and Sturla Þórðarson. The elder Sturla died in 1183, and it is assumed that his saga was written quite early in the thirteenth century. It gives a dense account of the interactions and rivalries in Sturla's region in northwestern Iceland, especially his antagonism with Einarr Þorgilsson. Guðmundr dýri died in 1212, and his saga is thought to have been written shortly after his death. It is somewhat shorter and not quite so genealogically overburdened as *Sturlu saga,* but both sagas give a good indication of what detailed information was retained and circulated about the personalities and events of a given district.

A saga entitled *Þorgils saga ok Hafliða,* this time about events around 1120, was perhaps written as early as 1220, although it is most often dated around 1240. It achieves the sort of dramatic effect characteristic of the best sagas. The three sagas referred to here, along with a number of others covering events of the mid-thirteenth century, were later collected in a compilation known as *Sturlunga saga* (The Saga of the Sturlungs), probably by a man named Þórðr Narfason (died 1308). The Sturlung compilation as a whole thus comprises an extensive record of personal and political events in twelfth- and thirteenth-century Iceland. The most extensive narrative was written by Sturla Þórðarson and is titled *Íslendinga saga*. It gives an account of Iceland from the death of the older Sturla in 1183 down to the middle of the thirteenth century. The style of these sagas is more chronicle-like and less dramatic than what we find in the sagas of the early Icelanders, but they provide something that more nearly approaches history, though a history certainly subjected to literary reformulation.

Sagas about Early Icelanders

The great triumph of Icelandic saga writing is found in the stories about the Saga Age (930–1030), that is, the period after the colonization when the commonwealth began to consolidate. The sagas about this period, sometimes called "sagas of Icelanders" or "family sagas," are scattered throughout the thirteenth century and are difficult to date because they are anonymous and make almost no reference to contemporary matters. As a result they are often discussed without chronological discriminations, but they too saw a development over time. That development may not have begun with the commitment of ink to parchment, but rather with the oral stories that preceded the sagas. That such stories circulated in Iceland between the Saga Age and the thirteenth century seems almost certain, but the form in which they circulated has been much debated. Some have thought that the sagas were substantially preformed in tradition, others that the traditions were slight and that saga composition was almost entirely a written exercise. In an important general study Carol Clover argues that there were only brief oral stories and that the stuff of the full sagas was merely potential in oral tradition, not realized until the act of writing occurred.

The oral forerunners of the sagas are largely inscrutable, but there is some semblance of chronology once the sagas are set down in writing. It appears that the so-called "skald sagas" were among the first to be written: *Bjarnar saga Hítdælakappa, Hallfreðar saga vandræðaskálds,* and *Kormáks saga Ögmundarsonar.* These sagas have several features in common. They celebrate noteworthy Icelandic poets biographically and record a good deal of their poetry, some of it amatory and some of it in praise of royal patrons. A special feature is the love triangle, which pits two poets against each other in an often bitter contest of words and arms. Björn loses his betrothed to a rival by deception and enters into a protracted exchange of poetic insults before finally succumbing to overwhelming odds in an ambush. Hallfreðr loses his beloved because of family intervention, travels abroad, devotes himself to Olaf Tryggvason, but then returns to Iceland and persists in his attentions to his lost love. Kormákr loses his betrothed to a rival, allegedly because of a curse placed upon him, and despite later opportunities he never recovers her. These replicating plots may derive from the love poetry of the skalds in question, but they may also owe something to the leveling of oral transmission.

A fourth saga that belongs in the same category is *Gunnlaugs saga ormstungu.* Unlike the first three, it is customarily dated in the latter part of the thirteenth century because of a romanticized tone and diction. A version of the story is, however, alluded to in *Egils saga* and must therefore have been in circulation before 1230 or so, whether in oral or written form we do not know. In this story the poets Gunnlaugr and Hrafn compete for the hand of Helga the Fair and are ultimately destined to kill each other in a duel. Another saga that may be very early, though, like *Bjarnar saga Hítdœlakappa,* it has also been dated late in the century, is *Fóstbrœðra saga,* a story that centers on the skald Þormóðr Bersason and his sworn brother Þorgeirr Hávarsson. Like the skald sagas it records a good deal of verse. It also recounts something of Þormóðr's amorous adventures and his close relationship to King Olaf Haraldsson.

Rather more remote from the core group of skald sagas is *Gísla saga Súrssonar,* which is difficult to date but may well be from the first half of the century. It focuses on the outlaw Gísli Súrsson, who is eventually tracked down and killed. A good deal of his verse is set down, but none of it is amatory, and rivalry in love is only a minor theme. In the prose, however, the erotic tensions are worked out with a suggestiveness found almost nowhere else, and marital love is celebrated more loftily than in any but the later epic sagas, *Laxdœla saga* and *Njáls saga. Gísla saga* may well be the most dramatic and most brilliantly crafted of all the sagas. A second saga focusing on an outlaw, though with less effect, is *Harðar saga Grímkelssonar.* It too must have been written in the first half of the century because it is ascribed to Styrmir Kárason (died 1245).

A special place in the development of the skald saga is occupied by *Egils saga Skallagrímssonar,* which, if it is correctly attributed to Snorri Sturluson, must have been written in the period 1220–40. Here the story is no longer about personal erotic rivalries or devotion to a Norwegian king. It is about poetry, character, and politics. The plot pits the great tenth-century Icelandic skald against a series of Norwegian kings and expands the biographical form into a historical canvas about Iceland and Norwegian kingship. It is several times longer than the other skald sagas and dwarfs their range of concerns. It also transfers epic form from the kings' sagas to the sagas of early Iceland.

We might surmise that *Egils saga* is the point of departure for the narrative of political conflict rather than personal conflict, but we cannot be certain that this was the sequence. It appears that at the same time, that is, in the 1220s, now in the north of Iceland rather than the west, there arose a narrative focusing on internal Icelandic conflicts. These sagas mark, in contrast to the twelfth century, a further turning inward, an Icelandic literature more exclusively about Iceland. *Reykdœla saga,* which has been dated between 1207 and 1222 by Dietrich Hofmann, relates feud events in northern Iceland in a serial manner reminiscent of the early texts in *Sturlunga saga.* There are no poets, no verses, no erotic complications, but there are a great many references to tradition, so that we can only conclude that the narrative was passed down by storytellers in the region.

Probably from the same time and a neighboring region is *Víga-Glúms saga*. Like *Reykdæla saga* it recounts a series of feuds and antagonisms, but unlike *Reykdæla saga* it maintains a constant focus on a single protagonist, Víga-Glúmr Eyjólfsson, whose dealings are traced down to the day of his death. Again there is almost no verse, and the saga can only be understood as the product of oral transmission. From the same region as *Víga-Glúms saga*, that is, Eyjafjörður in north-central Iceland, is another feud saga, *Ljósvetninga saga*. It is often dated to the middle of the thirteenth century, but there is some reason to believe that it too is from the 1220s. Any analysis is complicated by the fact that it is preserved in two differing redactions, but it too relates a complex feud between two families, one headed by the powerful chieftain in Eyjafjörður, Guðmundr ríki (the mighty), and the other clustered somewhat to the east around the lake Ljósavatn (hence the clan name Ljósvetningar). This saga is notable for attention to characterization and psychology and a number of vivid episodes.

Although the conflict saga is best represented in north-central Iceland, counterparts can be found in the west (*Heiðarvíga saga*) and in the east (*Droplaugarsona saga*). The former is not well preserved because a third of the sole manuscript was lost in a fire in 1728 and exists only in a reconstruction from memory, but there are some indications that the transcription from memory is surprisingly accurate. *Heiðarvíga saga* has often been considered the earliest of all the sagas because the manuscript has been dated ca. 1250 and the style seems undeveloped, but Bjarni Guðnason has suggested a later date for the manuscript and a date of composition around 1260. A date in the early thirteenth century may still be preferable. The saga tells the story of the ruffian Víga-Styrr (Killer Styrr), who is eventually slain by an improbably young avenger. But the bulk of the text focuses on the actions, both bold and sagacious, of Barði Guðmundarson in the ensuing feud. Although the style is rudimentary, the plot is at once complex and dramatically managed to a degree not surpassed in the later sagas. As in the previous conflict sagas, there is every reason to think that the tale was handed down in oral tradition.

The first saga from eastern Iceland is *Droplaugarsona saga*. A textually problematical reference to the teller of the story has on occasion suggested a very early date, but borrowings from *Gísla saga* (though borrowing in the opposite direction has also been argued) might rather place it in the middle of the century. Like *Heiðarvíga saga*, the tale concentrates on the mechanics of a feud, this time between a certain Helgi Droplaugarson and his antagonist Helgi Ásbjarnarson. Taken together with the four preceding sagas, *Droplaugarsonar saga* might well give the clearest index of the type of story that Icelanders told each other about their early ancestors from the Saga Age. What seems to have organized and preserved in memory the traditions of this period were accounts of antagonisms, feuds, slayings, and vengeances.

Such stories were presumably somewhat static, even hackneyed, but the practice of setting them down in literary form promoted a literary development that went beyond the maintenance of traditional feud yarns, as is already amply illustrated by *Egils saga*. The culmination of the early literary development is *Laxdœla saga* from the middle of the thirteenth century. It might in fact qualify as the first European novel. It dispenses with the *dróttkvætt* stanzas that are so characteristic of the first generation of skald sagas and are apt to alienate the modern reader of pure prose novels. It is by no means confined to the confrontational tactics of the earlier conflict sagas, though it practices this style as well as any previous text. Since it is two to four times longer than the older sagas, with the exception of *Egils saga*, it has latitude to unfold a broader panorama, and it does so with a certain deliberate grandeur, with fuller periods, fuller rhythms, and fuller narrative dimensions. Like *Egils saga*, it sets Iceland in an international frame, with visits to no fewer than six Norwegian courts and an Irish court to boot, but unlike the testing relations between Icelanders and Norwegians in *Egils saga*, the skald sagas, and the *þættir*, *Laxdœla saga* depicts Icelanders with a high status that provides instant, almost deferential, access to the Norwegian court. Since the time at which *Laxdœla saga* was written was also the time when King Hákon Hákonarson's plan to annex Iceland was nearing fulfillment, we cannot tell whether these status-conscious Icelanders betoken a new confidence in foreign affairs or an over-compensation for new apprehensions.

In addition to expanding the genealogical and historical range of the saga form, *Laxdœla saga* also deepens the personal and psychological portraiture. As in *Gísla saga* there are haunting glimpses of passion and family interactions. In fact the central and much discussed relationship between Kjartan Óláfsson and Guðrún Ósvífrsdóttir is modeled on the tale of consuming but thwarted passion between Brynhild and Sigurd in the *Poetic Edda* and *Völsunga saga*. *Laxdœla saga* thus subsumes not only the prior developments in the writing of the skald sagas, with their amatory emphases, and the conflict sagas, with their personal dissensions, but also the greatest poetic drama in the literature of early Iceland. Finally, this saga suggests the sort of moralizing stance to which readers of the modern novel are accustomed, the relativizing of social and material success by personal failure.

Part and parcel of the more generous dimensions in *Laxdœla saga* is a broader coverage of a particular region, in this case an area in northwestern Iceland. Two other sagas, longer than average but only half the size of *Laxdœla saga*, are also focused more on district than on conflict. *Eyrbyggja saga*, which plays in the same part of Iceland as *Laxdœla saga*, covers the career of the important chieftain Snorri goði. Rather than probing a particular contest, like the conflict sagas, it returns to a more biographical form and traces Snorri's dealings with a whole series of antagonists. It lacks the sharp edge of the best sagas and seems more intent on chronicling political interactions, in which Snorri proves to be a remarkable survivor. The form is somewhat akin to what we find in a text like *Sturlu saga,* that is, the history of a chieftain's dealings with his neighbors. Though located in the same region as *Laxdæla saga,* the coverage is complementary rather than overlapping, leaving open the question of priority in time. Whether a little earlier or a little later, *Eyrbyggja saga* is thought to belong to the same period as *Laxdæla saga,* that is, the middle of the thirteenth century.

The third regional saga, *Vatnsdæla saga,* located a little to the east of the previous sagas, seems to be later, perhaps considerably later. Rather than focusing on an individual, like *Eyrbyggja saga,* it chronicles the adventures of five generations of a family in Vatnsdalr. These adventures are frequently not so much political as supernatural, featuring Lapps with magical powers, thieves, raiders, and sorcerers in several iterations.

If *Egils saga* and *Laxdæla saga* can be seen as the first two highpoints in the saga-writing devoted to the early Icelanders, the second half of the thirteenth century can be seen as building toward the third and final crest in *Njáls saga,* but it also produced a series of remarkable smaller sagas: *Bandamanna saga, Hrafnkels saga, Hænsa-Þóris saga, Valla-Ljóts saga, Vápnfirðinga saga,* and *Þorsteins saga hvíta.* None is negligible, but the first three in particular have stood the test of time and commanded a steady readership. They are elegantly composed, and each raises questions of broad import. *Bandamanna saga* relates the discountenancing at law of eight chieftains by a sly old man with a sardonic view of human nature. If the chieftains are cast as the "establishment" and their antagonist as "the man of the people," the text can be read as a satirical exposé of the chieftain class in the waning days of the commonwealth institutions of Iceland. Even without that larger political context the comic treatment of human foibles and the verbal wit stand out in saga literature as a whole.

Hrafnkels saga may be the best known of all the sagas, partly because it is included in E. V. Gordon's *An Introduction to Old Norse* and is read first among the sagas by students of the language, and partly because it has received disproportionate critical attention. It tells the story of a chieftain in eastern Iceland who achieves prosperity and political dominion but carries autocracy too far and is unexpectedly toppled and exiled from the district by a much lesser man, only to reestablish himself in his former power and glory six years later. The text has been discussed more often than any other saga because it seems so overtly to suggest a moral paradigm, though the nature of the paradigm has proved elusive. Is the saga about a tyrant who is chastened and therefore reinstated, or is it about a politician who is ultimately able to maintain himself precisely because he understands how to subordinate morality to power? Is Hrafnkell a reincarnation of Nebuchadnezzar or a forerunner of Machiavelli's prince?

Hœnsa-Þóris saga is of special interest in the study of how the sagas evolved because it gives a full narrative of an incident mentioned by Ari Þorgilsson but seems clearly not to refer back to Ari. Presumably, then, there existed an oral version of the story alongside the literary reference provided by Ari. *Hœnsa-Þóris saga,* like the two preceding sagas, seems to be about chieftainship, the idealized chieftain Ketill Örnólfsson (Blund-Ketill) and the flawed chieftain Oddr Önundarson (Tungu-Oddr), abetted by his dull son Þorvaldr and the consummate scoundrel Hœnsa(Hen-)-Þórir. The saga becomes a study in how the outstanding personal and diplomatic qualities of a thoroughly admirable chieftain such as Blund-Ketill can be subverted by stupidity and malice. When Blund-Ketill succumbs in his house, set ablaze by his enemies, the message is obvious and bleak. Good will is no match for evil. The fact that these three late-thirteenth-century sagas all deal with the frailty of chieftains will inevitably suggest that Icelanders in this period were reflecting on the transition from the native oligarchy in the Sturlung period to royal hegemony after 1262–64.

The great monument of this post-commonwealth period, *Njáls saga,* is also haunted by such social and political questions. It brings the southern districts of Saga-Age Iceland onto the stage for the first time, reimagining the lives and destinies of the great hero Gunnarr Hámundarson and the great legal authority Njáll Þorgeirsson. The dimensions of the tale are even more generous than in *Laxdœla saga,* though reminiscent of that work in the inclusion of foreign travel and foreign favor, broad regional coverage, complex erotic relationships, family tensions, persistent feuding, and ineluctable fate. But there are new facets as well. Whereas *Laxdœla saga* distributes its narrative over a whole gallery of imposing men and women, *Njáls saga* places only a few characters in preeminent relief, chiefly Gunnarr and Njáll and their equally memorable wives Hallgerðr and Bergþora.

All four are problematical, with greater or lesser degrees of notoriety. Hallgerðr is celebrated as a psychologically opaque character, complicit in the death of two husbands, while Bergþóra is a paradox made up equally of uncompromising (and sanguinary) toughness on the one hand and wifely devotion on the other. Gunnarr is the pinnacle of male valor in the sagas, but he makes fatal errors that seem arbitrary. Njáll is a man of unparalleled wisdom, a devoted friend and father, but he perverts his learning for the purpose of legal advantage, and he too makes fatal errors. In this saga personal complexity seems to be the moving force, a quality that does not yield readily to analysis. It invites more rumination than explanation. Why Gunnarr, the greatest hero of the Saga Age, dies in an on-slaught on his house, and why Njáll, the greatest intellect of the Saga Age, dies, like Blund-Ketill, in an incendiary attack, are questions that are posed in terms of a puzzle. We may surmise, however, that *Njáls saga* not only queries the easy discrimination of good and bad characters or good and bad options, but also questions the most basic paradigms of the earlier Saga Age narratives, the paradigms of heroism and wisdom.

The last of the classical sagas, though it verges more than a little on the legendary sagas, is *Grettis saga*, dated to the early fourteenth century. Like a number of the conflict and regional sagas, it traces the hero's ancestry to the days of Harald Fairhair in Norway and the exodus to Iceland, but there the similarity stops. There is no counterpart to the family histories and family dissensions that characterize *Laxdœla saga* and *Njáls saga*, and the story passes quickly to Grettir himself. He is a strangely difficult child who advances rapidly to bloodshed, as a result of which he is exiled to Norway. Here he performs supernatural feats, commits more killings, and is exiled once again. Back in Iceland further adventures, some ghostly, lead to his permanent outlawry. He survives for nineteen years but is finally betrayed, cornered, and killed, although he is later avenged by his brother in Constantinople. In this story the historical and legal matrix of Saga-Age Iceland has loosened and shrunk, leaving an eccentric and isolated adventurer in a half-real setting. If the late thirteenth-century sagas suggest growing doubts about the commonwealth institutions, *Grettis saga* testifies to the diminishing hold that those institutions had on literature. The social novels of the commonwealth give way to an adventure fiction no longer anchored in the particularities of the Icelandic civic experience.[6]

Romances and Legendary Sagas

The cultivation of European romance in Iceland was by no means an afterthought. Romance did not enter a void left by a declining interest in native forms, but was largely contemporaneous with the development of indigenous sagas and the collection of indigenous verse.[7] A colophon informs us that a Norse translation of Thomas's *Tristan et Iseut* dates from 1226, and four other translations record that they were executed under the auspices of King Hákon Hákonarson (1217–63) in Norway. The period 1226–63 corresponds, as nearly as we can tell, to the full blossoming of the kings' sagas and the first period of the native sagas, culminating in *Laxdœla saga*. The coincidence is indeed so close that it was once proposed that medieval Arthurian romance provided the inspiration for the sagas of early Iceland. The proposal was only marginally serious. Not only are the differences palpable, but when it did come to reworking medieval romance, the Norwegian, and presumably soon thereafter, Icelandic adapters showed themselves to be less than imaginative. Unlike the situation in Germany, where gifted poets were truly inspired to rival or surpass their French models, the response in Scandinavia was only workmanlike. The lively verse of Chrétien's texts was converted into the prose that had already been established as the narrative medium in the north, and the psychological playfulness of the originals was not recaptured in Norse. In recent years there have been spirited defenses of Norse romance, notably by Marianne Kalinke, and there is no doubt that there was an eager readership for these tales in Iceland, but that interest should probably be understood in terms of the Icelandic fascination with foreign worlds, which originated in the twelfth century and persisted in later centuries. The perception that romances commanded equal time and attention in the thirteenth century and therefore might well command equal time and attention among modern literary historians is inspired more by a record of relative neglect than by the intrinsic qualities of the romance texts.

The "romance" translations carried out first in Norway include, somewhat paradoxically, romances proper, *chansons de geste,* Breton *lais,* and even a text that might be termed an Arthurian *fabliau.* The romances include *Tristrams saga, Erex saga* (Chrétien's *Erec et Enide*), *Ívens saga Artúskappa* (Chrétien's *Yvain*), *Parcevals saga* (Chrétien's *Perceval*), and *Flóres saga ok Blankiflúr* (*Floire et Blanchefleur* in the "aristocratic" version). Two *chanson de geste* texts appear as *Elis saga ok Rósamundu* (*Elie de St. Gille*) and *Flóvents saga* (from a lost French original). To these should be added an adventure tale titled *Bevers saga* (from an Anglo-Norman original that was also turned into the English *Bevis of Hampton*) and an extensive collection of translations from the French Charlemagne cycle known as *Karlamagnús saga ok kappa hans.* This latter collection is of particular interest because it preserves material that has been lost in French.

The prize exhibit in this group of works is a collection of twenty-one *lais* translated from the French and known as *Strengleikar* (string pieces). The collection is preserved in an early manuscript from ca. 1270, which also contains three other texts, including *Elis saga.* Eleven of the translated *lais* are those attributed to Marie de France, and there is indirect evidence that Marie's twelfth *lai* (*Eliduc*) was also known in Norse, though it does not appear in the collection. Ten other *lais* from other sources make up the total; for four of them the French originals are not known. In two other manuscripts a somewhat atypical *fabliau* is preserved under the title *Möttuls saga* (*Le mantel mautaillié*) and also attributed to the patronage of King Hákon Hákonarson. It relates a chastity test performed with a cloak that fits the ladies of King Arthur's court in revealing ways and exposes their infidelities, with the exception of just one flawless lady.

At some point these foreign romances dovetailed with romances composed in Iceland and variously known as Icelandic romances, *lygisögur* (lying sagas), or *Märchen*-sagas. As the last term suggests, they are put together from extravagant fictions and located in remote or imaginary realms. Though not much appreciated in our day, they were popular in earlier centuries. Marianne Kalinke has calculated that fifty were composed in the medieval period and that the vogue eventually produced some fifteen hundred texts preserved in more than eight hundred manuscripts. How we should date the onset of the fashion is unclear, but a typical example, *Klári saga,* is attributed to Jón Halldórsson, who was bishop in Skálholt in the years 1322–39. Like the translated romances, these Icelandic creations have suffered from neglect and some scorn, but attempts have been made to retrieve them from oblivion. Agnete Loth's five volumes of *Late Medieval Romances* (1962–65) have made a sample of fifteen texts accessible and Jürg Glauser's *Isländische Märchensagas* (1983) includes synopses of twenty-seven texts.

The native counterparts to the romances are the so-called *fornaldarsögur* or legendary sagas.[8] They do not in fact constitute a homogeneous literary genre but are a literary assemblage of texts first put together by Carl Christian Rafn in *Fornaldar sögur nordrlanda eptir gömlum handritum* (Copenhagen 1829–30). The collection continues to be available in a popular four-volume set and therefore has the appearance of being a separate class of sagas. What they have in common with the romances is a stereotypical recounting of largely supernatural adventures, but, unlike the romances, which are set in strange and distant locales, the *fornaldarsögur* celebrate Scandinavian heroes in known regions in northern Europe stretching as far as Germany and Russia, though in unspecified times. The heterogeneity of the group is illustrated by the traditional inclusion of *Völsunga saga,* which is no more than a prose paraphrase of the heroic poems later set down in the *Poetic Edda.*

A number of these texts were written at a relatively late date, with the result that the group as a whole has been considered late, but it is certain that these sagas, like the sagas about early Icelanders, had a prior existence in tradition. A famous passage in *Þorgils saga ok Hafliða* records the telling of such sagas at a wedding feast in 1119, assuming that there is truth in the incident. The Danish historian Saxo Grammaticus, working around 1200, made ample use of legendary materials and referred to the tales told by Icelanders. At the same time, or a little earlier, there was an Icelandic compilation on the legendary Danish kings with the title *Skjöldunga saga,* although only fragments survive. A full version of these narratives, titled *Hrólfs saga kraka,* was composed perhaps around 1400. *Jómsvíkinga saga* (ca. 1200), centering on the adventures of a band of Vikings in the Baltic, particularly their fateful attack on the Norwegian king in 986, is usually associated with the sagas of the outlying islands (*Orkneyinga saga* and *Færeyinga saga*), but it has a number of characteristics reminiscent of the *fornaldarsögur*. *Völsunga saga* is usually dated around 1260 but could be somewhat earlier. Torfi Tulinius has dated *Hervarar saga ok Heiðreks konungs* around 1240. All this suggests that such legendary sagas had a long prehistory. It is only the late examples that become, like the late romances, stereotypical, with repetitive encounters with giants, ghosts, revenants, and dragons.

Looking back on the development of Icelandic prose literature as a whole, we can generalize that it falls roughly into five periods:

1. a post-Bedan era in the twelfth century characterized chiefly by saints' lives and modest experiments in colonial history, first by Sæmundr and Ari and ultimately in *Landnámabók;*

2. a few echoes of the Renaissance of the Twelfth Century at the very end of the century, mostly in the form of translations of classical and medieval histories and pseudo-histories;

3. an appropriation of European romance alongside a burst of something akin to national romanticism, first in the skald sagas and kings' sagas, as well as the harvesting of native skaldic and Eddic verse, and culminating in the middle of the thirteenth century with the romantic novel *Laxdæla saga;*

4. a period of political uncertainty following the dissolution of the commonwealth in 1262–64 and marked by political sagas such as *Bandamanna saga, Hrafnkels saga, Hænsa-Þóris saga*, and *Njáls saga;*

5. a retreat from native poetic and prose forms and a growing cultivation of romance and legendary sagas in the fourteenth century and thereafter.

Conclusion

There has been a history of claims staked by non-Icelanders in what was perceived to be a common Scandinavian or even a common Germanic literary and cultural heritage. As early as the seventeenth century the Danes and Swedes felt that they shared a culture that was best represented by, but was by no means exclusive to, Iceland. In the nineteenth century the Norwegians believed that the sagas were a common Norwego-Icelandic phenomenon; thus Sir Walter Scott, in the second chapter of *The Pirate* (1822), could refer unhesitatingly to the "old Norwegian sagas." In the early twentieth century German scholars resorted to Icelandic literature in order to identify a Germanic ideology distinct from that of their Romance neighbors.[9]

But the more we study Icelandic letters, the more apparent it becomes that this literature is characteristically Icelandic and that the idea of a larger cultural heritage is an illusion. In England *Beowulf,* which is a Scandinavian story, may well have roots in something akin to a *fornaldarsaga,* but that form never took shape in England. Iceland clearly took over heroic themes from Germany, but the contrast between the German-derived *Þiðreks saga* and the cognate poems of the *Edda* shows how radically the German material was transformed in Iceland. Skaldic poetry originated in Norway but was rapidly transplanted to Iceland and flourished only there. As for the *þættir,* kings' sagas, and sagas about early Icelanders, they are the peculiar creations of Icelandic writers. By the same token attempts to link Icelandic letters to medieval literature in general have touched only a few externalities of form. The substance of the literary tradition in Iceland is remarkable for its independence in the early stages and for its strongly maintained continuity in the later stages. In the Germanic context Icelandic literature is not the hard core, as historians once supposed, but the most original, idiosyncratic, and autonomous offshoot.

The Texts

References to the primary sources discussed in this chapter, together with the most useful secondary studies, are supplied here as a guide for further reading, rather than being listed in the individual notes; these references are arranged to correspond to the sections of the text. The individual endnotes, containing references to other secondary literature, follow this section.

Skaldic Verse

The full corpus of skaldic poetry was edited by Finnur Jónsson in *Den norsk-islandske skjaldedigtning,* 4 vols. (2 vols. of diplomatic texts with variant readings and 2 vols. of normalized texts with Danish translations) (Copenhagen: Gyldendal, 1908–15; rpt. Rosenkilde & Bagger, 1967–73). For a brief anthology with introduction, commentary, and translations see E. O. G. Turville-Petre, *Scaldic Poetry* (Oxford: Clarendon, 1976). A considerable body of English translations can be assembled from the translations of *Heimskringla* and *Morkinskinna* noted below, and from the five-volume *Complete Sagas of Icelanders* (see under "The Sagas about Early Icelanders" below). See also Diana Whaley, *The Poetry of Arnórr jarlaskáld: An Edition and Study* (Turnhout: Brepols, 1998). A compact anthology of Christian skaldic verse done into German is Wolfgang Lange, *Christliche Skaldendichtung* (Göttingen: Vandenhoeck and Ruprecht, 1958). The simplest introduction to skaldic verse is Lee M. Hollander, *The Skalds: A Selection of Their Poems with Introduction and Notes* (Ann Arbor: U of Michigan P, 1968 [first publ. 1945]).

Eddic Verse

The standard edition of Eddic poetry is *Edda: Die Lieder des Codex Regius nebst verwandten Denkmälern,* ed. Gustav Neckel, rev. Hans Kuhn (Heidelberg: Winter, 1962). The glossary to this volume is now also available in English: Beatrice La Farge and John Tucker, *Glossary to the Poetic Edda, Based on Hans Kuhn's Kurzes Wörterbuch* (Heidelberg: Winter, 1992). So far two volumes of Ursula Dronke's edition with translations and commentary have appeared: *The Poetic Edda,* vol. I: *Heroic Poems,* and vol. II: *Mythological Poems* (including *Völuspá*) (Oxford: Clarendon, 1969 and 1997). At the same time a new German commentary is under way, of which two volumes have appeared: Klaus von See, Beatrice La Farge, Eve Picard, Ilona Priebe, Katja Schulz, *Kommentar zu den Liedern der Edda,* vol. II: *Götterlieder* (Heidelberg: Winter, 1997) and vol. III (2000). The poems of Codex Regius were supplemented by Andreas Heusler and Wilhelm Ranisch, *Eddica Minora: Dichtungen eddischer Art aus den Fornaldarsögur und anderen Prosawerken* (Dortmund: Ruhfus, 1903). There are a number of translations into English: Henry Adams Bellows, *The Poetic Edda* (New York: American-Scandinavian Foundation, 1923, and later reprints); Lee M. Hollander, *The Poetic Edda,* 2nd rev. ed. (Austin: U of Texas P, 1962); Patricia Terry, *Poems of the Vikings: The Elder Edda* (Indianapolis: Bobbs-Merrill, 1969); Carolyne Larrington, *The Poetic Edda* (Oxford and New York: OUP, 1996). *Þiðreks saga* has been translated by Edward R. Haymes, *The Saga of Thidrek of Bern* (New York: Garland, 1988). A full exposition of the problems in *Þiðreks saga* is provided by Susanne Kramarz-Bein, *Die Þiðreks saga im Kontext der altnorwegischen Literatur* (Tübingen and Basel: A. Francke Verlag, 2002).

Early Prose

An edition and translation of the *First Grammatical Treatise* are provided by Einar Haugen, *First Grammatical Treatise: The Earliest Germanic Philology, an Edition, Translation, and Commentary* (Baltimore: Linguistic Society of America, 1950). *Landnámabók* has been translated by Hermann Pálsson and Paul Edwards, *The Book of Settlements; Landnámabók* ([Winnipeg]: U of Manitoba P, 1972). *Ágrip* is available in an edition with facing English translation by M. J. Driscoll, *Ágrip af Nóregskonungasögum: A Twelfth-Century Synoptic History of Norway* ([London]: Viking Society for Northern Research, 1995). The two Latin synoptics have also been translated: *Theodoricus monachus, Historia de antiquitate regum norwagensium; An Account of the Ancient History of the Norwegian Kings,* trans. and annotated by David and Ian McDougall, with an introduction by Peter Foote ([London:] Viking Society for Northern Research, University College, London, 1998), and *A History of*

Norway and the Passion and Miracles of the Blessed Óláfr, trans. Devra Kunin, ed. with an introduction and notes by Carl Phelpstead ([London:] Viking Society for Northern Research, University College, London, 2001). Other translations are: *Morkinskinna: The Earliest Icelandic Chronicle of the Norwegian Kings (1030–1157),* trans. Theodore M. Andersson and Kari Ellen Gade (Ithaca, NY: Cornell UP, 2000), and *Heimskringla: History of the Kings of Norway by Snorri Sturluson,* trans. Lee M. Hollander (Austin: U of Texas P, 1964).

Snorri's *Prose Edda* has been translated by Anthony Faulkes, *Edda* (London: Dent, 1987). *Sturlunga saga* can be read in an English translation by Julia H. McGrew, *Sturlunga saga,* 2 vols. (New York: Twayne, 1970–74). The most recent general study of this text, specifically *Íslendinga saga,* is Guðrún Nordal, *Ethics and Action in Thirteenth-Century Iceland* (Odense: Odense UP, 1998). The Vinland sagas are conveniently accessible in *The Vinland Sagas: The Norse Discovery of America,* trans. Magnus Magnusson and Hermann Pálsson (Harmondsworth: Penguin, 1965 and New York: New York UP, 1966), and *Yngvars saga* in *Vikings in Russia: Yngvar's and Eymund's saga,* trans. Hermann Pálsson and Paul Edwards (Edinburgh: Edinburgh UP, 1989).

On *Trójumanna saga, Breta sögur,* and *Alexanders saga* see Stefanie Würth, *Der "Antikenroman" in der isländischen Literatur des Mittelalters: Eine Untersuchung zur Übersetzung und Rezeption lateinischer Literatur im Norden* (Basel and Frankfurt am Main: Helbing & Lichtenhahn Verlag, 1998). Würth has also provided German translations in *Isländische Antikensagas,* vol. 1: *Die Saga von den Trojanern; Die Saga von den britischen Königen; Die Saga von Alexander dem Grossen* (Munich: Diederichs, 1996). *Færeyinga saga* has been translated by George Johnston, *The Faroe Islanders' Saga* (N.p., Canada: Oberon Press, 1975), and *Orkneyinga saga* by Hermann Pálsson and Paul Edwards, *Orkneyinga saga: The History of the Earls of Orkney* (Harmondsworth: Penguin, 1981).

Sagas about the Early Icelanders

Most of the relevant texts, as well as many *þættir,* are available in English translation in *The Complete Sagas of Icelanders, Including 49 Tales,* 5 vols., ed. Viðar Hreinsson (Reykjavik: Leifur Eiríksson Publishing, 1997), with a selection in *The Sagas of Icelanders,* intr. Robert Kellog, preface by Jane Smiley (New York: Viking, 2000). A number of individual translations by Hermann Pálsson and associates are also available in Penguin paperbacks.

Romances and Legendary Sagas

A sample of the Norse translations from the French is provided in English by Foster W. Blaisdell, Jr., and Marianne E. Kalinke, *Erex saga and Ívens saga: The Old Norse Versions of Chrétien de Troyes's Erec and Yvain* (Lincoln, NE: U of Nebraska P, 1977). The *Strengleikar* have been edited with facing English translations by Robert Cook and Mattias Tveitane, *Strengleikar: An Old Norse Translation of Twenty-One Old French Lais* (Oslo: Kjeldeskriftfondet, 1979). Brother Robert's reworking of Thomas of Brittany's *Tristan* has been translated by Paul Schach, *The Saga of Tristram and Ísönd* (Lincoln NE: U of Nebraska P, 1973), and *Karlamagnús saga* by Constance B. Hieatt, *Karlamagnús saga: The Saga of Charlemagne and His Heroes,* 3 vols. (Toronto: The Pontifical Institute of Mediaeval Studies, 1975–80). Fifteen late romances with running paraphrases in English were printed from manuscripts by Agnete Loth in *Late Medieval Icelandic Romances,* 5 vols. (Copenhagen: Munksgaard, 1962–65). Most recently some of the texts above and some additional material have been gathered in a three-volume set with originals and facing translations, including a text from the Swedish *Eufemiavisor: Norse Romance,* ed. Marianne E. Kalinke (Cambridge: D.S. Brewer, 1999). Vol. I contains Tristan texts, vol. II Arthurian texts, and vol. III *Hærra Ivan* from the *Eufemiavisor.*

One version of *Jómsvíkinga saga* was translated by Lee M. Hollander, *The Saga of the Jómsvikings* (Austin: U of Texas P, 1955). A selection of the later *fornaldarsögur* may be found in *Gautrek's Saga and Other Medieval Tales,* trans. Hermann Pálsson and Paul Edwards (New York: New York UP, 1968), and *Seven Viking Romances,* trans. Hermann Pálsson and Paul Edwards (Harmondsworth: Penguin, 1985). The most useful version of *Völsunga saga* is the bilingual *The Saga of the Volsungs,* ed. and trans. R. G. Finch (London: Nelson, 1965).

Notes

[1] For a general history of early Iceland in English see Jón Jóhannesson, *A History of the Old Icelandic Commonwealth,* trans. Haraldur Bessason ([Winnipeg]: U Manitoba P, 1974). An excellent survey of how the medieval Icelandic polity evolved is Jón Viðar Sigurðsson, *Chieftains and Power in the Icelandic Commonwealth,* trans. Jean Lundskær-Nielsen (Odense: Odense UP, 1999). The most convenient survey of the literature in English is Jónas Kristjánsson, *Eddas and Sagas: Iceland's Medieval Literature,* trans. Peter Foote (Reykjavik: Hið íslenska bókmenntafélag, 1988). On individual texts and topics see also *Medieval Scandinavia: An Encyclopedia,* ed. Phillip Pulsiano (New York: Garland, 1993).

[2] A brief German introduction to skaldic verse is that by Klaus von See, *Skaldendichtung: Eine Einführung* (Munich and Zurich: Artemis Verlag, 1980). The best literary introduction, which also relates skaldic practice to other archaic verse traditions, is Roberta Frank, *Old Norse Court Poetry: The Dróttkvætt Stanza* (Ithaca, NY: Cornell UP, 1978). For an update on research see also her "Skaldic Poetry" in *Old Norse-Icelandic Literature: A Critical Guide,* ed. Carol J. Clover and John

Lindow (Ithaca, NY: Cornell UP, 1985), 157–96. For a specialized treatment of late skaldic poetry, see Guðrún Nordal, *Tools of Literacy: The Role of Skaldic Verse in Icelandic Textual Culture of the Twelfth and Thirteenth Centuries* (Toronto: U of Toronto P, 2001). Hallvard Lie's papers "Skaldestil-studier" and "'Natur' og 'unatur' i skaldekunsten" are reprinted in his collected papers: *Om sagakunst og skaldskap: Utvalgte avhandlinger* (Øvre Ervik: Alvheim & Eide, 1982), 109–200 and 201–315. For technical discussions of prosodic matters see Hans Kuhn, *Das Dróttkvætt* (Heidelberg: Winter, 1983); Kristján Árnason, *The Rhythms of Dróttkvætt and Other Old Icelandic Metres* (Reykjavik: Institute of Linguistics, 1991); Kari Ellen Gade, *The Structure of Old Norse Dróttkvætt Poetry* (Ithaca, NY: Cornell UP, 1995).

[3] For a full discussion of Eddic research see Joseph Harris, "Eddic Poetry" in Clover and Lindow, eds., *Old Norse-Icelandic Literature*, 68–156. On the dating problems see Bjarne Fidjestøl, *The Dating of Eddic Poetry: A Historical Survey and Methodological Investigation* (Copenhagen: Reitzel, 1999). On the heroic poems and their relationship to the German analogues see T. M. Andersson, *The Legend of Brynhild* (Ithaca, NY: Cornell UP, 1980). On the elegies see Daniel Sävborg, *Sorg och elegi i Eddans hjältediktning* (Stockholm: Almqvist and Wiksell, 1997). John Lindow has provided a compendious bibliography on the mythological materials in *Scandinavian Mythology: An Annotated Bibliography* (New York: Garland, 1988). See also his "Mythology and Mythography" in Clover and Lindow, *Old Norse-Icelandic Literature*, 21–67. The most recent general study of the mythological material is Margaret Clunies Ross, *Prolonged Echoes: Old Norse Myths in Medieval Northern Society*, I: *The Myths*, and II: *The Reception of Norse Myths in Medieval Iceland* (Odense: Odense UP, 1994 and 1998).

[4] On the early period of saga writing consult the still useful survey by G. Turville-Petre, *Origins of Icelandic Literature* (Oxford: Clarendon, 1953; rpt. 1967). For a repertory of saints' lives see Ole Widding, Hans Bekker-Nielsen, and L. K. Shook, "The Lives of the Saints in Old Norse Prose. A Handlist," *Mediaeval Studies*, 25 (1963): 294–337. On the early Icelandic geographical and encyclopedic literature see Rudolf Simek, *Altnordische Kosmographie: Studien und Quellen zu Weltbild und Weltbeschreibung in Norwegen und Island vom 12. bis 14. Jahrhundert* (Berlin and New York: de Gruyter, 1990).

[5] For a brief survey of the kings' sagas see T. M. Andersson, "Kings' Sagas (*Konungasögur*)" in Clover and Lindow, *Old Norse-Icelandic Literature*, 197–238. On the early kings' sagas see Gudrun Lange, *Die Anfänge der isländisch-norwegischen Geschichtsschreibung* (Reykjavik: Bókaútgáfa Menningarsjóðs, 1989), and on the full flowering see Ármann Jakobsson, *Í leit að konungi: Konungsmynd íslenskra konungasagna* (Reykjavik: Háskólaútgáfan, 1997). A re-evaluation of tradition in the kings' sagas and some of the special problems is Tommy Danielsson, *Sagorna om Norges kungar: Från Magnús góði till Magnús Erlingsson* (Hedemora: Gidlunds Förlag, 2002). On *Heimskringla* see Sverre Bagge, *Society and Politics in Snorri Sturluson's Heimskringla* (Berkeley: U of California P, 1991), and Diana Whaley, *Heimskringla: An Introduction* ([London]: Viking Society for Northern Research, 1991).

[6] The old classic on these sagas is W. P. Ker, *Epic and Romance* (London: Macmillan, 1896; rpt. New York: Dover, 1957). The most recent and up-to-date study is Véstcinn Ólason, *Dialogues with the Viking Age: Narration and Representation in the Sagas of the Icelanders* (Reykjavik: Heimskringla, 1998). For a detailed survey of research see Carol J. Clover, "Icelandic Family Sagas (*Íslendingasögur*)" in Clover and Lindow, eds., *Old Norse-Icelandic Literature*, 239–315. For an attempt to place the sagas in the context of medieval narrative see her *The Medieval Saga* (Ithaca, NY: Cornell UP, 1982), and on the perennial problem of origins see also her paper "The Long Prose Form," *Arkiv för nordisk filologi* 101 (1986): 10–39, and T. M. Andersson, "The Long Prose Form in Medieval Iceland," *JEGP* 101 (2001): 380–411. A very full survey of the problem and a radical reassessment of the oral tradition is offered by Tommy Danielsson, *Hrafnkels saga eller Fallet med den undflyende traditionen* (Hedemora: Gidlunds Förlag, 2002). An equally radical reassessment is offered by Gísli Sigurðsson, *Túlkun Íslendingasagna í ljósi munnlegrar hefðar* (Reykjavík: Stofnun Árna Magnússonar á Íslandi, 2002). Synopses of twenty-four classical sagas may be found in T. M. Andersson, *The Icelandic Family Saga: An Analytic Reading* (Cambridge, MA: Harvard UP, 1967). On the skald sagas see *Skaldsagas: Text, Vocation, and Desire in the Icelandic Sagas of Poets,* ed. Russell Poole (Berlin: de Gruyter, 2000). On *Njáls saga* see Richard F. Allen, *Fire and Iron: Critical Approaches to Njáls saga* (Pittsburgh: U of Pittsburgh P, 1971) and Lars Lönnroth, *Njáls saga: A Critical Introduction* (Berkeley: U of California P, 1976).

[7] The literature on the romances can be surveyed in Marianne E. Kalinke and P. M. Mitchell, *Bibliography of Old Norse-Icelandic Romances* (Ithaca, NY: Cornell UP, 1985). A particularly good and wide-ranging introduction to the translated romances is Geraldine Barnes, "Arthurian Chivalry in Old Norse," *Arthurian Literature* 7 (1987): 50–102. For an evaluation of the research see Marianne Kalinke, "Norse Romance (*Riddarasögur*)" in Clover and Lindow, eds., *Old Norse-Icelandic Literature* (as above), pp. 316–63. On the translated romances see her *King Arthur North-by-Northwest: The matière de Bretagne in Old Norse-Icelandic Romances* (Copenhagen: Reitzel, 1981). On *Karlamagnús saga* see Eyvind Fjeld Halvorsen, *The Norse Version of the Chanson de Roland* (Copenhagen: Munksgaard, 1959). On the late Icelandic romances see Jürg Glauser, *Isländische Märchensagas: Studien zur Prosaliteratur im späten mittelalterlichen Island* (Basel and Frankfurt am Main: Helbing und Lichtenhahn, 1983), and Marianne E. Kalinke, *Bridal-Quest Romance in Medieval Iceland* (Ithaca, NY: Cornell UP, 1990).

[8] The most recent survey of the *fornaldarsögur* is *Fornaldarsagornas struktur och ideologi*, ed. Ármann Jakobsson, Annette Lassen, and Agneta Ney (Uppsala: Institutionen för nordiska språk, 2003).

[9] On the Scandinavian and German appropriations of Icelandic literature see Oscar J. Falnes, *National Romanticism in Norway* (New York: Columbia UP, 1933), and Julia Zernack, *Geschichten aus Thule: Íslendingasögur in Übersetzungen deutscher Germanisten* (Berlin: Freie Universität Berlin, 1994). On the reception of Norse literature in Britain, see Andrew Wawn, *The Vikings and the Victorians: Inventing the Old North in 19th-Century Britain* (Cambridge: D. S. Brewer, 2000).

Old English

Fred C. Robinson

DURING THE FIFTH CENTURY A.D. Germanic tribes from around the north German littoral and the modern-day *Land* of Schleswig-Holstein migrated across the North Sea to the island of Britain. The occupants of Britain at that time were Romanized Celts, who were finding it difficult to defend themselves against invaders, the protecting Roman legions having been withdrawn early in the fifth century. The Germanic invaders — Angles, Saxons, Jutes, and probably some Frisians — conquered and peopled the island of Britain, which thereafter bore the name *Engla land* (land of the Angles), England. The Celts fled in large numbers into Wales, Cornwall, or across the English Channel into western Gaul.

The Germanic settlers or Anglo-Saxons (as they are usually called) spoke a language which we now call Old English. Between the time of their arrival in Britain and the end of the Old English period around A.D. 1100 they produced in that language a rich and varied literary corpus (and an even larger Latin corpus). Natural disasters and human folly both during and after the Old English period took a heavy toll on the vernacular corpus, but a substantial remnant totaling 3,895,061 words survives today in parchment manuscripts, Roman-letter inscriptions, and runic inscriptions.[1]

Runes are the Germanic epigraphic alphabet — designed, that is, for inscriptions — that the Anglo-Saxons brought with them to Britain, and inscriptions carved in runes date from the invaders' earliest years on the island. With the conversion of England to Christianity, which got underway near the beginning of the seventh century, the Anglo-Saxons were introduced by missionaries to the custom of writing in Roman letters on parchment with pen and ink, a writing system better suited than runes to recording extensive texts. Runes continued in epigraphic use throughout the Old English period, and scribes even developed a tradition of writing runes in manuscripts, but this is relatively rare and sporadic, as is the use of Roman letters for inscriptions.[2] The vast bulk of Old English literature is preserved in parchment manuscripts.[3]

Of the Germanic literatures Old English is one of the earliest and is probably the most varied. It includes some thirty thousand lines of verse;

hundreds of prose texts including everything from extensive works like *The Anglo-Saxon Chronicle* to a scribe's pathetic annotation in a manuscript he was copying, *god helpe minum handum* (God help my hands)[4]; over a million vernacular glosses — translations of individual Latin words — in Latin manuscripts; several Latin-English glossaries (forerunners of today's bilingual dictionaries); and an ever increasing tally of runic and non-runic inscriptions (846 words in runes and 796 in Roman at the last count). Over 400 manuscripts containing Old English survive, but more than half of these are primarily Latin with only a few vernacular glosses or notations. About 190 are substantially Old English. Most of these were copied in the eleventh century, but there are two from the eighth, six from the ninth, twenty-one from the tenth, and twenty-seven from the twelfth century.

Possibly the earliest recorded English word is the runic inscription spelling out *raihan* (roe deer) engraved on a gaming piece made from a roe deer's astragal (ankle-bone) in the early fifth century.[5] One of the runic letters shows that the inscription is "North Germanic in inspiration," a fact that reminds us of the Anglo-Saxon tribes' origins in northern Germany and southern Scandinavia.[6] Some have believed, apparently, that a runic inscription enables us to trace the beginnings of Old English back to the continental Anglo-Saxon homeland itself: the famous alliterative verse from the erstwhile horn of Gallehus in northern Schleswig could have been carved, it is suggested, by pre-migration Englishmen.[7] While it is pleasant to think that an Englishman-to-be may have composed *Ek Hlewagastir Holtijar horna tawido* (I, Hlegest of Holt, made the horn), it must be acknowledged that the language of the inscription is clearly proto-Norse, not primitive Old English.[8] We should therefore accept the fifth- and sixth-century inscriptions found in England as the earliest attestations of Old English.[9] The texts of runic and non-runic inscriptions are for the most part sub-literary, some consisting of no more than a proper name. But this is not always the case. The verse texts on the Ruthwell Cross and the Franks Casket are of distinct literary interest. In fact, at least nine of the surviving inscriptions in Anglo-Saxon England are in verse.[10]

The 178,128 Old English words found in Latin-Old English glossaries are of minimal literary interest, although they are often helpful in clarifying the meanings of words occurring in literary texts. The Epinal, Corpus, and Leiden glossaries are of great interest because they are early — the latter two from the ninth, the former possibly from the eighth century — and because they give valuable dialectal evidence.

The 1,036,533 words serving as Old English glosses (words in the vernacular language giving an equivalent for one of the Latin words, and added by contemporary readers) in Latin manuscripts (well over a quarter of the total corpus) are usually thought of as purely utilitarian usages — vernacular cribs to words in the Latin texts entered between the lines or occasionally in the margins near to the Latin words they are translating. They would appear to be of no literary interest. But in a brilliant and subtle study Mechthild Gretsch recently demonstrated that there can be a considerable aesthetic component in glossing.[11] In glosses such as those Gretsch notes in *The Royal Psalter, The Benedictine Rule,* and the Brussels Aldhelm manuscript, she discerns stylistic uses of loanwords, alliteration, use of words from the poetic register, striking neologisms, double glosses forming a hendiadys (one idea represented by two words joined by a conjunction), and many instances of what the great stylistic authority on the use of English, H. G. Fowler, memorably called "elegant variation." These effects present "precious evidence of the intellectual preoccupations of the scholars who devised them."[12] One might venture to suggest further that glosses can also give us insight into the literary temperament of the Anglo-Saxons, as when Aldhelm's flowery circumlocution expressing the idea that Circe chanted an incantation over a pool of water — *fontes liquidi maculabat flumina verbis* ([she] stained with words the flowing current of the liquid spring) — provokes from one glossator a clear specimen of impatient English downrightness: *þæt is sang on þæt wæter* (that is, [she] sang on the water).[13]

The largest portion of the Old English corpus by far is prose: more than 63 percent or 2,467,634 words. This fact bears witness to the remarkably advanced state of Anglo-Saxon culture. Virtually every society in its earliest attested state can boast an oral poetic tradition; a fully developed prose tradition is usually a much later development. Old English prose assumes definite shape as early as the ninth century with the anonymous *Martyrology, Life of St. Chad, Anglo-Saxon Chronicle,* and the prose translations by (or instigated by) King Alfred the Great, who ruled from 871 to 899. The tradition gathers strength in the tenth and eleventh centuries with several impressive writers using various distinctive prose styles.

Before we proceed to examine the prose corpus, something should be said about the dialects of Old English. Differences in spelling, grammar, and vocabulary demarcate four main dialects in Anglo-Saxon England. Northumbrian (spoken by Anglo-Saxons living north of the river Humber), Mercian (spoken by Anglo-Saxons living between the river Humber and the Thames), West Saxon (spoken by Anglo-Saxons living south and southwest of the Thames), and Kentish (spoken by Anglo-Saxons living in the southeastern corner of England in an area somewhat larger than the area of the modern county of Kent). The Northumbrian dialect is preserved in a few verse texts, glosses, and runic inscriptions starting as early as the eighth century. Mercian from as early as the eighth century is preserved in glosses, glossaries (compilations of separate glosses to make word lists) and a few other texts. Kentish survives in some ninth-century charters along with a pair of poems and some glosses. The vast majority of extant Old English texts are in the West Saxon dialect. Indeed, when people speak of "Old English," they are usually referring to the West Saxon corpus. It is Alfred the Great, ruler of the West Saxon kingdom, who gave the first major impetus to that dialect's move toward dominance. His leadership of the English resistance to Scandinavian invasions gave the West Saxons central status in ninth-century England, after which their power grew steadily in subsequent years. But also his program for translating important Latin books into the vernacular and for educating his subjects in the vernacular — about which more will be said — were factors in the growing importance of West Saxon. West Saxon book production was brisk in the tenth and eleventh centuries, and in the later Anglo-Saxon period, West Saxon became a standard written language used in all parts of Anglo-Saxon England.[14]

The earliest document written in Old English prose is the Laws of King Æthelbert of Kent, whose reign began in A.D. 560, but this text is preserved only in a twelfth-century manuscript (the *Textus Roffensis*) in which the language has been modernized. Bede in the early eighth century left translations in Old English, but these have not survived. A stirring prose narrative in the *Anglo-Saxon Chronicle* for the year 755 survives in a ninth-century telling which may be based on a story composed soon after 755, but the language is ninth-century Old English. A ninth-century Mercian author seems to have composed the notices of over two hundred saints called the *Martyrology*.[15] But it is in the West Saxon realm of King Alfred the Great that a major prose tradition really begins. His translation of Gregory the Great's *Cura pastoralis* (Pastoral Care), a manual for parish priests on the conduct of their duties, contains a preface in the form of a letter to each bishop in England to whom he is sending a copy of this book, and in the preface he describes his plan for initiating a cultural renewal in his kingdom. He regrets that the flowering of Latin learning that had taken place in England earlier has given way to neglect of learning and ignorance of Latin, even among the clergy. To restore learning in the land he proposes translating into English ("the language we can all understand") the books which are "the most necessary for all people to know" and then educating the youth of England in vernacular literacy (a revolutionary idea) so that they can read the translated books. This can be done, he says, "if we have sufficient peace." (He is drafting his plan for intellectual renewal in the intervals between leading his army against the invading Scandinavian armies.) He says that he himself has translated the *Cura pastoralis* for his people, and he closes his preface by urging the bishops to guard well the copies he is sending them.[16]

The other "most necessary" books that Alfred translated for his people are Boethius's *De consolatione philosophiae*, St. Augustine's *Soliloquia*, and the first fifty psalms from the Psalter. Whereas Alfred translates the *Cura pastoralis* fairly literally, his rendering of Boethius and the *Soliloquia* is much freer and in both cases results in "a Christian popularization of natural philosophy."[17] Not only does Alfred simplify Boethius's complex philosophical problems and domesticate the text with homely English analogies and comments, but he also conveys to the reader "the ideals of his life and work as king."[18] "Alfred's version of the *Soliloquies* is a free rendering of the original; in effect, Augustine's work serves as a point of departure for Alfred's reflections on the human soul, its immortality, and its knowledge of God after death."[19] The rendering of the Psalter is a faithful paraphrase, although Alfred composes explanatory introductions to each psalm and draws heavily on Psalter commentaries, especially those of Theodore of Mopsuestia.[20] It is reported that the king was translating the psalms at the time of his death and that the fifty paraphrases could be regarded as "a personal handbook of consolation and guidance in times of affliction."[21]

Three more "most necessary" books were executed by other translators as part of the king's educational program. He asked Bishop Werferth of Worcester, a Mercian, to translate Gregory the Great's *Dialogi,* an account of the inspiring deeds of a number of Italian saints, and in an Old English preface to the translation Alfred says that reading these accounts will help him "reflect in my mind on heavenly things amidst these earthly anxieties."[22] To provide his people with a comprehensive history of the known world, Alfred had a West Saxon scholar (whose name is unknown to us) translate the *Historiae adversus paganos* (Histories against the Pagans) by the fifth-century writer and friend of St. Augustine, Paulus Orosius. Coverage is from the creation to the year 417. The paraphrast deletes freely and also makes additions, as when he includes an extensive report to King Alfred by two Germanic seafarers who describe the geography and customs in parts of northern Europe; apparently Alfred thought that the Spaniard Orosius gave insufficient attention to the Germanic world.[23] To give his subjects a clear picture of their own history, Alfred secured a translation of the *Historia ecclesiastica gentis Anglorum* (Ecclesiastical History of the English People) by Bede (673–735), the learned and influential Northumbrian scholar. The translator deletes about a quarter of the Latin original which he deems of little interest to his contemporary countrymen, but otherwise his rendering is literal (at times awkwardly literal) but still quite readable.[24] This vernacular history of their nation continued to serve and to inspire Englishmen down to the end of the Anglo-Saxon period.[25]

Bede's *History* ends with the year 731. But Alfred's subjects would have found an account of subsequent events in their country's history in another work originating during the king's reign, *The Anglo-Saxon Chronicle*. This is a year-by-year record of events in Anglo-Saxon England. The early entries, starting with Julius Caesar's expedition to Britain, are often brief, many years being represented by a single event laconically reported (and some years left blank altogether). But when the annals reach the period of Alfred's lifetime and especially of his wars with the Scandinavian invaders, instead of the terse entries of earlier years, the *Chronicle* assumes the shape of full-blown history with detailed narrative and occasionally some analysis of events.[26] For modern historians the *Chronicle* "provides the basis for the greater part of our knowledge of Anglo-Saxon history."[27]

The style of the *Chronicle* is direct and expressive, while that of the Alfredian translations ranges from strictly literal to free and fluent. The reshaping of the Latin originals is sometimes so extensive that the rendering is virtually an original composition.[28] The range of subjects treated in the Alfredian books is impressive: historical narrative, theological reflection, anecdotal record, hagiography, philosophical reasoning, pastoral instruction, and biblical rhetoric. The books demonstrate the versatility and sophistication of Old English as an expressive medium and inaugurate a major prose tradition.[29]

The century after King Alfred's death in 899 saw a flowering of Old English prose that continued well into the eleventh century. A translation of the four Gospels survives (partially or whole) in six manuscripts, the latest of which was copied in the Middle English period. The most recent editor of the text suggests that "the Gospels are a sustained piece of Old English prose, whose proper historical and intellectual context is to be found in the Old English translations of Bede and Orosius, and the homilies of Ælfric and Wulfstan, rather than the glossed texts of the Lindisfarne and Macregol Gospels, Ulfila's Gothic translation, or — for that matter — the King James Bible."[30] Other translations of Biblical texts were made, most notably Ælfric's *Hexateuch*.[31] Apocrypha were included among the works translated, such as the *Vindicta Salvatoris,* the *Gospel of Pseudo-Matthew,* the *Apocalypse of Thomas,* and the *Vision of St. Paul.*[32]

The most important prose genre in post-Alfredian England is the homily or sermon. Twenty-three of these are preserved in a manuscript that somehow found its way to Vercelli, Italy.[33] Nineteen *Blickling Homilies* are preserved in a manuscript now in the Princeton University Library.[34] Both of these tenth-century collections contain prose texts of considerable power. But the homily form reaches its culmination in the work of two churchmen named Ælfric and Wulfstan.

Ælfric of Eynsham (ca. 950–ca. 1010) was the most learned and prolific writer of his time. Between 990 and 995 he composed two series of homilies, each containing forty sermons arranged according to the calendar of the church year.[35] Later he wrote thirty more homiletic texts, some for the proper of the season and some for unspecified occasions.[36] Forty more sermons for the church calendar are his well-told saints' lives.[37] In all these works Ælfric transforms his sources into idiomatic English prose that strives consistently for clarity. The patristic sources that he brings to the explication of doctrinal matters are simplified as much as possible, and he deletes from and expands the works that he paraphrases both to make them accessible to a vernacular audience and for heightened dramatic effects. At one point Ælfric began developing a unique prose style which he then used frequently for the rest of his writing career. His rhythmical prose is based loosely on the four-stress linear patterns of Old English poetry (see below) and also borrows from verse-form the use of alliteration, although he does not observe the strict rules governing the use of alliteration in verse. Neither does he use the distinctive poetic diction of Old English verse or the kennings, variations, and other elements of poetic style. The resulting prose combines a euphonious cadence with lucid, simple vocabulary. Ælfric's rhythmical prose would have been very effective, one suspects, when read from the pulpit, and his sermons and saints' lives were clearly designed for the use of parish priests, although his prefaces make clear that he anticipates a reading audience as well. (He does not use rhythmical prose exclusively for sermons.)[38]

Ælfric's contemporary Wulfstan composed twenty-two Old English sermons which will stand comparison with those of Ælfric.[39] Indeed, Wulfstan sometimes rewrote sermons by Ælfric, removing elements of Ælfric's style and recasting them in his own distinctive voice. He devotes his sermons to explaining elements of the Christian religion (the Creed, baptism, eschatology, etc.), to defining the duties of the clergy, and to condemning the evils of his times. He did not share Ælfric's enthusiasm for saints' lives and rarely even refers to saints. His style is very different from Ælfric's but just as individualistic. He had a special fondness for rhyming and alliterative pairs of words, for two-stress rhythms, and for the use of intensifiers like *æfre* (always), *swyðe* (very), and *ealles to swyðe* (entirely too much). He is fond of irony and frequently uses phrases like *ne beon ge naðor to swicole ne to ficole* (be neither too deceitful nor too untrustworthy). (Note the two-stress rhythm and the rhyme.) He often uses rhetorical questions, dramatic pauses, exclamations, and other tricks of oratory. He seems clearly to have fashioned his prose for declamation.

Homilies are not the only genre used by Ælfric and Wulfstan. Ælfric wrote a Latin grammar in Old English, the first European grammar composed in a vernacular language. He is sometimes called *Grammaticus* (the Grammarian). He translated the *Hexateuch* and wrote pastoral letters and prefaces.[40] He wrote an Old English treatise on the measurement of time, astronomy, and related scientific subjects (*De temporibus anni* [On the

Periods of the Year], which draws heavily on Bede's writings) and numerous works in Latin.

Wulfstan was more of a public figure than Ælfric. He contributed to the law codes of both Æthelred the Unready and Cnut, and he wrote *The Canons of Edgar,* a set of regulations for priests.[41] He wrote or revised *Rectitudines singularum personarum* (The Duties of Individual Persons) and *Gerefa* (The Reeve), which deal with the administration of an ecclesiastical fief. His unmistakable style is detected in other documents, like the so-called *Benedictine Office* and the *Chronicle.*[42] Toward the end of his life he wrote a comprehensive work on political theory, the orders of society, and especially the duties of secular leaders and the clergy and the obligation of all people to support the church. This is the *Institutes of Polity.*[43] A manuscript prepared at the direction of Wulfstan preserved now in Copenhagen contains works in Old English and in Latin by Wulfstan and others with annotations in the hand of Wulfstan himself.[44]

A substantial portion of Old English prose was devoted to scientific subjects. Around the year 1013 Byrhtferth of Ramsey completed his *Enchiridion* (Handbook), a treatise for instructing priests and monastic oblates in arithmology, computus, and time-reckoning (the subject of Ælfric's *De temporibus anni,* which is one of Byrhtferth's sources).[45] Byrhtferth's prose style is idiosyncratic, and the treatise seems somewhat disorganized. Anonymous writings on the same subject are scattered among surviving manuscripts,[46] as are writings about the weather, planets, precious stones, and other scientific topics.[47] The majority of Old English scientific prose is devoted to medicine, herbal remedies, surgery, and the like. Major texts are the *Leechbook* by a man named Bald and the anonymous treatises *Lacnunga* (Cures), *Herbarium* (Herbal), and *Medicina de Quadrupedibus* (Treatment of Domestic Animals). One part of the *Leechbook* begins with the grim observation *Gif þu mid þys ne meaht gelacnian ne meaht þu him æfre nahte* (If you can't cure him with this, then you never can do so). Folklore and superstition naturally color a fair amount of these texts.[48]

The prose corpus contains a large amount of legal writings. Laws, charters, writs, wills, and other legal instruments preserve utilitarian prose, often of a highly formulaic character.[49] A modest number of prose texts, however, are what we might think of as literature for entertainment. This would become a much larger number if we included saints' lives, which, for all we know, may have been found entertaining as well as exemplary by Anglo-Saxons. The earliest English prose romance is *Apollonius of Tyre,* a translation of the Latin *Historia Apollonii regis Tyri.*[50] This popular story is retold later in the *Gesta Romanorum* (Deeds of the Romans), in Gower's *Confessio Amantis* (The Lover's Confession), and in Shakespeare's *Pericles,* for which it is the main source. The tale brims with exotic romance motifs — wooing of beautiful damsels, exile, shipwreck, incest, and wanderings which take the hero from Phoenicia to Antioch to Libya to Ephesus and beyond until he finds eventual happiness as a family man and king. Although Chaucer's Man of Law describes the tale's contents as "unkynde abhomynacions" (1. 88), the story nonetheless can be seen as providing "a basis for moral instruction" which would explain its inclusion in a manuscript of sermons and other religious material.[51]

The localization of *Apollonius* in faraway eastern lands bespeaks an Anglo-Saxon interest in exotica, and this interest is present also in two prose texts included in the manuscript containing the poem *Beowulf* (British Library MS Cotton Vitellius A.xv). *The Wonders of the East* describes extraordinary peoples, animals, and customs in Near Eastern lands. Here is a translation of a typical specimen:

> Going east from there is a place where people are born who are in size fifteen feet tall and ten broad. They have large heads and ears like fans. They spread one ear beneath them at night, and they wrap themselves with the other . . . And if they see or perceive anyone in those lands, they take their ears in their hands and go far and flee . . .[52]

The Letter of Alexander to Aristotle in the same manuscript is a narration of the progress of Alexander the Great through Asia Minor to India and of what he found and did in India. The *Letter* is a free translation from the Latin of a fictitious report by the Macedonian conqueror to his old tutor, the philosopher Aristotle. There are descriptions of fantastic creatures much like that quoted above from the *Wonders,* but Alexander seems most intent on reporting the commands he gave, the victories he won, and the honors he earned. Toward the end of the narrative he receives a prophecy of his imminent death and closes with a statement not found in the Latin source: ". . . my memory shall forever stand and tower as an example for other earthly kings, so that they know the more readily that my power and my honor were greater than those of all the other kings who have ever lived in the world."[53] Andy Orchard argues (p. 139) that the English paraphrast curtails and shapes his source so as to depict Alexander as "a monstrous figure of pride" which would serve as a monitory example to the Christian Anglo-Saxon audience.

An exotic eastern orientation also characterizes four Old English texts based upon a supposed question-and-answer dialogue between a Chaldean prince named Saturn and the Old Testament King Solomon the Wise.[54] Two of these are in verse and will be discussed below. The other two are prose, one occurring among late (twelfth-century) texts now preserved together with the *Beowulf* manuscript, the other in a manuscript containing the poems about Solomon and Saturn. The former contains fifty-nine questions and answers introduced, respectively, by "Tell me

. . ." and "I tell you . . ." The pagan Saturn asks the questions, and Solomon provides the answers, as in the following translated examples:

> Sage me hwer god sete þa he geworhte heofonas and eorðan
> Ic þe secge, he sætt ofer winda feðerum.
> [Tell me where God sat when He made the heavens and the earth.
> I tell you, He sat on the wings of the wind.]

> Saga me hwæt ys betst and wyrst betwinan mannon.
> Ic þe secge, word ys betst and wyrst betwix mannon.
> [Tell me what is best and worst among men.
> I tell you, word is best and worst among men.]

> Saga me for hwan byð seo sunne read on æfen.
> Ic þe secge, for ðon heo locað on helle.
> [Tell me why the sun is red in the evening.
> I tell you, because it looks on hell.][55]

Twenty of the questions and answers are also found among forty-eight questions and answers in a similar text called *Adrian and Ritheus,* where Adrian is the questioner. Among questions unique to *Adrian and Ritheus* are:

> Saga me hu mycel seo sunne sy.
> Ic þe secge, heo ys mare þonne eorðe for þam heo byð on æl-
>   cum lande hat.
> [Tell me how big the sun is.
> I tell you it is larger than the earth because it is hot in every
>   country.]

> Saga me hwær byð mannes mod.
> Ic þe secge, on þam heafde and gæð ut þurh þone muð
> [Tell me where a man's intellect is.
> I tell you, in the head, and it goes out through the mouth.]

> Saga me hu wæs crist acenned of maria his meder.
> Ic þe secge, ðurc þat swiðre breost.
> [Tell me how Christ was born from His mother Mary.
> I tell you, through the right breast.][56]

The second prose *Solomon and Saturn* text consists of questions and answers about the Pater Noster. The prayer is presented as a sentient personification, and the questions deal with the stature and strength of the prayer, its clothing, and the guises in which it will do battle with the devil. This bizarre anatomization of a prayer personified is carried further in the verse *Solomon and Saturn* which precedes and follows the prose version in the manuscript.

Besides its eastern associations, the *Solomon and Saturn* texts bear the marks of what is called "wisdom literature." Proverbs, gnomes, and adages occur not infrequently in Old English, and there are at least two prose collections of such sayings. An Old English text called *Dicts of Cato* presents around ninety maxims, many but not all of them drawn from a third-century Latin text named *Disticha Catonis*.[57] They advise people not to talk too much or eat or sleep too much. One should speak of the good deeds of others more than of one's own. Think before you speak. Ignore the words of an angry woman. Take no bribes. And so on. Another text named *The Durham Proverbs* tells us that no one can have too many friends, that one should be neither too fearful nor too forward, that all the army is brave when its leader is brave, and so on.[58]

Altogether the Old English prose corpus consists of roughly two and a half million words. Compared with this, the poetic corpus is minuscule — 211,124 words. And yet this small verse corpus has received vastly more scholarly and critical attention than has the prose corpus. In the standard twentieth-century bibliography of publications on Old English literature there are nearly 3,800 entries for poetry listed but only 1,411 for the prose.[59] A corpus one-twelfth the size of the prose corpus received over two-and-a-half times as many studies.[60] Therefore, in the ensuing survey of the verse corpus citations of scholarship and criticism will have to be even more selective than it was in the foregoing survey of the prose corpus.

The one poem that has received by far the greatest amount of scholarly attention is *Beowulf*.[61] This anonymous work of 3,182 lines is a work by a Christian Anglo-Saxon poet describing heroic deeds performed by pagan Germanic peoples living in and around the areas on the continent whence the Anglo-Saxons migrated to Britain. The poem's action is set in the sixth century A.D., but there are allusions to much earlier heroic-age events. The time of the poem's composition was for most of the twentieth century generally held to be the eighth century, but the publication in 1981 of a volume reassessing the evidence for dating *Beowulf* introduced a period of doubt and disagreement over the poem's compositional date that persists to the present day.[62] There is general agreement, however, about the date of the manuscript containing *Beowulf*. It is of late tenth-century date or, possibly, from the first decade of the eleventh century. As is the case with most Old English poetry, the text is preserved in a single surviving manuscript, but there is strong evidence that this manuscript is a late copy and that pre-existing manuscripts of the poem have been lost.[63]

Beowulf has been accorded by some the status of English national epic, and yet its characters are not Englishmen but Germanic peoples, some of whom founded England. The hero of the poem is a member of a Scandinavian tribe called Geatas, who inhabited the southern part of

Sweden. In his youth he voyages to Denmark and rids the Danes of two
monstrous ogres who had been cannibalizing the Danish king's warrior
retinue. Returning home, Beowulf becomes the chief defender of his nation in its wars with aggressive neighbors. In his old age, after he has
served as his people's king for fifty years, he slays a fire-breathing dragon
that was intent on destroying the Geatas, but in doing so he receives a
wound which soon kills him. The poem closes with his solemn funeral
rites. The courtly splendor, lofty speeches, and heroic deeds that are described in the poem are given special poignancy by the poet's retrospective point of view. He is a Christian Anglo-Saxon looking back on his
people's lives as they were lived in pagan darkness centuries before his
time. Admiration for the ancestors' heroic achievements is mingled necessarily with pity and regret for their spiritual predicament.[64] The poet
communicates his story and his complex themes in style and language
which are superbly managed. In *Beowulf* one finds traditional Old English
poetic diction at its best.

Like all Old English poetry, *Beowulf* is written in the traditional allit-
erative-accentual meter of the Germanic people. Each line of the poetry
contains two verses linked by alliteration. Scansion of the first three lines
of *Beowulf* will illustrate the system:

> Hwæt we **Gar-Dena**   in **geardag**um
> þeodcyninga   þrym gefrunon,
> hu ða **æþeling**as   **ell**en **frem**edon.

[Now we have learned of the glory of the nation-kings of the spear-
Danes in olden days, [of] how noblemen then wrought deeds of valor.]

The stressed syllables are indicated in bold, and the third syllable of *þeod-
cyninga* in the second line is a half-stress. Others are unstressed. The verses
here are printed two to a line and are separated by a space in the middle of
each line. These are modern editorial conventions; in the Old English
manuscripts verse texts are written like prose margin-to-margin across the
page. The accented syllables are those that would be given emphasis in
natural speech. Each verse has a minimum of two unaccented (or less accented) syllables. The positions in a verse which accented and unaccented
syllables may occupy are strictly regulated, as is the addition and placing of
more than two unaccented syllables. In each of these lines the first accented
syllable in the first verse alliterates with the first accented syllable in the second verse. It is also permissible for the second accented syllable in the first
verse to alliterate instead of or along with the first accented syllable. But the
second accented syllable in the second verse must never alliterate (except in
lines with two sounds alliterating, as in the first line of *Beowulf*). The third
line shows that any vowel alliterates with any other vowel. Restrictions in-

volving syllable length and syntactic patterning are also an intimate part of the system. Toward the end of the Anglo-Saxon period some of the metrical rules begin to be violated. The prosody of *Beowulf* is generally regarded as classical Old English meter at its best.[65]

The only other long heroic poem for which we have evidence is *Waldere,* but only two fragments containing four pages of the poem (63 lines) survive.[66] We know the scope and content of the original poem because the same story is recounted in a (probably) tenth-century Latin verse-epic called *Waltharius,* and this survives in toto (1,455 dactylic hexameters). But we do not have enough of the old English poem to tell whether it was comparable in quality with *Beowulf.*

Other heroic poems are much shorter than *Beowulf* or the original *Waldere.* The best of these is *The Battle of Maldon* (with 325 lines), an account of an actual battle between Anglo-Saxons and Vikings fought on August 10 or 11, 991, near the town of Maldon. The poet treats his subject in the grand manner of the old heroic poems while at the same time suggesting the gritty realities of late tenth-century England. Through treachery as well as Viking power the English are defeated — and perhaps exterminated — but they fight tenaciously, and the poet memorializes their heroism with great skill and deep feeling.[67]

Another historical battle celebrated in verse is *The Battle of Brunnanburh.* In 937 the Anglo-Saxon King Æthelstan and his brother defeated an alliance of Vikings, Welsh, and Scots in the north of England. The poem takes the form of a panegyric, one of the oldest Germanic genres, and exults over the Anglo-Saxons' defeat and humiliation of their enemies. It is metrically and stylistically polished, but it lacks the depth of thought and feeling that dignifies *The Battle of Maldon. The Battle of Brunnanburh is* preserved as the sole entry in the *Anglo-Saxon Chronicle* for the year 937.

Other poems preserved as part of the *Chronicle* commemorate other events, and the titles that modern scholars have assigned to them make clear what those events are: *The Capture of the Five Boroughs* (942), *The Coronation of Edgar* (973), *The Death of Edgar* (975), *The Death of Alfred* (1036) (this Alfred is the son of Æthelred the Unready and is slain during the reign of Harold, son of Cnut), and *William the Conqueror.*[68] Although *The Death of Edward* (1065) is an orderly eulogy, most of the *Chronicle* poems are pedestrian performances often in imperfect verse. *William the Conqueror* is in such decayed verse as to be almost indistinguishable from prose, but it is interesting for having been composed by a man who had been a member of William's household. He remembers the king's harsh reign with some bitterness.

A poem in the Exeter Book[69] called *Widsith* is devoted primarily to keeping alive in memory the names of heroic-age men and women and nations and places on the continent in pre-migration times. Large parts of it are merely alliterating lists of names. The poem is usually thought to have been composed early in the Old English period, but its inclusion in the tenth-century Exeter Book shows that a keen interest in heroic-age origins persisted throughout the period. The poet of *Deor* (also in the Exeter Book) invokes the names of continental heroic-age men and women as well, but he employs these people and their stories in a strategy of self-consolation, noting that just as these people all passed through difficult experiences (which are specified) and lived to see better times, so the disconsolate poet, who has just lost his position as court poet, may live to see better times himself.

After *Beowulf* probably the most popular Old English poems are a set of short poems (none more than 124 lines) in the Exeter Book which modern scholars are accustomed to calling "elegies." This terminology is a somewhat loose application of the name of a classical verse genre to Germanic poems which are really *sui generis*. There is some disagreement as to what an elegy is and which poems belong in the grouping. The poems most frequently so designated are *The Seafarer, The Wanderer, Deor* (discussed above), *The Ruin, The Wife's Lament, Wulf and Eadwacer, The Rhyming Poem,* and *Resignation.*[70] The first two of these are among the strongest poems in the Old English canon. Both are monologues by an *isolato* — in the one case a veteran seaman accustomed to lonely nights on the watch in all weathers on the sea, and in the other a downcast nobleman who, having lost his lord and fellow warriors, is condemned to wandering alone across land and sea in futile quest of a friendly hearth. The seafarer emphasizes how in this transitory and treacherous world a person must embrace the rigors and challenges of life in order to struggle through to a better end. The wanderer's lament avers that in the heroic-age world a person must accept the hard blows of fate and the brevity of life with quiet dignity. Both poems conclude with the observation that the Christian Lord offers the only real remedy for the human predicament in a hostile world. *The Ruin* records the reflections of an Anglo-Saxon contemplating a Roman ruin in England and imagining the mirth and splendor that must once have attended this now desolate scene. *The Wife's Lament* and *Wulf and Eadwacer* are monologues by women suffering the torments of tragic loves. *The Rhyming Poem* is interesting mainly for its experimental form. In addition to following all the constrictive rules of Germanic alliterative verse, the poet adds copious end-rhymes to his verses, probably in imitation of Latin hymns. Having imposed such strenuous formal demands on himself, the poet has trouble making his message clear. The speaker seems to be a once powerful and affluent person bewailing his loss of youth and prosperity. *Resignation,* which is printed as a single poem in *ASPR* 3, appears actually to be the beginning of one poem and the end of another with loss of text in between them. In the manuscript a leaf has been lost between lines 69 and 70 of the *ASPR* text. The penitential tone in the first fragment and reference to a sea journey in the second give the fused texts a seeming resemblance to the so-called elegies.[71]

Sometimes seen as similar to the elegies is that portion of the verse corpus called wisdom literature. The series of versified maxims in the poems called *Maxims I* (in the Exeter Book) and *Maxims II* (in British Library MS Cotton Tiberius B.i, a *Chronicle* manuscript) show the characteristic formal features of the genre, such as the verbs *sceal* (must) and *byð* (is) used with gnomic force. The latter begins thus:

> Cyning sceal rice healdan.   Ceastra beoð feorran gesyne,
> orðanc enta geweorc,   þa þe on þisse eorðan syndon,
> wrætlic weallstan geweorc.   Wind byð on lyfte swiftust,
> þunar byð êragum hludast.   Þrymmas syndan Cristes myccle.
> Wyrd byð swiðost.

> [A king holds the power. Cities are seen from afar, the cunning constructions of giants who are on this earth, artful stone constructions. Wind is the swiftest thing in the heavens. Thunder is at times the loudest. Great are the powers of Christ. Fate is strongest.]

The stone constructions are Roman buildings, which overawed the Anglo-Saxons, who built only in wood and thought that giants must have made the stone buildings. The series of superlatives starting in the third line may seem like statements of the obvious, but they have cumulative power: if one is able to perceive that the wind is swift and thunder is loud, then the further declaration that fate is strong is perhaps to be believed. A wisdom poem which we call *The Fortunes of Men* describes the various fates awaiting various people: "Famine kills one man, storm does in another; the spear takes life from one, warfare destroys another. One goes through life deprived of sight, gropes with his hands," etc. Another poem called *The Gifts of Men* itemizes the various abilities of various people — athlete, harp player, seaman, gem cutter, etc. In *Precepts* a series of wise injunctions is presented dramatically as a father's counsels to his son. The poet of *Vainglory* reports the teachings of a wise man of his acquaintance who warns against drunkenness, violent behavior, arrogance and the like, all of which will receive divine retribution in the next world.

An even more elaborate dramatic situation is established for the presentation of lore and wisdom in the two verse texts called *Solomon and Saturn*. Here the same two figures we encountered in the prose literature engage in a verse dialogue. One text has Solomon explaining the mystic powers of the Pater Noster, while the other is an exchange of riddles, questions and answers, and sententious sayings. The 335 lines of the second text close with the assurance that "the wise son of David defeated and humbled the Chaldean earl." The poem is unlike any other in the Old English corpus, and an Irish provenance has been suggested for some of its stranger features.[72]

Several verse renderings of well-known Latin texts display a range of translation techniques in Old English. *Carmen de ave Phoenice* (Song of the Bird Phoenix — 170 lines) probably by the fourth-century Roman Christian Lactantius is paraphrased and greatly expanded into a 677-line Old English poem composed, perhaps, in the ninth century.[73] Lactantius tells the story of the mythical bird that lives in paradise and every thousand years, having grown old, flies to a lofty tree in Syria, where its nest is set afire by the sun, and the bird is consumed in flames. Then from its ashes the Phoenix is reborn and returns to Paradise. A little more than half of the Old English poem paraphrases this account expansively, using traditional Old English poetic diction. The remaining lines of the Old English poem are a Christian allegorization of Lactantius's narrative in which the poet draws on Ambrose's *Hexameron* and other patristic sources to posit an analogy between the Phoenix and, first, the resurrection of every good Christian, and, second, Christ's resurrection. The poem is a seamless and successful adaptation of Latin texts to Old English poetic conventions and Christian doctrine.

Similar to *The Phoenix* are the three sections of the Latin *Physiologus* (Bestiary) translated into Old English verse and preserved (like *The Phoenix*) in the Exeter Book. The *Physiologus* is an ancient genre consisting of a series of descriptions of animals, each being followed by a Christian allegorization of the spiritual significance of the beast. Three animals are described in the Old English translation: the panther (representing Christ), the whale (representing the devil), and a bird usually identified as the partridge, but the manuscript here is fragmentary and much of this part of the text is lost. The verse accounts are lively, as when sailors are described setting up camp on the whale, having mistaken him for an island; then the sinister beast plunges to the ocean's depths, downing them. But on the whole the *Physiologus* is much less impressive than *The Phoenix*.

When King Alfred the Great decided to translate Boethius's *De consolatione philosophiae* as part of his educational program, he was confronted with a Latin text written alternately in prose and verse. Apparently, he translated the entire text into Old English prose and then recast most of the metrical sections into Old English verse.[74] His verse paraphrase shows Alfred to be a competent if not inspired poet. He is in touch with the traditional poetic diction, and he manages the verse-form reasonably well, although expansions and fillers are not infrequently used to eke out the verse lines. Part of Alfred's problem was the philosophical content of the

Meters; Old English poetic diction was not fashioned for handling this kind of subject matter.

In the Exeter Book there are ninety-one verse riddles.[75] The Old English poet or poets who composed these almost certainly took the idea from the Latin collections of verse riddles such as the cycle of one hundred *Ænigmata* (Riddles) by the Anglo-Saxon poet Aldhelm and the one hundred riddles by Aldhelm's model, Symphosius. Indeed, a few of the Old English riddles are based on *ænigmata* of Symphosius and Aldhelm. It is very likely that the Exeter Book originally contained a complete cycle of one hundred riddles in imitation of the cycles of Symphosius and Aldhelm. In the course of the old English riddles there are losses of text in the manuscript: a folio has dropped out between fols. 111b and 112a and leaves between fols. 105b and 106a and between fols. 125b and 126a. These missing pages would have provided ample space for the riddles now missing from the original cycle of one hundred. Comparable with the Latin riddles is the broad range of subjects and styles in the Exeter Book riddles. The first, which is over one hundred lines long, has some of the solemn power of God's voice out of the whirlwind in the Book of Job (chaps. 38–41) with repeated questions and depictions of natural upheavals.[76] Other riddles are playful, with artfully misleading diction, wordplay, and even risqué double entendre. Yet others are whimsical paradoxes without any riddling element at *all*.[77] Were it not for the *Riddles* we might not have suspected that the Anglo-Saxons were capable of playfulness and whimsicality in their poetry.

The verse riddles are the product of the study or monastic library. The Old English verse charms, on the other hand, are very much the poetry of field and hearth. Composed in irregular meter sometimes trailing off into prose, the charms are attempts to use words to effect changes in the real world — to make fields fertile, to recover stolen cattle, to cure diseases or ensure a safe journey. The "Nine Herbs" charm seeking to provide an antidote for poison contains these startling lines:

> Wyrm com snican   toslat he man;
> ða genam Woden   viiii wuldortanas,
> sloh ða þa næddran   þæt he on viiii tofleah.

[A snake came sliding along, and he bit a person; then Woden took nine twigs of glory and struck that serpent so that it exploded into nine parts.]

The appearance of the heathen god Woden (Odin, Wodan) here suggests that the charms are a relic (in part at least) from the pre-Christian past. Another charm invokes an entity named *Erce,* who is identified as the earth-mother.[78] Since the copying of manuscripts was carried out primarily under the auspices of the church, and the church was normally disposed to suppress overt manifestations of Germanic paganism, it is remarkable that these references to Wodan and Erce were allowed to stand.

The verse texts which we have been considering thus far are what are usually designated "secular poetry."[79] This is the body of verse that has received the greatest amount of attention from scholars of Old English and has seemed accordingly to be the most prominent part of the verse corpus. It should therefore be emphasized that the secular poetry is in fact but a fraction of the verse corpus, the total size of which is just under thirty thousand lines. Of these thirty thousand, over twenty thousand are devoted to explicitly religious subjects.[80] The preponderance of religious poetry would be even greater if we redefined some of the texts here described as "secular" as religious. Because of their allegorizations *The Phoenix* and *Physiologus,* for example, could arguably be termed "religious."

Verse paraphrases of biblical narratives — the genre claiming the largest number of Old English verses — begin very early in the Anglo-Saxon period. In the seventh century an illiterate cow-herd named Cædmon was, according to the Venerable Bede, miraculously endowed with poetic powers and devoted his talents to translating biblical history (which literate monks read to him) into traditional Old English verse.[81] Bede says that Cædmon composed poems about "the whole history of Genesis, of the departure of Israel from Egypt and the entry into the promised land . . . of the incarnation, passion and resurrection of the Lord . . ."[82] This list of poems seems to agree remarkably well with the contents of a tenth-century manuscript now known as Bodley Library MS Junius 11, which contains four Old English verse narratives named *Genesis, Exodus, Daniel,* and *Christ and Satan.* In 1655 the scholar Franciscus Junius published these poems under the title *Cædmonis Monachi Paraphrasis Poetica Genesios ac præcipuarum Sacræ paginæ Historiarum* (The Monk Cædmon's Poetic Paraphrase of the Foremost Stories of Scripture). Subsequent scholars have shown conclusively that Junius's attribution is mistaken; the four long narratives in this manuscript are clearly of later date than Cædmon, and radical differences in style make clear that they are not all by one author. We may surmise, however, that these poems are the product of a school of biblical paraphrase that Cædmon founded. The only surviving verse known definitely to be by Cædmon is a nine-line hymn preserved in the manuscripts of Bede's *Historia ecclesiastica* translated into Old English.[83]

The most notable feature of the Old English verse paraphrases of biblical narrative is their cultural syncretism. When the Anglo-Saxon poets use the traditional heroic diction of their Germanic heritage to tell the stories of the Bible, the stories inevitably take on some of the coloring of the Germanic heroic world. Thus Moses in *Exodus* is described as a "leader of the army" and a "valiant commander of troops," and the children of Israel are "ironclad troops" and, when they start to cross the Red Sea, "sea-Vikings."[84] The poets also allow themselves to introduce into a paraphrase of one part of the Bible details from other parts, as when the *Genesis* translator adds to his narrative the Fall of Angels from the Apocrypha. The poets also Christianize the Old Testament somewhat. In *Genesis,* for example, God is frequently called *nergend* (Savior), a term usually reserved for Christ, and in *Exodus* critics have seen in the descriptions of the pillar of cloud proleptic allusions to the Cross. These details have prompted some scholars to undertake typological readings of Old Testament paraphrases. It should be noted that these Biblical narratives are selective, not complete. *Genesis* retells the biblical book only through 22:13. *Exodus* deals only with 12:29–30 and 13:17–14:31. *Daniel* paraphrases only chapters 1–5 of the Old Testament book, while *Christ and Satan* draws on the Gospels, Apocrypha, and a number of other sources. It is really a pastiche rather than a narrative paraphrase.

The quality of the four poems varies. *Exodus* is narrated with great force and vividness, and the diction is excited and highly metaphorical. "The hands of the laughter-smiths were locked" (43) is the poet's way of expressing the Egyptians' sorrow over the death of their first-born. *Genesis* is an orderly, fairly mechanical rendering, but at 235, where an account of the fall of the angels and the fall of man abruptly gets under way, the language suddenly becomes powerfully expressive and the narrative riveting. An heroically evil Satan, a dramatically rendered temptation, a daring interpretation of Eve's culpability, and a generally skillful narrative style command the greatest admiration, but then at 852 the verse returns to the orderly, humdrum tenor of 1–234 and continues thus to the poem's end at 2936. Scholars have determined that lines 235–851 are an Old English translation of a superb ninth-century Old Saxon poem which has been interpolated into the longer *Genesis* narrative. We refer to 1–234 and 852–2936 as *Genesis A,* the interpolation as *Genesis B. Daniel* has structural irregularities and ends abruptly but is otherwise reasonably well narrated. *Christ and Satan* is chronologically errant and somewhat jumbled but has moments of exclamatory power in some of the plaints of the fallen Satan.

The verse paraphrase of the Old Testament *Judith* (which is part of the Apocrypha in the Protestant Bible) comes at the end of the *Beowulf* manuscript. Although the beginning of the poem is missing, the story of Judith's beheading of Holofernes and the Hebrews' rout of the Assyrians is recounted effectively, the Old English poet skillfully reducing the narrative to the essential characters and heightening dramatic effects.[85]

The three-part poem *Christ* may be thought of as loosely based on the New Testament, but it draws most directly on the Breviary, some hymns, and a homily of Gregory the Great's. It has been said to "subsume the whole Scripture-based account of human history from Creation through present time and future Judgment into eternity."[86] Of the religious poems considered here it is the least like a scriptural translation, using rather a mélange of Latin sources.[87] The second section of the poem, usually called *The Ascension,* contains a series of eight runic letters starting sixty-nine lines before the end of the poem. The runes are woven artfully into the text so that their rune-names make textual sense in context. The runes spell the name Cynewulf, and this is the presumptive author of *The Ascension* and of three other, similarly "signed," poems to be discussed below. We know little about Cynewulf, except that he seems from his dialect to have been a Mercian living, possibly, in the ninth century. He is not thought to be the author of the first or the third and final part of *Christ,* the latter being a section on Judgment Day, which has been described as a "well-structured poem . . . marked by a masterly unity of images."[88]

The last major genre to be considered is that comprising the six verse saints' lives *Elene, Juliana, The Fates of the Apostles, Andreas, Guthlac A,* and *Guthlac B.* The first three all contain Cynewulf's runic signature and so are presumably by the same poet who composed the second part of *Christ.* All three are translations or paraphrases of Latin source texts. The best is probably the 1321-line poem *Elene,* which tells the story of St. Helena's quest for the Cross. A major theme in the poem is the willful blindness of the Jews when they are confronted with Christian illumination. *Juliana* is a well-told story of a Christian virgin's refusal to marry a pagan and her successful defense of her chastity before being martyred. But "as poetry, *Juliana* is the least impressive of the Cynewulf group, its diction being rather prosaic and repetitive, its syntax rather loose."[89] *The Fates of the Apostles* is a series of abbreviated accounts of the achievements and martyrdoms of the apostles. It is almost certainly a translation, like Cynewulf's other poems, but no source has been identified. In all four poems the section with Cynewulf's signature is, of course, the poet's own composition affixed to his foregoing translation.[90]

The other three saints' lives are anonymous. Of the three the amplest is *Andreas,* which recounts how St. Andrew is sent by God on a voyage to Mermedonia, where the cannibal population is about to take the life of St. Matthew. St. Andrew rescues Matthew and after many trials succeeds in eventually converting the Mermedonians. The style and diction of the poem, which has often been compared to that of *Beowulf,* is of high quality. The two *Guthlac* poems (apparently the work of two different poets) are about a Mercian saint who died in 714. The first, *Guthlac A,* describes how the saint withstands the onslaughts of demons trying to force him from the island retreat to which he has withdrawn for a life of prayer and fasting. *Guthlac B* is a moving account of the saint's death.[91]

Besides the two major genres of scriptural narrative and saints' lives, Old English religious verse includes a variety of shorter poems: two so-called *Homiletic Fragments,* two poems on *Judgment Day* (one of them a translation of a Latin poem probably by Bede), three versifications of The Lord's Prayer and two of the Gloria, a versification of the Creed, *The Menologium* (a verse calendar of the Christian year), two *Soul and Body* poems (including a dead man's laments for the sins he committed while alive), and a poem long mistaken for two separate poems called *An Exhortation to Christian Living* and *A Summons to Prayer* but now recognized to be a single text.[92] There are also some Old English versifications of portions of the Psalter, a hymn, a prayer, *The Descent into Hell, Alms-Giving,* and *The Seasons for Fasting.* Among all the Old English shorter religious poems one stands out as an especially important witness to the way in which Old English poetry at its very best could express the deepest thoughts and feelings of the Anglo-Saxons as they adjusted their Germanic culture to Christian ideals. This poem is *The Dream of the Rood.*

The Dream of the Rood is preserved in the Vercelli Book, a manuscript which also contains Cynewulf's *Elene, The Fates of the Apostles,* and *Andreas.* The first dream-vision in English literature, it begins with the narrator recalling an extraordinary vision he had of a jeweled Cross rising into the sky whose jewels melt into streaming blood and then congeal into jewels again. Suddenly, to his amazement, the Cross begins to speak, telling how it was forced to bear the body of Jesus during the crucifixion.[93] Conceiving of itself as a retainer of Christ, the Cross agonizes over having been made the instrument of his Lord's murder. Christ is described (39–42) not as a passive victim but as a valiant warrior embracing his fate:

> Ongyrede hine þa geong hæleð,   (þæt wæs god ælmihtig),
> strang and stiðmod.   Gestah he on gealgan heanne,
> modig on manigra gesyhðe,   þa he wolde mancyn lysan.
> Bifode ic þa me se beorn ymbclypte.

[Then the strong and firm-minded young hero stripped himself; that was the all-powerful God. Courageous in the presence of multitudes, He mounted the lofty gallows-tree when He wanted to redeem mankind. I trembled when the warrior embraced me.]

This martial heroicizing of Christ is an accurate reflection of early Christian conceptions of the Savior,[94] but the perfect meshing of this conception with the poet's native Germanic diction creates a heroicized Christ perfectly consonant with traditional Anglo-Saxon ideals. The passive figure in this Passion is the personified Cross; Christ is thereby freed to be active and heroic. This role is powerfully emphasized by the narrator's concluding depiction of Christ harrowing hell and leading the patriarchs triumphantly into heaven. The poet also achieves a poetic resolution of some of the current Christological disputes over the dual nature of the God-man; and he develops effectively the paradox of the ignominious instrument of Christ's crucifixion becoming the supreme symbol of the Christian religion.

The Dream of the Rood's success in bringing dissonant cultural themes into a memorable syncretism gives deeper meaning to the stylistic tension present in all Old English religious poems in which Christian themes are combined with martial diction. It also leaves a sublime example of that native heroic ideal that animates so much of what we have called secular poetry.

Notes

[1] Word counts have been kindly supplied by Professor Antonette DiPaolo Healey, Editor of *The Dictionary of Old English* project now underway at the University of Toronto. All word counts are as of January 21, 2002.

[2] For runic writing in England see R. I. Page, *An Introduction to English Runes* (London: Methuen, 1973) and *Runes and Runic Inscriptions* (Woodbridge: Boydell Press, 1995); for runic writing in manuscripts see René Derolez, *Runica Manuscripta* (Bruges: Sinte-Catharina Press, 1954); for Roman-letter inscriptions see Elizabeth Okasha, *Hand-List of Anglo-Saxon Non-Runic Inscriptions* (Cambridge: CUP, 1971). See also the chapter in the present volume on the problems associated with runes and runology.

[3] For a description of these, see N. R. Ker, *Catalogue of Manuscripts Containing Anglo-Saxon* (Oxford: Clarendon, 1957). For an excellent sampling of publications on this corpus, see *Old English Literature,* ed. R. M. Liuzza (New Haven: Yale UP, 2002).

[4] London, British Library, Cotton Tiberius B.v, fol. 28v.

[5] An important article by Alfred Bammesberger suggests that the inscription could be the owner's declaration "(This is) Raiha's (piece)" See *Old English Runes and Their Continental Background,* ed. A. Bammesberger (Heidelberg: Winter, 1991), 403.

[6] Page, *Introduction,* 20.

[7] Derek Pearsall, *Old English and Middle English Poetry* (London: Routledge and Kegan Paul, 1977), says tentatively, "English verse . . . would go back to the earliest recorded Germanic alliterative line, the runic inscription on the horn of Gallehus, dug up in 1734 on the German-Danish border, and dated to 400 A.D." S. B. Greenfield and D. G. Calder, *A New Critical History of Old English Literature* (New York: New York UP, 1986), 122–23, begin their discussion of Old English poetry with an analysis of the Gallehus inscription. B. Odenstedt, *The Inscription on the Undley Bracteate and the Beginnings of English Runic Writing* (Umeå Papers in English 5, 1983), 19, thinks that the Anglo-Frisian runic alphabet may have been created in Schleswig-Holstein.

[8] See, for example, Wolfgang Krause, *Die Sprache der urnordischen Runeninschriften* (Heidelberg: Winter, 1971), 148.

[9] For a tabulation of these, see J. Hines, "Some Observations on the Runic Inscriptions of Early Anglo-Saxon England," in *Old English Runes,* ed. Bammesberger, 83.

[10] These are listed (with photographs of each inscription) in *Old English Verse Texts from Many Sources,* ed. Fred C. Robinson and E. G. Stanley. (Copenhagen: Rosenkilde and Bagger, 1991 = EEMF 23), plates 37–46.4.23.

[11] Mechthild Gretsch, *The Intellectual Foundations of the English Benedictine Reform* (Cambridge: CUP, 1999).

[12] Gretsch, 426. For further discussion of glosses and their cultural context see *Anglo-Saxon Glossography,* ed. R. Derolez (Brussels: Paleis der Academiën, 1992).

[13] The comment occurs in a glossary preserved in the tenth-century British Library MS Cotton Cleopatra A.iii after the lemma *maculabat* (which occurs in Aldhelm's *Enigma* 95,1. 4 quoted above). See Thomas Wright, *Anglo-Saxon and Old English Vocabularies* 2nd ed. by Richard Paul Wülcker (London: Trübner, 1884), col. 447. The same spirit is expressed in another Anglo-Saxon's comment on another grandiloquent passage of Aldhelm's: namely, *gor* ("crap!"). See Fred C. Robinson, *The Editing of Old English* (Oxford: Blackwell, 1994), 34–35.

[14] Helmut Gneuss, "The Origin of Standard Old English and Æthelwold's School at Winchester," *ASE* 1 (1972): 63–83, [repr. in his *Language and History in Early England* (Aldershot: Variorum, 1996)] argues convincingly that those in authority in Winchester and especially the school of Æthelwold made deliberate efforts to spread the standard. See also Malcolm Godden, "Literary Language," in *The Cambridge History of the English Language,* ed. Richard M. Hogg, vol. 1 (Cambridge: CUP, 1992), 490–535, esp. 518–20. On books and book production see Gneuss, *Books and Libraries in Early England* (Aldershot: Variorum, 1996).

[15] *Die altenglische Martyrologium,* ed. Günter Kotzor (Munich: Bayerische Akademie, 1981).

[16] The easiest access to the material relating to Alfred and his program of learning is *Alfred the Great: Asser's "Life of King Alfred" and Other Contemporary Sources* trans. with an introduction and notes by Simon Keynes and Michael Lapidge (Harmondsworth: Penguin, 1983). See also J. Bately, "Old English Prose before and during the Reign of Alfred," *ASE* 17 (1988): 93–138, a magisterial survey.

[17] *King Alfred's Version of St. Augustine's Soliloquies,* ed. Thomas A. Carnicelli (Cambridge, MA: Harvard UP, 1969) 37. This is the standard edition. The standard edition of *Cura pastoralis* remains *King Alfred's West-Saxon Version of Gregory's Pastoral Care,* ed. Henry Sweet (London: OUP, 1871–72 = EETS/OS 45, 50).

[18] F. Anne Payne, *King Alfred and Boethius* (Madison: U of Wisconsin P, 1968) 134. The standard edition is still *King Alfred's Old English Version of Boethius,* ed. W. J. Sedgefield (Oxford: Clarendon, 1899). A second volume with a translation was published in 1900.

[19] Keynes and Lapidge, 138.

[20] *King Alfred's Old English Prose Translation of the First Fifty Psalms,* ed. Patrick P. O'Neill (Cambridge, MA: Medieval Academy of America, 2001). Alfredian authorship, long debated, is now virtually certain: see Janet M. Bately, "The Authorship of the Prose Psalms in the Paris Psalter," *ASE* 10 (1982): 69–95.

[21] Keynes and Lapidge 32.

[22] *Bischof Wærferths von Worcester Übersetzung der Dialoge Gregors des Grossen,* ed. Hans Hecht (Leipzig: G. H. Wigand, 1900–1907), 1.

[23] See the classic edition by Janet M. Bately, *The Old English Orosius* (London: OUP, 1980 = EETS/SS 6).

[24] *The Old English Version of Bede's Ecclesiastical History of the English People,* ed. Thomas Miller (London: OUP, 1890–98 = EETS/OS 95, 96, 110, 111). Alfred's association with this translation is not certain: see Bately, "Old English Prose," 103–4. For the Latin Version see *Bede: Ecclesiastical History of the English People,* ed. and trans. Bertram Colgrave and R. A. B. Mynors (Oxford: Clarendon, 1969), to be used with J. M. Wallace-Hadrill, *Bede's Ecclesiastical History of the English People: A Historical Commentary* (Oxford: Clarendon, 1988).

[25] As is attested by the eleventh-century scribe's addition of a poem spoken in the voice of Bede in one manuscript: see Fred C. Robinson, "Old English Literature in Its Most Immediate Context," in *The Editing of Old English* (Oxford: Blackwell, 1994), 3–24.

[26] The term *"Chronicle"* actually refers to seven different versions in as many manuscripts. The original compilation or "common stock" put together during Alfred's reign is more or less the same in all versions (although some begin with the Creation or Flood), but after 900 the continuations of the annals by various scribes in different areas of the country often diverge. The seven versions are being edited in *The Anglo-Saxon Chronicle: A Collaborative Edition* under the general editorship of David Dumville and Simon Keynes. An especially important version is Manuscript A edited in this series by Janet M. Bately (Cambridge: D. S. Brewer, 1986). Peter S. Baker's edition of Manuscript F (Cambridge: D. S. Brewer, 2000) is the first modern edition of that text. See further Janet M. Bately, *The Anglo-Saxon Chronicle: Texts and Relationships* (Reading: University of Reading Centre for Medieval Studies, 1991). One version, the *Peterborough Chronicle,* is continued into the Middle English period.

[27] Simon Keynes, "Anglo-Saxon Chronicle," in *The Blackwell Encyclopedia of Anglo-Saxon England,* ed. John Blair, Simon Keynes, and Donald Scragg (Oxford: Blackwell, 1999), 35.

[28] Janet M. Bately, *The Literary Prose of King Alfred's Reign: Translation or Transformation?* An Inaugural Lecture delivered on 4th March 1980 (London, 1980). See also Robert Stanton, *The Culture of Translation in Anglo-Saxon England* (Cambridge: Boydell and Brewer, 2002).

[29] See R. W. Chambers, *On the Continuity of English Prose from Alfred to More and His School* (London: OUP, 1932 = EETS/OS 191a). Cf. R. M. Wilson, "On the Continuity of English Prose," in *Mélanges de Linguistique et de Philologie: Fernand Mossé in Memoriam* (Paris: Didier, 1959), 486–94, and *Studies in Earlier Old English Prose,* ed. Paul E. Szarmach (Albany: State U of New York P, 1986).

[30] *The Old English Version of the Gospels,* ed. R. M. Liuzza (Oxford: OUP, 1994, 2000 = EETS/OS 304, 314), vol. 1, xvi. See also Liuzza's "Who Read the Gospels in Old English?" in *Words and Works: Studies in Medieval English Language and Literature in Honor of Fred C. Robinson,* ed. Peter S. Baker and Nicholas Howe (Toronto: U of Toronto P, 1998), 3–24.

[31] *The Old English Version of The Heptateuch,* ed. S. J. Crawford (London: OUP, 1922 = EETS/OS 160) repr. with additional manuscripts transcribed by N. R. Ker 1969; *The Old English Hexateuch: Aspects and Approaches,* ed. Rebecca Barnhouse and Benjamin C. Withers (Kalamazoo: Western Michigan UP, 2001).

[32] Antonette di Paolo Healey has published an excellent edition of *The Old English Vision of St. Paul* (Cambridge, MA: Medieval Academy of America, 1978); editions of the other translations are less satisfactory.

[33] *The Vercelli Homilies and Related Texts,* ed. D. G. Scragg (Oxford: OUP, 1992 = EETS/OS 300).

[34] A new edition is now in preparation by Milton McC. Gatch. Many anonymous homilies are scattered among various manuscripts; these have been collected and edited in several volumes over the years. A recent example is *Old English Homilies from MS Bodley 343,* ed. Susan Irvine (Oxford: OUP, 1993 = EETS/OS 302). For discussion of the homilies see *The Old English Homily and Its Backgrounds,* ed. Paul E. Szarmach and Bernard F. Huppé (Albany: State U of New York P, 1978).

[35] *Ælfric's Catholic Homilies: The First Series,* ed. Peter Clemoes (London: OUP, 1997 = EETS/SS 17); *Ælfric's Catholic Homilies: The Second Series,* ed. Malcolm Godden (London: OUP, 1979 = EETS/SS 5); *Ælfric's Catholic Homilies: Introduction, Commentary and Glossary* by Malcolm Godden (Oxford: OUP, 2000 = EETS/SS 18). *The First Series* was actually completed by Godden following Clemoes's editorial principles.

[36] *Homilies of Ælfric: A Supplementary Collection,* ed. John C. Pope (London: OUP, 1967–68 = EETS/OS 259 and 260).

[37] *Ælfric's Lives of the Saints,* ed. Walter W. Skeat (London: Trübner, 1881–1900 = EETS /OS. 76, 82, 94, 114). For discussion of the saints' lives see *Holy Men and Holy Women: Old English Prose Saints' Lives and Their Contexts,* ed. Paul E. Szarmach (Albany: State U of New York P, 1996).

[38] The best analysis and explication of Ælfric's rhythmical prose is Pope's in *Homilies of Ælfric,* 105–36.

[39] *The Homilies of Wulfstan,* ed. Dorothy Bethurum (Oxford: Clarendon, 1957).

[40] Especially useful as an edition and as a general introduction to Ælfric is *Ælfric's Prefaces,* ed. Jonathan Wilcox (Durham: Durham Medieval Texts no. 9, 1994).

[41] *Wulfstan's Canons of Edgar,* ed. Roger Fowler, EETS/OS 266 (1972).

[42] Bethurum, in the introduction to *The Homilies of Wulfstan,* discusses his non-homiletic works, 43–49.

[43] Karl Jost, *Die "Institutes of Polity, Civil and Ecclesiastical": Ein Werk Erzbischof Wulfstans von York* (Bern: Swiss Studies in English 47, 1959).

[44] *The Copenhagen Wulfstan Collection,* ed. J. E. Cross and Jennifer Morrish Tunberg, EEMF 25 (Copenhagen: Rosenkilde and Bagger, 1993).

[45] A superb recent edition is *Byrhtferth's Enchiridion,* ed. Peter S. Baker and Michael Lapidge (Oxford: OUP, 1995 = EETS/SS 15).

[46] Heinrich Henel, *Studien zum altenglischen Computus* (Leipzig: Tauchnitz, 1934).

[47] See S. B. Greenfield and Fred C. Robinson, *A Bibliography of Publications on Old English Literature to the End of 1972* (Toronto: U of Toronto P, 1980), 355–56, 370–73.

[48] For an overview of these subjects see M. L. Cameron, *Anglo-Saxon Medicine* (Cambridge: CUP, 1993) and Stephanie Hollis, "Scientific and Medical Writings," in *A Companion to Anglo-Saxon Literature,* ed. Phillip Pulsiano and Elaine Treharne (Oxford: Blackwell, 2001), 188–208.

[49] Carole Hough, "Legal and Documentary Writings," in *A Companion to Anglo-Saxon Literature,* 170–87 provides a good overview and names the relevant texts.

[50] *The Old English Apollonius of Tyre,* ed. Peter Gooldin (Oxford: OUP, 1958). A quire has been lost from the eleventh-century manuscript in which *Apollonius* is preserved, but the missing narrative can be recovered from the Latin source text.

[51] Donald G. Scragg, "Secular Prose," in *A Companion to Anglo-Saxon Literature,* 270.

[52] Andy Orchard, *Pride and Prodigies: Studies in the Monsters of the Beowulf-Manuscript* (Cambridge: D. S. Brewer, 1995), 197. Illustrations in this and in another manuscript containing this text form an integral part of the *Wonders.* These can be consulted in *The Nowell Codex,* ed. Kemp Malone, EEMF 12 (1963) and in *An Eleventh-Century Anglo-Saxon Illustrated Miscellany,* ed. P. McGurk et al. EEMF 21 (1983).

[53] Orchard, *Pride and Prodigies,* 253.

[54] Patrick P. O'Neill suggests that the various *Solomon and Saturn* texts are more closely integrated than previous scholars have led us to believe. See his "The 'Solomon and Saturn' Dialogues," *ASE* 26 (1997): 139–65.

[55] *The "Prose Solomon and Saturn" and "Adrian and Ritheus,"* ed. James E. Cross and Thomas D. Hill (Toronto: U of Toronto P, 1982), Numbers 1, 37 and 55.

[56] Cross and Hill, numbers 9, 23 and 41.

[57] R. S. Cox, "The Old English *Dicts of Cato,*" *Anglia* 90 (1972): 1–42.

[58] Olof Arngart, "The Durham Proverbs," *Speculum* 56 (1981): 288–300.

[59] S. B. Greenfield and Fred C. Robinson, *A Bibliography of Publications on Old English Literature.* These figures are approximate and uniformly understate the actual numbers of publications, for the tally is of *items* in the bibliography, and many items contain numerous individual publications — such as subsequent editions of a book listed and many reviews. Item 1637, for example, which is Moritz Heyne's edition of *Beowulf,* includes eighteen editions and about sixty reviews.

[60] Thanks to late twentieth-century scholars like Janet Bately and Paul Szarmach, the imbalance is beginning to be redressed now, but much of the prose is still relatively neglected.

[61] The poem has no name in the manuscript. Modern scholars have assigned the name *Beowulf* to it. The most recent edition is *Beowulf: An Edition,* ed. Bruce

Mitchell and Fred C. Robinson (Oxford: Blackwell, 1998). For two recent translations see *Beowulf: A New Verse Translation* by R. M. Liuzza (Peterborough, ON. Broadview, 2000) with superb introduction and apparatus, and *Beowulf: A Verse Translation* by Seamus Heaney, ed. Daniel Donoghue (New York: W. W. Norton, 2002) with excellent commentary and critical essays. A useful reference work is *A Beowulf Handbook*, ed. Robert E. Bjork and John D. Niles (Lincoln: U of Nebraska P, 1997).

[62] *The Dating of Beowulf*, ed. Colin Chase (Toronto: U of Toronto P, 1981), reprinted with an afterword by Nicholas P. Howe in 1997. See also R. M. Liuzza, "On the Dating of *Beowulf*," in *Beowulf: Basic Readings*, ed. Peter S. Baker (New York: Garland, 1995), 281–302, and the review article by Theodore M. Andersson in *University of Toronto Quarterly* 52 (1983): 288–301.

[63] See Mitchell and Robinson's edition 4–5. As the foregoing discussion indicated, prose texts often survive in multiple copies, but this is rare in the case of verse.

[64] Among the many studies examining these features are J. R. R. Tolkien, "*Beowulf: The Monsters and the Critics,*" *Proceedings of the British Academy* 22 (1936): 245–95 (and frequent reprints); Roberta Frank, "The *Beowulf* Poet's Sense of History," in *The Wisdom of Poetry: Essays in Early English Literature in Honor of Morton W. Bloomfield,* ed. L. D. Benson and Siegfried Wenzel (Kalamazoo: Medieval Institute Publications, 1982), 53–65; Fred C. Robinson, *Beowulf and the Appositive Style* (Knoxville: U of Tennessee P, 1985); and Nicholas Howe, *Migration and Mythmaking in Anglo-Saxon England* (New Haven: Yale UP, 1989), 143–79 and *passim.* For a judicious selection of essays on *Beowulf* see Baker, *Basic Readings.*

[65] For an elementary but authoritative explanation of the general features of Old English meter see C. S. Lewis, "The Alliterative Metre," in *Rehabilitations and Other Essays* (London: OUP, 1939), 117–32. Among many advanced studies one may consult Thomas Cable, *The English Alliterative Tradition* (Philadelphia: U of Pennsylvania P, 1991) and Geoffrey Russom, *Beowulf and Old Germanic Metre* (Cambridge: CUP, 1998). For a book relating meter to syntax and style see H. Momma, *The Composition of Old English Poetry* (Cambridge: CUP, 1997).

[66] *Old English Minor Heroic Poems*, ed. Joyce Hill (Durham: Durham and St. Andrews Medieval Texts, 1983).

[67] For text, translation, facsimiles, and a rich commentary by various hands see *The Battle of Maldon A.D. 991*, ed. Donald Scragg (Oxford: Blackwell, 1991). See also *The Battle of Maldon: Fiction and Fact,* ed. Janet Cooper (London: Hambledon, 1993), especially for the essays by Paul Szarmach, Ute Schwab, and Roberta Frank.

[68] All but the last are edited in volume 6 of *The Anglo-Saxon Poetic Records,* ed. George Philip Krapp and Elliott Van Kirk Dobbie (New York: Columbia UP, 1931–53). For *William the Conqueror* see *The Peterborough Chronicle 1070–1154,* ed. Cecily Clark (2nd ed., Oxford: Clarendon, 1970), 13–14. All the poems discussed below are available in *ASPR*. If no other edition is mentioned, reference is to *ASPR*.

[69] That is, Exeter Cathedral Manuscript 3501, a rich tenth-century anthology of Old English poems edited in *ASPR* vol. 3. A more recent independent edition is

The Exeter Anthology of Old English Poetry, ed. Bernard J. Muir (Exeter: U of Exeter P, 1994), 2 vols. For commentary on the shorter poems in the Exeter Book (and elsewhere) see *Old English Shorter Poems: Basic Readings,* ed. Katherine O'Brien O'Keeffe (New York: Garland, 1994).

[70] See Anne L. Klinck, *The Old English Elegies: A Critical Edition and Genre Study* (Montreal: McGill Queens UP, 1992), and *The Old English Elegies,* ed. Martin Green (London and Toronto: Fairleigh Dickinson UP, 1983).

[71] See Alan Bliss and Allen J. Frantzen, "The Integrity of *Resignation,*" *RES/NS.* 27 (1976) 385–402. Some scholars have wanted to add to the tally of elegies *The Husband's Message* and certain passages in *Beowulf* and *Guthlac.* See Klinck, *Elegies.*

[72] Charles D. Wright, "The Irish Tradition," in *A Companion to Anglo-Saxon Literature,* 360–61.

[73] *The Phoenix,* ed. N. F. Blake (Manchester: Manchester UP, 1964) has complete apparatus including the Latin text. For the most recent discussion see Ananya Jahanara Kabir, *Paradise, Death and Doomsday in Anglo-Saxon Literature* (Cambridge: CUP, 2001), 160–67 and *passim.*

[74] An early proem to the translation attests to Alfred's authorship and to this procedure. See Kenneth Sisam, *Studies in the History of Old English Literature* (Oxford: Clarendon Press, 1953), 293–97. For the verse itself, see *Alfred's Meters of Boethius,* ed. Bill Griffiths (rev. ed., Chippenham: Anglo-Saxon Books, 1994).

[75] *The Old English Riddles of the Exeter Book*, ed. Craig Williamson (Chapel Hill: U of North Carolina P, 1977).

[76] Michael Lapidge, "Stoic Cosmology and the Source of the First Old English Riddle," *Anglia* 112 (1994): 1–25, provides the solution to this riddle.

[77] Fred C. Robinson, "Artful Ambiguities in the Old English 'Book-Moth' Riddle," in *The Tomb of Beowulf* (Oxford: Blackwell, 1993), 98–104.

[78] See Richard North, *Heathen Gods in Old English Literature* (Cambridge: CUP, 1997) and Karen L. Jolly, *Popular Religion in Late Saxon England* (Chapel Hill: U of North Carolina P, 1996). See also the Old High German Merseburg Charms, where there is a similar reference in a clearly Christian context to various gods, including (in the continental form of the name), Wodan.

[79] Fred C. Robinson, "Secular Poetry," in *A Companion to Anglo-Saxon Literature,* 281–95.

[80] Translations or paraphrases of biblical narratives make up 12,658 lines of Old English verse, while 5,882 lines are devoted to saints' lives. Shorter texts like versifications of prayers, church calendars, the Creed and the like take up 1,647 lines. The total number of lines of religious poetry is 20,187.

[81] *Historia ecclesiastica* book 4, chap. 24. Colgrave and Mynors, 414–21.

[82] Colgrave and Mynors, 419.

[83] See C. L. Wrenn, "The Poetry of Cædmon," *Proceedings of the British Academy* 32 (1946): 277–95; see Kevin Kiernan, "Reading Cædmon's Hymn with Someone Else's Gloss," in *Old English Literature,* ed. Liuzza, 103–24.

[84] *herges wisa, freom folctoga* (13–14), *isernhergum* (348), *sæwicingas* (333).

[85] The most recent edition of *Judith* is in Bruce Mitchell and Fred C. Robinson, *A Guide to Old English* (6th ed., Oxford: Blackwell, 2001), 300–312.

[86] *Anglo-Saxon Poetry* trans. S. A. J. Bradley (London: J. M. Dent and Sons, 1982), 203.

[87] For an overview of the scriptural narratives see Paul G. Remly, *Old English Biblical Verse* (Cambridge: CUP, 1996).

[88] Jane Roberts in *The Blackwell Encyclopedia of Anglo-Saxon England*, 105.

[89] Greenfield and Calder, *A New Critical History* 167. In *The Cambridge Companion to Old English Literature,* ed. Malcolm Godden and Michael Lapidge (Cambridge: CUP, 1991), 259, Lapidge says that of the six texts being discussed here only *Juliana* "could properly be described as a saint's life."

[90] See further Daniel G. Calder, *Cynewulf* (Boston: Twayne, 1981); cf. H. L. C. Tristram's review in *Anglia* 102 (1984): 193–99.

[91] For an overview of the six saints' lives see Robert E. Bjork, *The Old English Verse Saints' Lives* (Toronto: U of Toronto P, 1985).

[92] See Fred C. Robinson, "'The Rewards of Piety': 'Two' Old English Poems in Their Manuscript Context," in *The Editing of Old English,* 180–95.

[93] Parts of the Rood's speech were carved in runes on an eighteen-foot high stone cross (ca. 700) in Ruthwell, Dumfriesshire, which is also decorated with Christian iconic artwork. Evidently this is an effort to create an actual Cross speaking its own words to viewers. For complete photographs of the inscription see Robinson and Stanley, *Old English Verse Texts,* plates 44.1–44.2.5.2.

[94] See *Sources and Analogues of Old English Poetry,* trans. D. G. Calder and M. J. B. Allen (Cambridge: D. S. Brewer, 1976), 53–58.

Old High German and
Continental Old Low German

Brian Murdoch

THERE ARE TWO WAYS of approaching the relatively limited amount of literature (a term usually extended to cover everything written down in the vernacular) that has survived from the earliest stages of High or Low German in continental Germania, from the Low Countries to Lombardy, between about 750 and around 1200. One approach places the greatest emphasis on the Germanic content and what those survivals can confirm or tell us about pre-Christian Germanic tribal culture. Since there is little directly relevant material for this approach beyond a few legal works, a couple of charms and one single short Old High German heroic poem, evidence has to be sought elsewhere, taking us beyond even that simple definition of "everything written down," and sometimes using methods which are, in the strictest sense of the word, speculative. The approach necessarily examines existing Christian texts; oaths forswearing pagan deities can provide clues to earlier beliefs, for example. Less concrete still is the (doubtless correct) assumption that literary works existed in oral form on the continent in German which matched texts that we have in Anglo-Saxon, Norse or Latin, or indeed later in Middle High German versions, dealing with the heroes of Germanic myth and legend. A case in point is the tale of Walther or Waltharius, a heroic story with Visigoth origins involving the hero Hagen, which was certainly known to the writer of the Middle High German *Nibelungenlied* (itself linked with early Germanic tribal history), but which survives in Latin, with analogues in several other languages, but not German. There may have been an oral Old High German Walther-poem, but — and this is crucial — we do not have it. Finally, a major collection of Old High German texts actually prints a piece of non-existent Old High German, even though it is a fairly convincing recreation of a little verse, based on a Latin text which *has* survived, and which *might* have been German in origin.[1] In recent years there has been interesting and important work on the interaction of orality and literacy, and there is much still to be done; the ultimate outcome is still inevitable, however — we cannot easily (and convincingly) examine what we do not have.[2]

The alternative approach is the pragmatic one that examines what we do possess in the light of the knowledge that Old High German (and Old Low German even more so) was completely subordinate to the dominant language of the Roman Empire and its Christian successors, Latin, and that, furthermore, everything we have in Old High and Old Low German depends upon the Christian Church, the body that introduced writing into Germany. Even the one heroic poem, the *Hildebrandlied,* and the so-called charms apparently invoking pagan deities were all written down by clerics. Interesting though the *Hildebrandlied* may be, it was also, when written down, a poetic anachronism in an archaic form already superseded by a rhymed verse based on Latin, which would remain the norm for centuries to come. The central work in this second approach is by a named writer, the monk Otfrid of Weissenburg, who around 860 completed a long and formally complex religious poem which he had deliberately chosen (again a crucial concept) to compose in High German. Although he wrote in a time in which Latin was the dominant language and in which vernacular German constitutes only a tiny fragment of what was being written, he too stands at the start of what would become German literature. Both approaches, whether the *Hildebrandlied* or Otfrid is placed at the head, have some validity, and they are not mutually exclusive. Both are German in a national sense, the *Hildebrandlied* naturally, Otfrid self-consciously.[3]

If we wish to refine the definition of Old High German literature (leaving Old Low German aside for the moment, although that chronology is not entirely justified) we may limit it initially to writings with some pretensions to poetic form, composed in what by an anachronistic shorthand is termed Old High German, by which is meant one of the dialects of the Western Germanic tribes that were affected after around A.D. 500, at least to some extent, by the consonant shift known as the High German Sound Shift, a set of sound-changes which moved from the southeast of present day Germany and Austria northwest across the country as far as a line roughly through Aachen, leaving the Germanic speakers above that line untouched. Thus it affected the soon-extinct dialect of Lombardic, the Upper-German dialects of Bavarian and Alemannic, and the central dialects of Thuringian, and especially Franconian — East, South Rhenish and Middle Franconian, the latter being divided into Ripuarian and Moselle Franconian, and the last-named being the High German dialect least affected by the sound shift. The Franks became the ruling political group. Beyond the Benrath-line came the continental Low German dialects, unaffected by the shift (though separated already from their more northerly Scandinavian neighbors): Old Saxon, Old Low Franconian and the various dialects of Frisian. Some of these dialects, High or Low, have no writing at all to show in the earliest period.

For most of the period in question, pretty well everything was written down and often originally composed at a monastery, and some of the monastic foundations in the Germanic world were clearly more interested in the writing of German than others. We cannot really think of these as centers of German, given the relatively small amount of material written at all in that language compared to the production of Latin. Nevertheless, certain monasteries, Fulda to the north and St. Gallen in the south, for example, produced more German than others, and again significantly, other relevant monasteries lay *outside* the Germanic part of Frankish territory. Murbach in Alsace and indeed Weissenburg are now outside Germany, but we know of German material from St. Amand in Picardy, for example, in what is and was Romance territory. Communication was not easy in any case. Finally, the transmission of the texts can be a problem in terms of preservation. Otfrid's text is consciously preserved in more than one manuscript, but that is an unusual situation at this period. Other texts have survived by chance, written down on spare pages or even in margins and blank spaces. That kind of extreme case is rare, although it does apply to one major work, the *Muspilli*. German works are typically afforded second class status in writing, and this matches the position of the language against Latin. It is important to remain aware of the influence of the Church and of the determining dominance of Latin as a literary language when assessing the few German survivals at the very start of German literature.

The ambitious history of medieval German literature by Rudolf Koegel, took account in a first volume of several hundred pages only of *one* extant Old High German text, the *Hildebrandlied* (St. I).[4] However reasonable the assumption that there were more German works than we have, this is the sole surviving Old High German heroic piece. It is damaged, it requires both historical background and considerable linguistic surgery to make it readable, and we can detect the hand of the church upon its content to a small extent. But it is still a story of vitality and importance, and it is (in one definition, at least) probably the oldest surviving example of Old High German literature. There is nothing to match it in continental Low German. The work was almost certainly oral in its original composition — it uses formulaic expressions associated with other oral traditions — but what we have is a text written down in a sequence of divided long-lines, with the two halves linked by alliteration rather than end-rhyme, a form found elsewhere in Old High German and far more frequently in other Germanic cultures (Old Norse, Anglo-Saxon), so presumably a native Germanic form. Some elements in the work as we have it hint at earlier stages, most notably names associated with the period of the Germanic tribal migrations in the fifth and sixth centuries, the enigmatic Odoacer and his Ostrogoth successor as ruler of Rome, Theoderic.

The text of the *Hildebrandlied* is an accidental survival: it was written down (rather than composed) by the only people with access to the wherewithal of preservation, the monks, so that one of the most fascinating speculations about the work is why the monks wrote it down. They did so at Fulda, where there was a tradition at least of using German, and they copied out a poem that had been written down before. One of the errors in the text we have is a repetition, which presupposes a written original. The way the alliteration works indicates a Bavarian copy-text, in an Upper German dialect; but in the text we have an attempt was made to adapt it into Low German. In one celebrated case a four-letter word begins in Upper German and ends in approximate Low German (*chud,* "known," High German *kund,* Bavarian *chund* and Anglo-Saxon *cuð*), and there are some Anglo-Saxon characters used. Presumably a High German text was intended to be transmitted to speakers of Low German, and the work, copied onto the front and back blank pages of a theological manuscript — space that was free in both senses of the word — has also been given a thin veneer of Christianity. At one point an unmetrical and hence noticeable *waltant got* (almighty God) appears, but it is also thematically unconvincing.[5]

We are shown in the fragment (of just over 60 lines) a battle between a father and his son, who are champions selected from two opposing armies. Probably the battle is a fictionalized version of the struggle at Ravenna in 493 between the Ostrogoth Theoderic and Odoacer, heir to the Visigoth rule in Rome. Theoderic (Dietrich) actually tricked and conquered Odoacer, but in the poem the old warrior Hildebrand is seen as having fled with Theoderic into exile; it is his job as a champion to help Theoderic regain what was seen in the fiction as his rightful throne. His adversary turns out to be the son he left behind. However far back in history we may wish to take the story,[6] and however much the themes reflect the ethos of a warrior caste, there are universal elements in the story. In style terms, however, the work was antiquated by the time it was copied, so that conservative nostalgia at Fulda may lie behind its survival.

There are several themes: reputation as a warrior, possessions, cowardice, inheritance, man versus fate, individual self-assertion, and the impossibility of human knowledge. The audience hears at the start that the two champions about to fight in single combat (while their own comrades watch) are a father and son, *sunufatarungo,* and their repeated and clearly related names underline this. Hildebrand, the older and, we are told with some irony, the wiser man first asks who his adversary is, claiming to know all men of that warrior class. Hadubrand promptly tells how his father, Hildebrand, had left a bride (so there were presumably no other children) and a baby without inheritance. Hadubrand assumes that his father, as a brave warrior, must be dead, and anyway, none of his own people (another irony) survives who might recognize Hildebrand. The latter now says, obliquely but absolutely clearly, who he is, but his son understandably does not believe him, but firms up instead his earlier assertion, stating that sailors (also unavailable as witnesses) have said that Hildebrand is dead. But he is not, and he tries to offer his son a gift, a little part of that lost inheritance, a gold arm-ring, a torque, that the audience hears came from Attila (with whom Theoderic was anachronistically supposed to have been in exile). The production of a Hunnish arm-ring (made incidentally from Roman imperial gold) serves only to identify Hildebrand as a Hun, which is what Hadubrand now assumes, thinking also that the older man is trying to trap him. It becomes clear that any *real* inheritance can only be genetic; the son will have to earn his gold as a warrior, by killing the older man.

The text is corrupt here; something is missing, and a case can be made for the younger man having called the older one a coward; the word *arg* "cowardly" is used reflectively by Hildebrand himself later on, who says that he would indeed be a most cowardly (*argosto*) Hun if he refused to fight. In known cases — Lombardic law, for example[7] — an insult of that nature led inevitably and indeed legally to a combat. Hildebrand now realizes that *wewurt skihit,* "cruel fate will take its course," and the battle begins. The ending is missing, but of the various possibilities for a conclusion, the only satisfactory (or even logical) one is that the father kills the son, as happens in various European analogues. The watching armies make sure that the two champions do their duty and fight, and only the tragedy of Hildebrand destroying his own posterity could have become known after the event. Hadubrand would have killed a treacherous Hun, and the death of both would be unrecorded horror. There are no ways out of the existential dilemma for the older man, except to prove that he *is* the great warrior Hildebrand by doing what he is supposed to do best: kill his opponent. The virtues implied are loyalty to the overlord regardless of the task required, and an acceptance of fate, however cruel.[8] Whether there are specifically *Christian* virtues here other than the somewhat clumsy attempt to impose the will of an all-powerful God onto a pessimistic view of cruel fate (*we-wurt*), so that what Hildebrand accepts is actually the will of God, is a matter of debate.

The *Hildebrandlied* is old and the material is undoubtedly Germanic, and the story as such has nothing at all to do with the Christian church. Of its transmission we can only say that someone wanted to try to preserve it;[9] but the attempt was not entirely successful. The Gospel poem written by Otfrid, a monk, librarian, and teacher at the monastery of Weissenburg, on the other hand, was very deliberately recorded. Standing at the beginning of a *self-aware* German literature, this work differs from the heroic poem in almost every respect. Otfrid's Gospel Book is known as the *Evangelienbuch*, although *Liber Evangeliorum* is its proper title, and there is still a lot of Latin involved in the work. It is long, seven thousand lines, in Latinate rhymed, not alliterative verse, it is framed by Latin, with Latin section headings and biblical citations; it is not a native story, but a biblical narrative plus commentary, and it was designed also for reading by eye rather than being an oral work captured in ink. But two features distinguish it from the heroic poem above all else: it was modern, and it was official. Modern, because German had not been used with end rhyme to that extent before (the theme and also the mixture of biblical narrative and explanation had been used earlier in the Low German *Heliand*, but that is not in rhymed verse); and official, because it had several manu-scripts dedicated to it, and hence seems to have circulated. The produc-tion of a book at this stage was a costly business, even one that was not expensively illustrated.[10] Otfrid's Gospel-book, which he provided with a dedicatory epistle in Latin, is even self-conscious about using rhymed verse in German, or rather (since Otfrid was aware of his identity as a South Rhenish Franconian), in Frankish.[11] Otfrid's consciousness of nov-elty is important; his dedicatory Latin letter, addressed to his archbishop, Liutbert of Mainz (and possibly intended for his former teacher at Fulda and Liutbert's predecessor, Hrabanus Maurus himself), apologizes for German as a rustic and barbaric language — by which he means that it is not the same as Latin — but he does use it, writing in long-line form, with rhyme at the end of each rhythmically balanced half-line, the long lines grouped in pairs by sense, like very short strophes. Apart from the Latin prose letter, there are dedications in German verse, first to the king, Ludwig the German (840–76), and then to other ecclesiastical associates, written in a highly complex form, with acrostics and telestichs — spelling out words with the first or last letters of a line or strophe; that to Ludwig spells out the Latin dedication with the initial and final letters of each two-line "strophe," and also with the letter at the end of the third half-line as well, giving an internal version of it.

An introduction to the whole work in German, however, also explains why Otfrid wrote in German, and without mentioning anything about barbarism. This section, the first "chapter" of the first of the five books into which the whole work is divided — remains important as a pro-grammatic justification of the use of German in the language, and its ar-gument is at its clearest when at its most simple:

> Wánana sculun Fránkon   éinon thaz biwánkon,
>   ni sie in frénkisgon bigínnen,   si gotes lób singen?

[Why should the Franks be the only ones not to do it, not to begin to sing the praise of God in Frankish?]

The *Evangelienbuch* is a Gospel harmony, although unlike the *Heliand*, its Low German predecessor by a generation, it is not based on the composite Gospel produced in the second century by Tatian, but represents Otfrid's own arrangement of the four Gospels in five books, themselves divided into chapters with Latin headings. The purity of the even number of Gospels, Otfrid tells us, cancels the impurity of the five senses. After his German introduction and an invocation which again indicates how much rooted in Church literature the text is (a reference to his mother in the opening led to some biographical speculation before it was pointed out that he is simply citing one of the Psalms), the events of the Gospels are narrated, moving freely from one Gospel to another. Otfrid stated his intentions of doing this in his Latin letter, but his structuring is selective: the second book opens with the *In principio* passage of John's Gospel, for example. The narrative of the Bible is usually provided with a commentary, however, which is either integral to the chapter (sometimes with a subheading or a comment by the poet to indicate that this *is* an interpretation) or as a chapter in its own right. The five books have as their basic themes the nativity, the ministry, the miracles, the passion and finally the resurrection, ascension and day of judgment. Otfrid expounds the Gospels according to the medieval system of classifiable hermeneutics, by which individual elements may be interpreted and expanded literally, or may be treated as moral sermons (headed *moraliter*), or as allegory (headed *spiritaliter* or *mystice*). Links to biblical verses are supplied in the manuscript, and it is likely that the whole object of the work was pedagogical, giving native speakers of German an introduction to the most important material of Christianity, with an emphasis on the introductory element; the tone is direct, somewhere between the classroom and the pulpit, so that there is always a clear pedagogic intent, with Otfrid frequently spending a long time telling his audience simply that there *is* a spiritual meaning. The commentary parts, too, are frequently small sermons, taking up biblical passages and interpreting them in various ways. The interpretative passages are not necessarily long, and IV, 25, on the crucifixion, with the title *pauca spiritaliter* "a little interpretative passage" has only 14 long-lines, opening with Otfrid explaining first, as so often, what he is going to do, namely, to make clear the mystery of the details. When he does so, it is done briefly:

> Thio súnta thio unsih stéchent   joh sih in úns rechent —
> bizéinont thaz thie thórna   thie wir hiar lasun fórna; IV 25 5f

[The sins that prick us and stick into us, that is what is meant by the thorns that we have just read about.]

The notion of interpreting the crown of thorns as human sins is not original, and Otfrid probably knew it from a Latin commentary by Hrabanus Maurus on Matthew; the passage ends, however, with an affirmation of Christ's having suffered in order to remove the sins of mankind, a reminder of the reality of what he is describing, and indeed Otfrid rarely forgets the human experience of the incarnation. The whole work is an artistic product as well, however. Although on occasion the style appears stolid and the technique of repetition with variation (used to fill half-lines) is foreign to modern tastes, Otfrid is capable of tour-de-force performances both in structure and in word-play. He uses repetitions and prayers almost as choruses, for example, in the long and impressive twenty-third chapter of the last book. In that chapter Otfrid contrasts the perfections of heaven with the imperfections of human life, and the repeated prayers alternate between the requests for protection from evil: *Biscírmi uns, druhtin gúato therero árabeito . . .* (protect us, O lord, from things that beset us), and the desire (which gradually takes precedence in the repetitions) to be led into the presence of God:

> Thára leiti, druhtin,   mit thínes selbes máhtin
>   zi thémo sconen libe   thie holdun skálka thine . . .

[Lead, O lord, in thine own power, thy faithful servants toward the blessed life.]

The work is a complex one, covering more than just the Gospels, and ranging from the beginning to the end of the world. The creation-passage at the start of John's Gospel is treated in the second book, and the last judgment (based on Old Testament apocalyptic) in V, 19. Both themes are taken up separately elsewhere in Old High German, but here the broadly conceived work uses the Gospels as the key to man's need to regain his true homeland, that of the lost paradise.

Otfrid did not create from nothing. Behind him lay not only the *Heliand,* a similar Low German narrative of the Gospels with commentary passages, albeit using the alliterative form, as indeed do similar Anglo-Saxon biblical poems, but, far more important, a wealth of Latin tradition, both in the use of poetry for the retelling of biblical books and in the biblical commentary. The use of end rhyme was presumably based on the example of Latin rhythmical hymns, though other sources have been suggested. The *Hildebrandlied* comes from one tradition, a native one of great antiquity; Otfrid comes from another, this time a relatively recently imported, learned and essentially written tradition (Otfrid's acrostics depend on sight rather than listening), but with the novelty that little of it before Otfrid was in

German. Otfrid's work is known to have been copied several times and sent to different parts of the German-speaking area — one of the manuscripts being of Bavarian rather than Rhenish-Franconian provenance.

However, there is not even a clear-cut division between works in Germanic alliterative verse and those composed using end-rhyme. Not all the former are concerned with German cultural material, and two texts referred to obliquely already treat in Old High German alliterative verse the creation and the end of the world respectively, although both are sty-listically somewhat problematic. The so-called *Wessobrunn Prayer* (from a monastery in Bavaria; St. II), is probably earlier than Otfrid, and has runic symbols in the manuscript. Furthermore, it is not clear whether some of it is in prose, or whether it is all in alliterative verse. At any rate, nine long lines describe the primeval emptiness, and following them is a prayer (which is either in verse or in balanced rhetorical prose) for grace to resist the devil and do God's will. A Latin prayer follows the German text with a demand for repentance. The effect of the piece is twofold: the vision of the uncreated world is striking, but the whole is really a prayer, compara-ble with Otfrid's treatment of John 1. There are several other prose prayers that have survived in Old High German, mostly translated from Latin, all of them brief, and there is one rhymed one, attached to the Freising manuscript of Otfrid's Gospel-poem, named for the scribe Sigi-hard (St. XX).

The poem of the end of the world, a text given as a title the word it uses for "the final destruction," *Muspilli* (St. XIV), is another accidental survival, copied in the spaces of a presentation manuscript of Latin theol-ogy dedicated to King Ludwig the German (while he was still a prince). It is difficult to sort out what the poem should look like. It is ostensibly al-literative, but there are also rhymes in the long-lines, almost as if there were a certain indecision about the form. The poem presents the war be-tween heaven and hell for the soul after death almost in an heroic fashion, but stressing (as Otfrid does) the implications of misdeeds on earth. We are then shown the end of the world, brought about when the Antichrist spills Elijah's blood, this being based perhaps on apocryphal writings. The finality of the judgment is stressed, and with that — importantly for the presumed audience — the need to judge honestly on earth. We are told how Christ will appear in majesty, but then the poem breaks off.

Once again the work is really a sermon, and if Otfrid's version of the last judgment in his final book was designed to instruct (novice) monks, the *Muspilli* is more certainly directed toward the same warrior-nobility that would have listened to poems like the *Hildebrandlied*. That audience is warned that it cannot hide behind relatives when Christ comes to judge *them*. The *Muspilli* provides evidence of poetic skill once again, but at the same time evidence for the lower status of German in its rather garbled transmission; and yet it *is* written on the pages of an important text, and that looks like an act of linguistic assertion at least.

The smaller Christian works that follow clearly from Otfrid (even though there are disputes about relative chronology) provide evidence of interest in developing a German literature within the framework of Christianity. Compared with contemporary Latin poetry these pieces are few and slight, and indeed the word *Denkmäler,* "monuments," is regularly used for them. The gradation between the small but more or less complete pieces that we have, and jottings in German, either legitimately included as quotations in Latin texts or written without official status in Latin manuscripts is slight. Thus beside Otfrid's large work we have a short Old High German rhymed fragment of the story of Christ and the Samaritan Woman (St. XVII) from John 4, 6–21, written down probably in the tenth century, and composed probably under the influence of the *Evangelienbuch,* although with some three-line strophes and offering a narrative only, rather than a mixture of narrative and commentary. The Gospel passage was a set piece for church reading, and is sometimes treated separately in other languages, but the idea was perhaps to stress that Christ's mission was not only to Jews, a useful point for the period. Contemporary with it or perhaps earlier is another biblical piece, a rhymed version of Psalm 138 (St. XXII; in the King James version it is Psalm 139), again almost certainly composed under the direct influence of Otfrid's work. It is Bavarian, and once more uses three-line strophes. The text we have urges us (as in one part of the original Psalm) to shun those who do murder, asks for protection against evil and then stresses God's control over man from conception onward. The work ends with a prayer, and indeed the whole text is more like a rhymed prayer than a translation. The *Petruslied* (St. XXI), finally, is a hymn to St. Peter (who controls entry to the kingdom of heaven), composed probably at the Bavarian monastery of Freising once more, although this time there has been some debate on whether it preceded Otfrid or was composed with knowledge of his work. However, it consists of only three rhymed pairs of long-lines, plus the liturgical refrain *kyrie eleison, christe eleison.* It ends with the communal effect regularly found in hymns: *pittemes . . . alla samant,* "let us pray . . . all together," and there is, interestingly, musical notation in the manuscript. It may have been associated with pilgrimages to St. Peter's in Rome, as there is evidence elsewhere of a German hymn being used as well as the more numerous Latin equivalents.

With these works — all tiny in comparison to Otfrid's — we have almost (though not quite) exhausted all that there is of Old High German poetry, at least in the period before the turn of the millennium. Some apparently secular remnants have survived, it is true, one for example apparently describing a giant boar, and used as an example of hyperbole within a

Latin school text, and another line-and-a-half about a hart and a hind; yet another looks like a lampoon concerning a daughter who is taken away and then returned. As an illustration of the problem of locating texts, there is even a brief verse that was once carved over (perhaps) a library entrance in Cologne, but which we know about only from a sixteenth-century engraving by the mapmaker Mercator. The size and nature of survival of these various pieces indicate again the relative status of German.[12]

A rather different position, however, is held by a work roughly the same size as the *Hildebrandlied*, but which, though important in literary terms and clearly in German, is difficult to integrate into a history of early German literature. The work is in Otfridian rhymed long-lines, in two or three-line strophes, and it is again "official" in that it is written out as poetry, albeit side-by-side with texts in Latin and French. The historical poem known in German as the *Ludwigslied* (St. XVI) was written down, however, in French-speaking territory by a French scribe, probably in the monastery of St. Amand, near Valenciennes. By the time the poem was composed, the Frankish empire of Charlemagne, which had effectively ceased to exist in political terms in 840, was divided very clearly into the ancestors of modern France and Germany, with a corresponding linguistic division.[13] Yet this poem is about a victory over Vikings invaders by the French king Louis III. Having ascended the throne while still in his teens in 879, he divided the West Frankish lands with his brother, Carloman, and was threatened both within his kingdom and from outside, in the latter case by Viking raids. Chronicles report how Louis and Carloman together defeated a would-be usurper, Boso, Duke of Provence, after which Louis rode north and defeated a Viking force at Saucourt in Picardy in August 881. However, Louis died almost exactly a year later, and the poem, when written down, had to be given the heading *in memoriam*. A lot of that historical sketch is reflected in the Old High German work. It has been argued[14] that the poem is about a different battle, fought by Ludwig the Younger, king of the East Franks, in 880, but this would make nonsense of the actual text, especially the first part, in which we are told (and the poet perhaps claims first-hand knowledge) how the young king lost his father but was "adopted" by God, shared his lands with his brother, and that the king was away when the Vikings attacked. The attacks are seen both as a punishment for the wickedness of the Franks and a test to see whether the king can suffer hardship at such a young age. The East Frankish king, already 40 when his father died, was about forty-five at the time of his battle, and he had two brothers with whom he shared lands, not one.

It is, of course, a religious work; there is a direct relationship between God and the king, and the Franks are referred to as God's people. As a further Old Testament parallel, the Vikings are instruments, used by God to punish the Franks, much as God sends Nebuchadnezzar to punish his people in the Book of Jeremiah. The ideas were common enough at the time of the work. The reason for the importance of the work is that it places an historical event in completely consistent theological-historical terms, showing *us* God's plan, but leaving the characters unaware of the outcome. Louis submits to God's will on behalf of himself and his men, and they all sing the *kyrie,* "Lord have mercy," as they ride into a battle in which God does in fact gives them victory. Making the young Louis into a king favored by divine power was useful propaganda, and this might have been the intent, but Louis's death in August 882 turned the work into a memorial.

Locating this work in the early stages of German literature depends, then, exclusively on the language, given that the work was composed with some certainty in what we can almost legitimately refer to as France, and thus raises a point about the nature of literature and nationality. Probably the poet was a German-speaking monk at the aristocratic monastery of St. Amand. The work also presupposes a German-speaking audience of some kind, however small, in Romance territory; at any rate, there is no evidence that the poem ever circulated in what is now Germany.

In his literary role as divinely supported king, Louis might perhaps have become a candidate for sainthood after his death, but the fact that he is reported to have been killed chasing a girl on horseback rather speaks against this. There is one Old High German text to do with a popular saint (even if Gibbon famously damned him as a parasite and profiteer), namely St. George of Cappadocia. The *Georgslied* (St. XIX), however, is a linguistic nightmare, a tenth-century poem, copied by a scribe who leaves us with a whole variety of garbled forms, into one of the manuscripts of Otfrid's Gospel-poem. The form of the work, as far as we can tell, is interesting in that the rhymed long-lines seem to be arranged in longer sense-groups, and the poem is probably based on one of the Latin lives of the saint. St. George appears here without his dragon (a story grafted on later probably from the classical Perseus legend), but he heals the sick, works miracles, and is martyred by the Romans — or at least, in the incomplete text we have, repeated attempts are made to kill him and repeatedly *uhffher stuont sihk goriio dhar* (George rose up again). The German has a number of even more distorted forms, which a modern mind might interpret as dyslexia; what is presumably *hellehunt,* "hellhound" appears in the manuscript as *ehtle unht.* Why this poem, composed perhaps at Prüm, was so badly transcribed is unclear. The only other saint's life we know of in OHG has been lost in the original, although this time there is more certainty that it existed. A monk in the monastery of St. Gall, which had a tradition of German, wrote a poem on the life of the founder of his monastery in

German verse at the end of the ninth century, but all that has survived of Ratpert's original is a Latin translation (which also fits the music, so it is probably pretty close) by a tenth/eleventh century monk at the same place, Ekkehart IV, who presumably disapproved of what he referred to as a *carmen barbaricum*.[15] Again the case points up the difficulty of defining German literature of the Old High German period and at the same time the dominance of Latin.

A different linguistic problem is presented by another historical work, also in the rhymed long-lines used by Otfrid, but this time macaronic, half Latin and half German. *De Heinrico* (On Heinrich, St. XXIII) once again has two- and three-line groupings, and the little poem (there are only twenty-seven lines) tells how Heinrich, Duke of Bavaria, was received by the emperor Otto, who seems in the poem to have welcomed two men "of that name," and honored Heinrich. This time it is genuinely unclear who the characters are. Otto I pardoned his younger brother, Henry of Bavaria, after a revolt in 941, but the work might equally well depict the reconciliation between the son of that particular Heinrich (known appropriately as "the Quarrelsome"), with the young Otto III in 985. The intent here is also hard to assess; it celebrates a specific event, but in literary terms it has the look of a formal learned exercise, something which is often the case with macaronic poetry, although at this period a conscious bridging of Latin and German has a rather different resonance. There is in fact another example of such verse in Old High German, a work of greater fascination but also provoking greater frustration, because it was deliberately damaged in the middle ages, possibly because it was felt to be obscene. *Suavissima nonna* (Sweetest of Nuns)[16] is a dialogue poem in which a man urges a nun to come with him. She resists, although she may have changed her mind at the end of the work, which — as is so often the case — we do not have. Again the nature of the piece is interesting; here it is more plausibly a bridge between vernacular and Latin poetry (and love poetry at that) than just a clerical exercise.

Around the middle of the eleventh century began a period of linguistic transition toward Middle High German, with the gradual weakening or loss of unstressed vowels its most striking feature (compare OHG *giuuisso*, MHG *gewis*, modern German *gewiss*), and coincident with these changes, between about 1050 and 1200, a wider variety of works begins to indicate that German has begun to establish itself more firmly. Although linguistically classified as early Middle High German, most of these eleventh-century texts develop the same theological content of the early pieces. The neat and hymnic balance of the Fall and the Redemption contained in the biblical *Ezzos Gesang*, and the ascetic poem *Memento Mori* are cases in point, and both are included in many editions of Braune's Old High German *Lesebuch*. Later still the historical chronicle of the bishop of Cologne, the *Annolied*, and the massive history of saints and emperors in the Regensburg *Kaiserchronik* can be linked with the *Ludwigslied*, while rhymed biblical narratives and commentaries on Genesis and Exodus continue Otfrid's work. The manuscript transmission also stabilizes as German becomes more acceptable.

Equally important for the emergence of German as a literary language in the long term is the development of prose, but it is far more difficult to assess Old High German prose as literature because we are dealing mostly with translations.[17] The early codifications of laws and customs, legal documents such as descriptions of land boundaries, or even something like the *Strasbourg Oaths,* are all valuable for demonstrating the vernacular in use, although all lie fairly clearly outside the literary sphere. The position with theological writings is less clear. The texts are functional in imparting knowledge, conveying the ideas of Latin theology in the vernacular; the enrichment of the German language in so doing is incidental, but it is nevertheless undeniable, and the notions of artistic prose in classical rhetoric can also transfer (at least later on) into German.

In terms of expansion of the German literary vocabulary, the simplest translation technique (and it should be stressed that no chronological development is implied here) is the process of glossing single Latin words with German ones. Glossing aids the understanding of the Latin upon which it depends, but it can also augment the native philosophical vocabulary, a basic tool for the construction of a vernacular literature. Sometimes entire Latin texts are glossed, provided, that is, with one or more German equivalents written in somewhere close to the original in the manuscript at some time after the writing of the original. Mostly the texts are useful ones, such as biblical books, or the Benedictine Rule, for example. Re-copying a manuscript that has already been glossed can, as it were, incorporate the German beside the Latin rather than above or near it.[18] Glosses can also be grouped later to make glossaries and dictionaries, alphabetic, thematic or both, and one of the earliest German texts is a glossing not of a continuous text, but of a *Latin* thesaurus, the so-called *Abrogans,* and the re-copied version of a text still based on alphabetized Latin headwords, but with integrated German, is a curious document. Phrase books exist too, based partly at least on a classical tradition, in fact, but with one interesting case in early German, the so-called *Pariser Gespräche* (the manuscript is in Paris, in this case appropriately, with a fragment in the Vatican). The text presents a series of what look like useful phrases for the traveler, plus a number of actively abusive ones not linked with any tradition. Unusually the German comes first, with Latin translations following, all written down with many features of what we would still recognize as a French accent, such as the dropped *h*. There is an enormous temptation to read these phrases, in which basic interrogation descends quickly and more than once into belligerence, as if they were reality, but we have no real ideas what lies behind the document.[19] The contribution to literary language of the early rendering of the phrase *Vndes ars in tine naso | canis culum in tuo naso* [dog's ass up your nose] is debatable; it does at least give us an idea of a different register.

With glosses, the German always depends on the Latin, and it is only vocabulary that is expanded, not continuous writing, since even collectively the German glosses do not constitute verse or prose, although in the case of the glossed Latin hymns from Murbach it can look like it, and there has been some debate over whether these glosses are merely aids to understanding the Latin or whether they might have an independent value.[20] Translations of complete texts take various forms. Scriptural texts tend (at least in the early stages) to be translated in way that we should call overly literal, though the translator would have called it faithful, while freer, and indeed well-translated versions of earlier theological works exist side by side both with these and with the glosses. That of the sixth-century Spanish Christian Isidore's treatise against the Jews (an argument for Christianity, that is, aimed at informed questioners), is well done, the translation expanded and clarified whenever necessary to make the text clear, and also varied, presumably for artistic effect. Although the manuscript shows that it was intended to be complete — German and Latin are in parallel columns — it was never finished. As an example of the literal/faithful technique there is one major contribution in the translation of a prose Gospel-harmony, a composite Gospel (called the *Diatessaron*) first compiled in the second century by Tatian, and, by way of a Latin translation, found in most western European vernaculars. The Old High German text, made at Fulda and written out by several scribes, often looks like an interlinear gloss, although this time it is not: the German version is given separate status in the manuscript, in a separate adjacent column, but it does adhere closely to the original, imitating Latin grammatical features, for example, like participial forms. This is especially clear with well-known passages and prayers, in which we can feel the reluctance of the translator to move too far away from what was felt to be a sacred text, much in the way that the Lord's Prayer is in German still called the *Vaterunser* in accord with Latin (and Greek) word-order, rather than, as in English: "Our Father."[21] Close in technique to the Tatian text, though not in the same sense a faithful translation, is the ninth century sermon text known in two manuscripts, the *Exhortatio ad plebem Christianam* (St. IX), and there are also some smaller translations of biblical texts associated with the translation of Isidore of Seville's tract, known as the *Monsee fragments*.

German prose *does* develop, however, and toward the end of the Old High German period and into the eleventh century two named writers command attention: Notker III of St. Gall (given the tag *labeo,* "thick-lipped," or more appropriately *teutonicus,* "German," to distinguish him from other monks of the same name), and Williram, abbot of Ebersberg. Both are conscious users of German,[22] but both employ what is known as *Mischsprache,* a deliberate mixture of German and Latin, a concept quite foreign to modern thought. Latin is still the official language of teaching.

Notker (ca. 950–1022) was a scholar and teacher at St. Gallen composing his own textbooks, sometimes in Latin, but in others making use of German, something he (like Otfrid) felt the need to justify to a superior, this time Bishop Hugo of Sion to whom he wrote in 1015 asking him to bear with the unusual idea of German as a medium for teaching. To that end he translated standard works, not only the Psalms, but perhaps most famously Boethius's *Consolation of Philosophy.* Often he would give a Latin sentence, then a translation into free German, then a commentary in Latin and German. Sometimes words are left in Latin even then, especially if they are obvious ones for a learner. Notker was concerned about the German language: he invented words when necessary, he translated freely and well, and he developed a consistent orthography, an unusual step at an early stage. His works, like Otfrid's so much earlier, were copied.

Notker wrote in the Alemannic dialect and spent his life in St. Gallen in what is now Switzerland. Around half a century after Notker's death Williram, who had, like Otfrid, studied in Fulda, and who was for many years abbot of Ebersberg in Bavaria, wrote a work on the biblical Song of Songs that is even harder to integrate into the history of German literature. Its form is quite unfamiliar to us now, and it was designed to be synoptically tripartite. Manuscripts of the texts are divided into three columns; in the middle is the Vulgate text of the biblical book, in large script. The left-hand column has a paraphrase in Latin verse, and on the right is a prose commentary in the same kind of *Mischsprache* as Notker used, in substance deriving from standard biblical commentaries on the Song of Songs, taking it as an allegory. The overall significance of this text is clear: it survived for a long time with fairly frequent copying, once as late as in 1523, and the German commentary section was copied on its own, and adapted later on in a work called the *St. Trudperter Hohelied.* Equally, though, the German elements were sometimes put into Latin.

Other later prose survivals are slighter. Otloh of St. Emmeram (ca. 1010–70), translated one of his prayers for the forgiveness of sins into Old High German (St. XXXV), and there is a short piece called *Himmel und Hölle* (St. XXIX), also written in the late eleventh century, which is of interest as an example of rhetorically balanced prose, the kind of thing taught in Latin rhetoric classes, only it is in German, contrasting heaven and hell, something not uncommon in medieval sermons.[23] The writing here is not unimpressive, however, and the work is worth noting in that we can begin to see the development of German prose (albeit with Latin underpinning still) rather more clearly.

One further late translation may, finally, be mentioned on thematic rather than on stylistic grounds. *Physiologus* (St. XXVII) is an ancient description of certain animals, to which religious interpretations have been added, and at the very end of the Old High German period in linguistic terms a German version with twelve animals was added to a theological manuscript. It is not a long text, and it is again functional theology, though it is also zoological. The *Physiologus* would be treated again in German more than once later on, but what is important is the thematic broadening of material in the German language.

One group of monuments bridges many of the divides in and between Old High and Old Low German and requires separate treatment.[24] The oppositions of Latin and German, pagan and Christian, prose and verse, oral and written, indeed, literary and functional are, however, all resolved by the invariably small texts usually (but not in fact very usefully) distinguished as charms or blessings. In chronological terms these are not only spread across the whole linguistic period, but go on almost to the present. The charms and the blessings are the most international survivals in Old High German, in that, with the exception of a very few Germanic elements in some pieces, they have parallels in a wide range of cultures from pre-classical times to the present. Since the whole context (rather than content) of Old High and also Low German is Christian, the charms and blessings are both really best described as specific prayers; non-specific prayers exist in any case, of course, and the most familiar of these, the Lord's Prayer, occurs regularly as part of the Old High German charms or blessings. If a division between the two latter terms is required, a charm is a prayer requesting amelioration of a problematic condition, usually a medical one, once it is already there, while a blessing is a specific request that something might not come about. The bulk of the charms are for medicinal purposes, are intended to be curative without the use of pharmaceutical (or at the period, herbal) ingredients, although actions are sometimes called for; blessings are prophylactic. It may be noted that there are a few actual medical recipes surviving in Old High German, those from the very end of the period being found in medical collections that also contain charms, which gives an indication of usage and indeed of status. There is even an indication in one manuscript that the charms are medicines for the poor.

The closest parallels to the charms are the collects in the Christian liturgy, and it should be noted that in what follows the word "magic" has deliberately been avoided; although a magical effect might have been hoped for (certainly in the earliest forms of these pieces), in the text we have the effect depends upon the attached prayer, and it is surely for this reason that charms were tolerated by the church and recorded regularly in ecclesiastical manuscripts. Even the word "charm" is problematic, but it is less clumsy than something like "thaumaturgic prayer." They are all prayers, in effect.

The format of a charm, however, is fairly regular. The fullest will usually have a Latin heading indicating the use (something like *Ad catarrhum,* "For nosebleeds"), and will then have a passage of Old High German in verse or in prose describing a situation in which a cure has been effected, or some action has been taken; then comes a command that the bleeding should stop, and this will be followed by a prayer such as the Our Father (often to be said three times). It contains, of course, the phrase "Thy will be done" or just the word *Amen* ("[Lord] let it be"). In a few cases the descriptive passage in Old High German is clearly pre-Christian. The Merseburg Charms, both probably designed to cure sprains, refer in the first to valkyries and in the second to Germanic gods like Wodan. The latter charm is also very clearly poetic, asking for the knitting of bone to bone, blood to blood, sinew to sinew in an incantatory passage known in cultures outside Germanic.[25] However, the references to the Germanic gods are not entirely clear, suggesting that when it was written down the references were no longer really understood, but that they were simply part of its antiquity. At any rate, the Christian prayer attached makes the whole thing into a request, whatever the narrative part might have been originally.[26] Although they have attracted disproportionate interest, the charms containing pre-Christian echoes are very few in number, while the charms themselves are very numerous, often containing in their narrative portions stories involving Christian figures, though rarely in biblical roles. Christ cures a sprain in a horse's foot once, for example, just as Wodan does in the second Merseburg Charm. Many of the bleeding charms refer to the incident with Longinus as the centurion at the crucifixion, but others use the apocryphal notion of the Jordan ceasing to flow while Christ is being baptized. These pieces are again essentially functional, designed to combat either temporary traumatic conditions, such as sprains or bleeding, or illnesses with passing symptoms (here epilepsy is the principal example). Such conditions (including epileptic fits) usually pass with time, and the calming effect of the familiar prayers probably played a part. General illness is also indicated in another charm of some antiquity, headed *pro nessia,* and often translated as "against worms," although "against germs" might be a better version. It is not always entirely clear what illness or condition is the target, or indeed whether humans, animals, or both are to be cured. Thus, the first Merseburg charm was long interpreted as a charm for the release of prisoners, but although that seems to be the content of the narrative section, such a charm would be unique, and, one has to add, surely not worth noting down in its new Christian context as something that would ever actually *work*. More likely it is a charm against cramp. In other cases the narrative is highly obscure. Some charms, too, seem to be concerned with adverse, but not medical conditions, to preventing bees from swarming, for example, or dogs from escaping.

These take us into the second category, that of the prophylactic blessing. One interesting example of these in a Zurich manuscript is even designed to be inscribed over a house to keep the devil away, but there is impressive poetry in one lorical piece — providing a *lorica*, a breastplate in defense of things that may happen. The so-called *Weingartner Reisesegen* (St. LXXVIII) is one of several rhymed prayers to guard travelers. After a formal blessing and what seems to be a hand gesture, angels are sent to protect the traveler and see that the doors of evil be closed to him, so that he return home safely.

Continental Old Low German, the other strand of West Germanic other than Old English/Anglo-Saxon, embraces three broad language groups, which do not demonstrate any of the effects of the High German consonant shift, and whose relationship with each other is also problematic in some respects. Again they have a small number of early written documents which, if not all literary, can be seen as proto-literary in the sense of helping to establish the medium for later literature.[27] The most interesting of the groups — Old Saxon — is that which is also closest to Old High German in geographical (and in some respects also in linguistic) terms, and it contains more early writing than the others, most notably the *Heliand*,[28] the importance of which merits a separate chapter in the present volume. The great biblical poem composed in the earlier part of the ninth century compares in size and content — narrative and exegesis — with Otfrid's later work, but it is composed in the alliterative longline that we saw in the *Hildebrandlied*. The same breadth is there, however, from the Fall to the Redemption, but the form might have had an easier appeal to an audience far more recently converted than Otfrid's.

There are other smaller remnants of Old Saxon, the most interesting being the fragmentary poem of *Genesis,* the subject of literary detective work at the end of the nineteenth century.[29] The Junius 11 Manuscript of Anglo-Saxon in Oxford contains a poem in alliterative long-lines about Genesis, which was soon recognized as a composite, one poem with a different Anglo-Saxon poem on the Fall of Man interpolated. The main Anglo-Saxon Genesis was designated *Genesis A,* while the interpolation became known as *Genesis B.* In 1875 Eduard Sievers determined on internal evidence that the latter had to be a translation or adaptation of an Old Saxon original, and in 1894 Karl Zangemeister proved him right when he discovered in the Vatican library fragments of that very original, with more of the same work, taking us down to the destruction of Sodom. The Old Saxon *Genesis* is similar to the *Heliand* in form, but it has long stood in the shadow of the larger work. Among the points of interest is the stress on how Eve was deceived into eating the fruit "in good faith" after a council of devils had decided that she should be tempted (this part only survives in the Anglo-Saxon version), and later on the sustained contrast of good and evil, with reference to Cain, to Cain's kindred, and to the people of Sodom. The existence of this text augments the *Heliand* with the awareness that other biblical materials were being adapted into poetic form. Beside the Gospels, Genesis was clearly vital to a full understanding of Christianity, and the importance of the Fall balanced by the Redemption is a recurrent theme.

In spite of the high level of literary skill represented by the *Heliand* and the *Genesis,* other surviving materials in Old Saxon are slight, and the conversion of the Saxons to Christianity by the Franks was a long and difficult process. While on the one hand this might well have furthered the need for vernacular Christian texts (and there was clearly also a connection with the insular Anglo-Saxon tradition), on the other, it exaggerated the loss of pre Christian material. Pagan material would hardly have been encouraged. As with High German, we have some small and mostly fragmentary monuments — the word is appropriate once more — including a small amount of glossing, some confessional and legal material, and a brief fragment of a translated homily by Bede. Some charms, finally, are interesting: one in prose relates how Christ healed a fish (a most unusual apocryphal motif) and requests the cure of a horse which has *spurihalz,* presumably some kind of lameness; another (to cure the same disease) is a Christianized version of the Wodan story in the second Merseburg piece. Beside a rhymed blood-charm, one final piece is a version of the incantatory "worm-charm" *pro nessia,* which conjures out the causes of disease from marrow, to bone, to flesh, to skin and then into an arrow, and which is known in Old High German too. It is one of the oldest forms of incantatory charms, with parallels in other cultures, although here once again it is supported by a concluding *Drohtin uuerthe so!* (Lord, let it be — the equivalent of Amen.)[30] The High German form calls for three Our Fathers.

Old Low Franconian is the ancestor, broadly speaking, of modern Dutch, but the earliest stage of the language has very little to offer in the way of written material, and what is more, its preservation is problematic. Effectively, all we have is a set of glosses including some interlinear Psalms, and it comes from a single, lost manuscript, the so-called Wachtendonck Codex, which may have been tenth century in its provenance. It was probably a Psalter with some other lyrical biblical passages and liturgical pieces, all glossed, with most of the Psalms fully glossed, that is, with every word given an Old Low Franconian equivalent (although Psalms 1–9 are in fact Middle Franconian, a High German dialect). The result is not a translation in the proper sense, and reprinting the texts without the Latin is as misleading as ever, although it does happen.[31] We only have post-sixteenth-century printed or transcribed extracts from this original codex, the whole offering us twenty-four of the interlinear Psalms and a set of glosses either from the Psalms or from the biblical canticles. It is a matter of some centuries before we can point to any further literature in Low Franconian.

Frisian represents the last and in many respects most difficult case of all in the establishing of early German literary history. The Frisii are mentioned in Pliny and in Tacitus, approximately in the geographical position with which they are to a large extent still associated, but their relationship to the Frisians of whom we hear later is unclear. Certainly the Frisians do not seem to have moved as part of the folk migrations. Furthermore, Old Frisian is an established, but not really a helpful designation, since it refers to writings that correspond by and large to the *Middle* High German period, so that we are forced, technically, beyond the chronological limits set for Old High German. The relatively numerous manuscripts in which Old Frisian texts are recorded are all late, although much of the material is clearly older. Old Frisian means Old East Frisian (around Ems and on some of the islands) and Old West Frisian (in the modern province of Noord-Holland in the Netherlands), the border being roughly the river Lauwers. The North Frisian dialect, spoken on the islands of Sylt, Föhr and Amrun, for example, is recorded only after the seventeenth century, and cannot be considered here. Early East and West Frisian is, however, conservative both in form and in content, and while most of that content is legal, it also contains material that is of considerable interest, even though it has been dismissed by most commentators as entirely lacking in literary value. Its proximity to English makes it of considerable linguistic interest, too.

The Law Code of the Frisians, the *Lex Frisionum*, dates from 802, but the principal documents in the vernacular are the so-called "Seventeen Statutes" plus the "Twenty-Four Land Laws," which contain material of considerable antiquity even though they are recorded no earlier than the twelfth century.[32] The laws themselves are of interest in their own right, but what is more significant, perhaps, is the presentation of those laws in a context of Frisian awareness. Much emphasis is laid in later works, too, upon the idea of Frisian freedom, and of the sources of the laws, presenting a supposedly unbroken chain of human law from ancient times down to the present. The various collections of the laws in Frisian are provided with prefaces detailing the authority on which those laws are based, from Old Testament to Roman times, and then the Carolingians. The lists are sometimes garbled, but the sense is there. The basic claim, too, is that the freedom of the Frisians, that is, the equality of Frisian landowners with the Frankish aristocracy, was laid down by Charlemagne. There is a complicated legend of how this came about, and there seems to have been a considerable cult of Charlemagne as late as the twelfth century. Later Frisian texts include a spurious *Privilegium* of Charlemagne and a rhymed tale of how the Frisians won their freedoms. Charlemagne, in fact, did not make any grants to them, although we are told in the life of Charlemagne's son, Louis the Pious, that it was he who in a lost capitulary of 814 granted that right to the Frisians. At all events, there is much consideration of the nature, origins, and right of law. Included among the legal writings, however, are some smaller texts that are still linked with legal issues, but which have other implications. Thus we have a small piece from apocryphal sources about the creation of Adam from eight elements, and also (linked with it) the pseudo-Augustinian description of the formation of the child in the womb; both underscore the equality of all men under the law. Of interest finally is the *fia eth,* the "chattel oath," an expansion of the "so help me God" formula, which refers to all the parts of the body, and is comparable to Latin and other lorical pieces (and indeed maledictions); the person taking the oath is to swear truly or else fall victim to a range of diseases (including *fallanda ewele,* presumably epilepsy) which will attack the whole body, *hit se a felle, hit se a flaske, hit se a edderun, hit si a sinum, hit se a herta* . . . (be it the skin, the flesh, the veins, the sinews, the heart . . .).[33]

Various features dominate the problem of how far it is possible to pin down an Old High (and even more so an Old Low) German literature: first the determining role of the Christian Church, and second, linked with it, the status of Latin, as the official and indeed one of the sacred languages, as against any of the dialects that make up the earliest stages of Old High or Low German. The Frankish hegemony also affects Low German. The nineteenth-century compilers of handbooks on early German literature clearly considered that the most interesting of the early German material is that which was given, in fact, the lowest status, so that the literature we have is strictly accidental. But it is important not to play down the conscious effort made by some writers to elevate German to the status of a written literary language *within* the framework of, rather than outside the Latin church. The conscious self-awareness of these writers (which is not quite divorced from national pride) is important; both Otfrid of Weissenburg and Notker of St. Gall were aware of the novelty of German, yet both promoted it and used their positions — pedagogical ones within the monastic world — to help to give it official status. The anonymous writers of the *Heliand* and Genesis, too, were making a statement by their choice of form and language. Otfrid and Notker were both successful, and they were successful precisely because they remained within the Latin context. Otfrid claims the right of a German dialect — Frankish — to be used for poetry, in a work which has, significantly, a Latin title. Notker also insisted on German as a viable tool and he used it well, but to the end — ostensibly at least — of teaching a Latin culture. Williram, finally, gave German prose a kind of status as part of a complex work. The importance of the *Hildebrandlied* is undeniable, but it is the three named writers who created Old High German literature, working in monasteries far apart and separated in time. Old High and Old Low German literature are literatures of isolation, but gradually Otfrid's work and that of Notker and Williram became known elsewhere, so that eventually the singing of songs in Frankish could indeed expand to become a German literature.

Notes

[1] There are individual editions of the longer surviving Old High German texts, but the standard collections of the smaller pieces are as follows: Wilhelm Braune, *Althochdeutsches Lesebuch* (Tübingen: Niemeyer, 16th. ed. Ernst Ebbinghaus, 1979; Karl Müllenhoff and Wilhelm Scherer, *Deutsche Poesie und Prosa aus dem VIII–XII Jahrhundert* (Berlin: Weidmann, 3rd. ed. Elias v. Steinmeyer, 1892, repr. 1964, cited as MSD); Horst Dieter Schlosser, *Althochdeutsche Literatur* (Frankfurt am Main: Fischer, 2nd ed. 1989; same title, Berlin: Schmidt, 1998) (with translations); Elias von Steinmeyer, *Die kleineren althochdeutschen Sprachdenkmäler* [1916] (Berlin and Zurich: Weidmann, repr. as 2nd ed. 1963, cited as St., and the basic text used here). Equally valuable as a reminder that these are texts surviving in manuscript is Hanns Fischer, *Schrifttafeln zum althochdeutschen Lesebuch* (Tübingen: Niemeyer, 1966). MSD VIII, "*Ein Spielmannsreim*" is not extant in German.

[2] See D. H. Green, *Medieval Listening and Reading: The Primary Reception of German Literature 800–1300* (Cambridge: CUP, 1994).

[3] In this introduction only a few of the most useful secondary works (with bibliographies) may be cited: *Althochdeutsch* (Festschrift Rudolf Schützeichel), ed. Rolf Bergmann, Heinrich Tiefenbach and Lothar Voetz (Heidelberg: Winter, 1982); Gustav Ehrismann, *Geschichte der deutschen Literatur bis zum Ausgang des Mittelalters 1. Die althochdeutsche Literatur* (Munich: Beck, 1932, repr. as 2nd ed. 1954); J. Sidney Groseclose and Brian O. Murdoch, *Die althochdeutschen poetischen Denkmäler* (Stuttgart: Metzler, 1976); Wolfgang Haubrichs, *Die Anfänge* (Frankfurt am Main: Athenäum, 1988); Stefan Sonderegger, *Althochdeutsche Sprache und Literatur* (Berlin: de Gruyter, 1974); Gisela Vollmann-Profe, *Von den Anfängen bis zum hohen Mittelalter* (Frankfurt am Main: Athenäum, 1986) *Theodisca: Beiträge zur althochdeutschen und altniederdeutschen Sprache und Literatur in der Kultur des frühen Mittellalters,* ed. Wolfgang Haubrichs, et al. (Berlin and New York: de Gruyter, 2000). In English, see J. Knight Bostock, *A Handbook on Old High German Literature,* ed. K. C. King and D. R. McLintock (2nd ed., Oxford: Clarendon, 1976); Cyril Edwards, "German Vernacular Literature," in Rosamond McKitterick, ed., *Carolingian Culture: Emulation and Inno-*

vation (Cambridge: CUP, 1994), 141–70; Will Hasty and James Hardin, *Dictionary of Literary Biography: German Writers and Works of the Early Middle Ages* (New York: Gale, 1995); Brian O. Murdoch, *Old High German Literature* (Boston: Twayne, 1983) and "The Carolingian Period and the Early Middle Ages," in Helen Watanabe, *Cambridge History of German Literature* (Cambridge: CUP, 1997), pp. 1–39; Cyril Edwards, *The Beginnings of German Literature: Comparative and Interdisciplinary Approaches to Old High German* (Rochester, NY: Camden House, 2002). Much of the material contained in the present chapter in introductory form is discussed in detail with a full bibliography in the second volume of the Camden House *History of German Literature*.

[4] Rudolf Koegel, *Geschichte der deutschen Litteratur bis zum Ausgang des Mittelalters,* Band I, Teil 1: *Die stabreimende Dichtung und die gotische Prosa* (Strasbourg: Trübner, 1894).

[5] This might once have alliterated on Wodan, as suggested in an attempt to create, or just possibly to re-create, a Lombardic *Urtext,* a nice, but entirely speculative idea: Willy Krogmann, *Das Hildebrandslied in der langobardischen Urfassung hergestellt* (Berlin: Schmidt 1959). Lombardic name-forms and Gothic historical figures seem to point to the story, at least, having moved from Gothic to Lombardic (in northern Italy) to Bavarian and finally to would-be Low German.

[6] See especially Siegfried Gutenbrunner, *Von Hildebrand und Hadubrand* (Heidelberg: Winter, 1976), and for secondary material the older but still useful survey by H. van der Kolk, *Das Hildebrandslied: Eine forschungsgeschichtliche Darstellung* (Amsterdam: Scheltema and Holkema, 1967). The scholarly equivalent to the law of diminishing returns tends to apply here: recent books on the *Hildebrandlied* include a study of whether or not it is a forgery (unlikely) and one on the proper names in the work (there are five).

[7] Section 381 of the *Edictum Rothari,* the Lombardic law book of the early seventh century, calls for a heavy fine at the use of the word *arga* or, if persistent, for combat. There is a convenient text in Hans Naumann and Werner Betz, *Althochdeutsches Elementarbuch* (Berlin: de Gruyter, 1962), 92–93 (with other legal extracts).

[8] See Brian Murdoch, *The Germanic Hero* (London and Rio Grande: Hambledon, 1996), 33–46.

[9] We are told by Einhard, Charlemagne's biographer, that Charlemagne was interested in collecting Germanic legends: see Paul Edward Dutton, *Charlemagne's Courtier* (Peterborough, ON: Broadview, 1998), 34. His son, Lewis the Pious, disapproved and did not continue the process.

[10] See Rosamond McKitterick, *The Carolingians and the Written Word* (Cambridge: CUP, 1989), 135–64 for an indispensable survey of the economic aspects of membranes and inks in the period.

[11] Otfrid von Weissenburg, *Evangelienharmonie* (manuscript), ed. Hans Butzmann (Graz: Akademische Druck- und Verlagsanstalt, 1972). There are various older editions, notably that by Oskar Erdmann (Halle: Waisenhaus, 1882), and the most convenient *Altdeutsche Textbibliothek* edition, 7th ed. by Ludwig Wolff (Tübingen: Niemeyer, 1973), is cited. Partial German translation by Gisela Voll-

mann-Profe (Stuttgart: Reclam, 1987). Designation is by book, chapter and line number. See Johanna Belkin and Jürgen Meier, *Bibliographie zu Otfrid von Weißenburg und zur altsächsischen Bibeldichtung* (Berlin: Schmidt, 1975). Of special value are: Wolfgang Kleiber, *Otfrid von Weißenburg* (Bern and Munich: Francke, 1971) and his edited collection: *Otfrid von Weißenburg* (Darmstadt: WBG, 1978).

[12] Most are in Steinmeyer (St. LXXXIX–LXXXVIII) and the other anthologies. For the inscription, see Rolf Bergmann, "Zu der althochdeutschen Inschrift aus Köln," *Rheinische Vierteljahresblätter* 30 (1965): 66–69.

[13] The *Strasbourg Oaths* of 842 (St. XV) underline the linguistic division already present in what was an official political reality; a French and a German king swear an oath of non-aggression in each other's language for the benefit of their respective followers, who do so in their own.

[14] McKitterick, *Written Word*, 232–35; the view is not widely held, but this is a prominent place. There is a useful genealogical table of the Carolingians in Timothy Reuter's translation of the *Annals of Fulda* (Manchester: Manchester UP 1992); French and German versions of the royal name Ludovicus are used here to distinguish the kings.

[15] Wolfgang Haubrichs, *Georgslied und Georgslegende im frühen Mittelalter* (Königsstein i. T.: Scriptor, 1979); P. Osterwalder, *Das althochdeutsche Galluslied Ratperts und seine lateinischen Übersetzungen durch Ekkehart IV* (Berlin and New York: de Gruyter, 1982) and MSD XII.

[16] There is a reconstructed text in Peter Dronke, *Medieval Latin and the Rise of the European Love-Lyric* (2nd ed., Oxford: Clarendon, 1968), II, 353–56. We may note that the Latin work *Ruodlieb* (the German name of the eponymous hero indicates a Germanic origin) contains a brief passage with some German words; the Latin *Waltharius* has a pun which only works in German (the hero Hagano is referred to as a hawthorn, the meaning of his name in German), and on one occasion there a warrior expostulates with the noise *Wah!*, which is in all conscience probably more Germanic than Latin!

[17] George Nordmeyer, "On the Old High German Isidor and its Significance for Early German Prose Writings," *PMLA* 73 (1958): 23–35, stresses the utilitarian nature of most Old High German prose and ventures the opinion that "it is absurd to begin the history of German literature with . . . exercises in translation" (23). The development of a literary vocabulary need, of course, be neither deliberate nor even conscious.

[18] The main collection remains that by Elias von Steinmeyer and Eduard Sievers, *Die althochdeutschen Glossen* (Berlin: Weidmann, 1879–1922), but many have been added since. See Rolf Bergmann, *Verzeichnis der althochdeutschen und altsächsischen Glossen-handschriften* (Berlin and New York: de Gruyter, 1973) and later individual studies. See too Alexander Schwarz, "Glossen als Texte," *PBB/T.* 99 (1977): 25–36; Gernot R. Wieland, "The Glossed Manuscript: Classbook or Library Book," *ASE* 14 (1986): 153–73 (Wieland's title is significant).

[19] Text in Wolfgang Haubrichs and Max Pfister, *In Francia fui* (Stuttgart: Steiner, 1989). There is an extract in Braune's *Lesebuch*, V.

[20] Text of the hymns ed. Eduard Sievers, *Die Murbacher Hymnen* (1874), repr. with an introduction by Evelyn Firchow (New York and London: Johnson, 1972). Some were written at the Reichenau, in fact. Even the most recent edition of Braune's *Lesebuch* prints the German glosses separately, the result looking indeed like verse, although they are headed 'Interlinearversion'; the anthology by Karl A. Wipf, *Althochdeutsche poetische Texte* (Stuttgart: Reclam, 1992) goes to some typographical trouble to ensure that the German words are more accurately shown, 16–45. In general terms Wipf's texts are close to the manuscript forms. See St. XXXVI–XXXIX for other interlinear glosses.

[21] *Der althochdeutsche Isidor,* ed. Hans Eggers (Tübingen: Niemeyer, 1964); *Tatian,* ed. Eduard Sievers (Paderborn: Schöningh, 1892, repr. 1966).

[22] *Notkers des Deutschen Werke,* ed. E. H. Sehrt and Taylor Starck (Halle/Saale: Niemeyer, 1933–35) and James C. King and Petrus Tax (Tübingen: Niemeyer, 1972ff.); Williram, *The Expositio in Cantica Canticorum,* ed. Erminnie H. Bartlemez (Philadelphia: American Philosophical Society, 1967).

[23] There is a ninth-century Irish sermon which is similar, for example: see J. Strachan, "An Old Irish Homily," *Ériu* 3 (1907): 1–7. See Brian Murdoch, "Preaching in Medieval Ireland," in *Irish Preaching 700–1700,* ed. Alan J. Fletcher and Raymond Gillespie (Dublin: Four Courts, 2001), 40–55.

[24] See Brian Murdoch, "*Peri hieres nousou.* Approaches to the Old High German Medical Charms," in *Mit regulu bithuungan,* ed. John L. Flood and David N. Yeandle (Göppingen: Kümmerle, 1988), 142–60; "But Did They Work? Interpreting the Old High German Merseburg Charms in their Medieval Context," *Neuphilologische Mitteilungen* 89 (1988): 358–69; and "*Drohtin, uuerthe so!* Zur Funktionsweise der althochdeutschen Zaubersprüche," *Jahrbuch der Görres-Gesellschaft* NS 32 (1991): 11–37. Most of the texts are in St. LXII–LXXVIII, the first being the Merseburg Charms.

[25] See Rolf Ködderitzsch, "Der 2. Merseburger Spruch und seine Parallele," *Zeitschrift für celtische Philologie* 33 (1974): 45–57.

[26] See Alf Önnerfors, *Antike Zaubersprüche* (Stuttgart: Reclam, 1991) for a collection of pre-Christian charms; the Christian contextualization of the Old High German pieces cannot be stressed strongly enough, however.

[27] See Willy Sanders, *Sachsensprache, Hansesprache, Niederdeutsch* (Göttingen: Vandenhoek und Ruprecht), 1982.

[28] *Heliand und Genesis,* ed. Otto Behaghel, 10. Ed. by Burkhard Taeger (Tübingen: Niemeyer, 1996); trans. into German Felix Genzmer, *Heliand* (Stuttgart: Reclam, n.d.), and into English with a commentary by G. Ronald Murphy, *The Heliand* (New York and Oxford: OUP, 1992). For secondary literature see Jürgen Eichhoff and Irmengard Rauch (eds.), *Der Heliand* (Darmstadt: WBG, 1973), as well as the final chapter of the present volume.

[29] There is a good edition with a detailed analysis and a vast bibliography by A. N. Doane, *The Saxon Genesis* (Madison: U of Wisconsin P, 1991). See Taeger's introduction to *Heliand und Genesis* on the various views of the way in which the original was put into Anglo-Saxon.

[30] Many of the smaller texts are in MSD and St., and the charms are in Braune's *Lesebuch* XXXI/4 and 9. See also Moritz Heyne, *Kleinere altniederdeutsche Denkmäler* (2nd ed., Paderborn: Schöningh, 1877, repr. Amsterdam: Rodopi, 1970) and F. Holthausen, *Altsächsisches Elementarbuch* (Heidelberg: Winter, 1900).

[31] Robert L. Kyes, *The Old Low Franconian Psalms and Glosses* (Ann Arbor: U of Michigan P, 1969).

[32] The standard text of the *Lex Frisionum* is that edited by Karl von Richthofen in MGH *Leges* III (Hannover: MGH, 1863), 630–710. For vernacular texts, see his *Friesische Rechtsquellen* (Berlin: 1840, repr. Aalen: Scientia, 1960). Details of the manuscripts are in Bo Sjölin, *Einführung in das Friesische* (Stuttgart: Metzler, 1969), pp. 10–12, and there are modern editions of nearly all the separate versions of the laws. See Sjölin, and my paper "Authority and Authenticity: Comments on the Prologues to the Old Frisian Laws," *ABäG* 49 (1998): 215–44, esp. note 7. For Frisian secondary literature see Rolf Bremmer, *A Bibliographical Guide to Old Frisian Studies* (Odense: Odense UP, 1992) and "Old Frisian Philology," *ABäG* 49 (1998): viii–xv.

[33] Thomas D. Hill, "Two Notes on the Fia-eth," *ABäG* 49 (1998): 169–78 and Eric G. Stanley "Alliterative Ornament and Alliterative Rhythmical Discourse in Old High German and Old Frisian," *PBB* 106 (1984), 184–217.

The Old Saxon *Heliand*

G. Ronald Murphy

T HE *HELIAND* IS OVER A THOUSAND YEARS OLD, and is the oldest epic work of German literature, antedating the *Nibelungenlied* by four centuries. It consists of approximately 6,000 lines of alliterative verse, twice the length of *Beowulf,* which shares just enough imagery and poetic phraseology with the *Heliand* that it might possibly be contemporary. The *Heliand* was written in Old Saxon,[1] possibly at the behest of the emperor Louis the Pious (Ludwig der Fromme), in the first half of the ninth century, around the year A.D. 830, near the beginning of the era of the Viking raids. That it is in continental Low German has probably been the reason for its neglect within the context of German literary history, but such neglect is hard to justify. The author has never been identified. His purpose seems to have been to make the Gospel story completely accessible and appealing to the Saxons through a depiction of Christ's life in the poetry of the North, recasting Jesus himself and his followers as Saxons, and thus to overcome Saxon ambivalence toward Christ caused by forced conversion to Christianity. That forced conversion was effected through thirty-three years of well-chronicled violence on the part of the Franks under Charlemagne,[2] and counter-violence by the Saxons under Widukind, and ended with the final but protracted defeat of the Saxons.

There must have still been resentment among the Saxons at the time of the composition of the *Heliand* since there was a revolt of the Saxon *stellinga,* what we might call the lower social castes, during this period. Whoever the poet of the *Heliand* was, he had his task cut out for him. His masterpiece shows that he was astonishingly gifted at intercultural communication in the religious realm. By the power of his imagination the poet-monk (perhaps also ex-warrior) created a unique cultural synthesis between Christianity and Germanic warrior society — a synthesis that would plant the seed that would one day blossom in the full-blown culture of knighthood and become the foundation of medieval Europe.[3]

The *Heliand* has come down to us in two almost complete manuscript versions, one housed now in Munich at the Bavarian State Library, designated *M,* and the other in London at the British Museum, designated *C.* Neither is held to be the author's original of circa 830, which was most likely composed by a monk in Fulda acting under the ecumenical aegis of the abbot (H)Rabanus Maurus.[4] It is now lost. The manuscript *M* is the older of the two extant and believed to have been written in the second half of the ninth century, ca. 850, in Corvey.[5] *C* is believed to have been written about a hundred years later, circa 950–1000 at an East Anglian monastery in England. Though later than *M*, *C* seems to have kept more to the original division of the Heliand into *fitts* or songs (as they will be referred to here).

The manuscript in Munich is in such excellent condition that one could almost believe it is a modern reproduction; its excellent condition seems to stem from the high quality calf-skin on which it was written. In several places neumes have been inserted above the text, giving sure evidence that the *Heliand* was chanted, as is also implied in the *Praefatio*. Unfortunately, the last two songs are missing from *M*. In addition to the two manuscripts there are also three fragments, named after their place of finding: *P* from Prague, *V* at the Vatican, and *S* from the binding of a book held in the Jesuit high school in Straubing.[6] The existence of three separate fragments as well as the two manuscripts, the one copied at Corvey (*M*) and the other at a monastery in East Anglia (*C*), as well as the presence of neumes in the texts, give evidence of wide-spread readership and use both in Germany and England in the ninth and tenth centuries and possibly beyond. We know that Martin Luther had a copy, and that it was used as a justification for the existence of a tradition of translation of the Gospels into the vernacular. It even seems that Luther admired the *Heliand*'s version of the angel's greeting to Mary as "full of grace." In the *Heliand* this becomes *thu bist thinon herron liof* (literally: *you are dear to your lord*, or *your lord is fond of you*). He uses this example to ridicule the idea of anyone being literally full of grace, as if they were a beer vat, and as if grace were something that could be poured into them. He insists instead on his preference for the German of *du bist deinem Herren lieb* taken from the *Heliand,* but unfortunately without attribution.

Where was the *Heliand* used? The audience of the *Heliand* was probably to be found in mead hall and monastery. The epic poem seems not to have been designed for use in the church as a part of official worship, but seems intended to bring the Gospel home to the Saxons in a poetic milieu, in a more familiar environment like the mead hall, in order to help the Saxons cease their vacillation between their loyalty to the sagas of Wodan and Thor, and loyalty to the epic of the mighty Christ. Some internal evidence, as well as liturgical tradition, would thus indicate that the *Heliand* epic was designed for after-dinner singing — in the poetic tradition of the scop, who sang in the mead hall of the nobility, and in Benedictine tradition in the monastic refectory of the monks.

The *Heliand* was first published by printing press in 1830, by Schmeller, a millennium after its composition, and immediately had an influence, among others, on the work of the Brothers Grimm. The first edition was dedicated by Schmeller to Jacob Grimm, and was read by Wilhelm Grimm when he was working on the editing and composition of the fairy tales. The *Heliand* has also been used by German nationalists in the nineteenth and twentieth centuries for their own pan-Germanic purposes, completely ignoring the great poem's historical context and Christian-Saxon origin.

The poetic technique of the author is centered on the use of analogy. In order to Saxonize the Gospel story, the author needed to find appropriate parallels for places and events of the evangelists' narrative. With regard to Bethlehem and Nazareth, for example, he is not interested in asking pilgrims what these places actually looked like. Instead, he attaches the Saxon word *burg* to each one. A *burg* at that time was a hill-fort, a local hilltop fortified with earthen embankments crowned with a palisade, a heavy wooden wall of sharpened pilings. Inside the fort was the hall of the chieftain. Outside the fort, often at the foot of the hill, were the smaller thatched-roof houses of those who were not of the warrior class. The warrior-nobility prided themselves, if we go by the account in the *Heliand*'s version of the nativity, on being born within the walls of the hill-fort. Some easier geographic analogies are readily provided by the location of Jesus' activities by the Sea of Galilee and the presence of the North Sea. Fishing scenes are frequent enough in the Gospel itself; the *Heliand* strengthens them by adding details of the apostles working on the nets and of implying that they are using the seine technique which must have been popular in the river regions of the north.

Finally the author finds not only cultural equivalencies for the events of the Gospel story, but often he sets them in parallel to a literal translation which he gives in the following line. "Your lord is fond of you" is followed by "woman full of grace." The poetic power of the *Heliand* lies in the unexpected parallel imagery and in the charm created by hearing northern equivalents for the Mediterranean concepts of the Bible in such close proximity to each other. The technique itself is biblical, and can be found in the Psalms, for example in ancient Hebrew poetry *mountain* can be "rhymed" with *hill* not on the basis of similarity of sound, but of similarity of image. Likewise, snow can be rhymed with hail, fish with whales, and more familiarly, "he leads me beside the still waters" can be rhymed with "he gives me repose." I call this technique concept alliteration. The Saxons did not know or practice Roman crucifixion, but they did punish criminals and make an offering to Wodan by hanging criminals and animals from the branches of sacred trees.[7] In the *Heliand*, therefore, crucifixion is "rhymed" in the following line with hanging. The arrogant thief crucified alongside Christ, is made in the *Heliand* to say "get down from the cross, slip out of the rope."

The poet worked in a number of categories in order to create a Saxon poetic equivalent to the Gospel. Since he was using the *Diatessaron,* a synthesis of the four Gospel narratives compiled originally in Greek by Tatian, a second-century Syrian Christian, and subsequently translated into Latin and most of the European vernaculars, including Old High German, he had all the known pericopes ("readings," biblical narrative units) of the story at hand, and he chose to leave out very few, notably those that had to do with examples that seemed to justify the taking of interest on loans. First, warrior equivalencies will be examined; second mythological incorporations; third, magic; fourth, epic structure, and fifth the enormous role of light in the *Heliand.*

The audience of the *Heliand* lived in an early feudal environment and thus might not have found the concept of rabbi and his disciples comprehensible. The author changes rabbi to chieftain, *drohtin,* and disciples to *gisiðos,* the young warrior companions of a chieftain. This translation makes the Gospel more at home sociologically, but it also makes the rela tionship of Christ to his disciples not one of teacher to students, but military leader to personal bodyguard. What is required then of disciples, faith in their teacher, becomes fidelity to one's leader in the *Heliand.* This Germanic reading of faith as personal fidelity will have far-reaching consequences that will extend from the piety of the medieval crusader to the Reformation's notion of faith.

The duty of a warrior/disciple is laid out both in the birth of John the Baptist and in the scene of Peter's drawing his sword at Jesus' arrest on Olivet. When the angel announces the birth of John the Baptist to his father Zachary in the temple he adds something significant:

> [God] Hêt that ic thi scol sagdi, that it scoldi gisîð uuesan
> heƀancuninges, hêt that git it helden uuel,
> tuhin thurh treuua, quað that he im tîras sô filu
> an godes rîkea forgeƀan uueldi.

> [God said that I should say to you that your child will be a warrior-companion of the King of Heaven. He said that you and your wife should care for him well and bring him up on loyalty, and that He would grant him many honors in God's kingdom. Song 2, 129–32][8]

In this remarkable passage we have the earliest known blending of Germanic warrior virtue with Christian religion. God the All-Ruler is made to request that John be raised specifically to practice the warrior virtue of *treuwa,* unflinching loyalty in battle to one's chieftain. God's reason is that He wishes to make John his *gesið.* In the original there is a truly

amazing linkage of two cultural worlds in two words: God wishes to make
John a *gesið hebancuninges,* a warrior-companion of the King of Heaven.
Discipleship has been reconceived as the author goes on to say that John's
chieftain will be Christ, and John will be *Kristes gesið* a warrior-
companion of Jesus.

The feudal world required reciprocity between chieftain and warrior
companion and the reciprocal relationship on the part of the chieftain was
that he care for his men, a care which the Heliand calls protection and
love. Thus, it does not come as a total surprise that, when Christ is born
and the shepherds have come and gone from the Christmas scene in
Bethlehem, Mary is described in the Gospel and in the *Heliand* as pon-
dering all these things in her heart, and in the *Heliand* the poet adds that
Jesus will be raised on the reciprocal virtue to John's *treuwa,* telling us
how the mother, — the loveliest of ladies — brought up the chieftain of
many men, the holy heavenly Child, on love, *minnea* (Song 6).

St. Peter, throughout the *Heliand,* is made into the ideal warrior-
companion of Christ, and the very model of a Saxon warrior-companion
of Christ. When Peter is about to drown due to lack of faith, or when he
disowns Christ three times as the cock crows, or when he draws his sword
to defend Christ, all are made into major epic scenes in the *Heliand.*
From the scene of his walking on the waters:

> the sêolîðanđean
> naht neƀulo biuuarp; nâðidun erlos
> forðuuardes an flod; uuarð thiu fiorðe tid
> thera nahtes cuman — neriendo Crist
> uuarode thea uuâglîðand —: tho uuarð uuind mikil,
> hôh uueder afhaƀen: hlamodun ûðeon,
> strôm an stamne; strîdiun feridun
> thea uueros uuiðer uuinde . . .
>   Thô gisâhun sie uualdand Krist
> an themu sêe uppan selƀum gangan,
> faran an fâðion . . .
>   "Nu gi môdes sculun
> fastes fâhen; ne sî iu forht hugi,
> gibâriad gi baldlîco: ik bium that barn godes,
> is selƀes sunu, the iu uuið thesumu sêe scal,
> mundon uuið thesan meristrôm.

[Night wrapped the seafarers in fog. The earls daringly kept on sail-
ing over the waters. The fourth hour of the night had come —
Christ the Helper was guarding the wave-riders — and the wind began to blow powerfully. A great storm arose, the waves of the sea
roared against the bow stem post, the men fought to steer the boat

into the wind . . . then they saw the Ruler himself walking on the sea, traveling on foot. . . ."Now you should be steadfast and brave, do not be fearful-minded, be courageous! I am the Child of God, his own Son, and I will defend you against the sea and protect you from the ocean waves." Song 35, 2909–30]

Jesus proclaims that he is aware of his duty to his men to extend his protection to them, even if the enemy is an ocean storm. Then Peter, his good thane, calls overboard to Christ and asks him to command him to come across the waves to him, ". . . tell me to walk to You across this seaway, dry across deep water, if You are my chieftain, protector of many people." Not only does Christ as chieftain of St. Peter have the right to tell him to come to him, but as chieftain, he also has the obligation to protect Peter as one of his men. As in the Gospel story, Peter does well walking on the water until he begins to doubt. The *Heliand* author makes the scene more vivid for his North Sea audience:

>   . . . he [Peter] *imu* an his môde bigan
> andrâden diap uuater,   thô he drîƀen gisah
> thene uuêg mid uuindu: uundun ina *ûðeon,*
> hôh strôm umbihring.   Reht sô he thô an is hugdi tuehode,
> sô uuêk imu that uuater under,   enti he an thene uuâg innan,
> sank an thene sêostrôm,   endi *he* hriop sân after thiu
> *gâhon* the themu godes sunie   endi gerno bad
> that he ine thô *generidi,*   *tho* he an *nôdiun* uuas,
> thegan an gethuinge.   Thiodo drohtin
> antfeng ine *mid* is faðmun   enti frâgode sâna,
> te huî he *thô getuehodi* . . .
>   Thô nam ine alomahtig,
> hêlag bi handun: thô uuarð imu eft hlutter uuater
> fast under fôtun,   endi sie an fâði samad
> bedea gengun,   antat sie oƀar bord skipes
> stôpun *fan* themu strôme.

[. . . in his emotions Peter began to feel the fear of deep water as he watched the waves being driven by the wind. The waves wound around him, the high seas surrounded the man. Just at that moment doubt came into his mind. The water underneath him became soft and he sank into a wave, he sank into the streaming sea! Very soon after that he called out quickly, asking earnestly that Christ rescue him, since he, his thane, was in distress and danger. The chieftain of peoples caught him with his outstretched arms and asked him immediately why he doubted. . . . Then the holy, all-mighty One took him by the hand and all at once clear water became solid under his feet, and went together on foot, both of them, walking, until they climbed on board the boat from the sea. Song 35, 2942–61]

The author has no difficulty recognizing, through Peter, the doubt that lay in the minds of many of the Saxons concerning the ability of their new chieftain, Christ, to protect them, but the author has shown them that Christ is not only willing to rescue them from death, drowning, but is also heartfelt enough to go hand in hand, something the author has touchingly inserted, walking with them, to the boat where all is safe and the storm is over.

The *Heliand* author might have been expected to delete the incident of Peter's triple denial of Christ, but he does not, true as it is to the Saxon warriors' own state of mind and behavior at the author's time. After having related the scene however he adds a compassionate explanation of Peter which is his own creation:

> Than ni thurbun thes luidio barn,
> uueros uundrioan, behuî it uueldi god,
> that sô lioben man leð gistôdi,
> that he sô hônlîco hêrron sînes
> thurh thera thiuun uuord, thegno snellost
> farlôgnide sô lioƀes: it uuas al bi thesun liudiun giduan,
> firiho barnun te *frumu*. He uuelde ina te furiston dôan,
> hêrost oƀar is hîuuiski, helag drohtin:
> lêt ina gekunnon, huilike craft haƀet
> the mennisca môd ano *the* maht godes;
> lêt ina gesundion, that he sîðor thiu bet
> liudiun gilôƀdi, huô liof is *thar*
> manno *gihuilicumu*, than he mên gefrumit,
> that man ina alâte lêðes thinges . . .

[People should not be amazed, warriors should not wonder, why God would have wanted such a loveable man and powerful thane to have such an evil thing happen to him (especially in the world of feudal loyalty) as to deny his beloved Chieftain so shamefully because of a servant-girl's words. It was done for the sake of those people, for the sake of the sons of men. The holy Chieftain intended to make Peter the first man in the leadership of his household, and wanted Peter to realize how much strength there is in the human spirit without the power of God. He let Peter commit sin so that afterward he would better appreciate people, how all human beings love to be forgiven when they have done something wrong . . . Song 59, 5023–36]

No scene in the *Heliand* makes such a warrior-like impression as when finally one of Jesus' disciple/warriors finally draws a sword in their Chieftain's defense. This scene may well be the one that helped make Peter the poet's favorite, and almost makes Peter sound like a Viking berserker:

> Thô gibolgan uuarð
> snel suerdthegan   Sîmon Petrus
> *uuell* imu innan hugi,   that he ni mahte ênig uuord sprekan:
> sô harm uuarð imu an is hertan,   that man is hêrron that
> binden *uuelde*.   Thô he gibolgan geng,
> suîðo thrîstmôd thegan   for is thiodan *standen*
> hard for is hêrron: ni uuas imu is hugi tuîfli,
> *blôð* an is breostun,   ac he is bil atôh,
> suerd bi sîdu,   slog imu tegegnes
> an thene furiston fiund   folmo crafto,
> that thô Malchus uuarð   mâkeas eggiun,
> an thea suîðaron half   suerdu gimâlod:
> thiu hlust uuarð imu farhauuan,   he uuarð an that hôƀid uund,
> that imu herudrôrag   hlear endi ôre
> beniuundun brast: blôd aftar sprang
> uuell fan uundun.   Thô uuas an is uuangun scard
> the furisto thero fiundo.   Thô stôd that folc an rûm:
> andrêdun im thes billes biti.

[Then Simon Peter, the mighty, noble swordsman flew into a rage; his mind was in such turmoil that he could not speak a single word. His heart became intensely bitter because they wanted to tie up his Lord there. So he strode over angrily, that very daring thane, to stand in front of his commander, right in front of his Lord. No doubting in him, no fearful hesitation in his chest, he drew his blade and struck straight ahead at the first man of the enemy with all the strength in his hands, so that Malchus was cut and wounded on the right side by the sword! His ear was chopped off, he was so badly wounded in the head that his cheek and ear burst open with a mortal wound! Blood gushed out, pouring from the wound! The men stood back — they were afraid of the slash of the sword. Song 58, 4865–82]

This is quite an expansion of the modest account in the Gospel, but much more in line with the grim battles in *Beowulf* and the *Battle of Maldon*.[9] To make for a better epic conflict, the religious enemies of Christ in the Gospel, the Sadducees, the Pharisees and the Torah scholars, have been combined by the author to create one hostile enemy military force, the Jewish army. This combination is required both by good epic form which requires a powerful antagonist, and by what I presume was the Saxons' general unfamiliarity with the Jews of their day, much less with the Jewish sects of the first century. The *Heliand* author has to give some identity to the Jewish "enemy force" and he does so in accord with northern European prejudices by describing them repeatedly as competent warriors but as "southern people, sneaky."[10]

The poet-monk who wrote the *Heliand* was quite familiar with Germanic mythology. Not only did he incorporate elements into the *Heliand* Gospel, he even tackled the theological problem of the role of fate, the highest Germanic religious power, in his Christian worldview. To begin with a familiar object from later German storytelling, the *Heliand* has the earliest instance of the invisibility cape or *Tarnkappe,* used by Siegfried in the *Nibelungenlied*. In the *Heliand* it is a magic helmet, the heliðhelm, and the author finds a place for it in the scene in which Pilate's wife is having bad dreams about her husband's actions toward his famous prisoner. The magic helmet is being worn by Satan to conceal his identity. He has come from hell with it to attempt to prevent the salvation of the world by opposing the crucifixion of Christ (Song 65). Even hell (*hel* in the *Heliand*), is the damp dark place of Germanic mythology and *Beowulf*'s monsters, it is not the fiery *inferno* of the Mediterranean tradition. Heaven too will be described as a place of light and green meadows (of Valhalla).

Fate as an absolute force beyond gods and men must have been a special challenge to the author. The three blind women, the Norns, who sit under the tree at the edge of the well of time, spin, measure, and cut the thread of all things. It would seem that a missionary would have to treat such a force as antithetical to the Trinity, but the *Heliand* author finds a place for "the workings of fate" and for its invisible spirit: time. When John the Baptist is born the author writes,

> Thô uuarð sân after thiu math godes,
> *gicûðid* is craft mikil: uuarð thiu *quân* ôcan,
> idis an ira eldiu: scolda im erðiuuard,
>
> suîðo godcund gumo giƀiðig uuerðan,
> barn an *burgun*. Bêd aftar thiu
> that uuîf *uuirðigiscapu*. Skred the uuintar forð,
> geng *thes* gêres gital. Iohannes quam
> an liudeo lioht.

[Soon thereafter the power of God, his mighty strength, was felt: the wife [Elizabeth], a woman in her old age, became pregnant — soon the husband, that godly man, would have an heir, an infant boy born in the hill-fort. The woman awaited the workings of fate. The winter skidded by and the year measured its way past. John came to the light of mankind. Song 3, 192–99].

Fate has been allotted a place in the *Heliand*'s scheme of things; it takes care of measuring the nine months of pregnancy. Fate attends to timing and to the accidentals, the color of John's hair, even his fingernails and the fairness of his skin. All the very things, one might reflect, that one day will become the realm of biology and history, are not excluded but are "co-workers" with God. Even the time of the passion and death of Christ are determined by the divine will working with fate. In the above scene when Peter draws his sword to prevent Christ's capture, when Christ tells him, in the Gospel, to sheath his sword because he who lives by the sword will die by the sword, this is expanded in the *Heliand* to have Christ clearly give fate its due:

> Thô sprak that barn godes
> selbo te Sîmon Petruse,   hêt that he is suerd dedi
> skarp an skêdia: "ef ik uuið thesa scola uueldi," quað he,
> "uuið theses uuerodes geuuin   uuîgsaca frummien,
> than manodi ik thene mâreon   mahtigne god,
> hêlagne fader   an himilrûkea,
> that he mi sô managan engil herod   obana sandi
> uuîges sô uuîsen,   sô ni *mahtin* iro *uuâpanthreki*
> man adôgen: iro ni stôdi gio sulic megin samad,
> folkes *gifastnod*,   that im iro ferh aftar thiu
> uuerðen mahti.   Ac it habad uualdand god,
> alomahtig fader   an oðar gimarkot,
> that uui *githoloian* sculun,   sô huat sô ûs *thius thioda* tô
> bittres brengit: ni sculun ûs belgan uuiht,
> uurêðean uuið iro geuuinne;   huand sô hue sô uuâpno nîð,
> grimman *gêrheti   uuili* gerno frummien,
> he suiltit imu *eft*   suerdes eggiun,
> *dôit* im *bidrôregan:*   uui mid ûsun dâdiun ni sculun
> uuiht auuerdian."

[Then the son of God spoke to Simon Peter and told him to put his sharp sword back into its sheath. "If I wanted to put up a fight against the attack of this band of warriors, I would make the great and mighty God, the holy Father in the kingdom of heaven, aware of it so that he would send me so many angels wise in warfare that no human beings could stand up to the force of their weapons. . . . But, the ruling God, the all-mighty Father, has determined it differently: we are to bear whatever bitter things this people does to us. We are not to become enraged or wrathful against their violence, since who-ever is eager and willing to practice the weapon's hatred, cruel spear-fighting, is often killed himself by the edge of the sword and dies dripping in his own blood. *We cannot by our own deeds avert any-thing*" (emphasis mine). Song 58, 4882–4900]

There is more than a little fatalism that will enter Germanic Christianity through the *Heliand,* since Christ himself is made to express sentiments that come close to equating fate, the events of this world, regardless of their bitterness, as part of the will of God. It is useless to resist them.

Even the raising of Lazarus from the dead, which shows the superiority of Christ to fate, is done with fate's cooperation (Song 49). The real test of course is the time of the death of Christ, and that is given the same treatment, with a twist. Christ is going to overturn fate by rising from the dead and unlocking the door to the road to heaven. The author knows his audience, and he knows that they want to have more assurance concerning Christ's non-resistance to fate and the attacking Jewish army, so he once again creates an apologetic for Christ's actions:

> Uuerod Iudeono
> sô manag mislic thing   an mahtigna Crist
> sagdun te sundiun.   He suîgondi stuod
> thuru ôðmuodi,   ne antuuordida *niouuiht*
> uuið iro uurêðun uuord: uuolda thesa uuerold alla
> lôsian mid is liƀu: bithiu liet hie ina thia lêðun thiod
> uuêgian te uundron,   all sô iro uuillio geng:
> ni uuolda im opanlîco   allon cûðian
> Iudeo liudeon,   that hie uuas god selƀo;
> huand uuissin sia that te uuâron,   that hie sulica giuuald habdi
> oƀar theson middilgard,   than uurði im iro muodseƀo
> giblôðit an iro brioston: *than* ne gidorstin sia that barn godes
> handon anthrînan: than ni uuurði heƀanrîki,
> antlocan liohto mêst   liudio barnon.
> Bethiu mêð hie is sô an is muode,   ne lêt that manno folc
> uuitan, huat sia uuarahtun.   Thiu uurd nâhida thuo,
> mâri math godes   endi middi dag,
> that sia thia ferahquâla   frummian scoldun.

[The Jewish people said many different sinful things about mighty Christ. He stood there, keeping silent in patient humility. He did not answer their hostile words, he wanted to free the whole world with his life — that is why he let the evil clan subject him to whatever terrible torture they desired. He did not want to let all the Jewish people know openly that he was God Himself. For, if they really knew how much power he had over this middle world, their feelings would turn cowardly within their breasts and they would never dare to lay their hands on the Son of God, and then the kingdom of heaven, the brightest of worlds, would never be unlocked to the sons of men. Because of this, he hid it in his heart and did not let the human clan know what they were doing. *Fate was coming closer then, and the great power of God, and midday,* when they were to bring his life-spirit to its death agony (emphasis mine). Song 64, 5379–96]

It seems that the Jews, as a stand-in for the human race, are the instruments of fate, but they could be deflected by intimidation, and so Christ conceals his identity from them. Meanwhile coming closer are: fate, God, and midday. As in the case of the date of the birth of John the Baptist, the nine-month period was within the realm of fate, and so also is the decision that the crucifixion should be on a Friday and at noon.

There is even some iconographic representation of Christ that leans on Germanic religious mythology. Wodan is typically pictured with the two ravens, Mind and Memory, *hugin* and *munin,* on his shoulder. They are the heart of his awareness of what is going on in *middilgard.* They fly about during the day observing the comings and goings of men and gods, and then return to their master to whisper in his ear all that they have observed. It seems that the *Heliand* author could not resist feeling that this function of Wodan's ravens seemed quite similar to the role of the dove, the Holy Spirit. The scene that is just made for his use is the incident of the baptism of Christ in the Jordan by John the Baptist. In Luke 3, as Christ comes up out of the waters a voice says "This is my beloved Son," and John says that he saw the Holy Spirit coming down from heaven upon Jesus in the form of a dove which remained above him (*mansit super eum,* in Tatian). In the *Heliand* the dove does not remain vaguely "above him":

> Krist up giuuêt
> fagar fon them flôde,   friðubarn godes,
> liof liudio uuard. Sô he thô that land *afstôp,*
> sô anthlidun thô himiles doru,   endi quam the hêlago gêst
> fon them alouualdon   oƀane te Kriste:
> — uuas im an gilîcnissie   *lungras* fugles,
> diurlîcara dûƀun —   endi sat im uppan uses drohtines *ahslu,*
> uuonoda im oƀar them uualdandes barne.

[Christ came up radiant out of the water, the Peace-Child of God, the beloved Protector of people. As he stepped out onto the land, the doors of heaven opened up and the Holy Spirit came down from the All-Ruler above to Christ — it was like a powerful bird, a magnificent dove — and it sat upon our Chieftain's shoulder [*uppan uses drohtines ahslu,*] remaining over the Ruler's Child. Song 12, 982–89].[11]

When it comes to finding equivalents for miraculous or sacramental incidents such as the multiplication of the loaves, or the institution of the Eucharist, or even explaining the divine inspiration of scripture, the poet seems to have had no difficulty. He simply alluded to the magic with which his audience was already familiar. Germanic religion was filled with magic spells and enchantments, magic objects that retained their ability to perform supernatural feats long after their connection to the god who made them had been severed. J. R. R. Tolkien's *Lord of the Rings* trilogy shows how a poet in the twentieth century can still draw successfully upon the ancient Germano-Christian forms of magic. Consider the origin of the runes, which are said to have been seized from the depths of the well of fate as Wodan hung himself as a sacrifice to divine the nature of reality. He reached down and grasped the runes, later giving them to mankind. Therefore writing itself is a divine institution and each letter can be used for magic. This makes the task of the *Heliand* poet easier. How does he explain that the Lord's prayer is a divine entity, taught by the God-man himself? He simply alludes to the story of Wodan and the runes. In the Gospel the disciples ask Christ to teach them to pray as John the Baptist taught his disciples to pray. In the *Heliand* the warrior companions phrase it differently: *gerihti us that geruni,* teach us the secret runes, and suddenly the *Our Father* becomes a magic spell capable of reaching God.

One might think that the Eucharist would offer more of a challenge to a group accustomed to treating food as something for the mead hall and not really for religion. The *Heliand* once again has Jesus say magic words. After Jesus has told his disciples that the bread is truly his body and the wine is truly his blood after a brief discourse he adds: *thit is mahtig thing,* this is a magic thing, this is a thing that has power. The word *mahtig* has been shown in Flowers' study[12] to be a word for magic, used to designate performative words (magic words) or performative persons or, here, things that possess an unusual strength, such as the ability of the magic helmet, the *heliðhelm,* to hide its wearer. The magic powers of the Eucharistic bread and wine are then explained in a way that enforces what Jesus said at the Last Supper. Where Jesus in the Gospel and in the liturgy asks his disciples to do the Eucharist in memory of me, the *Heliand* explains that the bread and wine of the Eucharist possess the power to help men remember what Jesus is doing out of love to give glory to the Lord. It possesses the magic power to give honor to the Chieftain. Thus repeating these magic words over the bread and wine fulfills a feudal obligation to honor one's Chieftain, and will enable Christ's men to repeat the magic of his words and defy time and the fates: "everyone all over *middilgard*" will come to know what he is doing. Truly a remarkable synthesis of Christianity and a beautiful concept of magic. Catholic sacramental theology will come to be very much influenced by this touching synthesis.

There is even some humor in the *Heliand*'s use of magic. When the disciple/warriors are distributing the miraculously multiplied loaves at the miracle of the feeding of the five thousand, the gospels say nothing about how or where the multiplication took place. The Heliand makes no such omission. As the warrior-companions go around among the crowd distributing the loaves they are shocked as they become aware that the bread *undar iro handun uuohs,* that the bread between their hands was growing!

If one were to object that there is no tradition in Christianity for seeing magic in God's words, and performative magic at that, it is easy to see what the response would have been, it is in the first song of the *Heliand*. The author describes creation itself as taking place though magic words. *Fiat lux,* Let there be light, and there was light. The words of God effect immediately what they say, that is, they are performative. "Your sins are forgiven you" and they are forgiven. "This is my body," and it is. The task of the Evangelists was to write down

> all so hie it fan them anginne   thuru is *ênes* craht,
> uualdand gisprak,   thuo hie êrist thesa uuerold giscuop
> endi thuo all bifieng   mid ênu uuordo,
> himil endi erða   endi al that sea bihlidan êgun
> giuuarahtes endi giuuahsanes: that uuarð thuo all mid
>   uuordon godas
> fasto bifangan

[all the things which the Ruler spoke from the beginning, when he, by his own power, first made the world and formed the universe with one word. The heavens and the earth and all that is contained within them, both inorganic and organic, everything was firmly held in place by Divine words. Song 1, 38–43]

Looked at through Germanic Christian eyes, the six days of creation in which the word of God uttered the magic words "Let there be . . ."[13] many times, the words of Christ at Cana, to the paralytic, to the blind, even to the three-days-dead Lazarus, "Lazarus, come forth," are all highly powerful magic, they are *mahtig*. The Saxons need not fear that they have been forced into a religion that knows far less of magic enchantment than their former faith. The whole Bible is a magic spell, a *geruni*.

To make his version of the Gospel into a magic and mythic spell, God's spell, the author also put the narrative into an epic structural frame centered on the scene which must have been of great significance for him, the Transfiguration on Mount Tabor. The monumental study made by Johannes Rathofer[14] attempted to establish the existence of four divisions in the *Heliand*, and was unable to do so, since he preferred to concentrate on numerical analysis rather than the content of the individual *fitts*. His ultimate contention that the *Heliand* is a centered composition with the Transfiguration, Song 38, as its middle point, has been accepted. If this is the case, then the events of the songs should end up in a balanced structure on either side of Song 38. In 1958 Cedric Whitman discovered this structuring pattern in the *Iliad,*[15] and it seems that the author of the *Heliand* was following the same ancient technique which facilitates both memorization and oral delivery.

The form of the arrangement rather nicely gives the events that follow the Transfiguration something of a Germanic feel of being fated by the events prior to the Transfiguration, blending in with the carefully allotted role of fate in the *Heliand*. In Song 33 we have the death of John the Baptist, in the parallel scene, Song 43, the death of Jesus is foretold. In Song 23 the Last Judgment is predicted; in Song 53 Doomsday is described. In a rather touching parallel in Song 19 Jesus teaches his disciples the magic runes of the Lord's prayer so that they can appeal to the Father, in Song 57 he himself is calling out in his agony in the garden to the Father. Even the nativity and the resurrection have been made parallel by describing both as a "coming," in the one case as a coming of God's child to this light, and in the other as the spirit of Christ coming back, making its way under the gravestone, to the body. For people whose lives have been influenced from time immemorial by the battles and events that occurred on crests of their hill-forts, this structure, anchored on three mountains, the mount of the sermon, Mount Tabor and Mount Olivet, becomes familiar. The events of Christ's life are made by the form of the tale to fit into a more northern religious emotional framework of invisible parallelism, a certain fatedness, in the realm of time.

The Transfiguration in the *Heliand* is a scene full of light, it is a key to the spiritual world of the poet and of his *Heliand* epic, and he has placed it in the very center of the *inclusio* structure of the poem so that it cannot be but felt by the hearer or reader.[16] The *Heliand* adds even more radiance to the scene than the Evangelists had done:

> Côs imu *iungarono* thô
> sân aftar thiu   Sîmon Petrus,
> Iacob endi Iohannes,   *thea* gumon tuêne,
> bêðea thea gibroðer,   endi imu thô uppen thene berg giuuêt
> sunder mid them gesiðun,   salig barn godes
> mid them thegnun thrim . . .
> Thô imu thar te bedu gihnêg,
> thô uuarð imu thar uppe   ôðarlîcora
> uuliti endi giuuâdi: uurðun imu is uuangun liohte,
> blîcandi sô *thiu berhte sunne:*   sô skên that barn godes,
> liuhte is lîchamo: liomon stôdun
> uuânamo fan themu uualdandes barne;   uuarð is geuuâdi sô huît
> sô snêu te sehanne.

[Then, soon after that, from among his followers he picked Simon Peter, James and John, the two men who were brothers, and with these happy warrior-companions set out to go up on a mountain on their own — the happy Child of God and the three thanes. . . . As he bowed down to pray up there his appearance and clothes became different ("other-like") His cheeks became shining light, radiating like the bright sun. The Son of God was shining! His body gave off light, brilliant rays came shining out of the Ruler's Son. His clothes were white as snow to look at. (Song 37, 3107–38, 3128)]

In the Gospel account (Mt 17:1–3: "He was transfigured before them. And his face shone as the sun, and his garments became white as snow," there is not quite as much enthusiasm, and there is far less emphasis on that fact not just his face but his entire body was emitting brilliant radiation. As the *Heliand* poet goes on, he makes a connection between Germanic and Christian images of heaven:

> sô blîði uuarð uupan themu berge: skên that berhte lioht,
> uuas thar gard gôdlic   endi groni *uuang,*
> paradise gelîc.   Petrus thô gimahalde,
> heliÐ hardmôdig   endi te is hêrron sprac,
> grôtte thene godes sunu: 'god is *it* hêr te uuesanne,
> ef thu it gikiosan uuili,   Crist alouualdo,
> that man thi hêr an thesaru hôhe   ên hûs geuuirkea,
> mârlico gemaco   endi Moysese ôðer
> endi Eliase thriddea: thit is ôdas hêm,
> uuelono uunsamost.'

[It became so blissful up there on the mountain — the bright light was shining, there was a magnificent garden there and the green meadow, it was like paradise! Peter the steady-minded hero then spoke up, addressed his Lord and said to God's Son, "This is a good place to live, Christ All-Ruler, if you should decide that a house be built for you up here on the mountain, a magnificent one, and another for Moses and a third for Elijah — this is the home of happiness, the most appealing thing anyone could have!" Song 38, 3134–43]

The poet has changed the top of the mountain to paradise. He has introduced the notion of a place where the light is always shining, and suggested both the Germanic and biblical images of heaven: the green meadow of Valhalla and the Garden of Eden. The light from heaven and the green of earthly meadows and garden combine to create the *Heliand*'s harmonized image of Paradise. Light shines everywhere and it comes both to the meadow of Valhalla and to the garden of Paradise from the shining light-person, Jesus Christ. This radiation is associated with bringing bliss to Peter the "Saxon warrior-companion" so that he is slightly beside himself. Peter's happiness is the "beaming" happiness of human beings that they are envel-oped in such a vast world of light, that they are part of the glowing com-munication between the two worlds of light, earth, this light, and heaven, the other light. At the end of the scene the poet adds his comment: "They saw God's Child standing there alone; that other light though, heaven's, was gone." This image of Germanic-Christian light and happiness, Paradise, is the center of the *Heliand*. In it Jesus is viewed as a kind of light bridge. He brings the light of the other world to *middilgard*, and makes it as bright as paradise. For a people accustomed by their religious mythology to the image of a shimmering light bridge connecting the two worlds of heaven and earth, the *bifrost*, the frosty Milky Way visible at night arching from the horizon across the sky, or the rainbow seen during the day, a bridge of pale light on which the gods, the giants, and souls of the dead, travel from this light to the other light, Christianity must have seemed po-etically barren of any inspiration from the natural world. The author of the *Heliand* fills in the missing gap and makes Jesus the bridge of light, the *bifrost* bringing otherworldly radiant happiness to our hilltops. In one of his more striking thoughts the author even adds: "*so lerde he in liohten uuor-dun*, he taught them in light-words."

In equidistant parallel on both sides of the Transfiguration scene's light, the author placed the brilliance of the light shining at the Nativity and the Resurrection. As in Luke's Gospel, when Jesus is born, men on night watch in the fields (in the *Heliand* they are not shepherds, they are St. Joseph's "horse-guards"!), see the angels from heaven. In the *He-liand*, though the awesomeness of the situation is not so much caused by the sudden appearance of the angels as on otherworldly light breaking through the night sky:

> gisâhun finistri an tuuê
> telâtan an lufte,   endi quam lioht godes
> uuânum thurh thiu uuolcan   endi thea uuardos that
> bifeng an them felda.   Sie *uurðun* an forhtun thô,
> thea *man* an ira môda: gisâhun that mahtigna
> godes engil cumin,   the im tegegnes sprac,
> hêt that im thea uuardos   uuiht ne antdrêdin
> lêðes fon *them liohta* . . .

[They saw the darkness split in two in the sky and the light of God came shining through the clouds and surrounded the guards out in the fields. They saw the mighty angel of God coming toward them. He spoke to the guards face to face and told them they should not fear any harm from the light. Song 5, 390–97]

In Luke's Gospel the angel simply tells the men not to be afraid, in the *Heliand* attention is called to the light by having the angel tell the men not to be afraid of the light.

In parallel, during the *Heliand*'s description of the Resurrection once again attention is called to the arrival of the light:

> Sia oƀar themo graƀe sâtun
> uueros an thero uuahtun   *uuannom* nahton
> bidun undar iro bordon,   huan êr thie berehto dag
> oƀar middilgard   mannon quâmi,
> liudon te liohte.   Thuo ni uuas lang te thiu
> that thar uuarð thie gêst cuman   be godes crafte,
> hâlag âðom   undar thena hardon stên
> an *thena* lichamon.   Lioht uuas thuo gopanod
> firio barnon te frumu: uuas fercal manag
> antheftid fan *helidoron*   endi te himile uueg
> giuuaraht fan thesaro uueroldi.   Uuânom *up* astuod,
> friðubarn godes . . .

[The warriors sat on top of the grave on their watch during the dark starlit night. They waited under their shields until bright day came to mankind all over the middle world bringing light to people. It was not long then until: there was the spirit coming, by God's power, the holy breath, going under the hard stone to the corpse! Light was at that moment opened up for the good of the sons of men; the many bolts on the doors of Hel were unlocked; the road from this world to heaven was built! Brilliantly radiating, God's Peace-Child rose up! Song 68, 5765–76]

As Christ rises, the light of paradise itself is transmitted from Christ's radiance at the Transfiguration and communicated to people, included those held captive like Balder under the earth in the dank realm of Loki's ugly sister Hel. The Christian *bifrost* is now in existence and functioning as He rises up.

Not only is the Christian Resurrection attributed to Christ but it is communicated to all. To the angels as brilliant radiance, to the grave guards as blinding light, to the women as beaming happiness:

> Rincos sâtun
> umbi that graf ûtan,   Iudeo liudi,
> scola mid iro scildion.   Scrêd forðuuardes
> suigli sunnun *lioht* . . .
> sân *up* ahlêd
> thie grôto stên fan them graƀe,   sô ina thie godes engil
> gihueriƀida an halƀa,   endi im uppan them *hlêuue* gisat
> diurlîc drohtines bodo.   Hie uuas an is dâdion gelîc,
> an is ansiunion, sô huem   sô ina *muosta* undar is ôgon scauuon,
> sô *bereht* endi sô blîði   all sô *blicsmun* lioht;

uuas im is giuuâdi   *uuintercaldon*
snêuue gilîcost.   Thuo sâuun sia ina sittian thar,
thiu uuîf uppan them giuuendidan stêne,   endi im fan them
        uulitie quâmun,
them idison sulica egison tegegnes . . .

[The Jewish warriors, the fighting men with their shields, were sitting outside around the grave. The brilliant sunlight continued to
glide upward. . . . suddenly the great stone lifted up, uncovering the
grave, as God's angel pushed it aside. The Chieftain's great messenger then sat down on the grave. In his movements and in his face,
for any one who attempted to look directly at him, he was as radiant
and blissfully beaming as brilliant lightning (*so bereht endi so blîði all
so blicsmun lioht*)! His clothes were like a cold winter's snow. The
women saw him sitting there on top of the stone which had been
removed, and terror came over them because of the nearness of such
radiance. Songs 68, 5779–82, 5803–12]

With their relief at hearing the news from the angel that Christ is
risen the three Marys who had come to the tomb to anoint the body
change from pale to radiant themselves, "The pale women, *bleca idisi,* felt
strong feelings of relief taking hold in their hearts — radiantly beautiful
women, *uuliti-sconi uuif*" (Song 69). It is interesting to see the psychological depth that the author attaches once again to *uuliti.* As in modern
English, the women are "beaming!" They are "radiant." And that seems
to be the chief reason for bringing the poet's fellow Saxons to Christianity, so that they may be a part of this beautiful structure centered on light,
and become a part of its radiant happiness.

Where did the author find inspiration for his light-filled version of
Germanic Christianity? Though it may have been mediated from the
Christian East, I believe it ultimately comes from the first chapter of
John's Gospel, in which the Evangelist alludes to the first verses of the
book of Genesis. John reminds the reader that "in the beginning" the
world was brought into being not by anything done by God, but simply
by his speaking performative words, and God's very first word was "Let
there be light." Christ is seen in the *Heliand* as one responsible for the
magic spoken light-word, "let there be light," in all its fullness of meaning, both radiation and happiness. It is he who brings himself to *middilgard,* to make Valhalla a Paradise beaming with happiness and light for
Peter and his Saxon warrior-companions. For the poet of the *Heliand*,
John the Evangelist's words about Christ were shaping and defining:

In the beginning was the Word, and the Word was with God, and
the Word was God. . . . all things were made through Him [and thus
the beginning of the Heliand in which all things are held together by

God's Words]. In him was life, and that life was the light of men.
And the light shines in the darkness and the darkness grasped it
not. . . . It was the true light, the light that enlightens every man,
that was coming into the world. He was in the world, and world was
made though him and the world knew him not, . . . but to as many a
received him he gave the power of becoming the sons of God.

The *Heliand* is one of the great hidden treasures, hard to fit into a
history of German(ic) literature and thus easily overlooked, yet clearly
part of it and a foundational document of Western culture. It deserves
much greater attention for the light it can shed on the roots and origins
of Germanic culture and Christianity. There is a great deal of value in
reading a document like the *Heliand* written at a time when English and
North German, Anglo-Saxon and Saxon, were not really two different
languages. It is impossible not to feel the power of the work, and there is
a great opportunity for those interested in cultural studies to begin to do
comparative work between the Anglo-Saxon *Beowulf* and the Saxon *Heliand*. In both works there is a confluence of Germanic and Christian culture in the poetry of two epic narratives. It is to be hoped that James E.
Cathey's recent annotated edition of the Old Saxon text of the *Heliand*
for students, and my translation and commentary, will be a help in making the Heliand more accessible, and that admirable philological scholarship continues to be pursued, notably in the work of D. H. Green[17] and
others, which will open up ever more of the hidden wealth waiting in the
words and worlds of the Old Saxon *Heliand*.

Notes

[1] For selections from the Old Saxon text with annotations and commentary, see
James E. Cathey, *Heliand: Text and Commentary* (Morgantown: U of West Virginia P, 2002). The standard edition of the entire Old Saxon text is given in note
6. There is a collection of essays on the text edited by Jürgen Eichhoff and Irmengard Rauch, *Der Heliand* (Darmstadt: WBG, 1973).

[2] For further detail see *The Saxon Savior, The Germanic Transformation of the Gospel
in the Ninth-century Heliand,* G. Ronald Murphy (New York: OUP, 1990), 11–31.

[3] For a description of the mutual influence of Germanic culture and Christianity
from a socio-historical point of view, see James C. Russell, *The Germanization of
Early Medieval Christianity* (New York: OUP, 1996).

[4] Some further circumstantial evidence for the association of the *Heliand* with Fulda
and with the patronage of Rabanus Maurus is the provenance of the very early *Heliand* fragment *V* (at the Vatican), which is believed to predate *M* and *C,* and is
much closer to the original, stemming from the first half of the ninth century — *V* is
from Mainz. Rabanus, abbot of Fulda and supporter of Louis the Pious, was made
archbishop of Mainz, after he had been abbot of Fulda from 822 to 841.

[5] See Bernhard Bischoff's discussion in "Die Schriftheimat der Münchener Heliand-Handschrift," *PBB/*T, 101 (1979): 161–70.

[6] For a suggestion concerning the relationship of the five manuscript texts to one another see *Heliand und Genesis,* ed. Otto Behaghel, 10th ed. by Burkhard Taeger (Tübingen: Niemeyer, 1996), xviii–xxix. Text citations are from this edition. Italicized words indicate existing manuscript variants.

[7] See the account by Adam of Bremen who came to Bremen in 1066 and wrote of Germanic religious customs that were still practiced in his time, especially at the temple in Uppsala, Sweden: *History of the Archbishops of Hamburg-Bremen,* trans. Francis J. Tschan (New York: Columbia UP, 1959), 10–11, 207–8.

[8] All English translations from the *Heliand* are taken from *The Heliand, The Saxon Gospel* trans. G. Ronald Murphy (New York: OUP, 1992).

[9] See "The Final Battle" in Murphy, *The Saxon Savior,* 95–117.

[10] The only place in the *Heliand* where contemporary Jews come under condemnation may be in the scene of the cleansing of the temple. (Song 45). Here the author criticizes Jews for being people who accept interest on loans, for practicing usury. Charlemagne had recently forbidden the practice of usury throughout the empire, and the *Heliand* condemns the practice in very absolute terms as *unreht enfald,* pure injustice.

[11] For a fuller look at the versions in *Tatian* and Old High German, see *The Saxon Savior,* 77–80.

[12] Stephen R. Flowers, *Runes and Magic, Magical Formulaic Elements in the Older Runic Tradition* (New York: Lang, 1986). For further discussion of Germanic magic see Jan de Vries, *Altgermanische Religionsgeschichte* (Berlin: de Gruyter, 1957). For the mutual effect of Germanic and Christian religious concepts and practices upon one another, see Valerie Flint, *The Rise of Magic in Early Medieval Europe* (Princeton: Princeton UP, 1991). Flint maintains that Christianity actually fostered magic rather than suppressing it. The *Heliand* seems to support her thesis in that magic was a convenient and familiar vehicle for expressing the sacred and sacramental mysteries to the Northern European mind.

[13] In the Latin text of the Bible this would be a single causative word: *Fiat.*

[14] *Der Heliand: theologischer Sinn als tektonischer Form* (Cologne: Böhlau, 1962).

[15] Cf. his *Homer and the Heroic Tradition* (Cambridge, MA: Harvard UP, 1958).

[16] For a fuller treatment of the light theme in the *Heliand,* including the role of sight and blindness see G. Ronald Murphy, "The Light Worlds of the *Heliand,*" *Monatshefte,* 89 (1997): 5–17.

[17] See D. H. Green, *The Carolingian Lord: Semantic Studies on four Old High German Words: balder, fro, truhtin, herro* (Cambridge: CUP, 1965). See also the valuable work on cultural confluence in the early medieval world made by James Russell, Stephen E. Flowers, and Valery Flint. A recent dissertation undertaken at Georgetown University, Washington DC, by Mark Dreisonstock initiates a fascinating new discussion of the opposition in the *Heliand* and in *Beowulf* to money and profit as a threat to the traditional warrior culture's concept of wealth as munificence.

Bibliography

IN A VOLUME covering a large range of discrete topics, a fairly large bibliography is inevitable. The distinction between primary and secondary literature, too, is not always entirely clear, but works have been cited once only. It is also impossible to be entirely consistent with the ordering of bibliographical items, although in the primary literature as far as possible the arrangement is according to the original author or the title of anonymous works (although dates are often approximate or disputed). Anthologies are listed under the modern editor. The secondary literature is very selective, concentrating upon the most important and most readily accessible studies; further and more specific literature on individual topics may be found in the detailed notes to the relevant chapters.

Primary Literature

Anthologies and Collections

Bradley, S. A. J. *Anglo-Saxon Poetry*. London: Dent, 1982.

Braune, Wilhelm. *Althochdeutsches Lesebuch*. Tübingen: Niemeyer, 16th. ed. Ernst Ebbinghaus, 1979.

Bugge, Sophus, and Magnus B. Olsen. *Norges Indskrifter med de ældre Runer*. Oslo: Brøgger, 1891–1924.

Calder, D. G., and M. J. B. Allen. *Sources and Analogues of Old English Poetry*. Cambridge: D. S. Brewer, 1983.

[Exeter Book, Cathedral Manuscript 3501:] *ASPR* vol. 3.

[Exeter Book, Cathedral Manuscript 3501:] *The Exeter Anthology of Old English Poetry*. Ed. Bernard J. Muir. Exeter: U Exeter P, 1994.

Fear, A. T. *Lives of the Visigothic Fathers*. Liverpool: Liverpool UP, 1997.

Fischer, Hanns. *Schrifttafeln zum althochdeutschen Lesebuch*. Tübingen: Niemeyer, 1966.

Green, Martin. *The Old English Elegies*. London and Toronto: Fairleigh Dickinson UP, 1983.

Herrmann, Joachim. *Griechische und Lateinische Quellen zur Frühgeschichte Mitteleuropas*. Berlin: Akademie, 1988–92 = Schriften und Quellen der alten Welt 37, 1–4.

Heusler, Andreas, and Wilhelm Ranisch. *Eddica Minora: Dichtungen eddischer Art aus den Fornaldarsögur und anderen Prosawerken.* Dortmund: Ruhfus, 1903.

Heyne, Moritz. *Kleinere altniederdeutsche Denkmäler.* Paderborn: Schöningh, 2nd ed. 1877, repr. Amsterdam: Rodopi, 1970.

Hill, Joyce. *Old English Minor Heroic Poems.* Durham: Durham and St. Andrews Medieval Texts, 1983.

Hollander, Lee M. *The Skalds: A Selection of Their Poems with Introduction and Notes.* Ann Arbor: U of Michigan P, 1968 (first published 1945).

Holthausen, F. *Altsächsisches Elementarbuch.* Heidelberg: Winter, 1900.

Hreinsson, Viðar. *The Complete Sagas of Icelanders, Including 49 Tales,* 5 vols. Reykjavik: Leifur Eiríksson, 1997; selected texts from this collection in *The Sagas of the Icelanders: A Selection,* preface by Jane Smiley and intro. by Robert Kellog. New York: Viking, 2000.

Isbell, Harold. *The Last Poets of Imperial Rome.* Harmondsworth: Penguin, 1971.

Jacobsen, Lis, and Erik Moltke. *Danmarks Runeindskrifter.* Copenhagen: Munksgaard, 1941–42.

Jónsson, Finnur. *Den norsk-islandske skjaldedigtning.* 4 vols. Copenhagen: Gyldendal, 1908–15; rpt. Rosenkilde & Bagger, 1967–73.

Kalinke, Marianne E. *Norse Romance.* Cambridge: D. S. Brewer, 1999.

Klinck, Anne L. *The Old English Elegies: A Critical Edition and Genre Study.* Montreal: McGill Queens UP, 1992.

Krapp, George Philip, and Elliott Van Kirk Dobbie. *The Anglo-Saxon Poetic Records.* New York: Columbia UP, 1931–53.

Kyes, Robert L. *The Old Low Franconian Psalms and Glosses.* Ann Arbor: U Michigan P, 1969.

Lange, Wolfgang. *Christliche Skaldendichtung.* Göttingen: Vandenhoeck and Ruprecht, 1958.

Loth, Agnete. *Late Medieval Icelandic Romances.* 5 vols. Copenhagen: Munksgaard, 1962–65.

Malone, Kemp. *The Nowell Codex.* Copenhagen: Rosenkilde and Bagger, 1963 = EEMF 12.

Massmann, H. F. *Die deutschen Abschwörungs-, Glaubens- Beicht- und Betformeln.* Quedlinburg and Leipzig: Basse, 1839.

Menéndez Pidal, Ramon. *Floresta des leyendas heroicas españolas: Rodrigo, el último godo* [1925–27]. 4th ed. Madrid: Espasa-Calpe, 1973.

Müllenhoff, Karl, and Wilhelm Scherer. *Deutsche Poesie und Prosa aus dem VIII– XII Jahrhundert.* Berlin: Weidmann, 3rd. ed. Elias v. Steinmeyer, 1892, repr. 1964.

Önnerfors, Alf. *Antike Zaubersprüche.* Stuttgart: Reclam, 1991.

Pálsson, Hermann, and Paul Edwards. *Seven Viking Romances*. Harmondsworth: Penguin, 1985.

Richthofen, Karl von. *Friesische Rechtsquellen*. Berlin, 1840, repr. Aalen: Scientia, 1960.

Robinson, Fred C., and E. G. Stanley. *Old English Verse Texts from Many Sources*. Copenhagen: Rosenkilde and Bagger, 1991 = EEMF 23.

Schlosser, Horst Dieter. *Althochdeutsche Literatur*. Frankfurt/M.: Fischer, 2nd ed. 1989; same title, Berlin: Schmidt, 1998 (with translations).

Steinmeyer, Elias von. *Die kleineren althochdeutschen Sprachdenkmäler* [1916]. Berlin and Zurich: Weidmann, repr. as 2nd ed. 1963.

Steinmeyer, Elias von, and Eduard Sievers. *Die althochdeutschen Glossen*. Berlin: Weidmann, 1879–1922.

Stubbs, William. *Select Charters* (1870), 9th ed. by H. W. C. Davis. Oxford: Clarendon, repr. 1966.

Sveriges Runinskrifter. Published by the Kungliga Vitterhets, Historie och Antikvitets Akademien. Stockholm: Almqvist & Wiksell International, 1900–1906.

Usener, Hermann. *Anecdoton Holderii*. Bonn: Georgi, 1877.

Williamson, Craig, ed. *The Old English Riddles of the Exeter Book*. Chapel Hill: U North Carolina P, 1977.

Wipf, Karl A. *Althochdeutsche poetische Texte*. Stuttgart: Reclam, 1992.

Wimmer, Ludvik F. A. *De Danske runemindesmærker*. 4 vols. Copenhagen: Gyldendal, 1893–1908.

Wolf, Kenneth Baxter. *Conqueror and Chroniclers of Early Medieval Spain*. Liverpool: Liverpool UP, 1999.

Wright, Thomas. *Anglo-Saxon and Old English Vocabularies*. 2nd ed. Richard Paul Wülcker. London: Trübner, 1884.

Würth, Stefanie. *Isländische Antikensagas I: Die Saga von den Trojanern; Die Saga von den britischen Königen; Die Saga von Alexander dem Grossen*. Munich: Diederichs, 1996.

Individual Authors and Texts

Adam of Bremen (d. ca. 1085)

Gesta Hammaburgensis ecclesiae pontificum. Ed. Bernhard Schmeidler. Hanover, 3rd ed. 1917, repr. Hanover: MGH, 1993. *History of the Archbishops of Hamburg-Bremen*, trans. Francis J. Tschan. New York: Columbia UP, 1959.

Ælfric (ca. 955–ca. 1010)

Ælfric's Catholic Homilies: The First Series. Ed. Peter Clemoes. Oxford: OUP, 1997 = EETS/SS 17. *Ælfric's Catholic Homilies: The Second Series.* Ed. Malcolm Godden. Oxford: OUP, 1979 = EETS/SS 5. *Ælfric's Catholic Homilies: Introduction, Commentary and Glossary.* By Malcolm Godden. Oxford: OUP, 2000 = EETS/SS 18. *Homilies of Ælfric: A Supplementary Collection.* Ed. John C. Pope. London: OUP, 1967–68 = EETS/OS 259–60.

Ælfric's Lives of the Saints. Ed. Walter W. Skeat. London: Trübner, 1881–1900 = EETS OS. 76, 82, 94, 114.

Ælfric's Prefaces. Ed. Jonathan Wilcox. Durham: Durham Medieval Texts, 1994.

The Old English Version of the Heptateuch. Ed. S. J. Crawford. London: Oxford UP, 1922 = EETS/OS 160; repr. with additional manuscripts transcribed by N. R. Ker, 1990.

Ágrip af Nóregskonungasögum (12th c.)

Ágrip af Nóregskonungasögum: A Twelfth-Century Synoptic History of Norway. Trans. M. J. Driscoll. London: Viking Society for Northern Research, University College London, 1995.

Alfred the Great (848–899)

King Alfred's West-Saxon Version of Gregory's Pastoral Care. Ed. Henry Sweet. London: OUP, 1871–72 = EETS/OS 45, 50.

King Alfred's Old English Version of Boethius. Ed. W. J. Sedgefield. Oxford: Clarendon, 1899–1900.

Alfred's Meters of Boethius. Ed. Bill Griffiths. Chippenham: Anglo-Saxon Books, rev. ed. 1994.

King Alfred's Version of St. Augustine's Soliloquies. Ed. Thomas A. Carnicelli. Cambridge, MA: Harvard UP, 1969.

King Alfred's Old English Prose Translation of the First Fifty Psalms. Ed. Patrick P. O'Neill. Cambridge, MA: Medieval Academy of America, 2001.

Ammianus Marcellinus (ca. A.D. 330–95)

Rerum gestarum libri XXXI. Ed. Wolfgang Seyfahrt. Leipzig: Teubner, 1978. Ed., trans. J. C. Rolfe. Loeb Classical Library. Cambridge, MA: Harvard UP; London: Heinemann, 1935–50. *The Later Roman Empire.* Trans. Walter Hamilton, notes by Andrew Wallace-Hadrill. Harmondsworth: Penguin, 1986.

Anglo-Saxon Chronicle (to 1154)

The Anglo-Saxon Chronicle: A Collaborative Edition under the editorship of David Dumville and Simon Keynes: Manuscript A, ed. Janet M. Bately. Cambridge: D.S. Brewer, 1986; Manuscript F, ed. Peter S. Baker. Cambridge: D.S. Brewer, 2000.

Apollonius of Tyre (11th c.)

The Old English Apollonius of Tyre. Ed. Peter Goolden. London: OUP, 1958.

Asser (d. 910)

Asser's "Life of King Alfred" and Other Contemporary Sources. Trans. with an introduction and notes by Simon Keynes and Michael Lapidge. Harmondsworth: Penguin Books, 1983.

Augustine (354–430)

Augustine. *De civitate Dei.* Ed. and trans. W. M. Green. Loeb Classical Library. Cambridge, MA; Harvard UP; London: Heinemann, 1957–63.

Bede (673–735)

Bede. *Historia ecclesiastica gentis Anglorum I–V.* Ed. Charles Plummer. Oxford: Clarendon, 1956. *Ecclesiastical History of the English People.* Ed. and trans. Bertram Colgrave and R. A. B. Mynors. Oxford: Clarendon, 1969.

The Old English Version of Bede's Ecclesiastical History of the English People. Ed. Thomas Miller. London: Trübner, 1890–98 = EETS/OS 95, 96, 110, 111.

Beowulf (8th c.)

Beowulf. Ed. Friedrich Klaeber. Boston: Heath, 3rd ed., 1950. New ed. Bruce Mitchell and Fred C. Robinson. Oxford: Blackwell, 1998. *Beowulf: A New Verse Translation.* Trans. R. M. Liuzza. Peterborough, ON: Broadview, 2000. *Beowulf: A Verse Translation.* Trans. Seamus Heaney. Ed. Daniel Donoghue. New York: W.W. Norton, 2002.

Bodley Homilies (12th c.)

Old English Homilies from MS Bodley 343. Ed. Susan Irvine. Oxford: OUP, 1993 = EETS/OS 302.

British Library, MS Cotton Tiberius B V (11th c.)

An Eleventh-Century Anglo-Saxon Illustrated Miscellany. Ed. P. McGurk et al. Copenhagen: Rosenkilde and Bagger, 1983 = EEMF 21.

Byrhtferth (late 10th c.)

Byrhtferth's Enchiridion. Ed. Peter S. Baker and Michael Lapidge. Oxford: OUP, 1995 = EETS/SS 15.

Gaius Julius Caesar (ca. 100–44 B.C.)

Caesar. *De bello Gallico libri VII.* Ed. Otto Seel. Leipzig: Teubner, 3rd ed. 1977 = C. Iulii Caesaris commentarii I. *The Conquest of Gaul.* Trans. S. A. Handford. Harmondsworth: Penguin, 1951.

Cassiodorus (487–583)

Cassiodorus. *Variae epistulae.* Ed. Theodor Mommsen. Berlin: MGH, 1894, Nachdruck Munich, 1981 = MGH AA 12. Ed. Åke J. Fridh. Turnhout: CCSL, 1973 = Corpus Christianorum, Series Latina 96.

Cassius Dio (ca A.D. 155–ca. 253)

Cassius Dio [Dio Cassius]. *Roman History.* Ed. and trans. Earnest Cary, based on that by Herbert B. Foster. Loeb Classical Library. Cambridge, MA; Harvard UP; London: Heinemann, 1914–27.

Cosmas of Prague (ca. 1045–1125)

Cosmas of Prague. *Chronik der Böhme.* Ed. Berthold Bretholz. Berlin: MGH, 1923, repr. Munich 1980 = MGH Scriptores rerum Germanicarum, NS 2.

Deor (9/10th c.)

Deor. Ed. Kemp Malone. London: Methuen, 1933.

Dream of the Rood (8th c.)

Dream of the Rood. Ed. Bruce Dickins and Alan S. C. Ross. London: Methuen, 1934.

Edda (Poetic, Elder, 9th–13th c.)

Die Lieder des Codex Regius nebst verwandten Denkmälern. Ed. Gustav Neckel, rev. Hans Kuhn. Heidelberg: Winter, 1962. *The Poetic Edda.* Ed. Ursula Dronke. I. *Heroic Poems* and II. *Mythological Poems.* Oxford: Clarendon, 1969–97. *The Poetic Edda.* Trans. Henry Adams Bellows. New York: American-Scandinavian Foundation, 1923 (and later rpts.). *The Poetic Edda.* Trans. Lee M. Hollander, 2nd rev. ed. . Austin: U Texas P, 1962. *Poems of the Vikings: The Elder Edd.*, Trans. Patricia Terry. Indianapolis: Bobbs-Merrill, 1969. *The Poetic Edda.* Trans. Carolyne Larrington. Oxford and New York: OUP, 1996.

Einhard (d. 844)

Paul Edward Dutton. *Charlemagne's Courtier.* Peterborough, ON: Broadview, 1998.

Erex Saga (13th c.)

Erex saga and Ívens saga: The Old Norse Versions of Chrétien de Troyes's Erec and Yvain. Trans. Foster W. Blaisdell, Jr., and Marianne E. Kalinke. Lincoln: U of Nebraska P, 1977.

Eusebius (ca. A.D. 260–ca. 340)

Hieronymi Chronica. Ed. Rudolf Helm. Berlin: Akademie, 1956.

Færeyinga Saga (ca. 1200)

The Faroe Islanders' Saga. Trans. George Johnston. N.p., Canada: Oberon Press, 1975.

First Grammatical Treatise (1170–80)

First Grammatical Treatise: The Earliest Germanic Philology, an Edition, Translation, and Commentary. Ed. and trans. Einar Haugen. Baltimore: Linguistic Society of America, 1950.

Fredegar(ius) (7th c.)

Fredegar, *Chronicae.* Ed. Bruno Krusch. Hanover: MGH, 1888, repr. Stuttgart, 1984 = MGH SS rerum Merovingicarum 2, 1–168. Ed. Andreas Kusternig. Darmstadt: WBG, 2nd ed. 1994 = Ausgewählte Quellen zur deutschen Geschichte des Mittelalters 4a, 3–271.

Annals of Fulda (9th c.)

Annals of Fulda. Trans. Timothy Reuter. Manchester: Manchester UP, 1992.

Gallus Anonymus (12th c.)

Gallus Anonymus. *Chronicon et gesta ducum sive principum Polonorum.* Ed. Karol Malezynski and Rudolf Köpke. Hanover: MGH, 1851, repr. Stuttgart 1983 = MGH SS 9, 418–78.

Galluslied (11th c.)

P. Osterwalder. *Das althochdeutsche Galluslied Ratperts und seine lateinischen Übersetzungen durch Ekkehart IV.* Berlin and New York: de Gruyter, 1982.

Gautreks Saga (13th c.)

Gautrek's Saga and Other Medieval Tales. Trans. Hermann Pálsson and Paul Edwards. New York: New York UP, 1968.

Gildas (ca. A.D. 540)

Gildas. *The Ruin of Britain.* Ed. and trans. Michael Winterbottom. Chichester: Phillimore, 1978.

Gospels (Old English, 10th c.)

The Old English Version of the Gospels. Ed. R. M. Liuzza. Oxford: OUP, 1994, 2000 = EETS/OS 304, 314.

Gregory of Tours (544–95)

Gregory of Tours. *Historia Francorum.* Ed. Bruno Krusch and Wilhelm Levison. Hanover: MGH, 2nd ed. 1951, repr. Hanover 1992 = MGH SS rerum Merovingicarum 1/i. Ed. Rudolf Buchner. Darmstadt: WBG, 1959 = Ausgewählte Quellen zur deutschen Geschichte des Mittelalters 2 and 3.

Heliand (ca. 850)

Heliand und Genesis. Ed. Otto Behaghel. 10th ed. by Burkhard Taeger. Tübingen: Niemeyer, 1996. *Heliand*. Trans. (German) Felix Genzmer. Stuttgart: Reclam, n.d. *The Heliand: The Saxon Gospel*. Trans. G. Ronald Murphy. New York and Oxford: OUP, 1992. James E. Cathey, *Heliand: Text and Commentary*. Morgantown: U of West Virginia P, 2002.

Historia Brittonum (Nennius? 9th c.)

Historia Brittonum. Ed. Theodor Mommsen. Berlin: MGH, 1898, repr. Munich, 1981 = MGH AA 13, 147–201. Nennius, *British History and the Welsh Annals*. Ed. and trans. John Morris. Chichester: Phillimore, 1980.

Isidore (ca. 560–636)

Isidore of Seville. *Etymologiarum sive originum libri XX*. Ed. Wallace Martin Lindsay. Oxford: Clarendon, 1911.

Isidore of Seville. *Historia vel Origo Gothorum*. Ed. Theodor Mommsen. Berlin: MGH, 1894, repr. Munich, 1981 = MGH AA 11. *History of the Goths, Vandals and Suevi*. Trans. G. Donini and G. B. Ford. Leiden: Brill, 2nd ed. 1970.

Isidor, Der althochdeutsche. Ed. Hans Eggers. Tübingen: Niemeyer, 1964.

Jerome (ca. 342–420)

Jerome. *Letters and Select Works*. Trans. W. H. Fremantle, G. Lewis, and W. G. Martley [1893]. Grand Rapids: MI: Eerdmans, 1979.

Jómsvíkinga Saga (12/13th c.)

The Saga of the Jómsvikings. Trans. Lee M. Hollander. Austin: U Texas P, 1955.

Jordanes (6th c.)

Jordanes. *Romana et Getica*. Ed. Theodor Mommsen. Hanover: MGH, 1882, repr. Munich, 1982 = MGH AA 5/i. *The Gothic History of Jordanes in English*. Trans. Charles Christopher Mierow. Princeton: UP, 1915; 2nd ed. Cambridge and New York: Barnes and Noble, 1966.

Julian (A.D. 331–63)

Julian. *Works*. Ed. and trans. Wilmer Cave Wright. Loeb Classical Library. Cambridge, MA: Harvard UP; London: Heinemann, 1913–23. *Oeuvres complètes*. Ed. and trans. [French] by J. Bidez, cont. by Gabriel Rochefort and Christian Lacombrade. Paris: Belles Lettres, 1924–63.

Karlamagnús saga (13th c.)

Karlamagnús saga: The Saga of Charlemagne and His Heroes. Trans. Constance B. Hieatt, 3 vols. Toronto: The Pontifical Institute of Mediaeval Studies, 1975–80.

Landnámabók (13th c.)

The Book of Settlements; Landnámubók. Trans. Hermann Pálsson and Paul Edwards. Winnipeg: U of Manitoba P, 1972.

Lex Frisionum (8/9th c.)

Lex Frisionum. Ed. Karl von Richthofen. Hanover: MGH, 1863 = MHG Leges 3, 630–710.

Livy (59 B.C. – A.D. 17)

Livy. *Ab urbe condita*. Ed. W. Weissenbron and M. Müller. Stuttgart: 1959–.

Luther, Martin (1483–1546)

Luther, Martin. *Sendbrief vom Dolmetschen* (1530). Ed. Karl Bischoff, 2nd ed. Tübingen: Niemeyer, 1965.

Maldon, Battle of (10th c.)

The Battle of Maldon, A.D. 991. Ed. Donald Scragg. Oxford: Blackwell, 1991.

Martyrologium, Old English (9th c.)

Das altenglische Martyrologium. Ed. Günter Kotzor. Munich: Bayrische Akademie, 1981.

Morkinskinna (12/13th c.)

Morkinskinna: The Earliest Icelandic Chronicle of the Norwegian Kings (1030–1157). Trans. Theodore M. Andersson and Kari Ellen Gade. Ithaca, NY: Cornell UP, 2000.

Murbach Hymns (9th c.)

Die Murbacher Hymnen. Ed. Eduard Sievers [1874], repr. with an introduction by Evelyn Firchow. New York and London: Johnson, 1972.

Notker the German (ca. 950–1022)

Notkers des Deutschen Werke. Ed. E. H. Sehrt and Taylor Starck. Halle/Saale: Niemeyer, 1933–35 and James C. King and Petrus Tax. Tübingen: Niemeyer, 1972–.

Óláfr, Passion of (13th c.)

A History of Norway and the Passion and Miracles of the Blessed Óláfr. Trans. Devra Kunin, ed. with intro. and notes by Carl Phelpstead. London: Viking Society for Northern Research, University College, London, 2001.

Orkneyinga Saga (ca. 1200)

Orkneyinga saga: The History of the Earls of Orkney. Trans. Hermann Pálsson and Paul Edwards. Harmondsworth: Penguin, 1981.

Orosius (5th c.)

Orosius. *Historiarum adversum paganos libri VII.* Ed. Karl Zangemeister, Leipzig: Teubner, 1889, repr. Hildesheim: Olms, 1967 = CSEL 5.

The Old English Orosius. Ed. Janet M. Bately. London: OUP, 1980 = EETS/SS 6.

Otfrid of Weissenburg (ca. 800–875)

Otfrid von Weissenburg. *Evangelienharmonie* (manuscript). Ed. Hans Butzmann. Graz: Akademische Druck- und Verlagsanstalt, 1972. Otfrid, *Evangelienbuch.* Ed. Oskar Erdmann. Halle: Waisenhaus, 1882, and in the *Altdeutsche Textbibliothek,* 7th ed. by Ludwig Wolff. Tübingen: Niemeyer, 1973. Otfrid, *Evangelienbuch.* Trans. [selection in German] Gisela Vollmann-Profe. Stuttgart, Reclam, 1987.

Pariser Gespräche (10th c.)

Wolfgang Haubrichs and Max Pfister. *In Francia fui.* Stuttgart: Steiner, 1989.

Paulus Diaconus (ca. 720–ca. 800)

Paulus Diaconus. *Historia Langobardorum.* Ed. Georg Waitz. Hanover: MGH, 1878, repr. Hanover, 1988 = MGH SS rerum Langobardicarum, 12–187.

Peterborough Chronicle 1070–1154 (12th c.)

The Peterborough Chronicle 1070–1154. Ed. Cecily Clark. Oxford: Clarendon, 2nd ed. 1970.

Phoenix (10th c.)

The Phoenix. Ed. N. F. Blake. Manchester: Manchester UP, 1964.

Pliny the Elder (A.D. 23–79)

Pliny the Elder. *Natural History.* Ed. H. Rackham, W. H. S. Jones, and D. E. Eichholz. Loeb Classical Library. Cambridge, MA: Harvard UP; London: Heinemann, 1938–52.

Ptolemy (2nd c. A.D.)

Ptolemy. *Geographica.* Ed. C. F. A. Nobbe (1843–45) repr. Hildesheim: Olms, 1966.

Brother Robert (early 13th c.)

The Saga of Tristram and Ísönd. Trans. Paul Schach. Lincoln: U Nebraska P, 1973.

Roland Saga (13th c.)

The Norse Version of the Chanson de Roland. Trans. Eyvind Fjeld Halvorsen. Copenhagen: Munksgaard, 1959.

Rudolf of Fulda (9th c.)

Rudolf von Fulda. *Translatio sancti Alexandri.* Ed. Bruno Krusch in *Nachrichten von der Gesellschaft der Wissenschaften zu Göttingen,* phil.-hist. Kl. II 13 (1933), 405–36.

Sallust (B.C. 86–34)

Sallust. *De Catilinae coniuratione.* Ed. Rudolf Dietsch. Leipzig: Teubner, 1859.

Salvian of Marseilles (Ca. 400–480)

Salvian of Marseilles. *De gubernatione Dei.* Ed. Karl Halm. Berlin: MGH, 1877, repr. Munich, 1991 = MGH AA 1.

Saxo Grammaticus (12/13th c.)

Saxo Grammaticus. *Gesta Danorum.* Ed. J. Olrik and H. Raeder. Copenhagen: Levin and Munksgaard, 2nd ed. 1931. *The History of the Danes.* Trans. Peter Fisher and ed. Hilda Ellis Davidson. Cambridge: Brewer, 1979–80.

Saxon Genesis (9th c.)

The Saxon Genesis. Ed. A. N. Doane. Madison: U of Wisconsin P, 1991.

Skeireins (4th c.)

Die Skeireins. Ed. Ernst A Kock. Lund: Gleerup, 1913. William Holmes Bennett, *The Gothic Commentary on the Gospel of St. John.* New York: MLA, 1960, repr. Kraus, 1966.

Solomon and Saturn (11th c.)

The "Prose Solomon and Saturn" and "Adrian and Ritheus." Ed. James E. Cross and Thomas D. Hill. Toronto: U of Toronto P, 1982.

Snorri Sturluson (1178/79–1241)

Heimskringla: History of the Kings of Norway by Snorri Sturluson. Trans. Lee M. Hollander. Austin: U of Texas P, 1964.

Edda. Trans. Anthony Faulkes. London: Dent, 1987.

Strengleikar (13th c.)

Strengleikar: An Old Norse Translation of Twenty-One Old French Lais. Ed. and trans. Robert Cook and Mattias Tveitane. Oslo: Kjeldeskriftfondet, 1979.

Sturlunga Saga (13th c.)

Sturlunga saga. Trans. Julia H. McGrew. New York: Twayne, 1970–74.

Suetonius (d. ca. A.D. 160)

Suetonius. *Lives of the Caesars.* Ed. and trans. J. C. Rolfe. Loeb Classical Library. Cambridge, MA: Harvard UP; London: Heinemann 1914.

Tacitus (ca. A.D. 55–ca. 130)

Tacitus. *Works.* Various edd. and trans. Loeb Classical Library. Cambridge, MA: Harvard UP; London: Heinemann, 1914–70.

Tacitus. *Germania* [etc.]. Ed. and trans. William Peterson, rev. Michael Winterbottom. Cambridge, MA: Harvard UP; London: Heinemann, 1970. *Germania.* Trans., intro., and commentary by J. B. Rives. Oxford: Clarendon, 1999. *Cornelii Taciti Opera Minora.* Ed. Henry Furneaux and J. G. C. Anderson. Oxford: Clarendon, 1900, repr. 1962. *Tacitus on Britain and Germany.* Trans. H. Mattingley. Harmondsworth: Penguin, 1948.

Tacitus. *Annales.* Trans. Michael Grant as *Tacitus: The Annals of Imperial Rome.* Harmondsworth: Penguin, 1956.

Tacitus, *Historiae.* Trans. Kenneth Wellesley as *The Histories.* Harmondsworth: Penguin, 1972.

Tatian (Old High German, 9th c.)

Tatian. Ed. Eduard Sievers. Paderborn: Schöningh, 1892, repr. 1966.

Theodericus Monachus (ca. 1180)

Theodericus Monachus. *Historia de antiquitate regum norwagensium; An Account of the Ancient History of the Norwegian Kings.* Trans. and annotated by David and Ian McDougall, intro. by Peter Foote. London: Viking Society for Northern Research, University College, London, 1998.

Þiðreks Saga (13th c.)

The Saga of Thidrek of Bern. Trans. Edward R. Haymes. New York: Garland, 1988.

Thietmar of Merseburg (975–1018)

Thietmar von Merseburg. *Chronicon.* Ed. Robert Holzmann. Berlin: MGH, 1935, repr. Munich, 1996 = MGH SS rerum Germanicarum NS 9. Ed. Werner Trillmich. Darmstadt: WBG, 6th ed., 1957 = Ausgewählte Quellen zur deutschen Geschichte des Mittelalters 9.

Ulfila (ca. 311–82)

Stamm-Heynes Ulfilas. New ed. by Ferdinand Wrede. Paderborn: Schöningh, 1920. *Die Gotische Bibel.* Ed. Wilhelm Streitberg. 5/6. ed. Heidelberg: Winter, 1920, repr. 1965; 7th ed. with new material by Piergiuseppe Scardigli, 2000. *Codex Argenteus Upsaliensis.* Ed. O. von Friesen and A. Grape. Uppsala: Malmogiae, 1927. *Wulfilae codices Ambrosiani rescripti.* Ed. Jan de Vries. Turin: Molfese, 1936.

Velleius Paterculus (1st c. A.D.)

C. Vellei Paterculi ex Historiae romanae libris duobus quae supersunt. Ed. C. Stegmann de Pritzwald. Leipzig: Teubner, 1968 (and see http://www.thelatinlibrary.com/). Ed. and trans. [into German] Marion Giebel. Stuttgart: Reclam, 1989. Ed. and trans. F. W. Shipley. Loeb Classical Library. Cambridge, MA: Harvard UP; Heinemann: London, 1924.

Vercelli Homilies (10th c.)

The Vercelli Homilies and Related Texts. Ed. D. G. Scragg. Oxford: OUP, 1992 = EETS/OS 300.

"Vinland Sagas" (12th c.)

The Vinland Sagas: The Norse Discovery of America: Graenlendinga Saga and Eirik's Saga. Trans. Magnus Magnusson and Hermann Pálsson. Harmondsworth: Penguin, 1965 and New York: New York UP, 1966.

Vision of St. Paul (Old English, 11th c.)

The Old English Vision of St. Paul. Ed. Antonette di Paolo Healey. Cambridge, MA: Medieval Academy of America, 1978.

Völsunga Saga (13th c.)

The Saga of the Volsungs. Ed. and trans. R. G. Finch. London: Nelson, 1965.

Wærferth of Worcester (9th c.)

Bischof Wærferths von Worcester Übersetzung der Dialoge Gregors des Grossen. Ed. Hans Hecht. Leipzig: G. H. Wigand, 1900–1907.

Waltharius (10th c.?)

Waltharius. Lateinisch/Deutsch. Ed. Gregor Vogt-Spira. Stuttgart: Reclam, 1994. *Walthari.* Trans. Brian Murdoch. Glasgow: Scottish Papers in Germanic Studies, 1989.

Widsith (7th c.)

Widsith. Ed. R. W. Chambers. Cambridge: CUP, 1912.

Widukind of Corvey (10th c.)

Widukind. *Res gestae Saxonicae.* Ed. Paul Hirsch. Hanover: MGH, 5th ed. 1935, repr. Hanover, 1989 = MGH SS rerum Germanicarum. Ed. Albert Bauer and Reinhold Rau. Darmstadt: WBG, 4th ed., 1992 = Ausgewählte Quellen zur deutschen Geschichte des Mittelalters 8, 1–183.

Williram of Ebersberg (d. 1085)

Williram. *The Expositio in Cantica Canticorum.* Ed. Erminnie H. Bartlemez. Philadelphia: American Philosophical Society, 1967.

Wulfstan (11th c.)

The Homilies of Wulfstan. Ed. Dorothy Bethurum. Oxford: Clarendon, 1957.

Jost, Karl. *Die "Institutes of Polity, Civil and Ecclesiastical": Ein Werk Erzbischof Wulfstans von York.* Bern: Swiss Studies in English 47, 1959.

Wulfstan: Canons of Edgar. Ed. Roger Fowler. London: OUP, 1972 = EETS/OS 266.

The Copenhagen Wulfstan Collection. Ed. J. E. Cross and Jennifer Morrish Tunberg = EEMF 25. Copenhagen: Rosenkilde and Bagger, 1993.

Yngvars Saga (13th c.)

Vikings in Russia: Yngvar's and Eymund's Saga. Trans. Hermann Pálsson and Paul Edwards. Edinburgh: Edinburgh UP, 1989.

Selected Secondary Texts

Reference Works

Aarne, Antti. *Verzeichnis der Märcheniypen* [1910]. Trans. Stith Thompson as *The Types of the Folk-Tale*. 2nd rev. ed. Helsinki: Suomalainen Tiedeakatemia, 1964.

Belkin, Johanna, and Jürgen Meier. *Bibliographie zu Otfrid von Weißenburg und zur altsächsischen Bibeldichtung.* Berlin: Schmidt, 1975.

Bergmann, Rolf. *Verzeichnis der althochdeutschen und altsächsischen Glossenhand-schriften.* Berlin and New York: de Gruyter, 1973.

Bremmer, Rolf. *A Bibliographical Guide to Old Frisian Studies.* Odense: Odense UP, 1992.

Caenegem, R. C. Van, with F. L. Ganshof. *Introduction aux sources de l'histoire médiévale.* New ed. by L. Jocqué, trans. B. van den Abele. Turnhout: Brepols, 1997 = Corpus Christianorum, Cont. med.

Feist, Sigmund. *Vergleichendes Wörterbuch der gotischen Sprache.* Leiden: Brill, 3rd ed. 1939. Adapted by Winfred P. Lehmann as *A Gothic Etymological Dictionary.* Leiden: Brill, 1986.

Greenfield, S. B., and Fred C. Robinson. *A Bibliography of Publications on Old English Literature to the End of 1972.* Toronto: U of Toronto P, 1980.

Holthausen, F. *Gotisches etymologisches Wörterbuch.* Heidelberg: Winter, 1934.

Hoops, Johannes, ed. *Reallexikon der germanischen Altertumskunde.* Strasbourg: Trübner, 1911–19; 2nd ed. by Heinrich Beck et al. Berlin and New York: de Gruyter, 1973–.

Kalinke, Marianne E., and P. M. Mitchell. *Bibliography of Old Norse-Icelandic Romances.* Ithaca, NY: Cornell UP, 1985.

Ker, N. R. *Catalogue of Manuscripts Containing Anglo-Saxon.* Oxford: Clarendon, 1957.

König, Werner. *dtv-Atlas zur deutschen Sprache.* Munich: dtv 1978.

Lindow, John. *Scandinavian Mythology: An Annotated Bibliography.* New York: Garland, 1988.

Marquardt, Hertha. *Bibliographie der Runeninschriften nach Fundorten.* Göttingen: Vandenhoeck and Ruprecht, 1961.

McEvedy, Colin. *The Penguin Atlas of Medieval History.* Harmondsworth: Penguin, 1961.

Mossé, Fernand. "Bibliographica Gothica," *Medieval Studies* 12 (1950): 237–324, "First Supplement," *Medieval Studies* 15 (1953): 169–83; "Second Supplement" completed by James W. Marchand, *Medieval Studies* 19 (1957): 174–96; "Third Supplement" by Ernst Ebbinghaus, *Medieval Studies* 29 (1967): 328–43.

Pokorny, Julius. *Indogermanisches etymologisches Wörterbuch.* Bern and Munich: Francke, 1959–69.

Pulsiano, Phillip, ed. *Medieval Scandinavia: An Encyclopedia*. New York: Garland, 1993.

Simek, Rudolf. *Dictionary of Northern Mythology*. Woodbridge: Boydell and Brewer, 1982.

Thompson, Stith. *Motif-Index of Folk Literature: A Classification of Narrative Elements in Folktales, Ballads, Myths, Fables, Medieval Romances, Exempla, Fabliaux, Jest-Books and Local Legends*. 6 vols. Rev. ed. Bloomington, IN: Indiana UP; Copenhagen: Rosenkilde and Bagger, 1955–58.

Tollenaere, Felicien de, and Randall L. Jones. *Word-Indices and Word-Lists to the Gothic Bible and Minor Fragments*. Leiden: Brill, 1976.

Language

Antonsen, E. H. *A Concise Grammar of the Older Runic Inscriptions*. Tübingen: Niemeyer, 1975.

Balg, Gerhard Hubert. *A Comparative Grammar of the Gothic Language*. London: Truebner, 1887–89.

Bennett, W. H. *An Introduction to the Gothic Language*. New York: MLA, 1980.

Borst, Arno. *Der Turmbau von Babel: Geschichte und Meinungen über Ursprung und Vielfalt der Sprachen und Völker*. Stuttgart: Hiersemann, 1957–63.

Braune, Wilhelm. *Gotische Grammatik*. 18th ed. by Ernst Ebbinghaus. Tübingen: Niemeyer, 1973.

Eggers, Hans. *Deutsche Sprachgeschichte I: Das Althochdeutsche*. Reinbek bei Hamburg: Rowohlt, 1963.

Friedrichsen, G. W. S. *Gothic Studies*. Oxford: Blackwell, 1961.

Frings, Theodor. *Grundlegung einer Geschichte der deutschen Sprache*. Halle/S.: Niemeyer, 3rd ed. 1957.

Green, D. H. *The Carolingian Lord: Semantic Studies on Four Old High German Words: balder, fro, truhtin, herro*. Cambridge: CUP, 1965.

———. *Language and History in the Early Germanic World*. Cambridge: CUP, 1998.

Grimm, Jacob. *Geschichte der Deutschen Sprache*. Leipzig: Weidmann, 1848.

Grønvik, O. *Runene på Tunesteinen: Alfabet — språkform — budskap* Oslo: Universitetsforlaget, 1981.

Hempel, Heinrich. *Gotisches Elementarbuch*. Berlin and New York: de Gruyter, 1962; 5th ed. by Wolfgang Binnig, 1999.

Hirt, Herman. *Geschichte der deutschen Sprache*. Munich: Beck, 1919.

———. *Handbuch des Urgermanischen I*. Heidelberg: Winter, 1931 = Sammlung Indogermanischer Lehr- und Handbücher; 1. Reihe: Grammatiken 21.

Keller, R. E. *The German Language*. London: Faber and Faber, 1978.

Kirk, Arthur. *An Introduction to the Historical Study of New High German*. Manchester: Manchester UP, 1923, repr. 1961.

Krause, Wolfgang. *Handbuch des Gothischen*. Munich: Beck, 3rd ed. 1968.

———. *Die Sprache der urnordischen Runeninschriften*. Heidelberg: Winter, 1971.

Lockwood, W. B. *An Informal History of the German Language*. London: Deutsch, 1976.

Mitchell, Bruce, and Fred C. Robinson. *A Guide to Old English*. 6th ed. Oxford: Blackwell, 2001.

Mitzka, Walther. *Deutsche Mundarten*. Heidelberg: Winter, 1943.

Morris, R. L. *Runic and Mediterranean Epigraphy*. Odense: Odense UP, 1988.

Mossé, Fernand. *Manuel de la langue Gothique*. Paris: Aubier, 2nd ed. 1956.

Naumann, Hans, and Werner Betz. *Althochdeutsches Elementarbuch*. Berlin and New York: de Gruyter, 1962.

Page, R. I. *An Introduction to English Runes*. 2nd ed. Woodbridge: Boydell, 1999.

———. *Runes and Runic Inscriptions*. Woodbridge: Boydell, 1995; paperback with new introductory chapter and postscripts appended by the author to most of the original chapters, 1999.

Palm, Rune. *Runor och regionalitet: studier av variation i de nordiska minnesinskrifterna*. Uppsala: Institutionen för nordiska språk, Uppsala universitet, 1992.

Sanders, Willy. *Sachsensprache, Hansesprache, Niederdeutsch*. Göttingen: Vandenhoek and Ruprecht, 1982.

Schaefer, Ursula. *Schriftlichkeit im frühen Mittelalter*. Tübingen: Narr, 1993 = ScriptOralia 53.

Sjölin, Bo. *Einführung in das Friesische*. Stuttgart: Metzler, 1969.

Sonderegger, Stefan. *Althochdeutsche Sprache und Literatur*. Berlin: de Gruyter, 1974.

Stanton, Robert. *The Culture of Translation in Anglo-Saxon England*. Cambridge: Brewer, 2002.

Vries, Jan de. *Altnordisches etymologisches Wörterbuch*. Leiden: Brill, 2nd ed. 1962.

Wessén, Elias. *Die nordischen Sprachen*. Berlin: de Gruyter, 1968.

Wimmer, Ludvik F. A. *Die Runenschrift*. Trans. F. Holthausen. Berlin: Weidmann, 1887.

Wright, Joseph. *Grammar of the Gothic Language*. 2nd ed. by O. L. Sayce. Oxford: Clarendon, 1954.

Mythological, Archeological, and Historical-Cultural Studies

Amory, Patrick. *People and Identity in Ostrogothic Italy, 489–554*. Cambridge: CUP, 1997.

Antonsen, E. H. "Runes and Romans on the Rhine." *ABäG* 45 (1996): 5–13 (= *Frisian Runes and Neighbouring Traditions,* ed. T. Looijenga and Arend Quak).

Axboe, Morten, Urs Clavadetscher, Klaus Düwel, Karl Hauck, and Lutz von Padberg, eds. *Die Goldbrakteaten der Völkerwanderungszeit: Ikonographischer Katalog.* Munich: Fink, 1985–89.

Baatz, Dietwulf. *Limeskastell Saalburg.* 8th ed. Bad Homburg: Saalburgmuseum, 1984.

———. *Der Römische Limes.* 4th ed. Berlin: Mann, 2000.

Baatz, Dietwulf, and Fritz-Rudolf Herrmann, eds. *Die Römer in Hessen.* Stuttgart: Theiss, 2nd ed. 1989.

Bammesberger, A., ed. *Old English Runes and Their Continental Background.* Heidelberg: Winter, 1991.

Barraclough, Geoffrey, ed. *Eastern and Western Europe in the Middle Ages.* London: Thames and Hudson, 1970.

Bickermann, Elias J. "*Origines gentium.*" *Classical Philology* 47 (1952): 65–81.

Birkhan, Helmut. *Germanen und Kelten bis zum Ausgang der Römerzeit.* Vienna: Akademie der Wissenschaften, 1970 = Sitzungsberichte 272.

Boetzkes, Manfred, and Helga Stein, eds. with Christian Weisker. *Der Hildesheimer Silberfund: Original und Nachbildung: vom Römerschatz zum Bürgerstolz.* Hildesheim: Gerstenberg, 1997.

Brøndsted, Johannes. *The Vikings.* Trans. Kalle Skov. Harmondsworth: Penguin, 1965.

Brown, Peter. *The World of Late Antiquity.* London: Thames and Hudson, 1971.

Burns, T. S. *A History of the Ostrogoths.* Bloomington, IN: Indiana UP.

Cameron, M. L. *Anglo-Saxon Medicine.* Cambridge: CUP, 1993.

Capelle, Torsten. *Anthropomorphe Holzidole in Mittel und Nordeuropa.* Stockholm, Almqvist and Wiksell, 1995.

Carroll, Maureen. *Romans, Celts and Germans: The German Provinces of Rome.* Stroud: Tempus, 2001.

Cavalli-Sforza, Luigi Luca. *Genes, People and Languages.* Trans. Mark Seielstad. New York: North Point Press, 2000.

Chadwick, Nora. *The Celts.* Harmondsworth: Penguin, 1970.

Clanchy, Michael. *From Memory to Written Record, 1066–1130.* London: Arnold, 1972.

Creighton, J. D., and R. J. A. Wilson, eds. *Roman Germany: Studies in Cultural Interaction.* Portsmouth, RI: Journal of Roman Archaeology, Supplementary Series 32, 1999.

Derolez, René. *The Origin of the Runes: An Alternative Approach.* Brussels; Koninklijke Academie voor Wetenschappen, Letteren en Schone Kunsten van België, 1998 = Academiae Analecta — Klasse der Letteren 60/1.

Dove, Alfred. *Studien zur Vorgeschichte des deutschen Volksnamens.* Heidelberg: Winter, 1916 = Sitzungberichte der Akademie der Wissenschaften 8.

Dumézil, Georges. *Gods of the Ancient Northmen.* Trans. Einar Haugen. Berkeley: U California P, 1977.

Dumville, David N. "*Historia Brittonum: an Insular History from the Carolingian Age.*" In *Historiographie im frühen Mittelalter,* ed. Anton Scharer and Georg Scheibelreiter. Vienna: Akademie der Wissenschaften 1994 = Veröffentlichungen des Instituts für Österreichische Geschichte 32, 406–34.

Düwel, Klaus. "Buchstabenmagie und Alphabetenzauber. Zu den Inschriften der Goldbrakteaten und ihrer Funktion als Amulette." *Frühmittelalerliche Studien* 22 (1988): 70–110.

———, ed. *Runeninschriften als Quellen interdisziplinärer Forschung.* Berlin and New York: de Gruyter, 1998 = Ergänzungsbände zum Reallexikon der Germanischen Altertumskunde 15.

Düwel, Klaus. *Runenkunde.* 3rd ed. Stuttgart and Weimar: Metzler, 2001.

Elbe, Joachim von. *Roman Germany: A Guide to Sites and Museums.* Mainz: Philipp von Zabern, 1977.

Elliot, Ralph W. V. *Runes.* Manchester: Manchester UP, 1959.

Enright, Michael J. "Lady With a Mead-Cup. Ritual, Group Cohesion and Hierarchy in the Germanic Warband." *Frühmittelalterliche Studien* 22 (1988): 170–203.

Ferreiro, A. *The Visigoths in Gaul and Spain, A.D. 418–711.* Leiden: Brill, 1988.

Flint, Valerie. *The Rise of Magic in Early Medieval Europe.* Princeton: Princeton UP, 1991.

Flowers, Stephen R. *Runes and Magic: Magical Formulaic Elements in the Older Runic Tradition.* New York: Lang, 1986.

García Moreno, Luis A. *Historia de España Visigoda.* Madrid: Cátedra, 1989.

Geary, Patrick J. "Land, Language and Memory in Europe 700–1100." *Transactions of the Royal Historical Society,* 6th Series, 9 (1999): 169–84.

Gelling, Margaret. *Signposts to the Past.* London: Dent, 1978.

Glob, P. V. *The Bog People.* Trans. Rupert Bruce-Mitford. London: Paladin, 1971.

Goez, Werner. *Translatio imperii: Ein Beitrag zur Geschichte des Geschichtsdenkens und der politischen Theorien im Mittelalter und der frühen Neuzeit.* Tübingen: Mohr, 1958.

Goetz, Hans-Werner. "Mediävistische Kulturwissenschaft als Herausforderung und Aufgabe." *Das Mittelalter* 5 (2000): 3–12.

Goffart, Walter. *The Narrators of Barbarian History (A.D. 550–800): Jordanes, Gregory of Tours, Bede and Paul the Deacon.* Princeton: Princeton UP, 1988.

Gordon, C. D. *The Age of Attila.* Ann Arbor: U Michigan P, 1960.

Grant, Michael. *The Fall of the Roman Empire.* London: Weidenfeld and Nicolson, new ed. 1990.

Gretsch, Mechthild. *The Intellectual Foundations of the English Benedictine Reform.* Cambridge: CUP, 1999.

Grimm, Jacob. *Deutsche Mythologie.* 4th ed. by Elard Hugo Meyer, 1875–78. Repr. Darmstadt: WBG, 1965.

Grundmann, Herbert. *Geschichtsschreibung im Mittelalter.* Göttingen: Vandenhoek und Ruprecht, 1965.

Gschwantler, Otto. "Christus, Thor und die Midgardschlange." In *Festschrift für Otto Höfler I,* ed. Helmut Birkhahn and Otto Gschwantler. Vienna: Notring, 1968, 145–68.

———. "Die Überwindung des Fenriswolfs und ihr christliches Gegenstück bei Frau Ava." In *Poetry in the Scandinavian Middle Ages, Spoleto, 4–10 Sept. 1988.* Spoleto: Presso la sede de Centro Studi, 1990, 1–26.

Haarnagel, Werner. *Feddersen Wierde: Die Ergebnisse der Ausgrabung der vorgeschichtlichen Wurt Feddersen Wierde bei Bremerhaven in den Jahren 1955–1963.* 4 vols. Wiesbaden: Steiner, 1967–91.

Hartner, Willy. *Die Goldhörner von Gallehus.* Wiesbaden: Steiner, 1969.

Hauck, Karl. *Goldbrakteaten aus Sievern.* Munich: Fink, 1970.

Heather, Peter. *The Goths.* Oxford: Blackwell, 1996.

———. *Goths and Romans 332–489.* Oxford: Clarendon, 1991.

———. *The Visigoths from the Migration Period to the Seventh Century.* Woodbridge: Boydell, 1999.

Heather, Peter, and J. F. Matthews. *The Goths in the Fourth Century.* Liverpool: Liverpool UP, 1991.

Hehn, Victor. *Kulturpflanzen und Haustiere in ihrem Übergang aus Asien nach Griechenland und Italien sowie in das übrige Europa: Historisch-linguistische Skizzen.* 8th ed. by O. Schrader. Berlin: Borntraeger, 1911, repr. 1963.

Heusler, Andreas. *Germanentum.* Heidelberg: Winter, 1934, 2nd ed. 1936.

Hirt, Herman, *Die Indogermanen: Ihre Verbreitung, ihre Urheimat und ihre Kultur I.* Strasbourg: Trübner, 1905.

———. *Indogermanica: Forschungen über Sprache und Geschichte Alteuropas.* Ed. Helmut Arntz. Halle/Saale: Niemeyer, 1940.

Holmes, George, ed. *The Oxford Illustrated History of Medieval Europe.* Oxford and New York: OUP, 1988.

Hoops, Johannes. *Waldbäume und Kulturpflanzen im germanischen Altertum.* Strasbourg: Trübner, 1905.

Howe, Nicholas. *Migration and Mythmaking in Anglo-Saxon England*. New Haven: Yale UP, 1989.

Ilkjær, Jørgen, and Jørn Lønstrup. "Der Moorfund im Tal der Illerup-Å bei Skanderborg in Ostjütland (Dänemark)." *Germania* 61 (1983): 95–116.

James, Edward. *Visigothic Spain*. Oxford: Clarendon, 1980.

Jankuhn, Herbert. *Archäologische Beobachtungen zu Tier- und Menschenopfern bei den Germanen in der Römischen Kaiserzeit*. Göttingen: Vandenhoek und Ruprecht, 1967 = Nachrichten der Akademie der Wissenschaften in Göttingen/Philologisch-Historische Klasse 1967/6.

———, ed. *Vorgeschichtliche Heiligtümer und Opferplätze in Mittel- und Nordeuropa*. Göttingen: Vandenhoek und Ruprecht, 1970.

Jolly, Karen L. *Popular Religion in Late Saxon England*. Chapel Hill: U North Carolina P, 1996.

Kingsley, Charles. *The Roman and the Teuton*. London: Macmillan, 1864; new edition with introduction by Max Müller, 1889 and many reprints.

Kunow, Jürgen. *Der römische Import in der Germania libera bis zu den Marcomannenkriegen*. Neumünster: Wachholtz, 1983.

Kurylowicz, Jerzy. *Etudes indoeuropeenes*. Krakow: Polska Akademija Umiejetnosci, 1935.

Lange, Gudrun. *Die Anfänge der isländisch-norwegischen Geschichtsschreibung*. Reykjavik: Bókaútgáfa Menningarsjóðs, 1989.

Looijenga, Jantina Helena. *Runes Around the North Sea and on the Continent A.D. 150–700: Texts and Contexts*. Diss. LittD, Groningen, 1997.

Lot, Ferdinand. *Les invasions Germaniques: La pénétration mutuelle du monde barbare et du monde romain*. Paris: Payot (1935), 1945.

Lund-Hansen, Ulla. *Römischer Import im Norden*. Copenhagen: Nordiske Fortidsminder, 1987.

Mallory, J. P. *In Search of the Indo-Europeans: Language, Archeology and Myth*. London: Thames and Hudson, 1989.

Maurer, Friedrich. *Nordgermanen und Alemanen: Studien zur germanischen und frühdeutschen Sprachgeschichte, Stammes- und Volkskunde*. Bern: Franke, 3rd ed. 1952 = Bibliotheca Germanica 3.

McKitterick, Rosamond. *The Carolingians and the Written Word*. Cambridge: CUP, 1989.

———, ed. *The Uses of Literacy in Early Medieval Europe*. Cambridge: CUP, 1990.

Meaney, A. L. "Woden in England: A Reconsideration of the Evidence." *Folklore* 77 (1966): 105–15.

Meulengracht Sørensen, Preben. "Thors's Fishing Expedition." In *Words and Objects; towards a Dialogue between Archaeology and History of Religion*, ed. Gro Steinsland. Oslo: Norwegian UP, 1986, 257–78.

Moltke, E. *Runes and their Origin: Denmark and Elsewhere.* Copenhagen: National Museum of Denmark, 1985.

Montelius, Oscar. *Sveriges historia från äldsta tid till våra dagar I: Sveriges hednatid, samt medeltid, förra skedet, från år 1060 till år 1350.* Stockholm: Linnström, 1877.

Morrall, John B. *The Medieval Imprint.* Penguin: Harmondsworth, 1970.

Moss, H. St. L. B. *The Birth of the Middle Ages 395–814.* London: OUP, 1935.

Motz, Lotte. "The Conquest of Death: The Myth of Baldr and its Middle Eastern Counterparts." *Collegium Medievale* 4 (1991): 99–116.

———. *The King, the Champion and the Sorcerer.* Vienna: Fassbaender, 1996.

Müllenhoff, Karl. *Deutsche Altertumskunde* (1870–1900). Berlin: Weidmann, 2nd ed. 1890–1929.

Müller-Wille, Michael. *Opferkulte der Germanen und Slawen.* Stuttgart: Theiss, 1999.

Murdoch, Adrian. *The Last Pagan: Julian the Apostate and the Death of the Ancient World.* Stroud: Sutton, 2003.

Nack, Emil. *Germanien: Länder und Völker.* Vienna: Ueberreuter, 1977.

Näsström, Britt-Mari. *Freyja — the Great Goddess of the North.* Lund: Department of History of Religions, University of Lund, 1995 = Lund Studies in History of Religions 5.

Nordal, Guðrún. *Ethics and Action in Thirteenth-Century Iceland.* Odense: Odense UP, 1998.

Norden, Eduard. *Die germanische Urgeschichte in Tacitus' Germania.* Stuttgart and Leipzig: Teubner, 5th ed. 1974.

North, Richard. *Heathen Gods in Old English Literature.* Cambridge: CUP, 1997.

Olsen, Magnus. *Farms and Fanes of Ancient Norway.* Oslo: H. Aschehoug, 1928.

Olsen, Olaf. *Hørg, hov og kirke.* Copenhagen: Det kongelige Nordiske oldskriftselskab, 1966.

———. "Vorchristliche Heiligtümer in Nordeuropa," in *Vorgeschichtliche Heiligtümer und Opferplätze in Mittel- und Nordeuropa,* ed. Herbert Jankuhn. Göttingen: Vandenhoek and Ruprecht, 1970 = Abhandlungen der Akademie der Wiss. Göttingen, Phil. hist. Kl. 3/74, 259–78.

Opie, Peter and Iona. *The Lore and Language of Schoolchildren.* Oxford: OUP, 1967.

Penka, Carl. *Die Heimat der Germanen.* Vienna: Mitteilungen der Wiener anthropologischen Gesellschaft 23, 1893.

Petrikovits, Harald von. "Fortifications in the North-Western Roman Empire from the Third to Fifth centuries A.D." *Journal of Roman Studies* 61 (1971): 178–218.

Pirenne, Henri. *Mohammed and Charlemagne.* Trans. Bernard Miall. London: Allen and Unwin, 1939.

Reuter, Timothy. *Germany in the Early Middle Ages.* London and New York: Longman, 1991.

Ross, Margaret Clunies. *Prolonged Echoes: Old Norse Myths in Medieval Northern Society,* I: *The Myths,* and: II: *The Reception of Norse Myths in Medieval Iceland.* Odense: Odense UP, 1994 and 1998.

Russell, James C. *The Germanization of Early Medieval Christianity.* New York: OUP, 1996.

Scardigli, Piergiuseppe, *Der Weg zur deutschen Sprache.* Bern: Lang, 1994.

Scheibelreiter, Georg. "Vom Mythos zur Geschichte. Überlegungen zu den Formen der Bewahrung von Vergangenheit im Frühmittelalter." In *Historiographie im frühen Mittelalter,* ed. Anton Scharer and Georg Scheibelreiter. Vienna: Akademie der Wissenschaften Wien, 1994 = Veröffentlichungen des Instituts für Österreichische Geschichte 32, 26–40.

Schlüter, Wolfgang, and Rainer Wiegels, eds. *Rom, Germanien und die Ausgrabungen von Kalkriese.* Osnabrück: Rasch, 1999.

Schmidt, Ludwig. *Die Ostgermanen.* 2nd ed. 1941; repr. Munich: Beck, 1969.

Schneider, Hermann. "Die germanische Altertumskunde." *Forschungen und Fortschritte* 15 (1939): 1–3.

———, ed. *Germanische Altertumskunde.* Munich: Beck, 1938.

Schwarz, Ernst. *Germanische Stammeskunde zwischen den Wissenschaften.* Constance and Stuttgart: Thorbecke, 1967.

———. *Goten, Nordgermanen, Angelsachsen.* Bern and Munich: Francke and Lehnen, 1951.

Simek, Rudolf. *Altnordische Kosmographie: Studien und Quellen zu Weltbild und Weltbeschreibung in Norwegen und Island vom 12. bis 14. Jahrhundert.* Berlin and New York: de Gruyter, 1990.

Simek, Rudolf, and Angela Simek. "Bog People Revisited: Iron Age Bog-Corpses and their Relevance for the History of Germanic Religion." In *Hugur: Mélanges [. . .] offerts à Régis Boyer pour son 65e anniversaire.* Paris: P de l'Université, 1997, 51–85.

Simpson, Jacqueline. "Some Scandinavian Sacrifices." *Folklore* 78 (1967): 190–202.

Ström, Folke. "Bog Corpses and Germania, Ch. 12." In *Words and Objects: Towards a Dialogue between Archaeology and History of Religion,* ed. Gro Steinsland. Oslo: Norwegian UP, 1986, 223–39.

Strömbäck, Dag. *The Conversion of Iceland.* London: Viking Society for Northern Research, 1975.

Suchenwirth, Richard. *Deutsche Geschichte: Von der germanischen Vorzeit bis zur Gegenwart.* Leipzig: Dollheimer, 1935.

Sveinsson, Einar Ólafur. "Celtic Elements in Icelandic Tradition." *Béaloideas* 15 (1959): 3–24.

Thompson, E. A. *The Early Germans.* Oxford: Clarendon, 1965.

————. *The Visigoths in the Time of Ulfila.* Oxford: Clarendon, 1966.

Thrane, H. "An Archaeologist's View of Runes." In *Runeninschriften als Quellen interdisziplinärer Forschung,* ed. K. Düwel. Berlin and New York: de Gruyter, 1998 = Ergänzungsbände zum Reallexikon der Germanischen Altertumskunde 15, 219–27.

Timpe, Dieter. "Die Schlacht im Teutoburger Wald: Geschichte, Tradition, Mythos." In *Rom, Germanien und die Ausgrabungen von Kalkriese,* ed. Schlüter and Wiegels, 717–37.

Todd, Malcolm. *The Early Germans.* Oxford: Blackwell, 1992.

Turville-Petre, and E. O. Gabriel. *Myth and Religion of the North.* London: Weidenfeld and Nicolson, 1964; repr. Westport 1975.

Ullmann, Walter. *Medieval Political Thought.* Harmondsworth: Penguin, 1975.

Vasiliev, A. A. *The Goths in the Crimea.* Cambridge, MA: Medieval Academy of America, 1936.

Vries, Jan de. *Altgermanische Religionsgeschichte.* Berlin: de Gruyter, 2nd ed. 1957.

————. *Die geistige Welt der Germanen.* Halle/Saale: Niemeyer, 1943.

————. "Heimdallr, dieu énigmatique," *Études Germaniques* 10 (1955): 257–68.

Wallace-Hadrill, J. M. *The Barbarian West 400–1000.* London: Hutchinson, revised ed. 1967.

Watt, Margarete. "Kings or Gods? Iconographic Evidence from Scandinavian Gold Foil Figures." In *The Making of Kingdoms,* ed. Tania Dickinson and David Griffiths. Oxford: University Committee for Archaeology, 1999 = Anglo-Saxon Studies in Archaeology and History 10, 173–83.

Wenskus, Reinhard. *Stammesbildung und Verfassung: Das Werden der frühmittelalterlichen gentes.* Cologne and Graz: Böhlau 1961; repr. 1977.

Werner, J. *Das Aufkommen von Bild und Schrift in Nordeuropa.* Munich: Verlag der Bayerischen Akademie der Wissenschaften, 1966 = Sitzungsberichte der Bayerischen Akademie der Wissenschaften, Phil.-hist. Kl. 1966/4.

Wickham, Chris. *Early Medieval Italy.* Totowa, NJ: Barnes and Noble, 1981.

Williams, H. "The Origin of the Runes," *ABäG* 45 (1996): 211–18 (= *Frisian Runes and Neighbouring Traditions,* ed. T. Looijenga and Arend Quak).

————. "The Romans and the Runes — Uses of Writing in Germania" In *Runor och ABC: Elva föreläsningar från ett symposium i Stockholm våren 1995* ed. S. Nyström. Stockholm: Sällskapet Runica et Mediævalia; Riksantikvarieämbetet; Stockholms Medeltidsmuseum, 1997 = Sällskapet Runica et Mediævalia, Opuscula 4, 177–92.

Wilson, David. *The Anglo-Saxons*. Harmondsworth: Penguin, rev. ed. 1971.

———. *The Vikings and their Origins*. London: Thames and Hudson, 1970.

Wolfram, Herwig. *Geschichte der Goten: Von den Anfängen bis zur Mitte des 6. Jahrhunderts: Entwurf einer historischen Ethnographie*. Munich: Beck, 4th ed., 2001; trans. from 2nd ed. by Thomas J. Dunlap as *History of the Goths*. Berkeley: U California P, 1987.

———. *"Origo et Religio*. Ethnic Traditions and Literature in Early Medieval Texts." *Early Medieval Europe* 3 (1994): 19–38.

———. *Das Reich und die Germanen: Zwischen Antike und Mittelalter*. Berlin: Siedler, 2nd ed. 1994; repr. 1998.

———. *Splendor Imperii*. Vienna: Akademie der Wissenschaften, 1963 = Mitteilungen des Instituts für Österreichische Geschichte, Ergänzungsband 20.

Literary Studies

Allen, Richard F. *Fire and Iron: Critical Approaches to Njáls saga*. Pittsburgh, PA: U Pittsburgh P, 1971.

Andersen, Flemming G., Otto Holzapfel, and Thomas Pettitt. *The Ballad as Narrative: Studies in the Ballad Traditions of England, Scotland, Germany, and Denmark*. Odense: Odense UP, 1982.

Andersson, T. M. *The Icelandic Family Saga: An Analytic Reading*. Cambridge, MA: Harvard UP, 1967.

———. *The Legend of Brynhild*. Ithaca, NY: Cornell UP, 1980.

Árnason, Kristján. *The Rhythms of Dróttkvætt and Other Old Icelandic Metres*. Reykjavik: Institute of Linguistics, 1991.

Bagge, Sverre. *Society and Politics in Snorri Sturluson's Heimskringla*. Berkeley: U of California P, 1991.

Barnes, Geraldine. "Arthurian Chivalry in Old Norse." *Arthurian Literature*, 7 (1987): 50–102.

Bately, Janet M. *The Anglo-Saxon Chronicle: Texts and Relationships*. Reading: Reading University Centre for Medieval Studies, 1991 = Reading Medieval Studies Monographs 3.

———. *The Literary Prose of King Alfred's Reign: Translation or Transformation? An Inaugural Lecture delivered on 4th March 1980*. London: King's College, 1980.

———. "Old English Prose before and during the Reign of Alfred." *ASE* 17 (1988): 93–138.

Bäuml, Franz. "The Oral Tradition and Middle High German Literature." *Oral Tradition* 12 (1986): 398–445.

———. "Varieties and Consequences of Medieval Literacy and Illiteracy." *Speculum* 55 (1980): 237–65.

Beck, Heinrich. "Germanische Menschenopfer in der literarischen Über-lieferung." In *Vorgeschichtliche Heiligtümer und Opferplätze in Mittel- und Nordeuropa,* ed. H. Jankuhn. Göttingen: Vandenhoek and Ruprecht, 1970, 240–58.

———. *Snorri Sturlusons Sicht der paganen Vorzeit.* Göttingen: Vandenhoek und Ruprecht, 1994 = Nachrichten der Akademie der Wissenschaften in Göttingen, Philol.-Hist. Kl. 1994, 1.

Bergmann, Rolf, Heinrich Tiefenbach, and Lothar Voetz, eds. *Althochdeutsch* (*Festschrift Rudolf Schützeichel*). Heidelberg: Winter, 1982.

Bertholet, Alfred. *Die Macht der Schrift in Glauben und Aberglauben.* Berlin: Akademie-Verlag, 1949 = Abhandlungen der Deutschen Akademie der Wissen-schaften zu Berlin, Phil.-hist. Kl., 1948/1.

Bjork, Robert E. *The Old English Verse Saints' Lives.* Toronto: U of Toronto P, 1985.

Bjork, Robert E., and John D. Niles. *A Beowulf Handbook.* Lincoln, NE: U Ne-braska P, 1997.

Boer, R. C. *Die Sagen von Ermanarich und Dietrich von Bern.* Halle/S: Waisen-haus, 1910.

Bostock, J. Knight. *A Handbook on Old High German Literature.* 2nd ed. by K. C. King and D. R. McLintock. Oxford: Clarendon, 1976.

Cable, Thomas. *The English Alliterative Tradition.* Philadelphia: U Pennsylvania P, 1991.

Calder, Daniel G. *Cynewulf.* Boston: Twayne, 1981: reviewed by H. L. C. Tris-tram, *Anglia* 102 (1984): 193–99.

Chambers, R. W. *On the Continuity of English Prose from Alfred to More and His School.* London: OUP, 1932 = EETS/OS 191a.

Chase, Colin. *The Dating of Beowulf.* Toronto: U of Toronto P, 1981; reprinted with an afterword by Nicholas P. Howe, 1997.

Clover, Carol. *The Medieval Saga.* Ithaca, NY: Cornell UP, 1982.

Clover, Carol J., and John Lindow. *Old Norse-Icelandic Literature: A Critical Guide.* Ithaca, NY: Cornell UP, 1985.

Cooper, Janet, ed. *The Battle of Maldon: Fiction and Fact.* London: Hambledon, 1993.

Curschmann, Michael. "The Concept of the Oral Formula as an Impediment to our Understanding of Medieval Oral Poetry." *Medievalia et Humanistica,* New Series 8 (1977): 63–76.

———. "Oral Poetry in Medieval English, French and German Literature: Some Notes on Recent Research." *Speculum* 43 (1967): 36–53.

Derolez, René. *Götter und Mythen der Germanen.* Trans. Julie von Wattenwyl. Zurich and Cologne: Benziger, 1963.

———. "Runic Literacy among the Anglo-Saxons." In *Britain 400–600: Language and History,* ed. A. Bammesberger. Heidelberg: Winter, 1990.

Dronke, Peter. *Medieval Latin and the Rise of the European Love-Lyric.* Oxford: Clarendon, 2nd ed. 1968.

Dronke, Ursula. "Eddic Poetry as a Source for the History of Germanic Religion." In *Germanische Religionsgeschichte: Quellen und Quellenprobleme,* ed. Heinrich Beck, Detlev Ellmers, and Kurt Schier. Berlin and New York: de Gruyter, 1992 = Ergänzungsbände zum Reallexikon der Germanischen Altertumskunde, 5, 656–84.

Edwards, Cyril. *The Beginnings of German Literature: Comparative and Interdisciplinary Approaches to Old High German.* Columbia, SC: Camden House, 2002 = Studies in German Literature, Linguistics and Culture.

———. "German Vernacular Literature." In *Carolingian Culture: Emulation and Innovation,* ed Rosamund McKitterick. Cambridge: CUP, 1994, 141–70.

Ehrismann, Gustav. *Geschichte der deutschen Literatur bis zum Ausgang des Mittelalters I: Die althochdeutsche Literatur.* Munich: Beck, 1932; repr. as 2nd ed. 1954.

Eichhoff, Jürgen, and Irmengard Rauch. *Der Heliand.* Darmstadt: WBG, 1973.

Elliott, Ralph W. V. "Byrhtnoth and Hildebrand: A Study in Heroic Technique." *Comparative Literature* 14 (1962): 53–70.

Erzgräber, Will, and Sabine Volk, eds. *Mündlichkeit und Schriftlichkeit im englischen Mittelalter.* Tübingen: Narr, 1988 = ScriptOralia 5.

Fidjestøl, Bjarne. *The Dating of Eddic Poetry: A Historical Survey and Methodological Investigation.* Copenhagen: Reitzel, 1999.

Foley, John Miles. *The Singer of Tales in Performance.* Bloomington and Indianapolis: Indiana UP, 1995.

———, ed. *Oral-Formulaic Theory: A Folklore Casebook.* New York and London: Garland, 1990.

Frank, Roberta. *Old Norse Court Poetry: The Dróttkvætt Stanza.* Ithaca, NY: Cornell UP, 1978.

Gade, Kari Ellen. *The Structure of Old Norse Dróttkvætt Poetry.* Ithaca, NY: Cornell UP, 1995.

Glauser, Jürg. *Isländische Märchensagas: Studien zur Prosaliteratur im späten mittelalterlichen Island.* Basel and Frankfurt am Main: Helbing und Lichtenhahn, 1983.

Gneuss, Helmut. *Books and Libraries in Early England.* Aldershot: Variorum, 1996.

Godden, Malcolm. "Literary Language." In *The Cambridge History of the English Language,* ed. Richard M. Hogg. Cambridge: CUP, 1992–2001, I, 490–535.

Godden, Malcolm, and Michael Lapidge, eds. *The Cambridge Companion to Old English Literature.* Cambridge: CUP, 1991.

Green, D. H. "The Beginnings of Literacy in the Early Germanic World." In *Varieties and Consequences of Literacy and Orality/Formen und Folgen von Schriftlichkeit und Mundlichkeit: Franz H. Bäuml zum 75. Geburtstag,* ed. Ursula Schaefer and Edda Spielmann. Tübingen: Narr, 2001, 185–98.

————. *Medieval Listening and Reading: The Primary Reception of German Literature 800–1300.* Cambridge: CUP, 1994.

————. "Orality and Reading. The State of Research in Medieval Studies." *Speculum* 65 (1990): 267–80.

Greenfield, S. B., and D. G. Calder. *A New Critical History of Old English Literature.* New York: New York UP, 1986.

Groseclose, J. Sidney, and Brian O. Murdoch. *Die althochdeutschen poetischen Denkmäler.* Stuttgart: Metzler, 1976.

Gutenbrunner, Siegfried. *Von Hildebrand und Hadubrand.* Heidelberg: Winter, 1976.

Hasty, Will, and James Hardin. *Dictionary of Literary Biography: German Writers and Works of the Early Middle Ages.* New York: Gale, 1995.

Haubrichs, Wolfgang. *Die Anfänge.* Frankfurt/M.: Athenäum, 1988 = Joachim Heinzle, ed., *Geschichte der deutschen Literatur von den Anfängen bis zum Beginn der Neuzeit,* I/i.

————. *Georgslied und Georgslegende im frühen Mittelalter.* Königsstein i. T.: Scriptor, 1979.

Haubrichs, Wolfgang, et al., eds. *Theodisca: Beiträge zur althochdeutschen und altniederdeutschen Sprache und Literatur.* Berlin and New York: de Gruyter, 2000.

Haymes, Edward R. "Oral Composition in Middle High German Epic Poetry" In *Oral Traditional Literature: A Festschrift for Albert Bates Lord,* ed. John Miles Foley, Columbus, OH: Slavica, 1980, 341–46.

Heinzle, Joachim. *Geschichte der deutschen Literatur von den Anfängen bis zum Beginn der Neuzeit,* vol. 2/2: *Wandlungen und Neuansätze im 13. Jahrhundert (1220/30–1280/90).* Königstein: Athenäum, 1984.

Honti, János. *Studies in Oral Epic Tradition.* Budapest: Akadémiai Kiadó, 1975.

Hunter, M. J. "The Gothic Bible." In *The Cambridge History of the Bible II: The West from the Fathers to the Reformation,* ed. G. W. H. Lampe. Cambridge: CUP, 1969, 338–62.

Jóhannesson, Jón. *A History of the Old Icelandic Commonwealth.* Trans. Haraldur Bessason. Winnipeg: U of Manitoba P, 1974.

Kabir, Ananya Jahanara. *Paradise, Death and Doomsday in Anglo-Saxon Literature.* Cambridge: CUP, 2001.

Kalinke, Marianne E. *Bridal-Quest Romance in Medieval Iceland.* Ithaca, NY: Cornell UP, 1990.

Ker, W. P. *Epic and Romance.* London: Macmillan, 1896; repr.ed New York: Dover, 1957.

Kleiber, Wolfgang. *Otfrid von Weissenburg.* Bern and Munich: Francke, 1971.

———, ed. *Otfrid von Weissenburg.* Darmstadt: WBG, 1978.

Ködderitzsch, Rolf. "Der 2. Merseburger Spruch und seine Parallele." *Zeitschrift für celtische Philologie* 33 (1974): 45–57.

Koegel, Rudolf. *Geschichte der deutschen Litteratur bis zum Ausgang des Mittelalters,* I/i: *Die stabreimende Dichtung und die gotische Prosa.* Strasbourg: Trübner, 1894.

Kolk, H. van der. *Das Hildebrandslied: Eine forschungsgeschichtliche Darstellung.* Amsterdam: Scheltema and Holkema, 1967.

Krause, W. *Die Runeninschriften im älteren Futhark.* 2 vols. Göttingen: Vandenhoeck and Ruprecht, 1966 = Abhandlungen der Akademie der Wissenschaften in Göttingen, Phil.-hist. Kl. 3/65.

Kristjánsson, Jónas. *Eddas and Sagas: Iceland's Medieval Literature.* Trans. Peter Foote. Reykjavik: Hið Íslenska Bókmenntafélag, 1988.

Kuhn, Hans. *Das Dróttkvætt.* Heidelberg: Winter, 1983.

Liebertz-Grün, Ursula. *Aus der Mündlichkeit in die Schriftlichkeit: Höfische und andere Literatur 750–1320.* Reinbek bei Hamburg: Rowohlt, 1988.

Liuzza, R. M. "On the Dating of *Beowulf.*" In *Beowulf: Basic Readings,* ed. Peter S. Baker. New York: Garland, 1995, 281–302; see the review article by Theodore M. Andersson, *University of Toronto Quarterly* 52 (1983): 288–301.

———, ed. *Old English Literature.* New Haven: Yale UP, 2002.

Lönnroth, Lars. *Njáls saga: A Critical Introduction.* Berkeley: U California P, 1976.

Lord, Albert B. *The Singer of Tales.* Cambridge, MA: Harvard UP, 1960.

Mitchell, Stephen A. *Heroic Sagas and Ballads.* Ithaca, NY: Cornell UP, 1991.

Momma, H. *The Composition of Old English Poetry.* Cambridge: CUP, 1997.

Morewedge, Rosmarie Thee. "Orality, Literacy, and the Medieval Folktale." In *Varieties and Consequences of Literacy and Orality/Formen und Folgen von Schriftlichkeit und Mundlichkeit: Franz H. Bäuml zum 75. Geburtstag,* ed. Ursula Schaefer and Edda Spielmann. Tübingen: Narr, 2001, 85–106.

Münkler, Herfried. *Das Blickfeld des Helden.* Göppingen: Kümmerle, 1983.

Murdoch, Brian. "The Carolingian Period and the Early Middle Ages." In *Cambridge History of German Literature,* ed. Helen Watanabe. Cambridge: CUP, 1997, 1–39.

———. "*Drohtin, uuerthe so!* Zur Funktionsweise der althochdeutschen Zaubersprüche." *Jahrbuch der Görres-Gesellschaft* NS 32 (1991): 11–37.

———. *The Germanic Hero.* London and Rio Grande: Hambledon, 1996.

———. *Old High German Literature.* Boston: Twayne, 1983.

Murphy, G. Ronald. *The Saxon Savior: The Germanic Transformation of the Gospel in the Ninth-century Heliand.* New York: OUP, 1990.

Nordal, Guðrún. *Tools of Literacy: The Role of Skaldic Verse in Icelandic Textual Culture of the Twelfth and Thirteenth Centuries.* Toronto: U Toronto P, 2001.

Ólason, Vésteinn. *Dialogues with the Viking Age: Narration and Representation in the Sagas of the Icelanders.* Reykjavik: Heimskringla, 1998.

Olson, David R., and Nancy Torrance, eds. *Literacy and Orality.* Cambridge: CUP, 1991.

O'Keeffe, Katherine O'Brien, ed. *Old English Shorter Poems: Basic Readings.* New York: Garland, 1994.

Ong, Walter J. *Orality and Literacy: The Technologizing of the Word.* London and New York: Methuen, 1984.

Opland, Jeff. *Anglo-Saxon Oral Poetry: A Study of the Traditions.* New Haven and London: Yale UP, 1980.

Orchard, Andy. *Pride and Prodigies: Studies in the Monsters of the Beowulf-Manuscript.* Cambridge: D. S. Brewer, 1995.

Parry, Milman. *The Making of Homeric Verse: The Collected Papers of Milman Parry.* Ed. Adam Parry. Oxford: Clarendon, 1971.

Payne, F. Anne. *King Alfred and Boethius.* Madison: U Wisconsin P, 1968.

Pearsall, Derek. *Old English and Middle English Poetry.* London: Routledge and Kegan Paul, 1977.

Poole, Russell, ed. *Skaldsagas: Text, Vocation, and Desire in the Icelandic Sagas of Poets.* Berlin: de Gruyter, 2000.

Pulsiano, Phillip, and Elaine Treharne, eds. *A Companion to Anglo-Saxon Literature.* Oxford: Blackwell, 2001.

Rathofer, Johannes. *Der Heliand: Theologischer Sinn als tektonischer Form.* Cologne: Böhlau, 1962.

Remly, Paul G. *Old English Biblical Verse.* Cambridge: CUP, 1996.

Renoir, Alain. "The Armor of the *Hildebrandslied:* An Oral-Formulaic Point of View." *Neuphilologische Mitteilungen* 78 (1977): 389–95.

Robinson, Fred C., ed. *The Editing of Old English.* Oxford: Blackwell, 1994.

Robinson, Orrin W. *Old English and its Closest Relatives.* Stanford: Stanford UP, 1992.

Röcke, Werner, and Ursula Schaefer, eds. *Mündlichkeit — Schriftlichkeit — Weltbildwandel: Literarische Kommunikation und Deutungsschemata von Wirklichkeit in der Literatur des Mittelalters und der frühen Neuzeit.* Tübingen: Narr, 1996 = ScriptOralia 71.

Russom, Geoffrey. *Beowulf and Old Germanic Metre.* Cambridge: CUP, 1998.

Scholz, Manfred Günter. *Hören und Lesen: Studien zur primären Rezeption der Literatur im 12. und 13. Jahrhundert.* Wiesbaden: Steiner, 1980.

Schwarz, Werner. *Schriften zur Bibelübersetzung und mittelalterlichen Übersetzungstheorie*. London: Institute of Germanic Studies, 1985.

See, Klaus von. *Skaldendichtung: Eine Einführung*. Munich and Zurich: Artemis, 1980.

See, Klaus von, Beatrice La Farge, Eve Picard, Ilona Priebe, Katja Schulz. *Kommentar zu den Liedern der Edda, II: Götterlieder (Skírnismál, Hárbarðsljóð, Hymiskviða, Lokasenna, Þrymskviða)*. Heidelberg: Winter, 1997 and *III*, 2000.

Sisam, Kenneth. *Studies in the History of Old English Literature*. Oxford: Clarendon, 1953.

Ström, Folke. "Poetry as an Instrument of Propaganda. Jarl Hakon and his Poets." In *Speculum Norroenum: Norse Studies in Memory of Gabriel Turville-Petre*, ed. Ursula Dronke et al. Odense: Odense UP, 1981, 440–58.

Stutz, Elfriede. *Gotische Literaturdenkmäler*. Stuttgart: Metzler, 1966.

Szarmach, Paul E., ed. *Holy Men and Holy Women: Old English Prose Saints' Lives and Their Contexts*. Albany, NY: State U New York P, 1996.

———, ed. *Studies in Earlier Old English Prose*. Albany, NY: State U New York P, 1986.

Szarmach, Paul E., and Bernard F. Huppé, eds. *The Old English Homily and Its Backgrounds*. Albany, NY: State U New York P, 1978.

Thomas, Rosalind. *Literacy and Orality in Ancient Greece*. Cambridge: CUP, 1992.

Tolkien, J. R. R. "*Beowulf: The Monsters and the Critics*": *Proceedings of the British Academy* 22 (1936): 245–95 (and frequent reprints).

Turville-Petre, E. O. Gabriel. *Origins of Icelandic Literature*. Oxford: Clarendon, 1953; rpt. 1967.

———. *Scaldic Poetry*. Oxford: Clarendon, 1976.

Uecker, Heiko. *Germanische Heldensage*. Stuttgart: Metzler, 1972.

Vollmann-Profe, Gisela. *Von den Anfängen bis zum hohen Mittelalter*. Frankfurt/M.: Athenäum, 1986 = Joachim Heinzle, ed., *Geschichte der deutschen Literatur von den Anfängen bis zum Beginn der Neuzeit*, I/ii.

Watkins, Calvert. *How to Kill a Dragon: Aspects of Indo-European Poetics*. New York: OUP, 1995.

Westra, Haijo J. "Literacy, Orality and Medieval Patronage." *Journal of Medieval Latin* 1 (1991): 52–59.

Whaley, Diana. *Heimskringla: An Introduction*. London: Viking Society for Northern Research, 1991.

Whitman, Cedric H. *Homer and the Heroic Tradition*. Cambridge, MA: Harvard UP, 1958.

Whitman, F. H. *Old English Riddles*. Ottawa: Canadian Federation for the Humanities, 1982.

Wilson, R. M. "On the Continuity of English Prose." In *Mélanges de Linguistique et de Philologie: Fernand Mossé in Memoriam*. Paris: Didier, 1959, 486–94.

Wolf, Alois. *Heldensage und Epos: Zur Konstituierung einer mittelalterlichen volkssprachlichen Gattung im Spannungsfeld von Mündlichkeit und Schriftlichkeit*. Tübingen: Narr, 1995= ScriptOralia 68.

Wrenn, C. L. "The Poetry of Cædmon," *Proceedings of the British Academy* 32 (1946): 277–95.

Würth, Stefanie. *Der "Antikenroman" in der isländischen Literatur des Mittelalters: Eine Untersuchung zur Übersetzung und Rezeption lateinischer Literatur im Norden*. Basel and Frankfurt am Main: Helbing and Lichtenhahn, 1998.

Contributors

THEODORE M. ANDERSSON is a Germanist specializing in the literature of medieval Iceland. He taught at Harvard (1960–75), Stanford (1975–95) and Indiana University (1995–99). He is the author of books on *Beowulf,* the legend of Brynhild, the *Nibelungenlied* and several on the Icelandic sagas. In 1998 he served as president of the Medieval Academy of America.

HEINRICH BECK is emeritus professor of Scandinavian Studies at the University of Bonn; his publications include monographs on the Old Icelandic *Konungsbók* and of Snorri Sturluson's view of the pagan world, and numerous articles on Old Norse literature. He has been co-editor of the *Reallexikon der Germanischen Altertumskunde* since 1973.

GRAEME DUNPHY was born in Glasgow and studied German at Stirling, then Hebrew and Old Testament in St. Andrews. He wrote his Stirling doctoral thesis on Jans Enikel's *Weltchronik.* Since 1993 he has been lecturing in EFL and in German literature at the University of Regensburg. He has worked mainly on medieval biblical and historical writing, but also on the Baroque period and on modern ethnic minority literature. Recent publications include an edition of the *Annolied*-commentary by Martin Opitz and an anthology of thirteenth-century verse chronicles.

KLAUS DÜWEL, professor of Germanic Philology (now emeritus) at the University of Göttingen, is a specialist on runology. His many publications on runes and runology include the Sammlung Metzler volume *Runenkunde,* much editorial work, and a large number of articles on all aspects of the subject.

ADRIAN MURDOCH studied ancient history at The Queen's College, Oxford and is now a writer and international print journalist working from Scotland. His book *The Last Pagan: Julian the Apostate and the Death of the Ancient World* is published by Sutton Press (2003).

BRIAN MURDOCH is professor of German at Stirling University, Scotland, and has held visiting fellowships at Oxford and Cambridge, where he has delivered the Waynflete, the Hulsean, and the Speaker's Lectures. His principal specialization is early medieval German and comparative literature, especially biblical and apocryphal writings and the Adam-legends. Recent books include *The Germanic Hero; Adam's Grace;* and *The Medieval Popular Bible.*

RON MURPHY was born in Trenton, NJ. He is a Jesuit priest and professor of German at Georgetown University. His publications include *Brecht and the Bible; The Saxon Savior;* a translation of *The Heliand — the Saxon Gospel;* and *The Owl, the Raven and the Dove: the Religious Meaning of the Grimms' Magic Fairy Tales.* He is currently working on a book on the Holy Grail in Wolfram's *Parzival.*

MALCOLM READ studied German and Swedish at Hull University, and has been head of the Department of German at Stirling University in Scotland. He writes principally on modern literature, most recently on Handke, Klabund, and Sperr, and is working at present on the novels of the Weimar Republic.

FRED C. ROBINSON began teaching at Yale in 1972, where he became Douglas Tracy Smith Professor of English. His many books include the collection of essays *The Tomb of Beowulf, The Editing of Old English,* and both his edition of *Beowulf* and the *Guide to Old English* co-authored with Bruce Mitchell. For his work in English studies he received the Sir Israel Gollancz Prize of the British Academy.

RUDOLF SIMEK is professor of Early German and Norse at Bonn University, and has published widely on many aspects of Norse life and literature, his works including lexica of Old Norse literature and of Germanic mythology.

HERWIG WOLFRAM was born in Vienna, and has been professor of Medieval History first in Los Angeles and then in Vienna, where since 1983 he has directed the Institut für Österreichische Geschichtsforschung (emeritus 2002). He is a member of many learned societies and academies in different parts of the world, and is the author of more than twenty books, many of which have been translated. He is the editor of a fourteen-volume history of Austria.

Index

Note: modern authors and critics are included by name in the index only when referred to directly in the body of the text; place-names are listed when the reference is significant; terms such as "German," "*Germani*," "Germany" are omitted for the most part.